EPIC OF SURVIVAL:
Twenty-Five Centuries of Anti-Semitism

Samuel Glassman

Bloch Publishing Company ● New York

Dedicated to my wife, Chana; my children, Shevi and Don; my grand-children, Billy, Bobby and Amy.

CONTENTS

Preface

This book uses the phrase "Jew-hatred" rather than "anti-Semitism" because, while Jew-hatred has a history of more than two thousand years, the term "anti-Semitism" has been in use for barely a century. (The word "anti-Semite" first appeared in a German pamphlet in 1879.) Anti-Semitism is a modern concept, closely associated with the race theory which spread throughout Europe in the mid-nineteenth century.

Modern anti-Semitism flared up suddenly in most European countries during the last quarter of the nineteenth century. It was brought about by a conjuncture of many factors. The capitalist system was then dominant in all phases of society. Finance capital had achieved preeminence in the social and economic life of most countries. Expanding industry drove most of the peasants from the villages and crowded them into the cities as proletarians. Exploitation went unchecked and unchallenged. The work-day was twelve to sixteen hours for starvation wages. The Franco-Prussian War of 1870 promised prosperity and brought with it unbridled German chauvinism. In France it resulted in bloodthirsty revanchism.

In 1873 the deepening economic crisis in Europe drove 40 percent of the German workers into the street with no means of livelihood. There were no trade unions of any consequence. Unemployment compensation and social security were still unheard of.

In most European countries the Jews were emancipated in the 1860s and 1870s. A bit earlier, Jews had begun to appear in industry, finance, and the professions. The Jewish stereotype remained the same as it had been throughout the Middle Ages. Always a "stranger," the Jew became the cause of all the misfortunes in the economic crisis of 1873. Anti-Jewish agitation emanated from both the Right and the Left. The anti-Jewish pamphlets of Richard Wagner were not a whit more "civilized" than the sermons of the preacher Adolph Stöcker or the diatribes of the "leftists" Dühring, Proudhon, or Bakunin. Karl Marx's *Zur Judenfrage*, in which he accuses the Jews of having no other god but money, also gained popularity.

The anti-Jewish agitation was now heard not only once a week—on Sunday in church, as in the Middle Ages—but every day of the week and everywhere: in the newspapers, in books and pamphlets, in the street and the marketplace, in the beer halls, wherever people gathered. The scope of this agitation was all the more frightening to the Jews because it was so unexpected.

Two hundred years earlier, in an era of enlightenment, the tide of Jew-hatred so characteristic of the second half of the Middle Ages had begun to recede. The anti-Jewish decrees, the expulsions and pogroms, had gradually diminished in central and western Europe, especially during the period of the French Revolution. In the first two-thirds of the nineteenth century, Jews struggled for and won their emancipation in almost all the countries of central and western Europe. Therefore they believed, quite justifiably, that with the growth of civilization, with the expansion of knowledge, with higher cultural levels among the people, Jew-hatred would eventually disappear altogether. Then all at once, a dense fog of Jew-hatred descended upon almost every country in Europe.

The center of the Jew-hatred, in the later Middle Ages, was again in Germany. From that country came the slogan: "The Jew is our misfortune." In 1881 *La France Juive* by Edouard Drumont appeared. The book warned the French people that Jews were well into the process of taking over France. A little over ten years later this agitation led to the notorious Dreyfus case. In Russia came the wave of pogroms organized by the czarist government. In the 1890s Russian and French anti-Semites joined together to produce the poisonous *Protocols of the Elders of Zion*. In many countries there was a rash of anti-Semitic congresses and organizations.

Throughout Jewish history, anti-Jewish agitation has always led to all sorts of decrees and violent attacks. The modern anti-Semitism of the late nineteenth and early twentieth centuries was no exception. In a very stormy historical climate, modern anti-Jewish agitation led to the bloodiest pogrom in Jewish history—the "Final Solution"—the massacre of six million defenseless Jewish men, women, and children.

Whatever form Jew-hatred takes, it is always an extremely serious problem. Jew-hatred is a misfortune not only for the Jews, but also for the people among whom the hatred is disseminated. They pay a heavy price for bearing this hatred. History has amply demonstrated that Jew-hatred always and everywhere nourishes only reaction, oppression, and Fascism. Some sociologists even believe that anti-

Semitism is a significant barometer of the social and political situation in any given country.

Sociologists who study the problem try to find the causes of this centuries-old plague, which shows no signs of disappearing. Research into the causes and effects of anti-Semitism has been intensified ever since Hitler started the worse conflagration in history with his Jew-baiting incantations.

Like all social phenomena, Judophobia has a genesis. Some sociologists lay all the blame for Jew-hatred on Christianity. It is indeed true that Christianity, for many centuries, contributed substantially to Jew-hatred. It is also a fact, however, the Christianity was not its originator. A study of history shows very clearly that Jew-hatred existed more than six hundred years prior to the rapid spread of Christianity. The new religion became widespread only in the second and third centuries of the Common Era, but Jew-hatred appears as early as 400 B.C.E.

Other scholars develop various theories for the rise of anti-Semitism—socio-political theories, national-ethnic theories, economic, cultural, psychological, anthropological, and racial theories. Most of these theories are not wrong in essence. Some of them are more valid historically than others. They all have one main weakness, however: the causes for the phenomenon of anti-Semitism are presented without the specific historical background in which they arose.

In order to place the problem of Jew-hatred in its proper historical perspective, the views of a profound Jewish historian, Yehezkel Kaufmann, are cited here. In 1932 he published his important work, *Goleh V'nekhar* (*Exile and Stranger*). Kaufmann reveals the causes which gave rise to Jew-hatred and shows why there has been no end to this sickness. He concludes that there is nothing supernatural or mysterious about these causes. Following are a few of his conclusions, here paraphrased and condensed.

> Jew-hatred is caused by religious rivalries, ethnic hostility, xenophobia, social and economic envy, and other natural reasons. Because of various historical circumstances, Jews have lived for many generations in strange lands among foreign peoples. For the sake of their religion they kept themselves apart from non-Jews.

> Just as everyone "struggles for survival," so Jews also have had to struggle for their livelihood. But Jews fought for their existence on foreign soil, and they competed with neighbors who were usually the

owners of that soil. This situation inflamed many peoples against "the stranger." The conflicts may have been economic, ethnic, religious or otherwise, but everywhere and always they led to Jew-hatred.

And because Jews were scattered in so many lands, among so many peoples, the contact between Jews and non-Jews continued to widen. But this contact always remained limited. *Nowhere was it ever close enough for the Jews to dissolve themselves and be swallowed up by the foreign body.* [Italics mine.] In all contact with strangers, Jews stubbornly remained separate. Consequently, the hatred did not remain isolated in any one place. It encompassed many peoples, almost the entire world, since Jews came into contact with many nations through the centuries.

The causes of Jew-hatred continued to multiply. New accusations were added, new fuel was added to the fire. When the object of the hatred was conspicuous and always the same—in medieval times the Jew was forced to wear distinctive clothing—the hatred became permanent, part of a way of life.

Among the peoples a certain opinion was formed concerning Jews, namely, that they follow wicked and odious ways. Mostly these "wicked ways" were fabricated, but their number continued to grow, until eventually there took shape a totally negative stereotype of the Jew, a creature without any redeeming human qualities, an inhuman, anti-human, destructive creature, a partner of the Devil himself.

This stereotype, as an idea, was then handed down almost as an inheritance from generation to generation. All those hate motifs combined and joined together, and what finally evolved was a fused mass of hatred that has persisted to our own day.

With this key to an understanding of the problem of Jew-hatred one must agree in every particular. This logical explanation is the only way to understand the persecutions, decrees, and pogroms visited upon Jews at various times in Europe and elsewhere. In "peaceful" times the accumulated Jew-hatred did not disappear, but only lay hidden in dark corners. In "troubled" times, during an economic crisis, a war, a revolution, civil strife, the fused mass of hatred then floated to the surface and the popular wrath was poured out upon the nearest Jews.

In this book, I highlight the main causes of Jew-hatred in all countries during the last twenty-four hundred years. Each of the thirty-one chapters deals with a section of Jewish history in different countries, in a particular period. All the decrees, libels, expulsions, and other tragedies which I discuss were always and everywhere a result of the "fused mass of hatred." In addition, Jew-hatred in every country, in every epoch, was influenced by the existing historical climate.

I wrote this book in Yiddish. My friend Max Rosenfeld translated it into English.* I have followed a chronological order in presenting the periods of Jewish history in Eretz Israel and throughout the Diaspora. The Jews were and still are a "world people." Not without reason did that great Jewish historian Simon Dubnow call his crowning work. "The World History of the Jewish People."

S. G.
Miami Beach
August 1979

*Most of the quotations in my manuscript were originally translated from English, Hebrew, and Russian into Yiddish, then retranslated into English. Therefore, quotations are not verbatim.

1

Beginnings of Jew-Hatred

The Dispersion

Hatred of Jews precedes Christianity. At the beginning of the third century B.C.E., writings were circulated in Egypt containing blatant anti-Jewish slanders.[1] Similar propaganda was widespread in almost every country where Jews lived in proximity with non-Jews, including cities in Judea itself.

Until the fifth century B.C.E., however, there is no evidence of Judophobia. The wars with the "Children of Israel" mentioned in the older writings of the Bible are not properly Judophobia. Quarrels among shepherds over wells, Esau's resentment of Jacob over Isaac's blessing, the war with Amalek, the battles with Canaanites and Philistines—these conflicts were not caused by Jew-hatred as we understand it today. In early times shepherds fought over pasture lands and water sources, nomadic tribes attacked farm settlements, peoples warred over borders and tribute. Even the comment in Genesis 43:32 that the Egyptians would not eat at the same table with Jews "because it was an abomination" cannot be considered Jew-hatred, since similar negative expressions are found in old Egyptian sources about Greeks and other peoples who had varying dietary customs.

From the end of the fifth century we begin to hear of prejudices, false accusations, even of pogroms against Jewish communities outside Judea. Before we examine the reasons for this, we shall first comment upon the emigration of Jews from their country and their dispersion in other lands.

Geographically, Palestine was not a place conducive to a peaceful existence. On the borders of large continents, surrounded on the north, east, and south by stronger and more warlike peoples, the small Hebrew kingdom had very little chance of remaining independent. When Egypt, Aram, Assyria, Babylonia, Persia, and later Greece and Rome, waged their wars against each other, the tiny Jewish country was a constant intrusion. The inhabitants of the Hebrew kingdoms were frequently despoiled by foreign armies who marched through their country. More often than not, the little country was under the heel of a neighboring power. Moreover, the Hebrew tribes split into two separate kingdoms—Israel and Judah[2]—which feuded for most of their existence.

In 722 B.C.E. Assyria attacked the northern kingdom, Israel, put many of its people to death, and took many captives. In 586 B.C.E. Babylonia conquered Judea, destroyed the Holy Temple in Jerusalem, and exiled much of its population. Within their communities in foreign lands the exiled Jews built synagogues to compensate for the loss of the Temple, and followed their traditional way of life as best they could. Because of their religious beliefs, they did not mingle with their pagan neighbors.

Some forty years after Babylonia conquered Judea, Persian armies overran Babylonia. The Persian kings permitted those Jews who wished to do so to return to their homeland. They also gave them the right to rebuild their Temple and even to restore and fortify the walls and gates of Jerusalem. While many Jews did return to Judea, most of the exiles stayed in Babylonia, where they had built new lives for themselves.

In addition to Assyria, Babylonia and Persia, Jewish settlements were also established around the Mediterranean and in Egypt. As opposed to the forced relocation of Jews in the northern countries, most Jews settled in Egypt voluntarily. Often they migrated to escape from famine or attacks on their own country. There were other reasons for these migrations. For example, it was then the practice for a victorious army to take young captives to sell in foreign slave marts. Jewish slaves were often ransomed by fellow Jews and many remained and became members of these foreign Jewish communities.

Through the centuries in which Palestine was the recognized land of the Jews it was seldom independent. From 586 B.C.E. to 135 C.E., a period of seven hundred and twenty years, Judea was subject to Babylonia, Persia, Greece, and Rome. The only exception is the seventy-eight years of Maccabean rule, from 141 to 63 B.C.E. Throughout this time the number of Jews in the Disaspora continually increased. The prophets from Isaiah on (mid-seventh century B.C.E.) already speak of *kibutz galiot* ("ingathering of the exiles") when Jews would return to Zion from Egypt, Assyria, Cush, the islands of the sea.

Jewish communities abounded. In the northeast, Jews were settled in Assyria, Babylonia and Persia; in the southwest, in Egypt; in the north, in Asia Minor and surrounding areas as far as the Black Sea; in the west they were already in the Aegean Islands and other islands in the Mediterranean. Jews had settled in North Africa, whence they migrated to Rome. When General Pompey, in 63 B.C.E., brought Jewish captives from Judea to Rome to sell them on the slave market, they were ransomed by the Jewish community there. From Rome, Jews migrated further west, to Gaul, Spain, and deeper into Europe.

Flavius Josephus, in his *Antiquities of the Jews*, cites the complaint of the Greek historian Strabo: "Jews can be found in all cities. There is practically no inhabited place in the world where that race has not penetrated and does not exercise its influence."[3]

In the days of Julius Caesar there were some two hundred Jewish communities in the lands ruled by Rome. It is estimated that at that time there were approximately five million Jews in the entire Roman Empire, including Judea, with four million living outside of the Jewish state. Philo of Alexandria reports, early in the first century C.E., that "Jerusalem is not only the capital of Judea, it is also the capital of the Jews of all countries, because Jews are scattered throughout all the lands."

Life of the Jews in the Diaspora

There is no reason to believe that the occupations of the Jews in the Diaspora were different from those of the people among whom they lived. Jews were farmers, cattle raisers, artisans. Living conditions were generally not easy. People earned their living by the sweat of their brow. In none of the denunciations of Jews in ancient times do we ever hear them charged with growing rich at the expense of others. No Jew-haters in ancient times ever accused Jews of practicing usury. Jews were the same as their neighbors in every respect except religion and traditional customs. The only complaint of that classic Jew-hater of antiquity, Haman, was: ". . . *v'dateyhem shonot mikol am*" (". . . their [religious] laws are different from those of all other peoples").[4]

Though the Jews in the Dispersion kept apart from their neighbors, they did become assimilated linguistically. In strange surroundings, they were compelled to adopt the foreign tongue in their social and economic life and give up the Hebrew language. Thus, when some Jews did return to Judea from Babylon (around 545 B.C.E.) they brought Aramaic with them and continued to use it for many centuries, creating in it many important cultural treasures.

In Alexandria, Egypt, the Jews spoke Greek as early as the second and third generations, even translating their sacred writings into that language. Of all their cultural possessions the Jews in foreign lands safeguarded only their religious laws and their traditional holidays and customs. To these values they held on assiduously. In order for them to do so (and also for convenience and safety), Jews in foreign lands stayed close together, separate from the non-Jews. They did not eat in the homes of the pagans, take part in their festivals, enter their temples, or intermarry with them.

Many other peoples in antiquity were conquered and exiled from their countries. Most of them, uprooted from their own soil, gradually assimilated with their neighbors. Not so the Jews. Through the centuries that Jews lived among foreign peoples, although they adopted foreign tongues and foreign names, they remained separate. Occasionally one can trace in Jewish customs and traditions certain foreign influences, but generally speaking, the Jewish religion was kept free of such influences. Jewish religious law surrounded itself with "fences."

During those centuries when primal Jew-hatred was being crystallized, many Jews were living among the Greeks. Like all idolworshipping peoples, the Greeks were firm believers in their Olympus, the home of their gods, and were zealots of their own traditional culture. The *polis*, the Greek city government, was closely tied to the religious cult. Public allegiance was given to the god Zeus. The Jews, even the assimilated ones, therefore avoided public meetings. They spoke Greek like other citizens, but they did not participate in the city's public life.

The Greeks could not understand how one could be a Greek and a Jew at the same time. Jewish apartness irritated them, Jewish customs seemed strange and bizarre. Circumcision, the Sabbath, ritual immersion, the dietary laws, the belief in "the Book," were held up to ridicule. The secretive Jewish way of whispering their prayers was viewed with suspicion. In addition, the Greek priests looked askance at the ornate temples built by Jews, certain that they were constructed for the purpose of attracting non-Jews, that Jews had been taught by Moses to destroy the religions of their neighbors.

Religious beliefs are essentially unprovable. Scientifically nothing about religion can really be tested or questioned. Any other's faith cannot be understood. Just as Jews could not understand how pagans could possibly believe in their inanimate idols, so non-Jews could not understand why Jews held fast to their faith in an unseen God. Jewish separateness was seen as arrogance. They may have deduced that Jews must hate other people; the Jewish God must hate other gods, witness that all the other peoples placed statues of their gods in Olympus.

The more the Jews kept themselves apart, the deeper grew the hostility toward them, and conversely. This vicious circle, together with natural socio-economic differences and dissensions that arose and the fact that Jews were strangers, created the first seeds of Jew-hatred within the peoples among whom the Jews lived.

Certain that theirs was the true faith, that sooner or later all the peoples would recognize the one true God, the Jews did look down on their idolatrous neighbors; they disparaged the "ignorant and the blind" who failed to recognize their own creator. Later, the Christians also looked down upon the idolators and considered them "ignorant and blind." But while the Christians, by certain "rights" of the Church, were able to absorb and dominate the idolators, first with the promise of "redemption" and later by force, the Jews were able only to disparage the idolators, without having any "right" to do so.

This belittling of their neighbors aroused a counter-feeling of hatred against the Jews, who were foreigners, subjects. There are remnants of Roman legislation which prohibit Jews from ridiculing the beliefs of others. The Roman emperor Claudius (41-54 C.E.) tells the Jews that he will permit them to observe their religious practices only if they agree not to deride the religion of other people.[5]

Because of the commandment against "graven images,"[6] Jews were granted permission not to place statues of emperors in their temples. These and other privileges—not given to other peoples—added to the anti-Jewish feelings already growing among their neighbors, and animosity which continued to mount without respite.

Jews as Missionaries

Quite early in the Dispersion there was a missionary tendency among the Jews. At every opportunity they endeavored to convert pagans to Judaism. The Jews of old were convinced that all the "non-believing" peoples would eventually turn to Judaism. In the mid-sixth century B.C.E. the prophet Zechariah, who returned to Judea from Babylonia, spoke of "strangers who will cleave to us." He consoles his brothers who had left Babylon with him: "It will yet come to pass that many mighty nations will seek the God of Jerusalem and worship Yahveh."[7]

In attempting to convert the idolaters, Jews engaged them in debates, deriding the hand-made gods of wood and stone which "have eyes and see not, which have ears and hear not" (Ps. 115:5-6). The pagan priests were incensed by this and attacked the foreign blasphemers by hurling counter-accusations against them. A cluster of libelous charges developed in those days, lies which Jew-haters repeated wherever Jews lived, and which continue to this day.

From 66 to 73 C.E., when Judea was destroyed by Rome, there was a large Jewish community in Alexandria. Many Greeks and Egyptians also lived there. Jews and Greeks had been brought here by Alexander of Macedonia when he conquered the area in 332 B.C.E. A considerable number of Jews were also brought here as captives during the long wars among Alexander's heirs.[8] Philo reports that in his time (20 B.C.E.–50 C.E.) approximately a million Jews resided in Egypt, out of a total population of eight million.[9]

In the mid-third century B.C.E. the Jews in Egypt translated their sacred writings into Greek, having forgotten the Hebrew in which the Torah was originally written. Thus appeared the famous Greek translation of the Bible know as the Septuagint. Another reason for this translation was the aforementioned tendency of the Jews of that time toward proselytism. Philo, who lived two hundred fifty years after the Bible was first translated, wrote: "The translation of the Jewish writings is a frontal attack on decadent paganism."

With the Holy Scriptures in Greek, the Jews in the Diaspora could more easily maintain their identity with the Jewish people. In turn, the non-Jewish world gained access to the source of the Jewish religion and its traditions and customs. This, then, was still another reason for translating the Bible—to refute the ugly libels that were already being widely disseminated wherever Jewish communities existed, but particularly in Egypt.

2

Jew-Hatred
in Antiquity

An account of the anti-Jewish feeling in Persia in the fourth century B.C.E. is the popular book that was incorporated into the Scriptures, the *Megillat Esther* (*Scroll of Esther*). It reflects the lot of the Jews in the Eastern Diaspora around the latter part of the fourth century. The story is well-known. The Jew-hater, Haman, persuades King Ahasuerus to issue a decree ordering the death of all the Jews in his 127 "provinces." The charges that Haman brings against the Jews are typical of the time: they observe different customs and do not keep the king's laws. Haman then casts lots to choose a lucky date for the massacre and it comes up the fourteenth of the Jewish month of Adar.

Ahasuerus had selected for a wife one of his comeliest concubines, the Jewish maiden, Esther, who has kept her origins secret. Some time earlier, Esther's uncle, Mordecai, had saved the king's life and he thus earned a place among the intimates of the royal court. Mordecai forms an alliance with his niece and they devise a plot to turn the king against Haman. Instead of executing Mordecai, Ahasuerus orders Haman hanged and grants the Jews permission to defend themselves. The Jews do so and slay many of their enemies who have come to exterminate them.

Most historians agree that even though the story of Esther may be fiction, it is based on historical fact. The author of *Megillat Esther* could not have invented a Haman had there not been Jew-haters in his time who sought the destruction of the entire Jewish people, a "final solution." That such hatred was widespread among the masses of people and not the chance feeling of a single individual is readily apparent from the writer's incidental but very significant observation.

In the message that Haman sends out to all the nations, we read: "The contents of the document were to be promulgated in every province and be published to all peoples, that they should be ready for that day" (Esther 3:14). This clearly refers to being ready to annihilate the Jews. The passage in the book in which the writer assigns this "noble" mission not to any organization of killers but "to all the peoples" shows that he was familiar with the violent nature of the Jew-hatred that manifested itself wherever Jewish communities evolved.

The second century of the Persian epoch (440-332 B.C.E.) is usually designated by Jewish historians as a "mute" century,[1] only a few authentic historical facts having come down to us from that period. The Scroll of Esther partially lifts this curtain and reveals the wall of hate that already existed between the Jews and their neighbors in the lands of the Middle East.

Ezra and Nehemiah

Until Joseph ben Mattathias (Flavius Josephus, 38-100 C.E.), there was no Jewish historiography as such. The biblical books of 2 Samuel and 1 and 2 Kings are considered to be the annals of the Hebrew kings, but these chronicles end with the exile to Babylon in 586 B.C.E. From around the mid-fifth century we have the writings of two important personalities, Ezra and Nehemiah, which were incorporated into the Scriptures.

In these two books we are told how the two leaders came from Persia to Judea with a mission assigned to them by the Persian ruler. With all the authority of royal satraps they instituted serious and strict reforms in Judea. One of these reforms was the forced dissolution of marriages between Jews and non-Jews or half-Jews. The people assembled at some time in the month of Kislev and stood for hours in a pouring rain to listen to Ezra's condemnation of mixed marriages. With solemn oaths they swore to cleanse themselves of this sin. Women who stemmed from non-Jewish backgrounds were forcibly separated from their Jewish families, along with their children, and cast out without a claim.

The reason for such an implacable step undoubtedly flowed from the assurance of these religious zealots that their faith was truer and more exalted than that of their pagan neighbors. It is also not inconceivable that this rigid posture of Ezra and Nehemiah toward "strangers" was in some degree a reaction to the animosity which the Jews were already experiencing themselves. Understandably, Jews have never felt friendly toward governments or peoples that have persecuted them. In any case, it is easy to imagine that this attitude only helped arouse more hatred against the Jews.

On the other hand, even in the ancient period under discussion, the Jews were already forced to depend on the protection of the rulers.[2] In the Persian epoch, they sought the protection of the emperors; later, of the Greek and Roman kings, their governors and satraps. By that time, the Jews had obtained privileges from these rulers that other conquered peoples did not have. The book of Nehemiah mentions that the Jews even obtained permission to secure Jerusalem from foreign invasion. Such magnanimous behavior toward conquered states is not encountered anywhere else in antiquity. Josephus tells us that when Alexander the Great captured a territory, he considered the Jewish inhabitants more trustworthy than the others and granted them all sorts of special privileges.[3] Such favors and privileges would have been sufficient to provoke feelings of envy, suspicion, and hostility.

Ezra's separatist reforms did not help the situation. As the Chronicles tell us, it was around that time that surprise armed attacks took place upon Jerusalem, and slanders against the Jews began to reach the ears of the Persian rulers. This hostility must have spilled over the borders of little Judea and into the Diaspora.

Early in the third century B.C.E. the Egyptian historian-priest Manetho rewrote the story of the Hebrew exodus from Egypt, incorporating the counter-legends to the original version which placed the Egyptians in an unfavorable light. An abridged version of his account follows: The Egyptian Pharaoh Amenophis I of the Eighteenth Dynasty dreamed that in order to serve god faithfully he had to purge his country of lepers. So he gathered all the lepers together—80,000 of them—and settled them in a separate city to work for him as slaves.

A renegade priest named Asarsif persuaded the lepers to rebel against the gods, kill the holy cattle, disobey the Pharaoh, and so on. As Amenophis prepared to punish them, the lepers sought the aid of the Hyksos in Syria, who arrived 200,000 strong and forced the armies of Egypt to flee to Ethiopia. The Hyksos and the lepers then plundered the land until the king was able to gather his forces and drive them out.

The renegade Asarsif then changed his name to Moses and composed a book of laws for the lepers, a corrupt tribe which gave itself the name "Hebrews." Among other things, he taught them to hate all other peoples. Their custom of avoiding contact with "foreigners" actually stemmed from the fact that they were lepers who no one would touch.

Very little remains today of Manetho's concoction. We know of them only through quotations in other works. Josephus quotes him at length in his book, *Against Apion*, in which he exposes the falsifications. Josephus wrote more than three hundred years after Manetho's death, but the slanders had not evaporated, nor have they yet.

At that time, Jews were actively converting pagans to Judaism. Concomitantly, the Greeks (among whom there were many Jewish communities) were striving to introduce their neighbors to the higher Greek culture. That Jews should spiritually influence others, including Greeks, shocked and infuriated the Greek intelligentsia, especially the priests. A process of disintegration had been going on for several decades in the pagan religions, and one of the contributing reasons was the preaching of the Jews against idolatry.

The Greeks not only considered their culture superior, but also saw themselves as the political guardian of the region, a position they actually held until Rome defeated them in the second century B.C.E. The Romans treated the Greeks with suspicion, granting them few privileges and curtailing their autonomy. At the same time, they granted the Jews many concessions, and in disputes between Greeks and Jews, interceded in behalf of the latter. In one instance, Josephus relates that a Jewish delegation from the Island of Pharos complained to the Roman proconsul about the curtailment of their religious and civil rights and that the proconsul reproached the Greeks for this state of affairs. "I am displeased," he wrote to them, "that you curb the rights of our friends and allies."[4]

This abnormal situation, where the former rulers of the region were stripped of their rights while their former subjects were now Roman citizens with special privileges, served only to exacerbate anti-Jewish feelings. Fighting broke out frequently in public places. Priests and orators kept adding fresh slanders against the Jews. Jew-haters even found "proof" of vile Jewish traits in the Septuagint, the Greek translation of the Bible. Chapter 7 of Deuteronomy plainly states that God warned the Jews not to mix with the Canaanites or intermarry with them because they were idolators.

In his polemics with these hate-mongers, Josephus disproved the lies and jibed at their perpetrators, such as Pasadonius, a highly esteemed scholar, who asserted that on the basis of their heinous customs, the Jews deserved to be destroyed. Josephus also challenged the Roman historian Diodorus of Sicily, who had fabricated a fresh commentary on the origin of the Jewish Sabbath. When the Hebrews were driven out of Egypt, he theorized, they ran for six days in the desert without stopping, until their feet were so cut and bruised that they were forced to stop and rest. In Egypt, such wounds were known as "Sabasosis" and since the Jews spoke Egyptian at that time, the custom of resting on the seventh day evolved into "*shabbat*."[5]

In *Against Apion,* Josephus tells us about one of the most rabid Jew-baiters of ancient times. Apion was born in Libya, settled in Alexandria, and then changed his nationality from Egyptian to Greek. A gifted orator, he considered himself one of the great Greek spirits of all time. In his speeches and writings he preached a hatred of Jews, but covered it up with many embellishments. His most "original" innovation was the story that Jews were cannibals.

One of the most potent causes of anti-Jewish prejudice lay in the socio-economic conditions of the time. The Greeks and Phoenicians were the acknowledged international merchants of the world. Following the Punic Wars and the fall of Carthage, the Greeks dominated this field. With the proliferation of Jewish settlements in the Diaspora, and with their contacts with fellow Jews in foreign lands, the Jews too had turned to world trade. In time the Greeks began to feel the competition of these "foreigners" and became further enraged against them.

From time to time an aroused mob would attack a Jewish quarter. Greeks and other nationalities who lived in the port cities in northern Judea were as inimical to the Jews as their brothers elsewhere. In the Syrian city of Antioch, where there was a large Jewish colony, hostility toward the Jews evolved just as it had in Alexandria. The Syrian armies which Antiochus led against the Jews were imbued with Jew-hatred. Contemporaneously with the wars against the Syrians, the Hasmoneans had to deal with uprisings in the border areas of their land by Ammonites, Edomites, Samaritans, and the remnants of the Philistines, as well as by Arab tribes in the surrounding deserts.[6]

These conflicts between Judea and its neighboring peoples never really ceased. Attacks on Jewish communities in the farflung areas of the Diaspora occurred more frequently,[7] except during the reigns of Julius Caesar and Augustus Caesar, both of whom maintained good relations with the Jews. The enmity did not vanish altogether, however, but continued to fester beneath the surface.

Development of Jew-Hatred: Destruction of Judea

The Jews did not remain silent in face of the slanders that were being spread against them. Their strongest weapon was religious propaganda. To the accusation of godlessness the Jews replied with their faith in the true God who had created the world. To the wild fabrications about Jewish "misanthropy" and "barbaric" customs, they responded with many examples from scholarly literature which emphasized the high moral standard of their behavior and way of life. Furthermore, they threw open the doors of their synagogues to anyone who wished to hear God's word. Thus, together with the intensification of Jew-hatred came an increase in Jewish proselytism resulting in many converts.

The first century B.C.E. and the first century C.E. also saw the emergence of all the factors which exacerbated anti-Jewish feelings: the Jewish dispersion to ever new lands; the self-imposed Jewish isolation; their derogatory attitude toward paganism (the religion of their conquerors); the resultant anti-Jewish activities of the pagan priests; and finally, the widespread anti-Jewish literature in all parts of the world. All these causes, multiplied by the socio-economic ones, served to intensify the anti-Jewish flames.

The general political situation in that part of the world in those centuries was hardly peaceful. Civil and foreign wars added to the suffering of people everywhere with a concomitant antipathy toward strangers. Hatred for the Jewish strangers began to find expression in deeds. Physical attacks upon Jews became a common occurrence.

The Jewish communities in Babylonia and Persia were older than those in Egypt, Syria, and the other lands around the Mediterranean. Rome had never entirely subjugated these "Parthians," as they called the nations of the Middle East. Jews lived there side-by-side with Syrians, Greeks, Persians, Armenians and other peoples. In some cities, entire sections were inhabited solely by Jews.

Among the Syrians and Greeks in those lands, feelings against Jews were the same as in Alexandria and Antioch. Josephus relates that early in the first century C.E., at Seleucia, a city of Syrians and Greeks, Jews who went there seeking refuge were murdered by the thousands.* While his figures may be exaggerated, the basic outline of the situation is clear.

3

The Jews in Rome

Jewish settlements appeared in Rome and the Phoenician Isles later than in the lands of the East. In the mid-second century B.C.E. the Roman rulers signed treaties of friendship with the Maccabees. During the civil war between Julius Caesar and Pompey in the first century B.C.E., the Jews fought on the side of Caesar. (They had never forgiven Pompey for the devastation of Jerusalem in 63 B.C.E.) Victorious in this struggle, Julius Caesar remained friendly to the Jews, granting Roman citizenship to Jews living in foreign lands. About twenty years later, Octavius Augustus confirmed all previous Jewish rights and added new ones.

In addition to having their own Jewish court and permission to observe the Sabbath, as well as exemption from certain taxes, the Jews also had the right to collect gifts for the Holy Temple in Jerusalem. Among the poorer classes, who were the majority of the population, Jew-baiters began to complain that their poverty was due to the scarcity of gold and silver, commodities which the Jews were sending to Jerusalem.

The same factors that gave rise to Jew-hatred in Egypt, Syria, and other places were at work in Rome, too, where it appeared particularly as a result of Jewish preachments against idolatry. Proof of the success of Jewish conversion efforts was found in the catacombs. In three Jewish cemeteries unearthed in 1602, 1859, and 1919, many of the graves bear inscriptions indicating that the deceased had been a convert.[1] Jewish proselytism reached into the highest strata of Roman society, including even the noble families of the Caesars.[2]

Concern over this state of affairs was expressed by some leading Romans of the period. The philosopher-statesman Seneca complained: "The customs of this despicable race have grown popular in all the lands."[3] The historian Tacitus charged: "The Roman conquest of the Jews has not eliminated their influence. Rather than slackening, the Jewish cultural offensive has grown even stronger."[4] The satirist Juvenal, mocking the Judaized Romans, sneered:

> A person whose father was too lazy to work on the seventh day of the week will come to revere the clouds and the heavenly spirits. . . . He would sooner eat human flesh than pork. He is likely to be circumcised as well. . . . Such a person will obey only the Judaic laws that Moses left his followers in some mysterious book.[5]

It was the same Seneca who calculated that a person who rests every seventh day loses one-seventh of his life!

Josephus taunts the Jew-baiters: "They complain that the Jews corrupt the morals of the Romans. But no one is being forced to adopt our customs—they do it of their own free will. And the wonder of it is that our temples do not lure them with pleasures."[6] (A reference to the practice of pagan priests who arranged sex orgies in their temples as a way of keeping their followers.)

Rome Destroys Judea

The fate of the Jews in all the lands of the Roman Empire, including Judea, deteriorated following the deaths of the Jewish king Herod and Augustus Caesar. The Jews hated King Herod, who stemmed from Idumean converts and had gained the throne with the help of the Roman army. Knowing he was intensely disliked by the people, and fearing that he would be replaced by a member of the Hasmonean family, he put to death every Hasmonean he could find, including his own wife Miriam and her two sons.

In his will, Herod divided the small Jewish nation into several parts to be ruled by each of his sons. This aroused such popular opposition that soon after his death, in 4 B.C.E., there were mass protests in Jerusalem. Archelaus, Herod's son, then sent a Roman legion against the demonstration, resulting in the deaths of three thousand Jews.[7] Seven weeks later, while Archelaus was in Rome awaiting Caesar's confirmation of his father's last will and testament, there were more demonstrations in Jerusalem. According to Josephus, two thousand Jews were crucified by the Roman troops who were dispatched to the scene.[8]

At the same time, two delegations arrived in Rome: a Jewish delegation, petitioned Caesar to free Judea from the Herodian dynasty and allow the land to be a Roman province without a king; a Greek-Syrian delegation, which petitioned that those cities in Judea populated by non-Jews also be permitted to secede from Judea.

The Roman authority confirmed Herod's will and Augustus Caesar divided Judea into three small states. He named Archelaus ruler over a small area with Jerusalem as capital. He also granted the petition severing Caesarea and two other cities on the Jordan River from Judea. A few years later, after Rome had exiled Archelaus, Judea was ruled by special Roman procurators whose function was to maintain the staus quo and collect taxes.

By that time, the mood in Rome was strongly anti-Jewish. The procurators were contemptuous of the Jews and their religion; their only interest in Judea was how much they could steal. During the period of the first procurators (7–26c.e.), the situation in Judea grew more and more strained. Impoverished by the heavy taxes, people went into debt; for not paying one's debts, one could be sold into slavery. Anti-Jewish provocations increased markedly.

From 26 to 36 C.E. the Procurator Pontius Pilate ruled Judea. Philo of Alexandria, a contemporary, related that Pilate was a man without scruples, cruel, wealthy, and totally devoid of conscience. Later historians described Pontius Pilate as the Roman representative who crucified Jesus, but in Christian theological literature of that time and since, he is not blamed for the murder. He did it, the Church insists, at the demand of the Jews, the priests, the Pharisees, the Elders.

In the ten years that Pilate was high commissioner of Judea, conditions there worsened significantly. The same was true of the Diaspora, where attempts to curb Jewish rights and physical attacks upon Jewish communities became more frequent. Rome at that time was ruled by Gaius Caligula, a psychopath with delusions of divinity, who ordered statues of himself erected in the temples of all the peoples in his empire. The Jews—for whom this would have been a grievous sin—refused to obey this order.

The then high commissioner of Egypt, Aulus Flaccus, a scoundrel and a Jew-hater, who was out of favor with the Roman authorities, sought to redeem himself by accusing the Jews of treason. The ensuing pogrom in Alexandria in 38 C.E., organized with Flaccus's assistance, served as a signal for attacks upon Jews in many other cities of the Diaspora, as well as in Judea. Flaccus abolished all Jewish privileges in Egypt, stripped the Jews of their Roman citizenship, and even tried to prevent them from observing the Sabbath.[9]

In 40 C.E. the Jews of Alexandria sent a delegation, led by Philo, to Rome to denounce the high commissioner and request permission to remove the statues from their places of worship. At the same time, a Greek delegation, led by the infamous Apion, arrived in Rome to urge the emperor to revoke the citizenship of the Jews, as well as their other rights and privileges. Caesar listened favorably to the Greeks and sent the Jewish delegation home empty-handed.

The decree placing statues of Caesar in the Jewish temples posed a mortal threat to Jerusalem, to the land of Judea, and to all the Jewish communities within the Roman Empire. Fortunately, Caligula was assassinated shortly thereafter and the new Caesar, Claudius, annulled his predecessor's orders. Claudius turned over the rule of an expanded and united Judea to his friend Agrippa, a grandson of King Herod. For four years the Jews were freed of the rule of Roman procurators, but after Agrippa's sudden death in 44 C.E., Rome reinstituted this method of government.

All the Roman commissioners in Judea from then on were reprobates who, instead of calming the uneasy land, only increased the disruptions. As a result, Jewish rebelliousness mounted. An important factor in aggravating the relations between the Jews and Rome, and leading to the tragic uprising in 66 C.E., was the provocation of Jew-haters in Judean cities with mixed populations. In Caesarea, for example, the Jews were in the majority, but anti-Jewish feelings often led to open fights which were joined by the Greek and Syrian members of the Roman legion stationed there.

During the rule of the Procurator Fadus, from 44 to 46 C.E., the non-Jewish population of Caesarea proposed that they be counted with the Roman legion, thus making them a majority and giving them the right to deprive the Jews of their citizenship. The result caused a series of clashes. During one such fight, the Roman legion inflicted a pogrom upon the Jews of Caesarea. When the Jews complained to Nero, he decided that Caesarea was really a Greek city and that the Jews were strangers there.[10]

This decision led to new provocations and new clashes, Jewish zealots called for an uprising against Roman rule. In 66 C.E. the Greeks set up an altar near a synagogue entrance and one Sabbath morning, as the Jews gathered there, a Greek conducted a sacrificial rite with a bird. This was an open act of contempt for the Jews, because in Jewish religious law, birds were sacrificed by lepers. When the Jews complained to the Roman Procurator Florus, he arrested the delegation and levied a huge tax upon the Jewish community. The resultant protest was met with an attack by the Roman legion. These and similar provocatons finally snapped the patience of the Jews.

The uprising of Judea against Rome lasted from 66 to 73 C.E. The second Temple in Jerusalem was destroyed. The Jewish population was decimated and many young Jews were dragged to Rome in chains and sold into slavery.

When the uprising began, attacks upon Jews took place in cities of Judea with a mixed population, as well as upon Jewish communities in the Diaspora. By that time, anti-Jewish enmity was ablaze in every corner of the Roman Empire and in most lands around the Mediterranean. A few generations later, Christianity encountered the hostility towards Jews already widespread in all the provinces of the Roman Empire. Added to the earlier causes of Jew-hatred was the agitation of this new faith which was expanding and striving to become master of the world.

4

Beginning and Spread of Christianity

From manuscripts unearthed in the Judean Desert in the mid-twentieth century, it is apparent that Christianity evolved from a schism in the Hasidic party in Judea some time around the Hasmonean revolt against the Greeks between 167 and 141 B.C.E. The schism was basically due to a religious dispute. Under the leadership of one called the "Teacher of Righteousness," a group of ultrapious Jews split away from the Hasidic party. They isolated themselves in the desert, where they proceeded to cleanse themselves of their sins and consecrate themselves to God.[1]

As votaries dedicated to obeying every single law of the Torah, they forged a "new covenant" with God because the old covenant had been nullified by the sinful Jews. In light of the evil decrees and the unending wars they were subjected to, these Zealots concluded that their era represented the "end of days" described in the sacred writings; that the "Day of Yahveh" forecast by the prophets would come in their time; and that it would be a day of judgment (Amos 5:18; Isa. 13:6; 46:10; 30:3; Joel 4:14).

Sticklers for the minutiae of the Torah, the Zealots were convinced that God had endowed their leader with the Holy Spirit, so that he would be enabled to reveal the secrets contained within the sacred writings. Perhaps, when making their predictions, the prophets had not even been aware of the truths hidden in their own words. From these prophetic passages the Teacher of Righteousness had gathered that the Zealots were God's chosen who would stand by His right hand when He judged the world.

During that time of torment and transition, the Zealots knew that a mighty confrontation was brewing between God's light and the darkness of Satan. Along with a redeemer they fashioned an "anti-redeemer." Setting himself against the Messiah was an "anti-Messiah," the embodiment of sin and evil who led human beings astray. God-fearing people had to drive him away, expunge him from their souls. Therefore, those who refused to enter into the "new covenant" were being led by Satan, the incarnation of sin, falsehood, darkness, impurity, wickedness, and death.

In addition to the idolatrous evildoers who oppressed the Jews, these Zealots also designated as Sons of Darkness their former brothers of the Hasidic party who had not joined them in forging the new covenant with God. Those who disbelieved that the Teacher of Righteousness interpreted the sacred writings with the help of a holy spirit were declared even more wicked than the idolators and the uncircumcised.[2]

The precise time and cause of this split in the Hasidic organization is unknown to us. Neither the Zealots nor their opponents, the Perushim, have left us a written history. But a few references concerning the dispute have remained in the literature written a few decades following the Maccabean revolt. The first book of Maccabees (end of second century B.C.E.) describes several events which provide reasons and motives for the sharp division among the Hasidim.[3]

Chapter 2 of the book tells of a thousand Jews—men, women and children—who hid in a cave to avoid the decrees of Antiochus Epiphanes. The Greeks found and murdered every one of them. The Jews offered no resistance whatever because it was the Sabbath day. We are also told that following this tragedy there was a great controversy among Jews as to whether it was moral to let people be slaughtered like sheep and not take up arms because of the Sabbath.[4]

The same book also contains an account which throws light on another vital motive for the split among the Hasidim. It had been a tradition for centuries that the post of high priest in the Temple pass by inheritance from father to son, or to the closest male relative in the priestly family, the Sons of Zadok. The family's claim to the position dated back to the days of the First Temple and had prevailed through many generations. The Hasmonean brothers, John and Simon, who were priests, but not the priestly family, abolished the ancient claim of the Sons of Zadok. Then Simon usurped this claim for himself, for his children, and his children's children, "until a prophet will arise and decide." Simon even threatened severe punishment against "the priests and anyone who will oppose this."[5]

Other signs of the schism are also present in the Book of Daniel, at least several chapters of which originate from the period of the Hasmonean struggle or soon afterward. The author of Daniel, evidently a Zealot, belittles the Maccabeans, describing their victories and newfound freedom as "a little help." Salvation, the author informs us, came not so much from the Hasmoneans as from divine intervention. "And the king shall do according to his will; and he shall exalt and magnify himself above every god, and shall speak strange things against the God of gods; and he shall prosper till the indignation be at an end, for that which is determined shall be accomplished" (11:36). The king (Antiochus) would be successful, but only until God's anger had subsided, because that is how it had been decided on high and that is how it would be.[6]

The split among the Hasidim, the fury of the sectarians against the "evildoers" (the Hasmoneans) and against the other Jews who followed and supported them, was no temporary pique. The Dead Sea Scrolls cast a clear light on just how deep this schism was. The Zealots speak of Judea in negative terms. They describe Jerusalem and even the Temple with intense hatred, since it had been "defiled" by the priests. They abuse and threaten the sinners with Judgment Day. They teach their followers never to stop hating the sinners. The pious ones were the only ones God had selected to survive. He had forged the new covenant with them and them alone.[7]

The Manual of Discipline (one of the scrolls) teaches the member of the new covenant how to behave toward the Sons of Darkness. "No one is to associate with them. They are to be ostracized. You may not eat or drink with them. You may not accept a thing from them. . . ."The new member had to swear an oath: "I will not still my rage against the corrupt people until the day of reckoning."[8]

From the ideology and the organizational structure of the Zealot sect it becomes evident that these ancient writings, several generations later, formed the basis for the New Testament. The terms and concepts in the Gospels—Day of Judgment, Kingdom of Heaven, the baptismal laws, the Critic (Episcopos) who keeps watch over his community, the awaited Messiah, rewarding good for evil, the struggle of the Sons of Light against the Sons of Darkness—and many other such phrases are found in the ancient scrolls. We even encounter in these scrolls a number of passages from the Five Books of Moses and the Prophets that were later incorporated into the New Testament as the most valid evidence in Jewish writings for the appearance of Jesus the Messiah.

Immediately after the destruction of Jerusalem from 66 to 73 C.E., Christian theologians declared that the catastrophe had been God's punishment upon the Jews who had condemned and crucified the "Redeemer." In order to strengthen and lend substance to the new religion, the founders of the new faith sought to disparage and eliminate the influence of Judaism. The slanders which helped to spread hatred of Jews now combined with the lagging political lot of the Jews under Roman rule and with the widespread Jew-hatred in the Diaspora, and it is here that Christianity began to take root. All the Christian groups originated in Jewish communities.

Following the defeat of the Jewish uprising against Rome, the Jewish settlements multiplied in the Diaspora as the number of exiles from Judea continued to increase. These communities contained many new converts. Oddly enough, in the first and second centuries of the Common Era, a period of severe political setbacks, the Jews continued to be active missionaries for their faith, and with considerable success.

Along with other Jews, many of the Zealots fled Judea. They believed that they alone would survive the wretched times. In their view, the "other Jews" had already lost all ties to the land of Judea and to Judaism. Their land of Judea was the celestial Kingdom of Heaven.

Their "Jewish People" was an imaginary one—a group that had forged a "new covenant" with God and was more concerned with the heavens than with the material world.[9] They had no contact with ordinary Jews. They never took part in the fight against Rome. It is easy to picture their members, refugees from Judea, espousing their cause from the synagogue pulpits, calling on the people to "repent" and to prepare for the terrible and imminent Day of Judgment. Their eschatological message that the "end of days" was already at hand—that the "end of the exile" was standing in the wings, that the Messiah would shortly arrive, or that he was already present, or that he had appeared and been crucified and would soon return "from there" or even that he had already been resurrected—was listened to by Jews in exile with much curiosity and fear, and not entirely without joy.

It was a bitter, troubled time. Along with the influx of converts to

Judaism there was a rise of Jew-hatred in the distant settlements, where refugees kept arriving from Judea. The news they brought was shattering, terrifying, and kept getting worse. Jews in synagogues trembled as they listened to soothing sermons by preachers who "revealed" secrets from the holy writings. Since these Zealot preachers based their sermons on passages from the Prophets, many Jews in the Diaspora accepted their conclusions readily, swallowing the comforting promises. It was already traditional among Jews to seek consolation in the predictions of the holy Prophets.[10]

The converts, moreover, were fertile soil for this apocalyptical solace. Former pagans, people of alien cultures, with a different world view than the Jews, they were much more receptive to the legendary half-god–half-man idea, the easy relationship between gods and earthlings. When the prophet Isaiah proclaimed: "Behold, the young woman shall conceive and bear a son," the Jews could readily accept the phrase in the allegorical sense, a customary mode of the prophetic style. But when such a phrase was dropped among converts who had grown up with pagan traditions, they understood it literally, as a definite sign from God that He was indeed sending the Redeemer down to earth. These "God-fearing" converts were thus easy prey for the preachers of the apocalypse, who spread their message with unflagging diligence as they raged against the wicked "Pharisees, scribes, and hypocrites" who had misled God's holy people.

This agitation must have extended over a long time prior to the destruction of Judea, long before the legendary birth and crucifixion of the Redeemer. The very fact that Saul of Tarsus was already communicating with avowed Christian groups in Asia Minor, Greece, and Rome in the years 40—60 C.E. makes it apparent that the Zealots in the distant Diaspora had been propagandizing there several generations earlier. This becomes more evident from the contents of the Dead Sea Scrolls, some of which were written (or copied) between 100 and 140 B.C.E.

The sermons of the Zealots in the far-off settlements must have led to religious debates in these communities. The tales of a Redeemer who had died on the cross and had come back to life, or was expected to come back to life, could not have been accepted by everyone as absolute truth. Those who had been born Jews would not casually have accepted the characterization of the Jews as an "evil people." Nor was it easy to swallow the dark and gloating prophecies that Judea would be destroyed along with its inhabitants. To most Jews, these interpretations of Scriptures must have appeared as lies or gross distortions.

That there were conflicts between those who believed in the Redeemer and those who did not is known from authentic sources. The Roman historian Suetonius, who left chronicles of all twelve Roman Caesars from Julius to Hadrian, reported that in the early years of the reign of Claudius Caesar (41–54 C.E.), Jews were driven from Rome because fights had broken out among them over a certain "Chrestus." (In the first two hundred years of Christianity, the Gentiles saw no diffrences between the Jewish groups. Suetonius therefore describes it as an intra-Jewish squabble.)

The story of a Jewish expulsion from Rome during the reign of Claudius is an exaggeration. There is no record of such an expulsion. Perhaps a few hundred Jews were exiled. The fact remains, however, that a few years following the legendary crucifixion of Jesus, there were already controversies in a Jewish community in distant Rome over the belief or non-belief in the crucifixion of a messiah.

The most important thrust toward the victory of the new Christian faith came from the unsuccessful Jewish uprising against Rome in 66–73 C.E. The destruction of Judea, the burning of Jerusalem and the Temple—as the Teacher of Righteousness had predicted—were the best arguments against those Jews who refused to "join and believe." These "proofs" that the Jewish prophets had foreseen the coming of the Redeemer remained the basis of the new religion. Along with this came their original opposition to those Jews whom they called evildoers, Sons of Darkness, accursed and damned. The entire hate vocabulary they employed at that time was incorporated into the sacred writings of the Christians and remains there to this day.[11]

In the sixty-five years from the destruction of Judea (70 C.E.) until the defeat of the Bar Kochba uprising in 135, a spiritual malaise lay heavily upon the Jews in Judea and in the Diaspora. The land was desolate. There was a shortage of young, able-bodied people; many had been killed or sold in the slave marts. All privately owned land was declared Roman property, for which the farmer had to pay a fee as if he were leasing it. The previous tax, which had gone toward the upkeep of the Temple, was not abolished. The Romans merely increased it to pay for the pagan temples in Rome.

The Diaspora was overrun with refugees. The "Jewish tax" was collected there just as in Judea. Many Jews who had been sold into slavery had to be ransomed. The hostility of the Gentiles had deepened. The Christians intensified their efforts to persuade the "lost sheep" that God had renounced His people forever.

The second and most powerful thrust toward Christianity's triumph over Judaism was engendered by the suppression of the Bar Kochba uprising and the total devastation which followed this tragic defeat. Very few Jews were left in Judea. Jews were even forbidden to come near the walls of the demolished Temple to weep for their lost glory. In the Diaspora, Jewish proselytism grew steadily weaker. With the Destruction came a decline of Jewish prestige. To the peoples of that time, might was right. The Jews had lost their independence. Such conditions were hardly conducive to proselytization.

On the other hand, with the fall of Judea, the Christian communities bloomed. The moment the news of the fall of Betar (Bar Kochba's last fortress) reached a distant settlement, the Christian preachers promptly began exploiting this as a sign that their prophecies had been vindicated, that Jesus was a true prophet. A stream of converts now flowed to the Christians. From the very start, they had been skillful missionaries.

When the Roman emperor Domitian (81-96) decreed that Jews were forbidden to circumcise pagans, the stream of converts must have come almost completely from the "God-fearing," most of whom were not circumcised. These converts perhaps were not aware that they were adopting another religion, since they still did not understand the difference between Judaism and Christianity. Once converted, they discovered that God had abandoned and damned the "other Jews." The "real" Jews were the God-fearing ones who believed in Jesus Christ the Messiah. Now they were the "true Israel," God's chosen.

5

The "Guilt" of the Jews in the Crucifixion

The New Testament account of the trial and crucifixion of Jesus is not authentic history, nor was it written as such. The story was composed around the mid-second century of the Common Era, that is, several generations after the event. Theophile of Antioch, one of the early Church Fathers, as late as the end of the second century still maintained that the Old Testament was the official doctrine of the Christian religion.[1]

That false prophets and messiahs were prevalent during the period when Judea was ruled by Roman procurators we know from reliable historical sources. These messiahs attracted masses of people who were yearning for a redeemer, and the Romans executed a number of them, together with their disciples, among whom were many Jews.[2]

The Sanhedrin in Judea, comprised of priests, elders, scholars, and other respected figures, had no choice but to look askance at these false messiahs, who persuaded their followers that they had been sent from heaven. While the Sanhedrin may have put such "messiahs" on trial and warned them, it did not have the power to execute them.

In the eyes of the Roman authorities, anyone who attracted followers was a rebel to be disposed of without benefit of trial. It is perfectly credible that such a notoriously heartless procurator as Pontius Pilate could have done this. (Philo of Alexandria relates that there was no Roman official more lawless than Pilate.[3])

However, whether the Jews brought such a "messiah" to trial or whether the story was fabricated, is no longer the point. What is important is that such a story was recorded in the sacred Christian books and was so embellished in the sermons of Christian priests that the guilt for the crucifixion was removed from Rome and placed upon the Jews. This shift of responsibility was necessary for the Christian leaders of that time for a number of reasons:

1. The Jewish religion, well established for centuries, had its own long history, heroes and prophets. The Christian faith was new, young, lacking historical tradition and saints. Its belief in a messiah was based entirely on the words of Jewish prophets.

2. Among the Jews, prayer was an established ritual. When the Temple in Jerusalem was still standing, the ritual consisted of sacrificial offerings. After the Destruction, it evolved into readings from the Torah and the recitation of prayers. The Christian Church had yet to create these customs. Their new rites still lacked the mystical aura which only time could create.

3. The Jews had a sacred Torah which, aside from its function as a code of law, was also the authority for a way of life. Christianity at that time still lacked such holy writ or any other recognized authority such as the popes were later to represent. Christian groups in various settlements conducted themselves more or less according to their own catechism, and they all based their rites on Jewish sources as the priests interpreted them.

Before the Nicaean Synod of 325 C.E. many Christian colonies conducted themselves very much like Jews, and even afterward many Christian groups still continued to function as Jews. They gathered in their synagogues on the Sabbath and holidays to listen to Christian sermons. Some believed in circumcision. Many maintained the dietary laws. Certain groups formulated their catechism so closely to the Jewish code of laws that they almost crossed over to the Jewish faith. Very definitely, Jewish influence at that time had not atrophied.

In order to eliminate this Jewish influence, the dominant Pauline faction did what all schismatic sects do vis-à-vis their former comrades and current opponents—they began to accuse the Jews of all kinds of crimes in order to besmirch them in the eyes of their followers. The most damning accusation was that the Jews had crucified the Redeemer.

To put the blame for Jesus' death on the Jews was not very difficult. The Jews refused to believe in Jesus. Their defeat and the destruction of Jerusalem was clearly a punishment for their crime, God's will through the hands of the Romans. In addition, the older writings of the Zealots were still in existence,[4] with their denunciations of those Jews who refused to associate. Most of these denunciations and doomsday predictions are repeated verbatim in the Gospel of St. John.

The Christians thus began to ascribe all sorts of sins and crimes to the Jews, which then found their way into the New Testament and became the "Gospel truth." The total separation from the Jews was a result of this unbridled hostility fostered by the Church Fathers.

After the destruction of Jerusalem, the deeply rooted Jew-hatred among the pagan peoples of the Roman Empire was intensified. There were many reasons for this. Jews fled their devastated country and flooded the Jewish settlements in the Diaspora, thus creating a good deal of economic competition for the indigenous population. As a people who suffered defeat, the Jews were expected to be humble and submissive. Instead, holding up their religion as the true one, they kept urging their pagan neighbors to forsake idolatry and accept the Jewish faith. Most telling were the lies and slanders that had been circulating about Jews for generations.

In 109–110 c.e., when the Roman Emperor Trajan was involved in a war in the farthest regions of the Empire, the Jews in North Africa and on the Island of Cyprus rebelled against the Roman garrisons. These uprisings were drowned by the Romans in rivers of blood.

In 111 c.e. Trajan launched a war against the Parthians in the east. His armies marched through Judea, Syria and Mesopotamia, treating the Jews in those regions most cruelly.

In Babylonia, which the Romans also invaded, the Jewish community was already six hundred years old and had grown significantly following the destruction of Jerusalem. The Roman march through Babylonia aroused the populous Jewish communities against this foe who had ravaged their homeland. Apparently this Jewish resistance helped to slow the advance of the Romans, since Trajan was forced to turn back without a victory over the Parthians.

Around the year 116 the Jewish population on Cyprus was exterminated. The inhabitants of the island, mainly Greeks, then institutionalized their hatred in a law forbidding any future Jewish settlement there.[5]

The Bar Kochba Uprising

As one more "unassailable proof" that God had forsaken the Jewish people forever, the Christian bishops could point to the failure of the Jewish uprising against Rome in 132–135 C.E.

Hadrian, who became emperor after Trajan, toyed with the notion of transforming Jerusalem into a center of Roman paganism. To the Jews, Jerusalem was the symbol of their nationhood, the center of their homeland where the Holy Temple had stood, the hope of their eventual return as a free and independent people, as well as a reminder to the other peoples of the world that Yahveh was the only, the true God.

The zealous and obstinate devotion of the Jews to their faith was well known to Rome. To prevent a revolt, the Roman authorities did not reveal their intentions. A rumor spread among the Jews that Hadrian was planning to reconstruct Jerusalem. How momentous must have been their disappointment, then, when it became clear that Jerusalem was to become—of all things—a center of idolatry. Enraged, the Jews promptly took up arms against the Romans.

The taunts of the Christians were surely a factor in the spontaneous uprising of the sparse Jewish population of Judea against the mighty forces of Rome. It is almost certain that it was this Christian agitation which compelled Rabbi Akiba to declare the military leader of the rebellion, Simon Bar Kochba, as a messiah.[6] The Jews displayed great valor as their meager military forces held out for three-and-a-half years against the power of Imperial Rome. In the end, the uprising was quenched in blood. According to Greek sources, half a million Jews were slain at that time in Judea.[7] The devastation was unparalleled in Jewish history.

After suppressing the rebellion, Hadrian issued a series of decrees against the Jews. Adherence to all Jewish religious law was forbidden. Circumcision, Sabbath observance, study of Torah, were declared capital crimes. Many Jewish scholars were killed. The academies of Jewish learning were shut down. Jews were not permitted within the limits of Jerusalem except for one day in the year, the Ninth of Av, a day of mourning for their destroyed Temple.

Jerusalem did in fact become a center of pagan worship. Hadrian built arenas for gladiatorial contests, with statues to the Roman gods. The mount on which the Temple had stood was leveled and a temple to Jupiter constructed in its place. Upon the site of Jesus' alleged grave a statue to Venus was erected. On the south gate leading to Bethlehem the figure of a pig was put up. The city was renamed Aelia Capitolina.

Until the Bar Kochba uprising, the Romans had considered the Christians to be Jews. The pagans, who could barely detect any difference between the two, cast the same kinds of aspersions against the Christians as Manetho and Apion had hurled at the Jews in earlier generations. Following the Bar Kochba rebellion, the Romans turned their wrath on the Jews, sparing the Christian groups, which had not participated in the revolt.

The division between the two faiths now deepened into an unbridgeable chasm, as the Christians gloatingly rubbed salt into Jewish wounds. Most of the anti-Jewish passages in the New Testament were composed following the Bar Kochba uprising. Justin Martyr, a Church Father who witnessed the fighting, wrote in his *Apologia*, "Jews must suffer eternally. Their priests murdered the Redeemer." Addressing a Jew, he says: "The judgment visited upon you is a just one. Your land is destroyed, your cities burned. Strangers eat the fruit of your labor even before your eyes. . . . No Jew may show his face in Jerusalem. . . ."[8]

Origen (185?–254?) another Church Father, wrote "We can state with assurance that the Jews will never return to their land, will never again have their own state. They committed the worst crime in the world: they murdered the redeemer of mankind. The city where Jesus was killed has been destroyed. The people are dispersed. God has chosen someone else to be His people."[9]

It was at this time also that Christian sacred writings began to absolve Rome of the guilt of crucifying Jesus. The Gospel of St. Luke, for instance, represents the Roman power as friendly to Jesus. When Jesus declares himself King of the Jews, Pilate says that he finds no fault in him. He even tries to convince the Jewish leaders that Jesus should be forgiven (23:3-4).

The sermons of Christian priests which were written down at that time are full of rabid anti-Jewish accusations. When they ran out of old charges they invented new ones. The more they reiterated these slanders, the more fixed they became in the folk memory.

A good example of this is the story of the mythical apostle, Judas Iscariot (Hebrew, Judah of Keriot), who allegedly betrayed the Nazarene for thirty pieces of silver and then kissed him in order to identify him to the Roman authorities. This legend is not mentioned anywhere in Christian sources until the mid-second century. The tale of a saint sold for thirty pieces of silver was taken from an ancient Jewish midrash. The original version, however, relates that when Jacob was on his deathbed, and his sons confessed that they had sold Joseph to the Egyptians, one of the sons, Gad, said, "We sold the pious man for thirty pieces of silver."[10] The name "Judas" was attached to the story for its symbolic significance: after all, was not the name of the people and its land also Judah?

The charge of "selling out" the Redeemer was one of the most popular in Christian lore. "Judas" became a slur to be hurled in the face of Jews, and remains so to this day. Saint Augustine (345–407), perhaps the most important Christian theologian, formulated it as follows: "Jews are descended from Judas Iscariot, who sold the Redeemer for thirty pieces of silver. . . . Jews cannot understand the prophecies of the sacred writings, for God has stopped up their brains. . . . They will forever bear upon their foreheads the mark: 'Killers of the Savior.'"[11]

The Christian historian Jusebius (263–339) already asserted "authoritatively" that "every year at Purim, Jews slay a Christian for their feast."[12] Even before Christianity became the dominant religion in the Roman Empire, it was already engaged in a holy war against the Jews, disseminating heinous and malevolent slanders among all the peoples of the world. Combined with other historical, socioeconomic, political and psychological factors, this hate-mongering has led, at various times, to the torture and slaughter of masses of Jews.

6

Christianity Becomes A Dominant Religion

The Bar Kochba rebellion against Rome (132–135 C.E.) was fierce and bitter, and its defeat shattered any hope of a Jewish political rebirth. Christian "proofs" that God had abandoned them must have sent the Jews into a mood of despair, a feeling that all the bloodshed and sacrifices had been for naught. Hadrian's decrees after the suppressed revolt only served to intensify Jew-hatred among pagans and Christians. The Jews had lost the contest. Hostility against them was well on the way toward becoming traditional.

In the almost two hundred more or less peaceful years after the rebellion, up until the time when the Christian faith combined with the Roman court in 315, Jewish scholars and sages occupied themselves with safeguarding Jewish distinctiveness so that it would not be swallowed up in the spiritual swamp of that era. The motto of the Talmudic sages, as the historian Simon Dubnow formulated it, was: "Oppose everything that can lead to fusion with the surrounding peoples."[1] Anything that could encourage an approbatory attitude toward foreign civilizations was declared idolatrous, and the worst form of idolatry was the Christian religion.

The commentaries on the Torah (the Mishnah and later the Gemara) were to some degree created as protection against a Christianity which was then extremely aggressive. The Jewish prayers which were introduced during that period were imbued with national motifs. A special prayer was composed against the Christians: "Let those who believe in Jesus [word obscured in the

Hebrew text] be dismayed; let them speedily be destroyed with all the enemies of your people. . . ."[2]

The struggle of Jew against pagan had grown feebler. The flow of converts had not ceased, but they were no great source of satisfaction to the Jews. Christianity had spread far and wide among the pagans in the Roman Empire. The persecution of Christians by the Roman authorities in the first few centuries had not succeeded in halting the advance of the new faith. The Roman cruelties against the Christians in the time of the Emperor Diocletian, at the end of the third century, were having less and less effect.

At the beginning of the fourth century there was already evident a political split between the two major divisions of the Roman Empire—the Greek East and the Roman West. Constantine, one of the new rulers, soon realized that he could overcome the opposition if he would ally himself with Christianity. He led his troops into battle under a banner bearing the symbol of the new faith, the Cross, defeated a rival for power, and in the year 312 was declared Emperor. Eleven years later his soldiers, again under the Cross, vanquished a second rival, and in 323 he became the sole head of the entire Roman Empire.[3]

The leaders of the Christian Church now began to exert their influence on the head of state. On October 18, 315, Constantine issued a decree against those Jews who harassed their brothers who had converted to Christianity. In 325 the first Synod of Christian leaders took place, with more than two hundred bishops meeting in Nicaea. The Synod discussed important problems of dogma around which differences of opinion had been developing.

It also dealt with the relationship between Christianity and Judaism. In order to sever Christianity from its roots completely, various decisions were adopted to drastically change those Christian religious customs that have some proximity to the Jewish ones. For example, the Passover holiday, which Christian communities had been celebrating at the same time as the Jews, was shortened from seven days to one, and it was calendared not on the fifteenth day of Nisan but the first Sunday after the full moon of the spring month. Sunday was sanctified because it was on that day, according to legend, that Jesus was resurrected. ("It is not seemly for us to keep the same holiday with the accursed Jews."[4]) It was also forbidden to consult the Jewish sacred books for answers to questions dealing with religious practices.[5] Debates on religious matters with Jews or visits to synagogues were prohibited. It was decided to take strong measures against Jews who circumcised converts.

Constantine also cleansed Jerusalem of idols, and on the spot where Jesus' legendary grave was located he built a church.

After Constantine, his son Constantius ruled the Roman Empire from 337 to 361. A pious Christian, Constantinius worked even more closely with the Church Fathers of his time, creating more anti-Jewish laws which guaranteed Jewish rightlessness in the Christian world for many years to come. Jews were prohibited from owning Christian slaves. "A pagan slave who is baptized ceases automatically to be the property of the Jew."[6] Since slave labor was then the general rule, these laws were an economic blow against Jews. A similarly harsh law was decreed against any Christian who converted to Judaism: his property was confiscated by the state, and the Jew who converted him could be punished by death.

At the same time as they were instituting these anti-Jewish laws, the Christian leaders never gave up hope of winning the Jews over to the Christian faith,[7] nor did they spare any efforts to do so. For example, they promised Jewish landowners that if they would convert, they would have their slaves returned to them. Those who leased farm land were promised a cut in taxes. New Jewish converts were promised great honors.

That these efforts had some successes we know from laws that were directed against Jews who harassed the converts. There was, for instance a law that a converted Jew could not be deprived of his share of an inheritance; the apostate could sue for his share in court.[8]

During the early centuries of its existence, there were a number of schisms within Christianity. First there were splits between the original Christians and the Disciples of Paul, and again later, among various "heretics" who continued to believe in the Jewish Scriptures. At the Nicaean Synod in 325 a schism took place between the Arians and the Athanasians. Arius (256–336), a Christian priest in Alexandria, contended that Jesus must not be compared to God the Father; the similarity is not total. It is also a desecration of God to say that He Himself was the husband of the Holy Virgin. It should be understood, rather, that God sent down an angel to fulfill this role. Athanasius (293–373), also of Alexandria, held the opposite view, that the Son was in all aspects as great and as holy as the Father, and that God Himself fathered the Son. The Nicaean Synod agreed with Athanasius. Arius and his followers were excommunicated.

In the local Christian communities there was a great deal of agreement with Arius's position. The newly migrating peoples into Europe in the fifth, sixth, and seventh centuries—the Visigoths, Ostrogoths, Huns, Franks, Burgundians, Vandals, and others—

were generally closer to Arius than to Athanasius, when they accepted Christianity. The conflict between these two main groups continued until around the eighth century, and although they were still split over other dogma, finally Christianity held with the Athanasian school.

The attitude of the Arians toward the Jews was not as hostile as that of the Athanasians. The new peoples in central and eastern Europe were, for the first few centuries, still not as steeped in Jew-hatred as the peoples of the Near East. The Christian bishops were afraid that the Arian heresy carried within it a seed which might grow into a compromise with Judaism. In the midst of their war against the Arians, therefore, they took time to continue their agitation against the Jews, too.

The missionary-priests were expert in the art of preaching. Traveling through various communities, they spoke to the Christian congregations, accusing the Arians and other heretics of being too friendly to the Jews, whom they portrayed as partners of the Devil, the source of all evil. These sermons, some of which were written down and remained in the Christian catechism for generations, rooted the poison of Jew-hatred in Christianity forever.

Chrysostom (344–407) was crowned as "the preacher with the Golden Tongue."[9] His sermons were filled with vivid metaphors and parables which he delivered with dramatic effect, sending his listeners into ecstasy. Upon Jews he hurled tons of fire and brimstone. One of his sermons says: "The Jews sacrifice their children to the Devil. They are worse than wild beasts. Their synagogue is a brothel, a gathering of clowns, a house of evil spirits, an assemblage of criminals and depraved sinners. It is a place of impurity. Believers in the unclean Jewish faith know only how to guzzle and gorge themselves. It is a people of the Sons of Baal. No Christian must enter their filthy place where animals and spirits live, lest they return with the Devil in their souls. For in the soul of every Jew lives an evil spirit."[10]

In Antioch, where he preached, the orthodox Christians had for many generations believed in the holiness of the Old Testament. The Christians were generally on friendly terms with the Jews and would often visit their synagogues on Jewish holidays.

Antioch was not the only place where the Nicaean Synod was challenged. Many Christian congregations in Babylonia and other eastern centers considered the decisions of that synod sinful and worthless and refused to obey them. During leap years they observed their Passover a month later, as did the Jews. The king and his Christian advisors tried to put a stop to this heresy, but they were afraid to punish the Christians in the east for fear of another schism. Too many Christian communities were acting in defiance of Nicaea. So they punished the Jews instead. They forbade them from scheduling a leap year.[11]

Another preacher whose words were immortalized in sacred Christian books was Gregory of Nyssa (331–396). In one of his sermons he described the Jews as follows: "The Jews are the murderers of God, murderers of the prophets, enemies of the Lord. They are enemies of God's grace, enemies of the faith of their fathers. They are allies of Satan, a nest of serpents, purveyors of slander, clowns, people who sin in the dark, Pharisees, a gang of devils. They are sinners and betrayers, decandants of Judas Iscariot."[12]

St. Augustine (354–430), a leading Christian theologian, described Jesus' death in these words: "The Jews seize him. They insult him. They 'crown' him with a wreath of thorns, they spit at him and humiliate him. They curse him. They hang him on the cross. They wound him with their spears. It was the Jews who murdered him."

Some of these sermons were written down immediately, others later by students who had committed them to memory. Many of the sermons in sacred books were quoted and preached for centuries, up to and including our own. No one questioned their "truth." Generations of Christians were brought up on these teachings which were offered as revelation. The "bible" of Jew-hatred was immortalized in Christianity.

The priests who allied themselves with the Roman rulers behaved not as equal partners in the Roman government, but as masters and final authorities. The honor of the Christian faith became the ideological essence, the spiritual philosophy of the Roman Empire. The Church Fathers became the self appointed guardians of this ideology. The internal politics and the legislation of the country had to go through the prism of their interpretation. Under the influence of priests, the Roman rulers created laws which left Jews rightless, defenseless, hated, and despised.

In the year 388 a Christian mob in Mesopotamia destroyed a synagogue. Under Roman law, the Jewish religion was still legal. King Theodosius I (374–395), a pious Christian, thereupon ordered the guilty parties to rebuild the synagogue. Bishop Ambrosius of Milan, an important Church Father, pointed out to the monarch that it is a sin for Christians to engage in constructing a Jewish house of worship, that it was a blatant insult to the honor of the Savior.

An even more vehement denunciation of the king's action, accompanied by a demand that the order be revoked immediately, was delivered by Simon Stylites, who became famous for living thirty-six years on a platform fifty feet in the air. He said about himself that he had given up all worldly pleasures and desires except the pleasure of hating the Jews. The king finally bowed to the pressure of these holy men and rescinded his order to rebuild the destroyed Jewish house of prayer.

When Christians asked why God did not destroy these sinful, unrepentant and accursed Jews once and for all, the pastors replied that God had not destroyed the murderer Cain either, but allowed him to wander through the world with the mark on his forehead. Similarly, Jews wander over foreign lands with the mark of Jesus' murder on their foreheads, in order to make manifest to the world their punishment by God.

The historian Eusebius, who was a participant in the Synod of 325, said: "What moved me to write the history of Christianity is that I wished to show that the misfortune which has come down upon the Jews is the punishment of God for murdering our Savior."[13] The most distinguished theologians of the time, Augustine and Jerome, also wrote and preached that God had allowed the Jews to live as witness to the Christian truth.[14]

Before his death, Emperor Theodosius divided the Roman Empire into two parts. The more important eastern part he left as an inheritance for his older son; the western part, which consisted of the Apennine Peninsula (Rome), Gaul (France) and some large, sparsely populated territories in central Europe, he left to his younger son.

In 410 the people of the North, the Visigoths, invaded the western kingdom and conquered Rome, Gaul and vast areas of central Europe. The Jews breathed a little easier; although they were still robbed and looted, at least they were not accused of murdering God's son. The invading peoples were pagans, but in the second and third generation they gradually turned to the Christian faith. However, they did not have the deep-rooted hatred of Jews which existed among the people of the Near East. It took a few hundred years until the priestly agitation infected them. Not until the ninth and tenth centuries did Jew-hatred in the west rise to the level it had reached among the eastern peoples in the fifth century.

In the early part of the fifth century, the Huns invaded the

Byzantine regions of the former Roman Empire. Several generations later they assimilated with the indigenous population and adopted Christianity. Theodosius II, who was emperor of the Eastern Roman Empire from 408 to 450, was an observant Christian. Despite the difficult problems resulting from the attacks on his kingdom, he did not neglect the commandment to persecute Jews. He collected all the old anti-Jewish laws, and added new ones, and issued his infamous Codex Theodosius.

Late in the sixth century the Byzantine rulers conquered the western kingdom and brought with them the Codex, which existed for centuries as a model for most of the anti-Jewish laws of the entire Christian world.

Continuous and unrelenting persecution had weakened the Jewish communities in the Eastern Roman Empire and they became more and more sparse and impoverished. However, that part of the empire was not completely free of Jews. During the first centuries of Christian rule, despite encirclement by enemies, despite rightlessness and degradation, Jews still took an active part in commerce in the most important trade centers such as Alexandria, Antioch, Constantinople, and other cities on the Mediterranean. Jews in the Byzantine section of the empire also had several creative centers of their own. Ultimately, weakened by centuries of persecution, these cultural centers were transferred to Babylonia, where there was a larger Jewish population.

In 415, as a result of mass rioting against the Jews of Alexandria, the Jewish community there declined precipitously and very little is heard from them until the advent of Islam in the seventh century, when Jews began to return to Alexandria in significant numbers. In that same year, there was also a pogrom in Antioch, after Jews there burned an effigy of Haman at a Purim celebration. Synagogues in Antioch and throughout Syria were expropriated from Jewish communities and turned into churches. Jewish homes were plundered. When Theodosius ordered the looting stopped and Jewish property returned, the Nazarenes threatened the king with damnation. The emperor's order had little effect, in any case.

From his study of the sacred writings Augustine had concluded that it is the fate of Jewry to be eternally subservient to Christianity. Isaac's granting of the birthright to his younger son was interpreted by the learned preacher to mean that the Jewish religion (the older one) must forever remain subject to the Christian faith, which came into the world later.[15]

During the twenty-one years from 486 to 507, the Christians staged one attack after another against the Jews of Antioch. Nor was the situation much better in North Africa, where Jewish communities had been in existence for a long time. With the rise of Christianity in the Near East, the Jewish communities in North Africa had grown as Jews fled from Palestine, Greece, and Rome.

The Emperor Justinian, who ruled the eastern Roman Empire from 527 to 565, was a pious Christian who determined to rid his country once and for all of heretics and other non-believers. One of his first acts was to outlaw the study of the Talmud which, he declared, had not been written by God-fearing men, but was full of gibberish concocted by swindlers and designed to turn people of little faith away from the path of righteousness.

In 553 there was a dispute among the Jews of Alexandria concerning the reading of the Torah. The assimilated Jews wanted it read from the Greek translation, which they could understand. Many copies of the Septuagint were already annotated with Christological phrases. Debates were then taking place between Jews and Christians about the true biblical text. Justinian interfered in the dispute with the royal decree that the Torah was to be read in the synagogues only from the Greek text, so that Jews would more rapidly forget the accursed Hebrew tongue and move closer to Christianity.

It was during Justinian's reign that we hear of the first instances of forced conversions of entire Jewish communities. In 534, when the emperor's general Belisarius defeated the Vandals in North Africa, he forcibly baptized the Jews of the city of Borion and turned their synagogues into churches. Belisarius then ordered his aides in Libya to do the same. In self-defense the Jews fled deeper into the desert.

In 534 Justinian issued his own Codex, a collection of anti-Jewish laws which had been adopted in Christian Rome in the preceding two hundred years. To those laws he added new ones. The Codes of Theodosius and Justinian had an extremely destructive effect on Jewish life throughout the long, dark Middle Ages in all the countries in Christendom. They also influenced the anti-Jewish laws later adopted in the countries of Islam.

Jews in Spain

In the sixth and seventh centuries, before Islam put its foot into the Iberian Peninsula, the Christian persecutions of the Spanish Jews had created a system of harrassments which the Christian countries of Europe adopted and practiced throughout the Middle Ages. The Visigoth rulers of Spain accepted Christianity long after the majority of their people had already done so. Here, too, the Christian priests preached the Gospel, built churches and baptized the last remaining pagan tribes of the newly migrated peoples.

Concerning the Jews in Spain in the first centuries of the Christian era we know very little. Nor do we know exactly when Jews began to settle there in large numbers. Jewish sources are silent about this, although there are legends that after the destruction of Judea by Babylonia in 586 B.C.E., ships carrying Jewish refugees anchored along the shores of Spain. Other legends relate that 80,000 Jewish prisoners were taken to Spain after the uprising against Rome was defeated in 73 C.E. It is safe to assume that during the Roman epoch, before and after the destruction of Jerusalem, when the Jewish dispersion had spread to distant points on the map, Jews settled in Spain. But we do not know it as a verified fact.

From Christian sources we learn that as early as the year 300, Spanish bishops issued a warning to their flocks against associating with Jews. We also know that in the first two centuries, all the Christian groups, almost without exception, originated only in Jewish communities. An anti-Jewish law in Spain in 300 C.E. is in itself evidence that Jewish communities existed there as early as the second and third centuries.

The Visigoth kings of Spain were, in the fifth and sixth centuries, already Christian, but they were Arian Christians. Persecution of Jews did not begin until the Spanish rulers became Athanasian Catholics. When King Reccared (586–601) became a Catholic in 587 he immediately began drafting anti-Jewish laws. It became illegal for a Jew to acquire a slave who was a Christian. Should the Jew convert a Christian slave, the latter would be automatically given his freedom and the Jew's property confiscated by the Crown.[16] Reccared also outlawed intermarriage with Jews and forbade Jews from holding public office. Since Jews were forbidden to imitate Christian customs, the king also outlawed reading the psalms at Jewish funerals.[17]

These laws were only a beginning. A decade later, when Sisebut was king of Spain, he issued a strict decree that all Jews in the country must become Christian. Since Jews did not have the right to leave the country, their alternative was apostasy or death. As an added encouragement, Sisebut announced that Jews who converted would have the right to keep or buy slaves. He of course renewed all the other anti-Jewish legislation of King Reccared I.

Many Jews at that time found ways to escape from Spain. Some went to North Africa, Italy, and France. Others reached Alsace and further into Germany, where Jewish communities were beginning to take shape. Some Jews evaded conversion by bribing local Church and government functionaries. In the larger centers of the country, however, large numbers of Jews had no choice but to convert. Like their brothers and sisters throughout the Middle Ages, they adopted the new faith only as a formality; secretly they remained Jews.

The step of forcible conversion, as well as the other anti-Jewish edicts, are explained by historians as a reaction to rumors which were then circulating in European countries that the Jews in Palestine had joined forces with the Persians, defeated the Christians there, looted Jerusalem, murdered a great many Christians, and burned down all the churches, including the Church of the Holy Sepulcher. These rumors were not complete fabrications. When Persia's king Khosrau II declared war on Christian Byzantium, the Jews in Palestine, who had endured so much at the hands of the Christians there, joined the Persians and together they overpowered the Byzantine armies, capturing Jerusalem in 614.

This alliance of Jews and Persians did not last very long. Three years after the victory over the Christians, the Persians drove the Jews out of Jerusalem. The Jews then allied themselves with the Byzantine king Heraclius (610–641), who swore a sacred oath that he would grant them amnesty, if they would help him drive the Persians out of Jerusalem. According to Christian sources, Heraclius would have kept his promise to the Jews had not the bishops talked him out of it. They declared a fast which absolved the king from his oath, and in 627 he had his revenge on the Jews of Jerusalem.[18] Many fled the country. A few years later Heraclius ordered the remaining Jews in his kingdom to submit to conversion.

The news that Jews had joined with the Persians to drive the Christians out of the Holy City had repercussions on the Jewish situation in all the Christian countries. In Spain, anti-Jewish decrees were intensified. Generally speaking, these laws kept changing at the caprice of the rulers, or as a result of the influence of the priests upon them. King Swinthila, for example, was a "liberal" in this regard. During his reign (621–631) many Jews who had fled returned to Spain. Baptized Jews even tried to revert to Judaism. The next king, however, meted out harsh punishment to converts who tried to return to Judaism, and rigorously enforced all the anti-Jewish laws.

The Marranos, the Jewish Christians, even those of the third and fourth generations, never ceased their attempts to return to their ancient faith. Whenever a king or a local ruler seemed a bit more liberal or was bribed to look the other way, they threw off the yoke of Christianity and became Jews again. King Chindaswinth (642–652), who was at odds with the clergy, was friendly toward the Jews, even permitting apostates to publicly renounce their conversion. Many Marranos reentered the Jewish fold at that time. However, when his son took the throne, he brutally reversed the situation; for renouncing the Christian faith the punishment was death, plus the confiscation of the victims' property by the royal treasury or the Church.

Even in their third and fourth generations, Jewish converts were not recognized as true Christians by their neighbors or by the Church. As Jewish Christians, they were not trusted, they were spied upon, they were continuously threatened by the authorities. Edict after edict was issued against "the contagious pestilence" (as the Marranos were called by the synods). Jews who held fast to their faith could be forgiven, although they were hated; but those who had been baptized and had already taken part in a sacred Christian rite would not be permitted to dishonor their new faith.

This problem was always on the agenda of the synods.[19] Special measures were adopted to bring the lost souls back. A law was passed to prohibit marriage between children of converts, and of course between them and Jews. Converts must marry only real Christians. Young children of converts were taken away from their parents and placed in the homes of true Christians. Converts must spend the Jewish and Christian holidays, as well as Saturdays and Sundays, in church or in the homes of priests. A convert was not permitted to leave his city of residence without permission of the Church. The priest would attest to the convert's good behavior in a special document. The Jewish Christian must then take this document to the priest in the place of his destination, and this priest must observe him and record the details of his conduct in the new location.

Converts and their descendants must take a special oath to be good and pious Christians. One such oath, sworn by a group of Marranos in 654, reads in part:

To our noble and pious lord and ruler, King Recenswinth: We, the undersigned Jewish Christians of Toledo, remember that we once were commanded to deliver a petition to King Chintila. . . . At that time, in the year 637, we promised to be good Christians. However, we were then still strongly influenced by the falsity which stems from our own obstinacy, from the ugliness in our viscera which stems from our corrupt parents. At that time we did not really believe in our Lord God Jesus Christ. We were not yet good Christians.

Now, however, we pledge that we and our wives and children will henceforth no longer observe any Jewish laws and customs, nor associate in any way with unbaptized Jews. We will not marry them nor will we betroth our children to each other's children nor to blood relatives unto the sixth generation. . . . We will not celebrate the Jewish Passover. . . . We will not keep the dietary laws or any other Jewish customs.

We believe with complete faith that Jesus Christ is the Son of the true God. . . . We promise to keep all the Christian commandments, the Christian holy days, the marriage laws. . . . We shall observe everything precisely and with all our hearts and without reservations.

Should any one of us break these pledges . . . we swear by everything holy, by the Holy Trinity, that we will, with our own hands, burn such a person at the stake or stone him to death. . . . [20]

Between 672 and 680, during the reign of King Wamba, the Jews, as well as the Marranos, enjoyed a brief period of peace. But the thirty-one years preceding the invasion of the Iberian Peninsula, from 680 to 711, were the worst in Jewish history up to that time. The kings introduced a system of spying, and the priests, the true Christians, and even the Marranos, were compelled to search for sins among their neighbors and friends. Informers were promised part of the property of their victims as a reward.

In the year 711 Muslim armies from North Africa began occupying larger areas of the Iberian Peninsula. With the victory of Islam, the Spanish Jews were released from the worst persecution they had suffered in Christian Spain up to that time.

Jews in France

Undoubtedly there were Jewish communities in France several centuries before the spread of Christianity to that part of the world. Again, whatever information we have comes from Christian sources.

For the Jews of France, the fifth century was a more or less peaceful period. The Roman institutions which had existed prior to the migrations of the European peoples were almost completely abolished, and with them went the anti-Jewish codes. Even the Christian clergy did not treat the Jews too badly. The Church assemblies in that part of the world were busy converting the new tribes and safeguarding them from Jewish propaganda.

Around the first quarter of the sixth century, King Sigismund, a Christian zealot, began turning the screws more tightly on both Jews and Arians. Laws were passed in France prohibiting Jews from appearing in the street on Christian holidays, from constructing their synagogues near churches, and so on. In 576 there was a pogrom in Clermont after a Jew killed an apostate during a Christian procession. The Christians retaliated by attacking Jews and looting their property. The local bishop, Gregory of Tours, gave the Jews a choice: conversion or expulsion. According to the bishop's report, more than five hundred Jews converted. Others fled to Marseilles. The synagogue at Clermont was sacked by a mob. A few days later a synagogue in Orleans was similarly destroyed.

In 582 King Chilperic I decreed that all "non-believers" in France must become Christian, that those who refused to do so would either be expelled or have their eyes put out. Many Jews converted, as the Jews in Spain had done, only *pro forma.* Bishop Gregory writes about them in his *History of the Franks,* "They observe two days of rest, Saturday and Sunday."[21]

The news of the Persian-Jewish alliance in Palestine eventually reached France. The Spanish Jews who had fled to France to find peace found the atmosphere charged with hate instead.

In 629 King Dagobert ordered the Jews of his country to convert to Christianity, otherwise they would be considered enemies of France and would be expelled or executed. Many French Jews, including the new refugees from Spain, then migrated to other regions. Jews are not heard from in France for over a hundred years, until the middle of the eighth century.

Jews in Italy

A Jewish community in Italy must have existed even before Pompey's destruction of Jerusalem in 63 B.C.E., since many Jewish captives that he brought from Jerusalem were ransomed by the Roman Jews.

During the sixth and seventh centuries the Jews in Rome experienced lesser persecution than the Jews in Byzantium. Roman Jews defended their country when the Byzantine general Belisarius attacked in 554. After Rome fell, Belisarius introduced the anti-Jewish laws of the Justinian Code and levied heavy taxes upon the Jews in Italy. Many fled to North Africa or deeper into Europe.

In 568 the Lombards invaded the region and drove out the Byzantine armies. Eventually the Lombards also became Christian, but not Athanasian. As Arians they abolished most of the anti-Jewish laws and reinstituted Jewish civil rights. In the middle of the next century, when the Lombards had become Catholic, and the bishops were the real rulers of Rome, the Jews there also suffered forced conversions and bloody pogroms.

Jews in Germany

During the fourth, fifth and sixth centuries, when Christianity gained dominance in Europe, the Jewish communities in Germany were still small. We know that there was a Jewish community in Cologne even before Constantine, and certainly long before the Germans migrated there.[22]

Beginning with the seventh and eighth centuries, there are references to large Jewish communities in Germany. Charlemagne entrusted important government posts to Jews. Through the reign of his heir, Louis the Pious, the situation remained about the same. Up until the end of the tenth century, Jews lived in western and central Europe much more freely and peacefully than in the eastern areas. The palpable hatred which enveloped the Jews in the Byzantine Empire did not reach central Europe until the tenth century.

Not every king or local prince permitted the priests to dictate his actions. Many rulers maintained Jewish advisors and physicians in their courts. Among the common folk, incited by the clergy, hostility would sometimes erupt against the "enemies of Jesus." But the king was not required to listen to his subjects. The people had no say either in the government or the Church.

While Pope Gregory I did indeed complain about Jewish "obstinacy and superstition," he also defended Jews against physical attack or conversion which local bishops tried to force upon them. He even went so far as to order a destroyed synagogue rebuilt and instructed one bishop to return a synagogue to the Jewish community.

Jews in the Balkan Peninsula

The Balkan Peninsula and the lands to the north remained part of the Byzantine Empire. Jewish communities had existed there for several centuries before Christianity became the dominant religion. During the first centuries of the Common Era, the anti-Jewish laws gradually drove out and killed many Jews and forced many others to convert. The Jewish communities there became progressively sparse as the codes of Theodosius and Justinian were enforced more cruelly.

In 723 King Leo Isaurian ordered the forcible conversion of the Jews of the entire Byzantine Empire, with strict punishment for violators. As everywhere else, many Jews converted as a matter of form. Many others migrated to the Crimean Peninsula.

Conditions were no better under King Basil I the Macedonian (867–886). A Christian zealot, Basil undertook to convert all the Jews of his kingdom. First he tried kind words and promises. Then he arranged debates between rabbis and priests. When all these attempts failed and the Jews did not convert voluntarily, he turned to force.

During the Middle Ages, in particular, and in the preceding centuries, the Jews in Europe sought protection with the rulers— kings, princes, bishops, and popes. Often it was to the ruler's advantage to help the Jews, but not always. Whenever a ruler found himself in need of funds, he could always issue a decree of conversion or expulsion against the defenseless Jews and take every last penny away from them.

When the Jews came to Europe from the Near East and Rome they were no longer a vigorous people but a despised tribe, dependent on foreign rulers. They had lost all hope of ever standing bravely on their own feet. Their belief in ultimate salvation now depended not on a Bar Kochba but on a supernatural, heaven-sent messiah.

7

Jews in the East Before Islam and Under the Rule of the Arabs

Because of Christian persecutions of Jews in the Near East, the center of the Jewish historical arena had already moved from there to more distant lands as early as the sixth century. Jewish communities arose further east in Babylonia and Persia and also in Western Europe.[1] The Jewish population in Byzantium was dwindling. Christianity had even erased the word "Judea" from the language: the ravaged land of Judea was already referred to in Rome as "Palestine."[2] In Christian writings Judea is known as "the Holy Land" because Jesus was born there.

The life of the Jews in Babylonia under the Persians and later under the Arabs was not overly restricted. Jews lived more or less freely. From the fourth century onward, cultural hegemony over the Jewish Diaspora, which had previously been centered in Judea, had moved gradually to Babylonia. However, the frequent and protracted wars between Roman Byzantium and Parthia would not permit a completely peaceful situation. In the days of the Persian king Shapur II, for example, a war between Persia and Rome lasted fully twenty-five years, from 338 to 363. Jews suffered from this war like everyone else. Persecutions of Jews in particular also took place, but they were not systematic or long-lasting.

During the Sassanid dynasty in Persia, from the mid-third to the seventh century, the situation of the Jews continuously vacillated between good and bad. This depended on the mood of the ruler or to what extent he was influenced by the Magians, the Persian priests, zealots for the Ahura Mazda religion (Zoroastrianism). Throughout the fifth and sixth centuries there was strong pressure from the Zoroastrian priests upon the Persian king. All infidels were then being harassed, Jews as well as Christians. In addition, there were frequent wars between the Parthians and the Christian countries in the Near East, as well as uprisings in Persia itself.

In the reign of King Firuz (459–484) the situation of the Jews deteriorated rapidly. In ancient Jewish writings the name Firuz is always coupled with the words "the Wicked." The Magians compelled Jews to engage in religious debates, which frequently ended in violence. In 472, three Magians were killed in a fight in Ispahan, a city with a large Jewish population. In retaliation, King Firuz ordered half the city's Jewish population executed.[3] He also decreed that the Jews must convert to the Zoroastrian religion. When they refused, he ordered their young children taken away from them, to be brought up in the Magian temples. The Jews fled to nearby Arab countries.

From 531 to 579, under King Khosrau I, Jews lived in peace in the Persian countries. Many who had fled during the time of Firuz and his successors now returned. The academies which had been closed were reopened. Many Jews migrated from the Christian countries to Babylonia and Persia. At that time Byzantium was ruled by the tyrant Justinian.

Under the reign of King Harmisd IV (579–589) the Jews again were persecuted. In 581 the academies were shut down and the scholars fled the country. Harmisd's dominion was of short duration, and in the violent uprisings against him, the Jews supported one of the generals.[4] The king's son, Khosrau II, suppressed the rebellion and punished the Jews, executing many. Others escaped by fleeing the country.

Khosrau II, however, was able to reestablish peace in his country and even displayed some tolerance for infidels. Jews returned to their former homes.[5] For the Jewish communities in Babylonia and Persia there was peace, but not for long. The entire East was about to be invaded by Arab armies under the flag of Islam.

Jews in Arab Countries Before Islam

For many centuries Arab tribes had lived in compact communities on the Arabian Peninsula. Most of them were pagans. Jewish communities were also well established there, in such cities as Khaibar, Mecca, and Yatrib. The Jews in these communities were a mixture of old settlers and recent immigrants, refugees from Christian or Persian persecution. The old settlers spoke Arabic and, like their neighbors, lived in large family clans headed by an elder.

The Jews in the Arab countries preached their religious truth to the Arabs, many of whom were familiar with the biblical tales and the epics of the Fathers. The Arabs believed that Ishmael, son of Abraham and Hagar, was the forefather of their tribes, and that the Jews were therefore blood-relatives.

At the beginning of the sixth century an Arab tribe in Yemen, the Himyarites, adopted Judaism. The leader of this tribe, Dhu-Nuwas (516–525) became a priest of the Jewish faith and began to harass Christians in retaliation for their anti-Jewish decrees in Byzantium. He even expelled some Christian merchants from Yemen who had come there on business. Abyssinia then attacked the Himyarites and defeated them, killing Dhu-Nuwas. Many Jews died in the battles and others fled. A few years later the Persians drove the Abyssinians out of Yemen, but very few Jews had remained there, most of them having escaped to Yatrib.

A number of Jewish families had been residing in and around Yatrib for generations—the Benu Kainuka, the Benu Nadir, and the Benu Kuraiza, for example. In addition, there were other Jewish communities in towns and villages in Northern Arabia, the largest one being in the city of Khaibar. For the most part, Jews lived amicably with the Arab tribes around them. The Arab clans waged frequent wars with each other, and Jewish clans often entered into alliances with them, taking an active part in the fighting.

Early in the seventh century the Jews in Yatrib were confronted with a difficult problem. From Mecca came the Messenger of Allah, the Prophet Muhammad.

Muhammad and the Jews

Born in Mecca, Muhammad became the manager of a camel caravan and crossed the Arabian deserts several times, visiting far-off countries. On the roads and at fairs he heard many tales and legends of various peoples. He was familiar with the biblical stories of Creation, with the Jewish belief in one God, and with the Prophets. Since he himself could not read or write, his knowledge of the Old Testament was gained by listening to storytellers, Jewish as well as Christian. His perception of Jewish history was thus a mixture of Midrashic legends and Christian mythology.

Muhammad was impressed by the idea of one God who had created the world. Jews and Christians had such a God; the Arabs did not. Blessed with a fertile imagination, he soon became convinced that he, Muhammad, had been called to spread the monotheistic idea among the Arabs. He began to see visions and to confide in trusted friends about an angel named Gabriel who had instructed him to spread the message of one God among his people. In Mecca he gained a few disciples, but most of the people mocked him and he was driven out of the city.[6]

With his small group of followers Muhammad went to Yatrib, hoping that the learned Jews there would come to his support. After all, he was disseminating the teaching that God is one, which was the message of Father Abraham, whom the Jews had sanctified. He also strongly opposed the pagan idol-worshippers, whom the Jews deprecated. Muhammad arrived in Yatrib on a Yom Kippur and found the Jews there fasting and praying in their synagogues. He immediately added to the "revelation" which the angel Gabriel had entrusted to him that the tenth day of the month of Tishri is a day of fasting, and that the worshippers must face the holy city of Jerusalem.[7] To write down his visions and prophecies, Muhammad employed a Jewish secretary.

Initially the Jews of Yatrib considered him one of their own, virtually a proselyte. But Muhammad soon proclaimed himself a Messiah, and his sermons, in which he claimed to be God's last prophet after Moses and Jesus, estranged him from the Jews. They laughed at this new "Prophet of Allah" and disparaged him, which naturally incensed Muhammad and insulted his disciples.

Not all the Arabs became followers of Muhammad immediately. It took several years and, more importantly, several victories over Jewish clans, to win the allegiance of a growing number of believers in the new religion of Islam.

Muslim Wars Against the Jews

Angry with the Jews, the new prophet now looked for opportunities for vengeance. A master strategist, he knew how to prevent his various enemies from uniting against him. When he felt that the weaker Jewish clan, the Benu Kainuka, was isolated, he found an excuse to attack them. The Jews of that clan, as well as the other Jewish clans, made the mistake of underrating this "Prophet of Allah" and allowed themselves to be drawn into a war with

Muhammad and his followers. This battle was looked upon as a commonplace dispute among Arab tribes.

As the victor, Muhammad was prepared to kill all the males of the Jewish tribe. However, an Arab tribe with whom the Benu Kainuka had an alliance prevented this. The several hundred Jews of the clan were compelled only to turn over their homes and fields to the Arabs and leave the area. They were permitted, however, to take along their movable property. With all their belongings on their camels, the Jews set out for Palestine, then a Persian possession. This was in 624, ten years after the Persians and the Jews had captured Jerusalem.[8]

The other Jewish clans—the Benu Nadir and the Benu Kuraiza—suffered the same fate. The former was vanquished by Muhammad in 625 and forced to leave Yatrib, but was not permitted to take with it more than one camel-load per family. Only a few members of this clan migrated to Palestine. Apparently the news had reached them that the Persians were expelling the Jews from Jerusalem.[9] Most of the families of the Benu Nadir settled in the other Jewish communities on the Arabian Peninsula, mainly in Khaibar. The Jews of this city began to gather allies among those Jewish and Arab tribes hostile to the prophet, with the intent of revenge. They succeeded in assembling an army of 10,000 warriors who besieged Muhammad and his followers in Medina. However, there was a sad lack of unity among them and after a few days some of the tribes went home. The remaining Benu Nadir then fled to more distant areas.

The Muslims pursued their enemies, inflicting great losses on the Benu Kuraiza. Initially this tribe had formed an alliance with the followers of Muhammad and had hesitated to join the coalition against him. Now Muhammad beleagured their fortress. Although completely isolated, the Benu Kuraiza held out for several weeks, while the Muslims chopped down all the date-trees around the stronghold.[10] When the Jews surrendered, seven hundred men of the clan were killed and the women were divided up among the victors. For his own harem, Muhammad selected the prettiest girls.[11]

One year later the Prophet of Allah and his greatly strengthened armies overpowered the Jews of Khaibar. With several strongholds in that city, the Jews put up stubborn resistance, but when the largest fortress fell, the smaller one surrendered under condition that they be allowed to leave their homes. Later they were permitted to remain, providing that they pay an annual tribute of half their agricultural yield to the victorious Arab army. (This was in 628. In that same year, the Christians, with the help of the Jews, again became masters of Palestine, but they punished the Jews for siding with the Persians fourteen years earlier.)

After this victory over the Jews of Khaibar, Muhammad added a few anti-Jewish complaints to his Koran. Most of these charges he apparently had heard someone read from the New Testament. He noted that Allah had punished the Jews for not believing in His Prophet, and that the Jews are a stiff-necked people.[12]

Following Muhammad's death in 632, the Muslim armies grew in number. The wars expanded and they went from victory to victory. Only twenty years later the Islamic warriors, led by caliphs (Muhammad's representatives) were in control of almost all the countries bordering on Arabia, having overrun Persia, Babylonia, Syria, Palestine, Egypt, and even the more distant lands of North Africa. In many of these countries there were Jewish communities. In their victories over the Christian armies, the Arabs had received help from the Jews, who had been suffering at the hands of the Christians. The attitude of the Arab conquerors toward the Jews was therefore rather tolerant.

The edicts of the great Caliph Omar were directed against all infidels. Non-Muslims were not permitted to build new churches or synagogues, or to repair old ones. They were not permitted to sing during worship. They were not permitted to prevent anyone from converting to Islam. They could not serve as officers in the army or as public officials. They could not ride horseback, this being a mark of honor. They had to wear special clothing and pay a head tax. These restrictions, however, were mostly observed in the breach, except for the taxes.[13]

Muhammad's prophecies were inscribed in the sacred books of Islam. In the Koran he immortalized his anger against the Jews. After his victories over the Jewish clans, the prophet of Allah taught his followers:

> Believers, do not be friends of Jews and Christians. They are friendly to each other. A true believer who becomes friendly with them will become one of them. Know that Allah is with the righteous and against the wicked.[14]

Jews Under Arab Rule

Jewish sources say very little about how Jews lived in Syria and

Palestine under the reign of the first Arab rulers, the orthodox caliphs (632–661) and their successors, the Ommayads (661–750). Under the laws against infidels, as written in the Islamic religious books, Jews could not hold important public positions, they could not wear expensive clothing, and generally could do nothing that would raise their social status above that of the Arabs. For the right to keep their own faith, infidels paid a special head tax.

The Arab rulers, who waged many wars, needed large sums of money. In 711, after defeating various peoples in North Africa, they invaded Spain. The march of Arab armies through countries where there were Jewish communities gave the Jews no peace. During the reign of Omar II (717–720), who was a firm believer in all the Koran's strictures against infidels, Jews also suffered from Muslim repression.[15]

The cruel Islamic persecution of Jews occurs later. In the first few centuries of their reign, the Ommayad caliphs (and after them the Abbasids, 750–1000) conquered many lands and united the scattered Jewish communities under one political roof. The tolerant attitude of several Arab rulers toward other faiths and the cultural collaboration which occasionally took place between some caliphs and the Jews, elevated and benefitted both. Unfortunately, this state of affairs was of brief duration.

The Arab armies had very little rest. The wars of the caliphs against each other, as well as the conflicts on their borders, were incessant. In the mid-eighth century a new dynasty of caliphs, the Abbasids, defeated the Ommayads and, like their predecessors, took to the sword to conquer new territories. They took possession of most of the islands in the Mediterranean and established themselves firmly in the largest part of the Iberian Peninsula, which they conquered with the help of the Jews there.[16] The Abbasids chose Baghdad for their capital, rather than Damascus. Baghdad was the residence of the Jewish Exilarch, who had the duty of collecting taxes from the Jews. The Arabs had no special Jewish or anti-Jewish policy. For them it was simply a matter of believers and infidels.

As always among foreign peoples, Jews in Arab lands adopted the language of their environment and spoke Arabic. Despite the prohibition in the Koran against Jews holding public office, they often became officials in cities or countries with friendly Arab rulers. In the reign of certain caliphs, when there was a cultural renaissance among the Arabs, Jews advanced to higher positions in both the economic and intellectual world. At the same time, the Jews in Arab lands did not neglect their own culture.

The gold age of the Abbasid dynasty occurred during the reign of the caliphs Aroun al-Rashid (786–809) and his son, Al-Mamun (813–833). The first half of the ninth century marked the cultural renaissance of Islam. And it was even during this period that the Jews suffered persecution at the hands of the Arabs. As Islamic zealots, the enlightened caliphs also oppressed the infidels.

From 809 to 813 a bitter civil war raged in the eastern countries under the Abbasids as the two sons of Aroun al-Rashid, Al-Mamun and Aleimin, fought over the right to rule. Looting and murder became the order of the day, and since the Abbasids at that time ruled over quite a few countries, many cities and entire regions were ravaged.

The caliph Al-Mamun is known as the most prominent representative of the Arab renaissance in the Abbasid dynasty. Poet and philosopher, he encouraged and disseminated knowledge, established libraries, and engaged in scholarly discourse. He even characterized the Koran as a work composed by human beings rather than a supernatural power. A zealot of Islam, he nevertheless appointed Jews and Christians to posts in his government.

It is said that a fakir once asked him why he allowed infidels to hold public office. The caliph confessed that it was indeed a sin. He ordered the immediate dismissal of all non-Muslims, imprisoned twenty-eight hundred Christians and drove many Jews out of Baghdad.[17] The same account tells us also that the caliph called the Jews "that most depraved people."

Especially severe were the anti-Jewish decrees of the caliph Al-Mutawakkil (847–861). A religious fanatic and a tyrant, he revived all the old anti-Jewish laws of the Koran and the Sunna (the later commentaries on the Koran) and in 850 drafted new laws against the infidels which emphasized their inferiority to Muslims. He decreed that infidels must wear a prominent yellow patch on their clothing; on women's garments one sleeve must be yellow; hats must contain visible yellow spots.[18] Muhammad's warning about not fraternizing with Jews was strictly enforced. "Aliens" who rode horseback or who lived in better homes were dismissed from jobs and taxed a tenth of the yield of their fields and gardens. Old houses of worship used by infidels were destroyed and newer ones were turned into mosques. Graves of infidels had to be level with the ground.[19]

During the ninth century most Arab tribes gradually wearied of their long and costly wars. In the tenth century the caliphate of Baghdad was in decline. Disturbances throughout the widespread areas were frequent and serious. From Persia and Central Asia came pressure of the Turks. In North Africa and Egypt the Berbers established a new caliphate, the Fatimids.

In 996 a fanatical Shiite by the name of Al-Hakim[20] became caliph of the Fatimids in Egypt. He was a member of one of the two great religious divisions of Islam that regard Muhammad's son-in-law, Ali, as the legitimate successor of Muhammad and disregard the three caliphs who actually did succeed him. Hakim, like Caligula, was convinced that he was a divine being and punished anyone who did not believe in his divinity. In 1008 he decreed that all infidels in his kingdom must become Muslims. Those who refused were compelled to wear clothing with colored patches and a picture of a calf's head around their neck. Violators of these laws were liable to expropriation and expulsion.[21] When Hakim discovered that Jews were wearing a gold or silver figurine of a calf's head as an ornament, he decreed that the figurine must be made of wood and weigh no less than six pounds, and that Jews must sew bells on their clothing, to inform everyone that infidels were in the vicinity. He also ordered all synagogues and churches in his kingdom razed.[22]

The caliph at that time reigned over Egypt, Palestine, Syria, and a large part of North Africa. Some Jews converted to Islam, pro forma, others fled in all directions, looking for a place of refuge. Although some Jews reached India and Tibet, the majority went westward, even back to Christian Byzantium and eventually Eastern Europe. A lesser number settled in central and western Europe, where the situation was not unfavorable, and where, as a result, large Jewish communities began and grew. The Jewish population in North Africa and Spain also increased.

Jews Under the Arabs in Spain

In the tenth and eleventh centuries the Jews of Spain experienced another Arab-Jewish cultural renaissance under the caliphs of Cordoba and Granada. However, in this golden epoch the Jews also suffered bloody attacks and forcible conversion.

We have very little authoritative information about the Jewish community in Spain during the first two centuries of the Cordoban caliphate, that is, the eighth and ninth centuries. From Arab sources we know that Jews helped the Arabs capture Toledo, Cordoba, Seville, Granada, and other cities.[23] From Jewish sources we have few details as to what constituted this help. We also know nothing of the Jewish achievements or misfortunes there during the first two centuries of Arab rule. The facts are, however, that the decline of the Baghdad caliphate drove many Jews out of the eastern countries and that the Jewish community in Spain continued to grow.

In 912 Abdul Rahman III became caliph. An intelligent and tolerant individual, he took it upon himself to establish Cordoba as an example of the progressive Arab world. His chief advisor was Hasdai ibn Shaprut, a Jew. Hasdai began as a court physician to the caliph, but was soon appointed financial overseer. A tactful man, well versed in Arabic and Latin, Hasdai became the caliph's diplomatic representative. He maneuvered among the rulers of the various Arab tribes and negotiated with the Christian neighbors in northern Spain and more distant lands. Hasdai unified the separate Arab principalities under the Cordoban caliphate and established normal relationships with the Christian neighbors, even extending the borders of the caliphate itself. As a result, he was recognized and lauded.

Hasdai utilized the tolerant attitude of the caliph to establish institutions of Jewish learning in Cordoba and other Spanish cities. These academies eventually took over the functions of the older Jewish schools in Babylonia, where a process of deterioration had already set in.

The Golden Age of Spanish Jewry was interrupted by periods of violence and unrest. In the reign of the Cordoban caliph Hashim (976–1009) and his devout vizier Manzur, restrictions against infidels were reinstituted. During that period, battles were fought with Castilian Christians in Northern Spain. To defray the costs of this war and the construction of an ornate Islamic Temple, the infidels of Cordoba and other cities were heavily and unconscionably taxed.

The Cordoban caliphate was then in a period of decline, having been divided into smaller principalities such as Toledo, Seville, and Saragossa. Christian Spain in the north now launched attacks on these weakened Arab centers. Cordoba appealed to the Berbers in North Africa for help. The Berbers agreed, helped to beat off the Christian armies, and became masters over the Spanish Muslims.

In 1013 the Berber king Sulaiman defeated the caliph of Cordoba, destroying and looting the city.[24] Many Jews fled to Christian Castile, where the old anti-Jewish laws had become inoperative. Most Jews of Cordoba fled to other Arab cities in Spain. A large Jewish community survived in Granada, where a Berber emir, Habus, proclaimed himself caliph and Granada a caliphate.[25]

Among the refugees in the city of Malaga, in Granada, was a Jew named Samuel ibn Nagdela (993–1055). A scholar in Jewish and general studies, a linguist, and a calligrapher, he became the vizier's secretary and advisor. Not long after his appointment, the vizier was stricken with a fatal illness. On his deathbed he advised the caliph that the Jew Samuel would serve him well as vizier. Thus, in 1027, Samuel ibn Nagdela became vizier of Granada. He served in that position for twenty-eight years, until his death. (When the caliph died in 1038, his son Badis kept Samuel on as vizier.)

Like Hasdai ibn Shaprut in Cordoba, Samuel ibn Nagdela was eminently successful in his handling of government affairs for the caliph. During that period unnecessary wars were avoided and the country prospered. Samuel was liked and respected in the court despite the ever-present enemies, particularly since he was an infidel Jew. Like Hasdai, too, Samuel took advantage of the opportunity to improve the life of the Jews in the caliphate and other cities where his authority carried weight. The Jews of Granada crowned him with the title of *Nagid*, by which name he is known in Jewish history.[26]

After Samuel's death in 1055 the caliph appointed his son, Joseph, to be vizier. Times were bad. The devout and impoverished Berbers were already agitating against the "Jewish rulers" and the "rich Jews" in their caliphate. A fanatic Muslim poet who had tried in vain to become an official in the court issued a challenge to the caliph and the people—to all believers—which spewed hatred and lies against Jews:

> The caliph could have chosen a secretary from among the believers, but he chose to select an infidel. Thanks to his secretary, the Jews—an inferior people—have become great lords. . . . Badis, do you not see the evil these devils are doing? Their horns are prominent in all your provinces. How can you trust this criminal and even become his close friend? [An allusion to the stricture in the Koran. S.G.] Turn your eyes to other countries and you will see that everywhere they treat Jews like dogs and keep them out of public life.

> O Muslims, Jews are in control here! They eat the best foods and dress in elegant clothing, while your garments are old and tattered. . . . Believers go hungry while Jews enjoy sumptuous feasts in their palaces. . . . Look around, bring the vizier as a sacrifice, slaughter the fat sheep and don't spare his family! The Jews have piled up countless treasures. Take their money—you have more right to it than they! Don't be afraid to kill them. Who will condemn you if you punish them?[27]

In 1066 an emir from a neighboring province invaded Granada with his army. The foreign soldiers spread a rumor that it was the Jewish vizier who had invited them. A mob surrounded Joseph's castle, broke in and murdered him. From there they proceeded to the Jewish streets, looting and burning, and slaughtered fifteen hundred people.[28] Those Jews who were able to escape fled to Christian Castile; others to Seville, Lucena, Saragossa, Toledo, and Cordoba. As time went on, the Jewish communities in Arab Spain were more and more spread out among the separate principalities.

Early in the twelfth century, fanatically religious Berber tribes, the Almoravides from Morocco, invaded Spain and defeated the splintered Arab princedoms. They reestablished the old "true" Islamic faith which, they charged, had been seriously weakened and corrupted. Of the infidels, both Jews and Christians, they demanded that they renounce their faith and become Muslims. Against the Jews they had a special complaint. According to a legend then current in Islam, the Prophet Muhammad in his time had let the Jews alone and not demanded that they become believers, but only on condition that after five hundred years—if the Jewish Messiah had not appeared—the Jews must then acknowledge Muhammad as their prophet and convert to Islam. According to this legend, the Jews had agreed to this condition. Now, in the first quarter of the twelfth century, five hundred years had elapsed since the prophet had made the alleged agreement with the Jews.

When the leader of the Almoravides entered the city of Lucena in 1105, he summoned the Jews, explained the charge against them, and demanded that they convert. The Jews bought their way out of this trap with a large "gift" of money.[29] It is not known how the Jewish communities in other cities in southern Spain averted the terms of this five-hundred-year-old agreement. There is no reason to believe, however, that the Jews under Almoravide rule escaped with only fear and bribes. We do know that this was a troubled period for the Jews in the Spanish cities. The Arab emirs were then at war with each other more often than not. The Christian reconquest had begun in earnest. Cities changed hands from Christian to Muslim and back again. When the fighting was over, many of the Spanish cities lay in ruin.

Around the mid-twelfth century another sect of ultrafanatic Muslim Berbers, the Almohades (also from North Africa), attacked the already corrupted Islamic rulers of Spain, the Almoravides, and began an intensive effort to convert the sinful Muslims, as well as the infidels, to the true and pure Islamic faith. They had the same five-hundred-year-old complaint against the Jews, but this time the Jews could not buy their way out. The alternative to conversion was death.[30] Many Jews converted and stayed alive. Others chose martyrdom.

The persecutions, pogroms, and forced conversions in Arab Spain during the twelfth century sharply reduced and weakened the Jewish population in Islam. Only a trace remained of the once flourishing Jewish communities in Spain and North Africa. Many Jews returned to Christian Castile in the north. Some went to the already existing Jewish communities in southern France; others went to central and eastern Europe. Many Jewish scholars who left their mark on later Jewish history fled Spain; among them was Moses Maimonides (1135–1204) whose family emigrated to North Africa and thence to Egypt.[31]

Around the time this was happening, the Jews in western and central Europe were being subjected to the barbarities of the Crusades.

8

Jews in Christian Europe at the Beginning of the Middle Ages

The Jews who fled from Muslim Spain at the turn of the twelfth century found refuge in Castile and southern France, which were then Christian. Officially the Visigoth anti-Jewish laws of the seventh century were still in force in Castile and the kingdom of the Franks. The Christian bishops in those countries had not changed a hair of their hate-propaganda against the "murderers of our Lord."

Nevertheless, something had changed there. Governmental power was in the hands of central rulers. The king and his nobles, like the pope and his bishops, were complete masters of the land, the cities, and the people in their particular areas. And these rulers needed the Jews. Much of the trade and commerce of the time was in the hands of Jews, who exchanged the products of the feudal estates for currency. The ruling castes in Europe at that time regarded the Jews as a group whose special function was to develop the economy of their countries.

The kings, albeit devout Christians, paid little attention to the anti-Jewish agitation of fanatical priests. Even the popes in Rome—almost all of them, from Gregory I (590–604) to Gregory VII (1073–1085), for a period of five hundred years—did not persecute the Jews. Although they very much wanted the Jews to become Christians, and they strove mightily toward this end, they were opposed to forcible conversion. In 937, when the Archbishop of Mainz asked Pope Leo VII which was preferable, to convert the Jews forcibly or to expel them from the city, the pope replied that the former was forbidden, that it was much more Christian to expel them.[1]

In the eighth century there were already well established Jewish communities in western and central Europe. Most of the Jews in those communities were recent immigrants, refugees from persecutions in Byzantium, where the anti-Jewish codes of Theodosius and Justinian were in full force. Large Jewish communities sprang up on the Rhine, in Metz, Mainz, Worms, Speyer, Cologne, and other cities in France and Germany.

During the eighth and ninth centuries the Carolingian dynasty, builders of a new empire, in need of Jewish economic expertise, protected the Jews. The first of the Carolingians, Pepin the Short (751–768), forbade the destruction of synagogues and encouraged the immigration of Jews into his kingdom.[2] His son Charlemagne (768–814), the chief architect of the new empire, which comprised almost all western and central Europe, provided even more protection for Jews than had his father. Evidently the emperor paid very little attention to the anti-Jewish propaganda of the priests and the Church.[3]

Official protection of Jews was instituted in the time of Charlemagne's son, Louis the Pious (814–840), who gave the Jewish community the requisite documents to show that they were under the king's protection.[4] He also permitted Jews to keep Christian servants. Economically, the Jews prospered. They engaged in handicrafts, and in trade and money-exchange. Jews had also been landowners, but gradually fewer and fewer were found in agriculture. Owning land in those days was associated with an oath which Jews could not take. Most legal oaths (as they are today) were couched in religious terms, and these terms were unequivocally Christian.

In the European cities, Jews lived close together around a synagogue, in their own neighborhoods in order that they might be better able to observe their customs. However, many Jews lived among non-Jews. The wall between Jews and their Christian neighbors in those years before the Crusades was not yet so high and thick. Jewish communities in central and western Europe continued to grow. New streams of Jews flowed into Europe from Asia and Africa. Large Jewish communities arose in Mainz, Speyer, Worms and many other cities in that part of the world.

Through four centuries, from the eighth to the eleventh, the hatred of Jews in the western European countries was expressed mostly in moderate legal and political restrictions. Here and there Jews suffered physical abuse, but these manifestations were local and of short duration. The pressure of the clergy, although at times quite strong, was restrained by several basic factors: (1) the pagan peoples who had poured into Europe a few centuries earlier; (2) the great Arian heresy among the new peoples; (3) the heresy of the Nestorians in the eastern lands; and (4) the victorious advance of Islam. All this created serious problems for the Church in Europe. The kings, themselves devout Christians, were not required to abide by the decisions of the synods and they protected the Jews who were then vital to the economy and well-being of their countries.

When the central authority was strong and could control local vassals and bishops, the Jews were relatively safe. Whenever the local princes had more power in their own provinces, the protection of the Jews by the central authority was ineffectual. Some of the princes, influenced by the clergy, even issued their own edicts of expulsion and forcible conversion against the Jews.

From around 810 to 850 the Bishop Agobard and his disciple Amulo conducted a consistent anti-Jewish campaign in France. Both of them tried unsuccessfully to influence the Carolingian King Louis the Pious. Incensed by the security and prosperity of the Jews, Bishop Agobard appealed to the king for permission to baptize the pagan slaves of the Jews in Lyon.[5] The ruler rejected the request. Furious, Agobard now began preaching against the king himself. He refused to believe, he protested, that a Christian sovereign would defend the accursed murderers of the Savior, an attitude which could only strengthen Jewish insolence. The Jews were now boasting, he claimed, that the king had taken their side against the bishop. All this had an adverse effect on Christians, the Lord's people, who were beginning to regard the sinful Jews as being more correct in their beliefs than the Christian clergy.

Five of the bishop's pamphlets have survived. In them Agobard collected all the old anti-Jewish slanders, all the "sins" which the early Church Fathers had accused the Jews of when Christianity was struggling to become a dominant religion half a millenium earlier. In a letter to the bishop of Narbonne, who treated the Jews of his province fairly humanely, Agobard warned him to reconsider his actions and to recognize the danger in time. In the language of a Chrysostum,[6] Agobard pointed out to him how sinful and accursed the Jews really were:

> The curse upon the Jews has penetrated their innards like water, like oil in their bones . . . accursed are their homes and their gardens, their

goings and their comings, accursed is the fruit of their womb, their fields and their flocks, their cellars and their storehouses, and even their food. None of them can free themselves of the curses, so awful is their sin.[7]

In Agobard's pamphlets the Jews are referred to as "Sons of Satan, Sons of Darkness who contend against the Sons of Light [the Christians]." In the letters which the bishop wrote to the king he accused the Jews of violating Christian women, kidnapping Christian children and selling them as slaves to Muslims. The pamphlets were disseminated from France into other countries. In the monasteries, hundreds of copies were made. Priests everywhere read and preached from them for many generations after Agobard's death. Hundreds and thousands of times these lies about Jews were told to the people.

Bishop Amulo (840–852) was no less a Jew-baiter than his teacher. In his pamphlet, *Contra Judaeas*, which was very popular in Catholic Europe, Amulo poured out his wrath upon a Christian clergyman named Bodo, an advisor to the king, who had converted to Judaism and lived among the Jews of Spain. In letters to his friends, Bodo had described his revulsion at the scandalous and immoral life of the clergy; he related how he had traveled to Rome to confer with the heads of the Church about restoring the purity of the Christian faith, starting with the priests themselves; but the degeneration which he found in Rome, in the "suite" of the pope himself, had driven him away from Christianity completely.[8] Bishop Amulo, in his pamphlet, raged against the deadly witchcraft of the sinful Jews which was able to mislead even a Christian priest.

These anti-Jewish pamphlets were popular in their time and all through the Middle Ages. Historical researchers of the Jewish travail in medieval Europe are of the opinion that the inferno into which the Jews were cast in the second half of the Middle Ages was rooted more than anywhere else in the sermons of Agobard and Amulo, the Catholic bishops of Lyon.[9]

After Louis' death his kingdom was divided among his sons. France remained under the rule of Charles the Bald. Like his father, he also protected the Jews of his country. His heirs, however, were already under the influence of the incessant clerical propaganda. Charles III (the Simple) made a gift of all the Jewish fields to the bishop of Narbonne. With the division of the Carolingian kingdom, the central authority was abolished, along with its control over the local princes. From then on the Jews in these lands remained under the authority—and the caprice—of the local feudal lords who, as time went on, fell more and more under the influence of the Church and its campaign of incitement against the Jews.

In Toulouse, in southern France, at the end of the ninth century, an Easter custom was introduced by which the rabbi, or another leader of the Jewish community, was compelled to come to the nobleman or the bishop and be slapped in the face, as punishment for the suffering of Jesus on that day. The Jews tried unsuccessfully to buy their way out of this practice, but the bishop of Narbonne insisted that it be observed. He also added that the Jew who was being punished must call out three times, "It is right for Jews to be slapped by Christians because they have refused to accept the Christian faith!" Not until the eleventh century did the Jews manage to evade this humiliating practice by paying a special tax to the Church. It frequently happened, however, that around Easter-time, after the church sermons about the sufferings of Jesus, attacks took place upon Jews in their neighborhoods.

In the year 1012 a certain priest converted to Judaism and wrote a pamphlet criticizing Catholicism. King Henry II of Germany, a devout Catholic, replied by expelling the Jews from Mainz. Only those Jews who agreed to convert were permitted to remain in the city. Among those who did so was the son of Rabeynu Gershon, a leader of the Jewish community. Several years later the Jews were allowed to return to Mainz, and the converts rejoined their faith. Rabeynu Gershon, whose son had died in the interim, warned the Jews not to insult the apostates or to torment them about their sin.[10]

Early in the eleventh century, stories were being spread in France to the effect that Jews in the East were conspiring with the Fatimite caliph Al-Hakim (996–1021) in the persecution of Christians in Jerusalem. In actual fact, Hakim was cruelly persecuting both Christians and Jews in Egypt, Palestine, and Syria. The caliph, as we have noted, was a madman.[11] As a result of the rumors, the bishop of Orleans expelled the Jews from that city in 1012.[12] A few years later they were allowed to return, but many had already migrated to safer areas. Thus, in the first half of the eleventh century, Jewish communities arose further east, in Bohemia and Poland.

Around 1007 there were attacks upon Jews in Rouen in northern France. Later in the century, a detachment of volunteers was organized in France to drive the godless Muslims out of Spain. On the way, the marchers massacred Jewish communities. This was the first rehearsal for the Crusades which began in Europe later and which shed so much Jewish blood. However, these persecutions, expulsions, and forced conversions were, at that time, mainly of a local nature. Most of the Jewish communities in central and western Europe, during the troubled and hate-filled eleventh century, became even more firmly established and generally showed no signs of weakness or attrition.

Jews in Italy and Byzantium

Through the Middle Ages and later, Italy was not a united country. In the ninth, tenth, and eleventh centuries the southern Apennine Peninsula and the island of Sicily were often in the hands of Muslims, but at times under the rule of Byzantium. Jews who fled from Byzantium to the west would generally go through Italy. However, no sizable Jewish communities developed there.

During the eleventh and twelfth centuries, there was a Jewish community in Rome. In times of trouble, the wealthier Jewish merchants there would often intercede with the pope to rescind a decree issued against Jews in the Catholic countries.

In the eastern part of the former Roman Empire, the situation of the Jews under Christian rule deteriorated rapidly. In the seventh century, after the Muslims occupied Syria, Palestine, and Egypt, the Jews of Byzantium were subjected to all sorts of harassment, including expulsion and forced conversion. This situation became most critical when the Muslims, at the beginning of the eighth century, invaded Asia Minor and stood before the gates of Constantinople, the capital of Christendom. Naturally, the Jews hoped for the defeat of their Christian oppressors.

And so, to the list of Jewish "sins" was now added the worst accusation of all—treason. As soon as the Muslims were driven off, a pogrom erupted against the Jews of Constantinople.[13] Leo III decreed that if the Jews refused to convert they would be severely punished. The Jews fled in all directions, some to Syria, others to more distant places.

In the course of three centuries, from the ninth to the eleventh, the situation of the Jews in Byzantium never improved, with the exception of several years under the Amorio dynasty.[14] During the reign of Basil I (867–886) the situation again worsened. Many Jews at that time fled to the southern regions of eastern Europe, in the valleys between the Don and Volga Rivers, to the Khazars, whose rulers had adopted Judaism in the eighth century.[15] The Khazars had dominated the region for several centuries, subjecting the peoples on their borders.

It was somewhere in the middle of the eighth century that a king of the Khazars named Bulan was converted to the Jewish faith, and along with him, several hundred of his royal family. To what extent Judaism began to spread among the people of the area is not known. Bulan's descendants called themselves Jews. We can assume that in the land of the Khazars there were many Jewish refugees from other countries. Authoritative sources provide no verification.

Late in the eleventh century the Khazars were conquered by the Russians. For a time they remained on the Crimean Peninsula. When the Tatars invaded the area in the thirteenth century, the Khazars disappeared. It is reported that a number of them escaped to the Jewish community in Spain.[16]

Upon King Basil's death his son, Leon VI (886–911), became ruler of Byzantium. The author of the *Book of Yochsin* relates that Leon permitted the Jews to observe their religion. However, the laws of the Justinian Code against, among other things, studying Talmud and against preaching in synagogues remained in force, as did a degrading procedure whereby any Jew who appeared in court against a non-Jew had to wrap himself in thorns during the taking of the legal oath.

From the mid-tenth century on, we again hear of forced conversion decrees in Byzantium. In this part of the world these decrees never stopped. The Jewish community in Byzantine countries continued to shrink.

The Church and the Middle Ages

Up until the end of the ninth century the Jews in Europe were still seeking and finding proselytes, a phenomenon which outraged the Church. At Christian conclaves priests warned their flocks not to be friendly with Jews, not to conduct debates with them; in their sermons the priests continually insulted the Jews and accused them of all sorts of heinous sins. In great detail they described how the Jews had tortured and crucified the Savior, how Pontius Pilate had pleaded with the Jews not to condemn the innocent Jesus, and how the Jews had insisted that he be crucified.

In the New Testament the Jews are called *B'nai Belial*, Sons of the Devil. During the tenth and eleventh centuries the word "Devil" was already so closely associated with the word "Jew" that it was almost synonymous. Judaism was then regarded not as another religion but as an anti-religion, the Antichrist. To kill a Jew was equivalent to destroying the Devil. About this Devil-Jew, stories were told, sermons were preached, songs sung, and pictures painted.

Artists and sculptors took their themes mainly from Christian symbols approved by the Church. On large canvasses they depicted the stories of the New Testament, the Apostles, the Church Fathers. Along with these positive church images they portrayed the negative Antichrist. As a model for the Devil they used the Jew. The Jew-Devil was pictured as grotesque, ugly, with an exaggeratedly hooked nose, and frequently with horns protruding from his head.[17] The Jews in the paintings always wore bizarre clothing, and later, when Jews were compelled to wear the yellow patch, this feature was prominent in the portrayals. These huge canvasses, which hung in the churches, visually complemented the word-pictures of the Jew, the Antichrist, the Devil, which the priests drew in their sermons.

Conversely, the pictures of the Christian saints were cleancut, graceful, honest and innocent, with noble features in shining countenances.

The prayers in the church services complemented the hate themes. In the early Christian centuries the churches had introduced special prayers on Good Friday which the worshippers offered up for people who were not yet Christians—Jews, pagans, and other infidels. They prayed that God would open the eyes of these "blind" unbelievers, and after each prayer the worshipper was to kneel. From the ninth century on, in many liturgical books, we find the prescription, "*Pro Judaeis non flectant*" ("for Jews, do not kneel"). For pagans they knelt, for all sorts of heretics they knelt, but not for Jews. Jews were infidels too, but they were different, worse.[18]

Up until the ninth century it was forbidden to hold celebrations in a church. This prohibition was gradually lifted. At first, smaller celebrations took place, such as christenings. Not long afterward, wedding feasts were permitted, at which there was wine, music, and dancing. Eventually, theatrical performances were introduced. In the spirit of the times, these presentations were on religious themes such as the apostolic legends. During Easter, plays were produced showing the trial, crucifixion, and resurrection of Jesus. In these plays the villains, who looked exactly like the Jews in the city, wearing the same kind of clothing, mocked and tortured Jesus, spat upon him, stoned him, and crowned him with the wreath of thorns.

The people who witnessed these performances saw Pontius Pilate trying to free Jesus, while the Jews kept clamoring for his death; they watched the Jews rejoice and dance for joy when the Savior was crucified.

During the showing of these plays Jews were usually forbidden to appear in the street. It was dangerous anyway for Jews to appear in public at such times. The emotions of the agitated Christian population reached a fever pitch after such performances. Gangs roamed the Jewish streets and beat Jesus' enemies, robbing and murdering in revenge. These crucifixion dramas were repeated every year. In time they were improved and refined, more cruelties were added to the scenes, stirring up more Jew-hatred.

These impassioned, rabid presentations were staged in the German town of Oberammergau and have been renewed every ten years even to this day. Adolf Hitler admired this play: "It is vital that the Passion play be continued in Oberammergau, for never has the menace of Jewry been so convincingly portrayed."[19]

During the tenth and eleventh centuries the Church in central and western Europe achieved its goal. Among the Christian masses of many nations it created a fire-spitting volcano of Jew-hatred. From the twelfth through the sixteenth centuries this volcano poured its death-dealing lava upon the Jews of Europe, degrading, robbing, expelling, torturing, and murdering them in the towns and cities of Roman-German Europe. With the exception of the few years of the twentieth century under the arch-murderer Adolf Hitler, these five hundred years were the most horror-filled in Jewish history.

9

The Century
of the Crusades

Two hundred years before the twelfth century the Jews of Europe were already surrounded by enemies. The only protection they had was what they could buy from their rulers; the right of Jews to arm themselves in their own defense had long since been taken away from them.

The situation of the Jews was not the same everywhere, however. In France, Jew-hatred in the tenth and eleventh centuries was deeper and more widespread than in the Germanic lands or in Lotharingia (Lorraine). Christendom took hold in France earlier than in Germany. Bishops Agobard and Amulo, the worst anti-Semites of the ninth century, did their preaching in France. As early as 1084, twelve years before the first crusade, Bishop Rudiger of Speyer on the Rhine invited Jews to settle in a new area of his city, even granting them a charter which stated that they were a blessing for the city. Jews would not be prohibited from keeping Christian servants, as they were elsewhere.

In Germany, relations between Jews and their Christian neighbors were cool but correct. It might have appeared that Jew-hatred was only a surface phenomenon. However, the seeds of animosity which the Church had sown for so many generations had penetrated deeply into the minds and hearts of the masses in Germany, too, but up until the end of the eleventh century the feudal lords and their knights saw to it that the Jews were not harmed. The masses were well disciplined; an order from the lord or bishop could keep them in check. So long as the political and social life was more or less calm,

Jew-hatred smoldered internally and very rarely erupted. No one anticipated the black clouds which were soon to descend upon the Jews.

The First Crusade

In 1071 the Seljuks (Turks) conquered Byzantium, occupying Asia Minor and all the smaller Christian countries in the area, including Palestine. The Seljuks were orthodox Muslims with no toleration for other faiths. They introduced and strictly enforced the old laws of Omar against the *Dhimmis* or infidels. Christians who made the pilgrimage to Jerusalem on the observances marking Jesus' birth, crucifixion, and resurrection were punished. Pilgrims returning to Europe told of persecutions of Christians at the hands of the "heathen" in the Holy Land. These stories spread throughout Christian Europe and soon Jews were being blamed for these persecutions more often than were the Muslims. In the churches, monks preached about the enemies of Jesus—the Saracens and the Jews—who were persecuting Christians.

During the later decades of the eleventh century, a bitter struggle took place between Gregory VII and Emperor Henry IV over control of civil as well as religious authority: the Church wanted control of the land along with the peasants who worked it. The emperor would have none of it. He tried to depose Gregory, banished him, and appointed another pope in his place. For a time there was a pope and an antipope each excommunicating each other. Christian religious circles were in turmoil and many synods were called to deal with these serious problems.

At the synod of November 1095, in Clermont, France, Pope Urban II raised the issue of the dishonored Church of the Holy Sepulcher in Jerusalem. He called for a religious march to the Holy Land, with the objective of rebuilding the church on the most sacred spot in Jerusalem, Jesus' grave. His proposal was adopted immediately. For such a mission there were plenty of volunteers, especially when the pope promised them that all their sins, past or future, would be forgiven and that they would all be assured of eternal life.

All sorts of adventurers joined the crusade: knights with dreams of shining victories, paupers (many of them criminals) from the towns and villages, and still others for want of something to do. The various armies were not organized by a general staff with a central plan. Separate groups formed here and there, headed by princes, abbots, bishops. Nor did they wait for orders from a leader. As soon as a group of "Zealots for the Lord" was organized, they sewed crosses on their shirts and started out. In the towns and villages along the way they were joined by local Christians. Their numbers multiplied.

From the start the "holy army" engaged in looting. In need of food and supplies, they stole from the population in every town and village they passed through, at first from Jews and non-Jews alike. Several prosperous villages in Lorraine were plundered this way. In France the local lords and bishops were sufficiently in control of the "soldiers of God" to restrain them from robbing Christians. From the Jews, however, crusaders could demand whatever they pleased, including money. With each passing day the anti-Jewish mood among the armies grew more rabid. The Jews of Lorraine managed to buy their way out with money and provisions. In Metz, twenty-two Jews were killed and many others forced to convert.[1] In Rouen crusaders drove the Jews into a church and forced them to convert at swords' points.

The Jews of northern France immediately sent messages to the larger and better established Jewish communities in the German cities of Trier, Speyer, Worms, Mainz, and Cologne to prepare for the worst. Based on the experience in Lorraine, they advised them to have ransom money and provisions ready for the marauders. The Jews of the Rhine communities took the advice. They also proclaimed fast days and, as was the practice in those days, bought protection from the local lords and bishops. Henry IV, well-disposed toward the Jews, was then in Italy with his army, busy with the papal dispute. The leader of the Jewish community in Mainz, Rabbi Klonimos, sent messages to Henry that his vassal, Prince Godfrey of Bouillon, was leading a large army of crusaders and that he had sworn to exterminate all the Jews. The king in turn sent orders to all his vassals to protect the Jews against looting and murder. But his orders were not heeded. The marchers knew they could get away with their pillage now without fear of punishment. Some of them, right from the start, had been preaching that it was foolish to travel to distant lands to fight the well-armed Lord's enemies when there were plenty of Jews closer at hand. Many of the crusaders swore that they would go to the next world with that highest of good deeds to their credit—the killing of Jews.

On 3 May 1096, a Sabbath, the marchers arrived at Speyer, where there was an old, established Jewish community. Joined by Christians in the city, they seized Jews and forced them to convert; eleven who refused to do so were killed on the spot. Bishop Johann of Speyer who, like his predecessor Rudiger, believed that the Jews were a boon to the city, arrived quickly with his knights and drove off the killers. He permitted the Jews to take refuge in his castle and even punished several of the murderers by cutting off their hands.[2]

On 18 May a large army of crusaders entered Worms. The Jews of that city had already heard the tragic news from Speyer and were seeking ways to save the community. The wealthier Jews were given refuge in Bishop Allebrand's castle.[3] The army of marchers that entered Worms was larger than the one that had invaded Speyer, criminals in the city having swelled their ranks. A rumor spread that the Jews had murdered a Christian. Pogroms flared up. Jewish homes were plundered. Most Jews committed suicide rather than submit to conversion. Mothers killed their own children, husbands and wives killed each other. Those who did not manage to take their own lives were killed by the crusaders.

As soon as they were finished with the defenseless Jews of the city the crusaders besieged the castle and demanded that the Jews inside be handed over to them. The bishop informed the Jews that he could no longer protect them unless they converted. They asked for a few days to discuss it. Outside, the mobs waited at the gates. On 25 May, after the stipulated time had elapsed, the bishop opened the gates. When the attackers rushed into the castle they found their would-be victims in a pool of blood. The Jews of Worms had perished by their own hand in defense of their faith. It required more than a hundred wagons to move the bodies outside the city, where approximately eight hundred Jews were buried. Only a very few converted in order to save themselves. One young man whose fathers and brothers had been murdered by the crusaders slipped a knife out of his sleeve as he was being baptized and killed two of his tormenters. He was cut to pieces on the spot.[4]

The day after the massacre in Worms the "wolves of the desert" (historian Eliezer ben Nathan's phrase) arrived at Mainz, led by the bloodthirsty Baron Emicho. The Jews of Mainz, whose community was the largest on the Rhine, had already heard the shocking news from Worms. They begged Bishop Rothard to protect them. He demanded payment and advised them to place all their valuables in his treasury for safekeeping. Upon payment of a large sum of money they were permitted to take refuge in his castle.

Emicho and his killers found the city gates locked, but the

Christians there soon opened them. The Jews in the castle took up arms alongside the bishop's guard, prepared to resist. The guard, however, did not stay at their posts for very long. The bishop also disappeared. Weakened by fasting, the Jews were no match for the armed mobs outside. Some of them committed suicide; others fought to the end. One group of fifty Jews, who had been hidden in a cellar, slipped out during the night and escaped to a nearby village. Discovered by the villagers, the bishop offered them safety if they would convert. All but a few refused. Most of them were killed. Several who had converted soon regretted it. A man named Isaac, after his conversion, killed his two children and burned down his house. The fire spread through the city. Isaac perished in the synagogue with the *Shema* on his lips as a large area of Mainz went up in flames.[5]

Thirteen hundred Jewish martyrs were buried outside the city in a mass grave, for many years referred to as "Jews' Hill." In many cities and towns of Germany, similar place names have remained as signs of Jewish mass burials.

After Mainz it was the turn of the Jews in Cologne. The local bishop and many of the city's residents hid Jews in the castle and in their homes. On 30 May (on Shavuot) the crusaders invaded the city, looting Jewish homes at will. Enraged because they could find no Jews to kill, they burned down the city along with the synagogue. In order to save the Jews the bishop moved many of them secretly into some of his villages near Cologne. From 3 to 24 June the Jews stayed in their hiding places. Eventually, however, they were discovered and given the alternatives of conversion or death. Most of them chose the latter.

From the Rhine and the Moselle the gangs went eastward to the Danube, devastating Jewish communities along the way. In Regensburg, Bavaria, the entire Jewish population was converted under one cross as they were forced into the Danube and declared to be Christians. When the "Lord's messengers" left the area, the Jews returned to their own faith.

All through the months of May, June, and July 1096 the crusaders terrorized Germany and the surrounding lands. At the end of July they arrived in Bohemia. At that time Prague already had a large Jewish community. Christianity in those areas was less than a hundred years old and had not yet managed to implant a hatred against Jews. There are confused accounts about one town in Bohemia where five hundred Jews, together with the baron's soldiers, overpowered a band of crusaders, killed some of them and drove the rest away.[6] In Prague the crusaders put many Jews to death and forced others to convert. When the crusaders left, the Jews renounced their conversion.

Prince Broneslaw of Prague was out of the city when the murderers entered. When he returned, he would not allow the converts to rejoin their faith, but sent them to the bishop for permission. Not trusting the bishop's brand of "justice" the Jews quietly prepared to migrate to Hungary and Poland. When the prince discovered their intention he stationed troops in the Jewish homes to prevent them from leaving with their possessions. Summoning the representatives of the Prague Jewish community, he told them:

> You were driven out of Jerusalem and condemned to slavery. You brought nothing here with you from Jerusalem. I forbid you to take anything out. You can go wherever you please, but without your property. As naked as you came here, that's how you can leave.[7]

Most of the Jews abandoned everything they owned and escaped to neighboring countries where they could live as Jews. Only a few individuals stayed behind with their possessions.

No less than 300,000 crusaders gathered in Europe in 1096 for their "sacred mission." For three years they struggled against all sorts of obstacles on the way. Many of them returned to their homes with sacks full of spoil. Many died from disease. Others fell in battle against armies which refused to let them pass, as happened in Hungary.

In Christian Constantinople the ranks of the crusaders were strengthened. From Constantinople, 150,000 of them continued their march to Jerusalem. For a full two years they fought the Muslims in Asia Minor and Syria. In May 1099 some 20,000 crusaders, led by Prince Godfrey, reached the gates of the Holy City, For more than a month they besieged Jerusalem. At the end of June they broke through, killing whoever got in their way. One group of Jews was at worship in a synagogue. The battlers for Jesus, Prince of Peace, set fire to the synagogue, burning the Jews alive.[8] In the streets, in homes, in mosques, the murderers rampaged, killing old and young, men, women, and children.

One priest who accompanied the army that invaded Jerusalem wrote in his memoirs: "The bloodbath lasted till evening. The bloodstained conquerors then went to the Church of the Holy Sepulcher and wept for joy. They kneeled and sang, 'This is the day which the Lord hath made; we will be glad and rejoice thereon' "—a verse from Psalm 118!

There are accounts which relate that 10,000 Muslims were slaughtered in the Islamic temple, in addition to the thousands killed in the city. After this victory, Prince Godfrey wrote to the pope in Rome: "The blood of our slain foes was up to the knees of horse and rider."[9]

The number of Jews murdered during the first crusade is estimated to be between ten and twenty thousand. The number converted is unknown. When Henry IV returned from Italy he permitted the Marranos to revert to Judaism. He also ordered the bishop of Mainz to return the property which they had stored in the treasury vaults. In the religious writings of the time there are arguments against the king's granting permission to Jews to return to their faith. It is true, the argument went, that according to Christian law no one must be baptized against his will. However, the subject must state during baptism that he does not wish to be baptized. Those who did say that are dead. Those who did not say it thus agreed to their conversion voluntarily, were sprinkled with holy water, and became Christians, and Christians are not permitted to convert.

After the bloodbath of the first crusade, the relationship between Jews and their Christian neighbors became more strained. Understandably, Jews began looking at every non-Jew as a potential murderer. They kept to themselves even more than they had before. The "protection" of the Crown now became for Jews a matter of life and death.

For several decades after the first crusade there is no mention either of new drastic decrees against Jews in Europe or of any massacres. Despoiled, degraded, Jews gradually and hesitantly returned to their daily pursuits. Those who had previously engaged in a commercial undertaking which made it necessary for them to travel to distant places on unfamiliar roads now began to look for safer occupations closer to home.

The Church did not cease its agitation against the "Killers of our Lord." Rumors were spread that Jews kidnapped Christian children, crucified them, and drained their blood. Any rumor which supported the "guilt of the Jews" theory was readily believed by the ignorant masses. Apparently these rumors provided exoneration for their own guilt. The blood accusation against Jews originated during the first century of the crusades. The victims themselves were now being accused of murder.

The Second Crusade

The Christian state which was established in Jerusalem in 1099 was not very secure. The Islamic rulers of the surrounding countries, Syria and Egypt, continued their attacks on the borders of Palestine and in 1140 defeated the Christians in several battles. A cry for help went out to Christendom. In 1146 the pope issued a call for a second crusade. To attract volunteers, the Papal Bull announced that all crusaders who were in debt would be absolved from paying interest. This was a blow to those Jews whose livelihood at that time was dependent on money-lending.[10] The volunteers not only stopped paying interest, but ignored the debts altogether. Worse than this nonpayment of debts was the anti-Jewish agitation which spread mainly in the same areas where the ashes of the first crusade, fifty years earlier, were still smoldering.

The organization of the newest holy mission was undertaken by the kings of France and Germany. The ravaged cities of the first crusade had not yet been forgotten. To prevent a repetition of that havoc, the rulers prohibited attacks against the Jews of their countries. The pope, in his call, also renewed his prohibition against the killing or forcible conversion of Jews.

Among the preachers of the second crusade of 1146 was the abbot, Peter of Cluny. Peter's sermons were full of venomous attacks on the Jews. In a letter to King Louis VII he "proved" that Jews were worse enemies of Jesus than the Saracens. The Muslims believed partially in the divine mission of Jesus, that he was a prophet born of the Holy Ghost. Jews, however, are contemptuous of Jesus and his origin. Therefore, it was more important, wrote the abbot, to settle accounts with the Jews first. It was not necessary to exterminate them—there is, after all, a commandment against murder—but they must be made to live in penury and darkness, amid hatred and contumely, as did the eternal wanderer Cain, with the mark of murder on his forehead. Their wealth must be taken away from them; it was only fitting that the murderers of the Lord pay the cost of the holy war against the Saracens. It was certainly contrary to God's will that for such an inspired expedition, with Christians sacrificing so much, the Jews should fail to contribute their share.

The monk Rudolph traveled throughout the Rhine region inciting the population against Jews with the same sermons Baron Emicho had used in the first crusade:

The Jews must either be converted or destroyed. The name Jew must no longer be heard among us. We do not need to travel to the ends of the earth to fight the enemies of Jesus. God's worst enemies, the Jews, live in our cities, right in our own midst.[11]

Another abbot, Bernard of Clairvaux, has gone down in history as the "conscience of the Second Crusade." His sermons enlisted many volunteers. However, he opposed any unbridled anti-Jewish incitement. His "defense" of the Jews was characterized by the medieval clerical denunciation of their "perfidy." The abbot argued that Jews must remain alive as witnesses to the fact that by denying Jesus they had sinned. Furthermore, as long as the Jews were alive there was still hope that they would at some time accept Christianity.

After the tragic experience of the first crusade and upon hearing of a second, the Jews began seeking ways to save themselves. For large sums of money Jews were allowed into the fortresses of the nobles, in most cases with permission to offer armed resistance. Many Jews did survive this way. Outside the fortresses, Jews were completely defenseless.

When King Conrad III left Germany, many of his subjects vented their anger against the Jews in the towns and villages, dragging them to churches to be baptized. Several hundred Jews died on the roads and in discovered hiding places. Jews were massacred in Cologne, Speyer, Mainz, and other German cities. In Würzburg the crusaders found the corpse of a Christian and were told it was the victim of a Jew. A hysterical mob broke into the fortress and slaughtered twenty Jews.[12]

In France in 1147 Jews were killed in Rameru, Carentan, and other cities. Rabbeynu Tam, grandson of Rashi, and a spiritual leader of French Jewry, fell into murderous hands and was wounded five times in the head, as a symbol of the wounds Jesus suffered during his crucifixion. A prominent knight rescued him from further injury and possible death.[13] In Bohemia five hundred Jews were killed. Several thousand Jews perished in the second crusade, and thousands more were converted. Untold amounts of Jewish property was stolen.

When the crusaders finally left Europe the situation grew calmer.

Jews returned to their despoiled homes, but relationships with their Christian neighbors became strained. The chasm between Jew and Christian widened. At that time a Jewish migration began from Central Europe to Bohemia, Hungary, and even farther toward Poland. The Jewish communities in the better fortified cities of western Europe grew larger at the expense of the smaller communities, where the risks of life among the Christians had increased. In their more protected habitats Jews grew accustomed to living amid thick clouds of hostility. They composed elegies in which they mourned for their dead on memorial days and sanctified their martyrs who had died for their faith.

The second crusade reached the borders of Palestine and for several decades strengthened the position of the Christian state in Jerusalem. In 1187 the leader of the Islamic sect of the Fatimids, the heroic Sultan Saladin, vanquished the Christian kingdom in Palestine and put an end to its government in Jerusalem. The news of this defeat shocked Christian Europe into action. The agitation for a new crusade began.

In the crusades of 1096 and 1147 the volunteers came mostly from France and Germany. In the third crusade of 1189 England also participated, but in the midst of preparations for the expedition, King Henry II suddenly died. His son, Richard Coeur de Lion, took over the holy mission. Before his departure, the celebration of the coronation took place, and on that day pogroms against the Jews of England began.

Jews in Twelfth Century England

The Jewish communities in England in the twelfth century were not yet well established. It is not known whether there were Jews in England before 1066, when William the Conqueror became ruler. With the conquest of the islands by the Normans in 1066, many of the Jews suffering persecution in France and Spain emigrated to the new country. From Rouen in Normandy, where there had been a pogrom during the first crusade, many Jews fled to England and established communities in London, York, Lincoln, Cambridge, and other cities.

In the interest of developing their country, the English kings granted the Jews a charter in which they were promised the right to engage in any occupation they chose, including landowning and farming with the help of slave labor. Jews also engaged in commerce and moneylending. Since the Church still forbade the taking of interest, moneylending remained almost entirely in Jewish hands. Protected by the Crown, Jews felt safe from attack. As dealers in money, they were brought into close contact with princes and feudal lords, who became their debtors. Some Jews even became owners of large estates which landowners had pledged as security for loans.

In exchange for a large portion of the recovered monies, the government helped Jews collect their debts. Under English law at that time, when a Jew died and left no heirs, his entire estate went to the Crown, as happened with Aaron of Lincoln in 1186.[14]

It was not only feudal lords and knights who became indebted to Jews but craftsmen and merchants who borrowed money to conduct their business. To the "traditional" Jew-baiting sermons of the Christian clergy was now added envy and hatred of the "heartless Jewish usurers." A vast reserve of anti-Jewish hostility had accumulated among the Christian population in the cities.

The coronation of the young King Richard was attended by representatives of the nobility. Many Londoners and nearby villagers, eager to get a glimpse of the new king, stood outside Westminster Abbey, where the festive ceremony took place. Several wealthy Jews, bearing gifts for the new sovereign (he was supposed to renew the "Jewish charter") also came to the gates of the Abbey. A priest of the church refused them admittance. Knowing that the clergy was attempting to influence the king against renewing the charter, the Jews insisted on their right to attend the coronation.

At a sign from the priest, the guards roughed them up and threw them out. A rumor quickly spread among the crowd that the new ruler had ordered the beating of Jews. Several Jews at the gate were killed on the spot. The aroused mob now took off on a Jew-hunt, setting homes on fire, killing and looting without hindrance all day and part of the night.

When Richard learned what was going on in the city he sent out emissaries to stop the violence, but their efforts failed. The rioting continued until dawn. The looters made off with their spoil. The king then dispatched a proclamation to all his cities ordering that the Jews were not to be molested, and that any violator of this decree would be punished.

One of the Jewish delegation at the coronation was the wealthy Benedict of York, who had been savagely beaten by the mob at the Westminster gate while pleading with them that he was ready to convert. They had taken him to a church and baptized him. A few days later Benedict complained to the king that he had been converted against his will. The king asked the bishop for guidance. "If he doesn't wish to serve God," replied the bishop, "let him serve the Devil."[15] On the way home, Benedict died of his wounds.

So long as Richard was in the country, his order was obeyed. No sooner had he and his army crossed the channel than Jews were attacked in a number of cities. In Bury, fifty-seven Jews were murdered. The worst riot took place in York on 16–17 March 1190. An account of this tragedy was left by the monk, William of Newburgh.[16]

When the king discovered what had taken place during his absence, he was furious, especially because of the serious harm done to the royal treasury. As William of Newburgh noted: "Everything the Jewish moneylenders owned was really the property of the royal treasury." The king sent a bishop, accompanied by an army, to investigate and punish the guilty. Upon investigation, the bishop found no one guilty. All he did was tax the citizens of York for disturbing the peace. The chronicler concluded: "No one has ever been punished for the murder of Jews."

The crusade of 1189–92 failed to expel the Muslims from the Holy Land. The chief accomplishment of the expedition was the concession that Christian pilgrims could now visit the shrines. On the way home, the English king was captured by a German prince and helf for a ransom of 100,000 pounds. The English lords squeezed the money out of the country, mainly from the Jews. These taxes, and the pogroms, soon impoverished the Jewish population of England to a point beyond recovery. When the king was freed he did not lower the taxes which had been levied against the Jews, but in order to make sure that notes which might be burned would not go uncollected, he ordered a special registration taken of the loans and the payments.

Jews in France and Germany

In France the rulers of the various provinces which had allowed the return of Jews expelled in 1182 were quite happy with the additional income they were receiving, and during the third crusade they prevented violence against Jews. In several cities, however, the crusaders killed a number of Jews, and before he left France for the Holy Land, King Philip Augustus himself led a murderous attack on the Jews of Breil in Champagne province. One hundred Jews were burned at the stake.

In Germany the situation was under tighter control than it had been during the first two crusades. As soon as the clamor began for the third crusade, Emperor Frederick Barbarossa decreed that murdering a Jew would be punishable by death. For injuring a Jew the offender would have his hand cut off.[17] The local rulers also notified the population in their cities, as well as the crusaders, that crimes against Jews would be severely punished. In addition, for a price, Jews were given the right to take refuge in the fortified castles when the crusaders entered their neighborhoods. As a result, there was no serious violence against Jews during the third crusade.

Here and there an individual Jew was killed and looting took place. One serious episode, not directly connected with the crusade, occurred in Speyer. A Christian woman was found dead near the city. Rumors spread that she had been killed by Jews for ritual purposes. Enraged mobs attacked the Jews of Speyer, killed the rabbi and eight other Jews, and set fire to buildings.

The local bishop, who had given his blessing to the pogrom, taxed the Jews for the "crime" and demanded payment for burying their dead. The king's brother, Otto, who was left in command while the king was off on the crusade, came to Speyer with his troops and destroyed the bishop's property, fields and vineyards. When the new king, Frederick Barbarossa's son, Henry VI, returned from the east, he compelled all those guilty of organizing the violence against the Jews to rebuild the burned down houses in Speyer and pay damages to the Jews.[18]

Other Crusades

The Catholic expeditions to the east did not stop with the third crusade. Jerusalem had remained under Saracen rule. In 1199 Pope Innocent III called for a fourth crusade. This, too, was a failure. In 1218 the fifth crusade was launched, an expedition in which the crusaders suffered such heavy losses that they barely managed to return.

In the sixth crusade (1228–29) Emperor Frederick II recaptured Jerusalem, but without firing a shot. The caliphs of Islam were then feuding among themselves, and Frederick took diplomatic advantage of the situation to win concessions. After the crusaders returned to Europe, the Holy Land was invaded by Muslims.

The seventh crusade took place in 1248–54, the eighth in 1270. By that time, the whole idea of the crusades had been discredited. With the ninth crusade the Catholic wars in the eastern countries came to an end. During the thirteenth, fourteenth, and fifteenth centuries there were several more crusades in Europe, but these were waged by Catholics against Christian heretics, as well as against Jews and Muslims.

In 1209 Pope Innocent III (1198–1216) issued a call for a crusade against the Albigensian "heretics" in southern France. Fanatical monks led the marchers in exterminating tens of thousands of these Christians, many of them devout Catholics. The leaders of the crusade ordered their followers to kill everyone without distinction. The angels in heaven, they said, would sort out the guilty souls for punishment in Hell.

In this "holy war" many Jews also perished. Neither the Jews nor their murderers kept count. Jewish children were torn out of the arms of their parents and taken to churches and monasteries to be baptized and brought up as Christians. From the inquisitorial trial of an Albigensian noble there has survived an oath in which he swore to keep all Jews out of public places in his province, to prohibit Jews from working on Sundays or Christian holy days, to prohibit Jews from eating meat on Christian fast days, and to prohibit Jews from keeping Christian servants.

At the Ecumenical Council in 1212 Innocent III organized the Dominican Order. A few years later Pope Gregory IX instructed the Domincans to spy upon and punish those Albigensians who had promised to be good, devout Catholics but who had remained heretics at heart. This was the beginning of the idea of the Inquisition which two centuries later perpetrated unspeakable horrors upon thousands of Jews.

In addition to the major crusades against Islam in the east and against Christian heretics in Europe, there were many local crusades against Jews from the thirteenth century onward. Bands of "crusaders" would sew crosses on their shirts and set out to rob, kill, and convert Jews. There were also crusades which marched to Spain to drive out the Saracens. One of these was the Crusade of the Shepherds in France in 1251. A mad shepherd, convinced he was King of Hungary, reported that he had seen a vision. The Virgin Mary had instructed him to gather an army and liberate Spain from the Saracens. In a short time, he had 30,000 followers. They set out to rob and murder Jews in the cities of southern France. The local lords and bishops gave battle to the crusaders and dispersed them, but not before they had destroyed one hundred forty Jewish communities.[19]

In 1320 an army of young Christians gathered in France and set out to expel the Saracens from Spain. This crusade had some definite social overtones. Around the year 1300 the peasant protest against the feudal system had begun to mature.[20] The young crusaders were shouting slogans about getting rid of the rich nobles who were oppressing the poor. The Jew-hatred which the Church had been sowing now led the protesting crusaders to seek vengeance first on the Jews. A total of one hundred twenty Jewish communities were laid waste. In Verdun the crusaders slaughtered more than five hundred Jews; in Toulouse more than a hundred. Many were forcibly converted, but this time, when the baptized Jews tried to rejoin their faith, the now powerful Dominicans prevented it.

The Christians among whom the Jews lived in central and western Europe were permeated with Jew-hatred. Large, wealthy, and highly cultured Jewish communities were harassed, pillaged, and impoverished in Germany, France, England, Spain, in the Danube region, in Jerusalem, wherever the crusaders set foot. Marranos and converts by the tens of thousands remained in Europe at the mercy of the Christian pastors, bishops, and popes, and later the Dominican overseers of the Inquisition. Thousands of Jews chose suicide rather than submit to the soldiers of the Cross.

Some historians maintain that the overall effect of the crusades was positive and progressive. The crusaders, we are told, opened the windows of a backward Christian Europe to the fresh air from the outside, and ushered in the dawn of the Renaissance. The armies that marched off to foreign lands not only brought about increased production and trade in Europe, but important contact with foreign peoples, which broadened the cultural horizons of Europe.

All this may be partially true, but there were undoubtedly negative results, too. In addition to destroying Jewish communities, in addition to killing, raping, and torturing tens of thousands of Jews, the Catholic Church, with the help of the crusaders, became the sole master over the minds and bodies of the Christian masses in Europe. The feudal order entrenched and fortified itself with the blessing of the Church, while the blame for the poverty and suffering of the common people was placed upon the defenseless Jews, the "murderers of our Lord."

In the Jewish communities that survived the crusades, these experiences of the twelfth and thirteenth centuries left a tragic, anguished memory for many generations. They created an abyss between Jew and Christian in Europe. The difference between the two religions ceased to be a theological one. The Jews now saw the Cross not as the emblem of another faith, but as a pirate's flag, a symbol of violence, murder, torture, and death, and those who carried it, as raging, predatory beasts.

At that time, too, Jews began to move in masses toward Poland and other eastern European lands. Most of the Jews who remained in western Europe settled in fortified cities where, in times of danger, they could take refuge, of course, for a price. Jews were pushed out of land ownership and out of occupations and endeavors in which they had been engaged for many generations. Travel became perilous and Jews could no longer move about freely. Because the Church, as well as the guilds and trade associations, excluded Jews from all legitimate livelihoods, more and more Jews began to engage in the hated occupation of moneylending, which only served to add fuel to the fires of Jew-hatred still smoldering from previous generations.

In the propaganda of the crusades, scare stories were spread about the infidel Saracens. A lie, that those "cannibals" were roasting Christian children on spikes and eating their flesh, was broadened to include Jews among the villains. Christians were convinced that Jews were in the habit of murdering non-Jews, poisoning wells, and crucifying Christian children for their blood. With the crusades also begins the monstrous blood libel; the tormented and decimated Jews themselves began to be accused of murder. The crusades ushered in the second half of the Middle Ages in Europe, which degraded the Jews, demeaned them, and deprived them of all elementary human rights for several centuries to come.

10

The Middle Ages: Jews in the Money-Economy

Around the eleventh century, another important factor was added toward the heating up of Jew-hatred in Europe. For a number of reasons, Jews found themselves more and more in the business of handling money. In no anti-Jewish writings up to the end of the tenth century, even in the slanders of the bishops Agobard and Amulo in France, are Jews accused of being usurers. But beginning with the eleventh century, and especially in the time of the second crusade, Jews are charged with exploiting poor Christians, with "tearing the last bite of bread out of the mouths of God's people."[1] "Jew-moneylender" became the leitmotif of the hate-mongering sermons in the churches, of the talk in the taverns, of the discussions at all sorts of assemblies. "Jew" and "moneylender" became synonymous epithets.

The expulsion of Jews from various legitimate occupations in the European economy proceeded in different ways, depending on the location. In most European countries, Jewish ownership of land was virtually outlawed. In some areas this was a direct ban by a bishop or other feudal lord; in other places the Jews themselves were compelled to relinquish this source of income because they were forbidden to own slaves,[2] and because of the Christian oath they were required to take as landowners. The chief reason, however, seems to have been that as a farmer, a Jew would have had to live far from a Jewish community, in an environment that was growing more hostile.

In the cities, the Christian artisans, during the ninth and tenth centuries, were organized into guilds which did not admit Jewish craftsmen. Petty trade, as well as the importing and exporting of goods—an occupation which had previously been mostly in Jewish hands—had gradually been taken over by non-Jews. The Christian merchant, who was not taxed as heavily as his Jewish counterpart and who was in less danger of being robbed on the road, found it easy to drive his Jewish competitor out of business. The German-Hanseatic and Italian port cities gradually forced Jews out of foreign trade. In Venice in 945, a law was passed prohibiting Jews from owning ships or transporting goods to and from eastern lands.[3]

In the late eleventh century and during the entire twelfth, the century of the crusades, with vast armies of Europeans moving back and forth through far-off lands, there was a revival of commerce and industry in the European cities. Since gold and silver (the only currency in circulation) were in short supply, credit became a necessity. Not only the artisans, merchants, and farmers, but also the feudal lords and sometimes even the king himself had to rely on loans.

When travel in distant, unfamiliar areas became too risky for Jewish merchants, they sought occupations closer to home. Particularly since the first crusade in 1096, the pogroms had taught the Jews not to spread their capital over too large an area. Exchanging their goods for cash, which they could hide more easily and which would be transportable if they were uprooted, they found that this type of "liquid capital" could earn income.

Christians and Muslims were forbidden by their religion to lend money at interest. The demand for loans and the high profit to be made on them induced many non-Jews to violate this proscription, but the Church was able, to some degree, to prevent Christians from participating in the moneylending business. On occasion, a Christian moneylender would be excommunicated. Christian moneylenders usually charged higher rates of interest than Jews and often falsified their accounts to cheat their customers. In 1306, when the Jews were driven out of several French provinces, indebted peasants and handicraftsmen complained that the Christian moneylenders were impoverishing them, that the Jews had treated them much more humanely. In the summer of 1315, when the exiled French Jews were invited to resettle in the provinces from which they had been expelled, the reason given was that "the people had demanded it."[4]

The various rulers kept a close check on the Jews in the money business in order to ascertain how much they could squeeze out of them. In return for a sizable "commission" a king or nobleman would even help the Jewish moneylender collect his debts. The portion of the profit which went into the royal treasury was determined by the ruler himself. The Jewish moneylenders acted as a sort of sponge which absorbed the wealth of the local population; whenever the ruler wished, he squeezed the sponge out into his treasury.

Taxes collected from the Jews were much higher than their proportionate share. In England, for example, where the Jews were barely one percent of the population, they contributed about ten percent of the king's income. Whenever taxes were raised, the interest rate had to follow suit. The greatest portion of the profits from moneylending thus went to the "senior partner"—the king, the bishop, or the baron. The population did not see the guilt of these chief culprits in raising the interest rates; all they saw was the sponge, the "heartless, grasping Jewish villains." And Jew-hatred increased.

Jewish law also forbids the taking of interest on money; the Torah contains three separate passages on the subject.[5] It is true that these verses refer specifically to taking interest from "your brother," that is, another Jew. Deuteronomy 23 states clearly: "Unto a foreigner thou mayest lend upon interest, but unto thy brother thou shalt not lend upon interest. . . ." Up until the eleventh century the rabbis prohibited Jews from engaging in moneylending.

In the eleventh and twelfth centuries, however, leading rabbis began to ease this ban. Rabbeynu Tam (1100–1171), Rashi's grandson and an important authority in his time, who was himself engaged in moneylending, wrote: "Today Jews are generally lending money at interest to Jews and non-Jews because we are compelled to pay high taxes to the king and other rulers, and we have to live too."[6]

The *Sefer HaHasidim*, a deeply ethical book which teaches the Jew to live honorably with Jews and non-Jews, also permitted moneylending, but on one condition: "If a Jew has another source of income, he must not take interest either from Jews or non-Jews. He may do so only when he has no other livelihood."[7]

By reason of the oppression which the Jews experienced in those years, the high taxes and the frequent bribes they were forced to pay, and primarily because they were kept out of all the "legitimate" occupations, Jews began to deal more frequently in money. Life simply compelled them to do so. The combination of "Jew" and "moneylender" strengthened the already negative stereotype of the

Jew in the Middle Ages, and the fever of hostility against Jews in the Christian world continued to rise.

The Blood Libel

As partners of Satan, as sorcerers, as Christ-killers, the Jews certainly were regarded as mortal enemies of their neighbors. The ignorant Christian masses, sunk in superstition, believed every story, no matter how fanciful, that showed the evil ways of the Jews. That Jewish doctors were magicians, that they tore the hearts out of Christian children and used them in healing Jewish patients, was proven fact to the Christians. Two centuries before the crusades, stories were already circulating that Jews could do unnatural tricks with animals and humans, such as casting the evil eye.

In the mid-twelfth century the slander gained currency that a group of leading rabbis gathered periodically and drew lots to select a city or a village where Jews would kidnap a Christian child, crucify it, drain its blood, tear out its heart, and commit similar atrocities. By means of this crucifixion Jews placed their curse upon Christendom. To this was added various reports of Jewish sorcery which would bring further misfortune down upon Christians. One story explained that by crucifying a Christian child, Jews were trying to bring their messiah to the world, the Antichrist, who would destroy all of Christendom.

During the early centuries when Rome was persecuting Christians, these and similar stories were spread among the pagans against Christians.[8] In the twelfth century the same accusation was made by Christians against Jews and was being spread far and wide. In 1144 the body of a twelve-year-old boy named William was found in a woods near Norwich, England. A rumor spread that the murder had been done by Jews. The local judge and guardian of the peace, as well as the bishop of Norwich, were able to prevent any "disturbances" and did not call any of the Jews in for questioning. Evidently they had good reason to believe that the Jews were not involved.

However, the legend of Jewish guilt in the boy's death evolved quickly into a horror story which circulated among the people for many generations. In 1173 a document appeared, written by a Norwich monk, Thomas of Monmouth, who had bequeathed to future generations a record of the Jewish "crime." In his account Thomas lists all the grisly details of the Jewish deed, including the draining of the boy's blood. And he wrote this not from memory but through "witnesses"—Jews who had had a part in the "murder" and who later accepted the "true faith."

One such convert, Theobald of Cambridge, even knew the real reason why Jews killed Christian children. It seems that in ancient Jewish books it is written that the Jews will never be redeemed unless they shed the blood of Christian children. Jews believe, said Theobald, that by crucifying Christian children they will cleanse themselves of the sin of crucifying Jesus. Furthermore, the rabbis of Spain gather periodically in Narbonne, where they draw lots to see which place would be the site of the crucifixion that year. In 1144, chance chose Norwich. All the synagogues in Norwich (the monk continued in the name of the convert) were notified about this by special messenger:

> I was then a Jew like all other Jews. I too knew about this crime which they were planning to commit. Later, when I learned about the miracles which were taking place at the grave of the holy martyr William, and I listened to my own conscience, I left that false religion and joined the true faith of Jesus.

Thomas concluded: "These words from a former Jewish enemy of Christendom, a man who knew all the Jewish secrets, are absolutely true."[9]

On the spot where the body of the boy was found a church was built, bearing the name of St. William. To this church, for centuries, Christian pilgrims streamed to commune with the holy spirit of the "crucified" saint. Many miracles are said to have happened there. The stories about these miracles entered the folklore of the people and were retold many generations later in England and other countries.

In 1147, three years after the blood libel in Norwich, a similar accusation was made against the Jews in Würzburg. As a result, a number of Jews there were killed. In 1168, Jews were put to death in Gloucester for a similar reason.

A blood accusation struck a community of Jews in Blois, France, in 1171 and resulted in the burning of thirty-eight Jews at the stake. The "evidence" against the accused is incredible. It seems that one evening a servant of the mayor of Blois was watering his master's horse at the river. On the bank stood a Jew, holding something white in his hand. The horse, startled by the white object in the dark, broke away from the servant, who then told his master that he had seen an unfamiliar Jew throw a Christian into the water. The mayor repeated the story to the count, who ordered all the leaders of the Jewish community of Blois put in prison.

A Jewish woman who was friendly with the count convinced him of the ludicrousness of the charge and, after the river had been dredged for several days without turning up any sign of a body, the count was ready to set the Jews free. At this point the local priest persuaded him to investigate the matter further, and the inquiry proceeded in the following manner. The servant, the only witness of the "crime," was placed in a rowboat. After a little holy water had been poured into the boat, it was pushed into the river. The understanding was that if the boat, with the servant in it, would sink, that would prove he had lied and the Jews were innocent. However, the boat did not sink, demonstrating conclusively that he had told the truth!

On the basis of this "proof" the Jews were sentenced to death. It was then proposed to the Jews that if they would convert, their lives would be spared. The Jews refused. They were all placed into a wooden structure, which was set afire. The thirty-eight martyrs were burned to death on 26 May 1171.[10]

In 1182, during a pogrom in Saragossa, Spain, over a blood libel, a number of Jews were killed. The survivors bought their way out either by converting or by paying a large ransom. In 1191, in the city of Breil, a hundred Jews were burned to death. The slaughter of those innocents took place in the following manner:

A Christian in Breil killed a Jew. The Jewish community appealed to the countess to punish the murderer. The guilty man was hung. King Philip Augustus was told about this with a few added details, namely, that it was the Jews who had hung the Christian after crowning him with a wreath of thorns. The king (who was then at odds with some of his vassals) used the incident as a pretext to march into Breil with an army. Besieging the Jewish homes, he issued an ultimatum: Conversion or death. The Jews held fast to their faith. A hundred of them were burned alive.[11]

The blood libels spread throughout all the Christian countries. In 1221 twenty-six Jews were murdered in Erfurt. In 1235 the leaders of two Jewish communities were killed in Baden province over a blood libel. In the same year a tragic incident led to a massacre of Jews in Fulda. On Christmas Eve, while the miller of Fulda and his wife were in church, their home burned down with their five children inside. A rumor started that Jews had killed the children and set the fire to cover up the crime. Twenty-two Jews of that city were arrested and horribly tortured. Two "confessed." The enraged mob murdered all twenty-two Jews and their families.

While the blood accusation spread in all the Germanic countries, King Frederick II, who apparently did not believe the charge himself, undertook to discover the truth. He appointed a commission of priests and nobles to study the matter. The commission duly investigated, but could not agree. The king thereupon called together a larger group of scholars (several of them converted Jews) to research the Jewish texts. The second commission unanimously agreed that the charge was false. On the basis of their findings the king issued an edict in 1236 prohibiting any further such accusations against Jews. (Church chronicles mention this decree with the comment that the king received payment from the Jews for absolving them from guilt.)

The royal decree, however, corrected nothing. The blood libels continued to spread. The Jews of Germany and France appealed to Pope Innocent IV in Rome to explain to the Christians that the accusation was a lie. The pope in turn appointed a special commission which investigated and arrived at the same conclusion: there was no truth to the charge. The pope then issued a Bull requesting his bishops and cardinals to stop accusing Jews of this crime. Like Frederick's decree, this too fell on deaf ears. The blood libel became further entrenched in the minds of the people. There were instances where a Christian would hide a child and come to a Jewish home looking for it. While searching he would rob the frightened Jews of everything he could carry, and then demand that they pay him to stop searching. There were cases when the bodies of dead children were placed near Jewish homes and then "found"—with the resultant robbing, torturing, and burning of Jews.

The blood libel crossed the borders of Christian Europe into the Islamic lands and later spread among the Slavs and other peoples. In all countries it became an important weapon in the arsenal of Jew-haters for many years. Even today, in the last quarter of the twentieth century, Jews have been accused of ritual murder in some parts of the world.

Desecration of the Host

At the same time the blood libel was "in vogue," another lie was being disseminated among the ignorant masses of Christendom: Jews were desecrating the Christian Host, the ritual wafer which is the symbol of Christ's body. ("Host" comes from the Greek word for "sacrifice.") The New Testament relates that Jesus distributed pieces of matzo, or unleavened bread, to the Apostles at the Last Supper, saying, "Take it and eat, this is my body (Matt. 26:26)." Then he served them cups of wine and said, "Drink all of you from this, for this is my blood, the blood of the covenant" (Matt. 26:27). Very early in Christian practice the custom arose whereby at Easter-time the priest distributed the wafer to his congregants as he recited the above verses. Christians paid for the Eucharist and tasted the Savior's body.

During the mid-twelfth century, rumors began spreading among Christians that whenever the Jews got such a wafer into their hands they would desecrate it, torture it, burn it, stab it, and the Host would bleed. As early as the fifth and sixth centuries legends circulated about miracles that took place with desecrated Hosts in far-off lands, where the wafer would turn into a dove or an angel and fly up to heaven. Those tales have been in Christian folklore ever since. In the century of the crusades, the story of a Host which turned into an angel was completely identified with "Jewish perfidy," and thousands of Jews were executed for this "desecration."

Joseph HaCohen (1496–1575) wrote in his book, *Emek Habokha* (*Vale of Tears*), about a Jewish family which was accused of torturing the wafer and how they were punished:

In the days when Henry IV reigned in Germany [1056–1106], ten corrupt people accused a French Jew of torturing the Host. They said that the Jew put the holy wafer into a pot of boiling oil and that they saw a little child fly out of the pot and ascend to heaven. The judge ordered the Jew arrested.

Despite cruel torture, he denied everything; he would not confess to something he had not done. They then tortured his wife and children, who confessed to everything their tormentors told them to. The Jew was burned alive with a Talmud in his hands. His wife and children abandoned the Jewish faith.

The chronicler tells us further that on the basis of this story, repeated in many lands, Christians attacked Jews, put them to the sword and stole their possessions.[12]

In the thirteenth century Christendom went through a crisis of mass disillusionment and desertion. The impoverished and starving people were enslaved body and soul by both their secular and religious rulers. Jesus Christ the Redeemer had not appeared. The crusades to the Near East had not liberated his holy grave. The infidel Saracens were again masters of Jerusalem. The Holy Fathers, the priests and the bishops, were themselves sinful and corrupt. Superstition was the daily spiritual fare of the people. The Church was in dire need of miracles.

The grave of a child "crucified by Jews," the place where "the Host had bled"—such phenomena attracted masses of Christian pilgrims from near and far. The Christians who came to kneel and pray at these holy shrines also brought gifts, a source of income for the Church.

The miracle tales were written down and repeated in many variations. The historians Graetz, Dubnow, and Roth tell about a large number of "Host" libels which led to the killing of many Jews. The monstrous Rindfleisch massacres in Germany in 1298, which annihilated 146 Jewish communities in six months, began over a Host desecration charge. (Rindfleisch was a Bavarian noble who instigated the pogroms.) Yehezkel Kornhendler, in his book, *Yidn in Pariz* (*The Jews of Paris*), relates that as a result of such an accusation, a Jew named Jonathan and his family were burned to death near their home. Several years later the Temple du Billet was built on the spot where the Host "bled." This church stood for five hundred years, attracting many pilgrims. There are a great number of variations on this particular libel, but the basic story is this:

Jonathan the Jew had been a moneylender. A poor Christian woman to whom he had loaned money came to him one Easter eve and begged him to let her have the dress which she had given as a pledge, promising to return it immediately after the holiday. The loan on the dress amounted to thirty coins. (A correlation with the "thirty pieces of silver" theme.) Jonathan entrusted the dress to the woman on condition that she bring him a Host from her church. When he received the wafer he pierced it with needles and cut it with knives, and the wafer bled so profusely that streams of blood poured out of the house into the street.

The end of this story, in all the variations, is that Jonathan and his family were burned to death. The first chronicle of this event was composed around 1330, forty years after the wafer "bled." News of the miracle spread far and wide. For several hundred years artists painted pictures of the Jew Jonathan beating the Host, sticking it with spears, while the blood gushed from the wafer. A play was written about the event and presented in churches. In this play the Jew, with horns on his head and wearing the yellow patch, stabs the Host, tears it to pieces, boils it in oil, and out of the boiling oil flies an angel which floats in the air. (The very same miracle "happened" in Brussels in 1369, again to a Jew named Jonathan.)[12]

This canard, together with the other lies that were spread about Jews, resulted in tragic losses to the Jewish population over the centuries. At the beginning of the Common Era, when according to all estimates, the Jewish population of the world numbered eight million.[13] In 1650, according to various estimates, there were less than a million Jews in all the countries of the world.

The compulsory wearing of the yellow patch, adopted by the Christian synod in 1215, was copied by Pope Innocent III from an old Muslim decree issued by a fanatical caliph in Baghdad, Al-Mutawakkil, in the middle of the ninth century, and reissued by another caliph, the mad Hakim, early in the eleventh century.[14] The Islamic rulers, however, did not enforce this law very strictly. The Christian Church in the thirteenth century, on the other hand, which had greater power than the secular rulers, watched very closely over the enforcement of the laws passed at the synod at 1215, but the wearing of a compulsory symbol on their clothing was the most degrading blow of all to the Jews. They began to avoid appearing in the street. After the crusades, the hatred for them on the part of their Christian neighbors ate deeply into the Jewish psyche.

With the passage of time, all the anti-Jewish laws of 1215 were enforced more stringently, with the exception of the yellow patch, which Jews fought and resisted for many years. Eventually, however, it became an integral part of law and custom in most Christian countries. King Philip the Fair even required the Jews to purchase the cloth for the patch from the prince or bishop.[15]

The Negative Stereotype of the Jew

During the thirteenth century many churches and cathedrals were built in Europe. From 1170 to 1270, in France alone, eighty mammoth cathedrals went up, plus about five hundred larger churches.[16] Like museums, these edifices were filled with paintings and sculptures, all of them on religious themes. They contained positive and negative portrayals. Those which depicted Jesus, Mary, the Apostles, and the saints were positive, radiating honest splendor, glory, and charm. The negative portrayals were mostly of figures from anti-Jewish legends and the Old Testament.

During the thirteenth century Jews were forced to take part in debates with Christian scholars (many of them Jewish converts) concerning the truth of their beliefs. The debates were presented as being between the Church and the Synagogue. Many paintings and sculptures were produced about this "pair"—the Church and the Synagogue—which were usually pictured as two women. The Church, as the victor, stood proudly, with an open and friendly countenance, with a crown on her head and a crucifix in her hand. The vanquished Synagogue stood with bowed head, her crown fallen to the ground, a beaten, dejected woman. Around her head was a serpent, covering her eyes so she would not "see the light." Nearby, on the ground, lay the broken tablets of the Law.

These works of art complemented the negative stereotype of the Jew already current among Christians for several generations. In addition to works depicting Jews insulting Jesus, there were also images from the Christian mythology of the ritual murder, the desecration of the Host, and other fabricated anti-Jewish legends, for example, that Jews had obstructed the funeral of the holy Mother Mary. Artists created paintings showing a Jewish high priest hurling himself upon the coffin, attempting to push it to the ground. Miraculously, his hands stick to the coffin and his arms are torn away; another Jew tries it, with the same result.[17] Similar paintings and sculptures of Jews without hands were still to be found in churches in Belgium and Switzerland in the twentieth century.

To the older, negative representations of the Jewish character was now added the vision of the Jewish moneylender rapaciously shoveling in his gold coins, or else it was an ugly Jew with a large beak-like nose and a cold, inhuman face, draining the blood out of a dead Christian child. Julius Streicher, the ideologue of Nazi Germany, copied all his Jewish caricatures from these medieval prototypes.

Another popular painting in the cathedrals showed Jews suckling at a pig's teats, licking the hole under her tail, smacking their lips over her urine. In short, anything that added to the negative view of the Jew, anything that pictured him as hideous, dishonorable, and despised, was used in the sermons of the priests, in the paintings, in the plays which were presented on Christian holidays in the churches. No method was too base, too dishonest. The Jew had to appear to his neighbors as less than human, as a vile and disgusting creature.

This abnormal situation of the Jews—their rightlessness, the hatred that enveloped them, the insecurity in which they lived out their lives—made them increasingly dependent upon the protection of the ruler, who might be king, bishop or baron. The Jews were his chattel, and he could do anything he wished with them. He taxed them to the limit. He had the right to confiscate their property without stating any reasons. He could expel them from his cities and provinces. In short, they were "his" Jews.

In 1210 John Lackland, king of England, placed a heavy tax upon his Jews. From the wealthy Abraham of Bristol he demanded such a large sum that the Jews could not pay it. The king put Abraham in jail and every day they pulled another tooth out of his mouth. It took seven days before his family could raise the money to ransom him.[18]

11

Jews in France and England in the Thirteenth and Fourteenth Centuries

When Philip Augustus was named king of France in 1181 he was fifteen years old and his ears had already been filled with outrageous lies about Jews. No sooner had he been crowned than he ordered the arrest of the wealthy Jews in his provinces, setting an exorbitant sum for their release. A few months later he absolved all Christians from their debts to Jews. In return for this the debtor had to pay one-fifth of his debt to the royal treasury. A year later the king expelled all the Jews from his provinces, permitting them to take with them only what they could carry; everything else became the property of the Crown.[1]

A large portion of the money which Philip Augustus stole from the Jews went toward building churches and cathedrals. Notre Dame, whose foundations were laid in 1163, was built almost entirely with Jewish money.[2] The synagogues which were left in the empty Jewish cities were turned over to the Catholic Church.

The Jews who were expelled from Paris, Orleans, and other cities moved to neighboring areas under the rule of local feudal lords, who welcomed the Jews into their lands. More Jews in a province meant more income for the ruler. In 1198, sixteen years after he expelled them, Philip Augustus invited the Jews back; he realized that the expulsion had dried up an important source of his income. He no longer enforced most of the anti-Jewish decrees issued by the Synod of 1215,[3] nor did he compel the Jews to wear the yellow patch, but he did place strict regulations on Jewish moneylending. The interest rate was fixed in accordance with Church strictures, and royal officials kept a close watch on the records. The Crown's income from this source of revenue increased every year, reaching a total of 1200 livres in 1202 and 7550 livres in 1217.[4]

Between the king and his vassals, and among the nobles themselves, there were agreements to restrict the movement of Jews from one province to another unless they received special permission from the given ruler. The Jews in France thus became bound to their dwelling places and their lords.

Under Louis IX, who ruled from 1226 to 1270, the situation of the the Jews in France continued to worsen. A devout Catholic, his primary ambition was to baptize all the Jews in his kingdom. It was a period in which there were many heretics among the Christians, such as the Waldensians and the Albigenses. Among the Jews, too, a certain amount of heresy was prevalent. Some rabbis opposed Moses Maimonides's rationalization of the biblical miracles. Rabbis Shlomo ben Avrom and Jonah Grondi appealed in 1233 to the Dominican Order to ban the works of Maimonides as heretical. The priests gladly granted the request. In 1234, Jewish homes were searched and anything written by Maimonides was confiscated and publicly burned.

The leaders of the Christian Church had long realized that the source of Jewish religious pride lay more in the Talmud than in the Bible. Like many other accusations against the Jews in their long history, the denunciation of the Talmud came from an apostate French Jew, Nicholas Donin. In 1238 he came before Pope Gregory IX and charged that the Talmud insulted Jesus and Mary and that it commanded Jews to kill *goyim*. Were it not for the Talmud, Donin charged, Jews would not be so stubborn in their faith and would gladly accept Christianity.

Two years later the pope dispatched orders to the elders of the Church in all Catholic countries to confiscate all copies of the Talmud found in Jewish homes and synagogues. This encyclical was carried out only in France, where Louis IX ordered a trial held of the Talmud. Four rabbis, headed by Yehiel of Paris, were invited to conduct the defense. The outcome was predictable. The Talmud was found guilty of defaming the Christian faith and was sentenced to burning. The Dominican Inquisitors made a search of Jewish homes in Paris and other cities, confiscating many volumes of the Talmud. For two years the Jews strove by various means to save their cultural treasure. By bribing a priest who was close to the king, they were able to get the books back.

A year later, however, the devout monarch ordered the reconfiscation of the Talmud. On 6 June 1242 the original sentence was carried out; twenty-four wagonloads of Jewish books were burned in a marketplace in Paris.[5] Many Jewish communities declared a fast day and recited lamentations. The loss was extremely grave.[6] For a number of years the Inquisitors continued their search, and in 1248 three more wagonloads of books were burned.

In 1247, St. Louis, preparing for the seventh crusade, ordered the Jews expelled from his cities and confiscated their property. Actually, only a few wealthy Jews were expelled; the decree was not carried out because the king was already on his way to do battle with the Saracens. In 1269 St. Louis decreed that every Saturday, in their synagogue, the Jews must listen to a sermon by a Christian priest.

Louis's son, Philip III, continued to enforce the anti-Jewish laws of the Synod of 1215. The Inquisition was already in full bloom. The Dominicans paid special attention to Jewish converts, who were always seeking ways to return to Judaism. In 1277 the Inquisitors delivered Rabbi Isaac Moll into the hands of the civilian authorities for execution because he had converted a dying Marrano back to his faith, so he could be buried in a Jewish cemetery.[7]

Under Philip the Fair (1285–1314) the Jewish situation deteriorated further. In 1288, in the city of Troyes, an aroused mob stormed out of the churches on Easter Sunday and conveniently found a murdered Christian near the home of Isaac Chatelen, a wealthy Jew. They beat up Chatelen and his family and arrested them. The Inquisitors "tried" several other Jews in the city, found them guilty, burned thirteen of them to death and confiscated their property. Infuriated by this, the king decreed that henceforth the priests no longer had any authority over Jewish property in his cities.

In 1290 Philip ordered a Jewish couple in Paris burned on the charge of desecrating a Host.[8] This time it was the king who confiscated the Jew's property. As usual after such an accusation, rumors spread that blood had spurted from the wafer. At the site of the "miracle" a church was built, to which devout Christians made pilgrimages for many years.

The rulers of France in those days regarded the Jews as their personal property. In 1297 a court arranged a compromise between King Philip IV and his brother Carl, a baron in one of the royal provinces, between whom there had been a dispute over the "ownership" of forty-three Jewish families. In 1299 Carl sold all two thousand Jewish families in his province to King Philip for 20,000 livres. The king immediately placed a residence tax upon the Jews. The tax collectors had the right to inspect all Jewish credit operations; if they found any "irregularities," they were authorized to confiscate the Jew's property, arrest him, and even beat him to death. In 1295 inspectors arrested the well-to-do Jews of Beaucaire province and kept them in prison until they paid the exact sum of the profit which they had made in their business, according to the calculations of the authorities.

In 1306 King Philip issued an expulsion decree against the Jews of France, and to prevent them from hiding any of their property he kept the announcement secret until the day of the expulsion. On 22 July 1306 all the wealthy Jews in many French cities were suddenly arrested and informed that they must be out of the king's domains within a month, leaving all their property behind. They were permitted to take with them only the clothes on their backs and a small amount of cash. Only those Jews who agreed to convert were allowed to remain.[9]

The most important provinces were then under the rule of the Crown. Thousands of Jews, impoverished and humiliated, were driven from the French cities. Those in the north went to Lorraine, to Germany, to Italy, and as far as Bohemia. From the south many Jews went to Provence, which was still an independent territory. Others went farther south to Spain.

In 1315, ten years after the explusion, the new king, Louis X, invited back those Jews who had settled in the French provinces outside the king's jurisdiction. How many Jews returned to their former homes is not known. It stands to reason that some of them would have tried to get their homes back or recoup some of the debts owed to them. In the contract of return, several conditions were set forth. One condition was that the Jews would have a "grace period" of twelve years. At the end of that time, if the king decided to expel them again, he must give them twelve months' notice.

Inside France the Church continued its agitation against the infidels who had "crucified the Savior." In 1317, in Chinon, two Jews were sentenced to death on a ritual murder charge. In 1320 a peasant uprising broke out in France and a band of shepherds, together with various vagrants and criminals, began a pogrom of the Jewish communities. In Toulouse a group of five hundred Jews took refuge in a fortress and defended themselves. When the attackers set fire to the fortress the Jews committed suicide rather than fall into their hands. The children were dragged to churches and converted. These "shepherds" brought much misery upon the Jews of Bordeaux, Albi, and other cities in southern France and northern Spain. Dubnow cites a reliable source to the effect that one hundred twenty Jewish communities were ravaged by these "shepherds."[10]

After the shepherds a new misfortune came down upon the Jews of France—the leper libel. The people in the cities and villages suffered frequent epidemics. Among the common folk rumors spread that the lepers, kept isolated from the rest of the population, were resentful of their treatment and in revenge were poisoning the wells. A number of lepers were tortured to admit their crime. They confessed, adding that they had obtained the poison from Jews, a story which found ready acceptance among the people.

Jews in many places were killed as a result of this lie. In Chinon a bonfire was lit in a deep ditch and the Jews were thrown into the flames.[11] In Paris Jews were arrested and "investigated." Philip V, the new king, punished the Jewish community with a heavy fine. Under Carl IV, who became king in 1322, conditions were no better. Jews began to emigrate to the independent French provinces Avignon and Provence.

In 1358 a widespread peasant revolt, known as the Jacquerie, erupted throughout the countryside. Many of the fortified courts of the nobility were burned down. After a great effort the Crown finally suppressed the rebellion, but the royal treasury was left empty. In 1360 the king invited the Jews to return, promising them many privileges. On resettling, they would have to pay only a residence tax and the annual tax.

A number of wealthier Jews came from other neighboring areas to settle in France, with a residence contract that was to be in force for twenty years. In 1368, eight years after the return, they were again threatened with expulsion, but on payment of a large sum of money, this order was rescinded. When the twenty-year period came to an end in 1380, the Crown renewed the privileges for another twenty years, but that same year a revolt broke out in Paris, and one of the demands was that the Jewish moneylenders be expelled. Mobs looted the government treasury, attacked the Jewish quarter, and killed many Jews. On 17 September 1394 the king ordered all the

Jews expelled. By the end of the year—and for three centuries thereafter—France was *Judenrein*.

But during those three hundred years, while the Jews were absent from France, Jew-hatred was not. If anything, it intensified, as the folklore created an imaginary Jew who was a frightening devil, a hideous ogre, the incarnation of evil. From childhood the French, like the Germans and the Spaniards, grew up under the influence of these folktales that were repeated over and over again by family, friends, and priests, stories of evil spirits called "Jews," who had murdered God's only begotten Son. This "cultural heritage" became part of the national mythos.

Jews in England in the Thirteenth Century

When John Lackland became king of England in 1199, he started his reign with a "Charter of Freedoms" for the Jews, promising them a life more or less free from harassment. Soon, however, the king's avarice nullified the Charter, as he again taxed his Jews unmercifully, piling tax upon tax. During the historic struggle of the nobles in 1215 for the Magna Carta, the Jews in England were hit by riots and by the concessions which the king made to his vassals, who were in debt to the Jews. The nobleman, the urban landowner, the smaller gentry, and the clergy, all of them now the new partners in state power, looked upon the Jew as the financial power that had supported the king against the interests of the vassals, the merchants, and the common people.

Under the reign of Henry III, who ruled from 1216 to 1272, the situation of the Jews steadily deteriorated. While he was still a boy-king, power was in the hands of his guardians, who represented the classes that had imposed the Magna Carta upon the king. Now they tried to force all sorts of decrees upon the king's servants. The king, who could no longer tax his vassals as freely as he wished, kept squeezing "contributions" out of his Jews. In 1226, for example, the taxes on Jews amounted to 4,000 livres; in 1230 they were 6,000; from 1232 to 1239 they rose to 18,000 livres.

In order to keep tighter control on Jewish property, the authorities compelled the Jews to live in a few selected cities, where the royal tax collectors could watch them more closely. In 1231 the Jews were expelled from Newcastle; in 1236 from Southampton; in 1244 from Newbury and other cities. By 1253 the Jews were concentrated in only a few places and were forbidden to move from one town to another. It became extremely difficult for them to leave England with any of their property. In short, they were in captivity.[12]

Throughout England robberies and violence upon Jews grew in frequency. The priests in the churches continuously spread their poison of hatred. The ritual murder charge became more common. In 1230 the Jews of Norwich were charged with kidnapping a five-year-old Christian boy and circumcising him. Thirteen leaders of the Jewish community were imprisoned for ten years; several of them were hung. Before the execution they were tied to horses and dragged through the streets from the prison to the gallows.

In 1244 a Christian child was dug out of a grave in London. Wounds were found on the body and it was reinterred in St. Paul's Cathedral. For the payment of 60,000 livres the king absolved the Jews of London from their "guilt." This payment was in addition to the annual tax.[13]

In 1255, in the city of Lincoln, an eight-year-old Christian boy by the name of Hugh disappeared. After a search of several days he was found drowned in a well near a Jewish home. The rumor of a ritual murder spread quickly throughout the city. The Jew who lived in the house confessed under torture that every year the Jews murdered a Christian child in order to dishonor the Savior. King Henry III ordered a trial of the "guilty" Jews. Ninety-two respected members of the Jewish community of Lincoln were arrested. Eighteen of them were hung immediately. The rest were kept in prison for many years until the king's brother interceded and they were released. The body of the drowned child was buried in the courtyard of the church, which soon was called "The Church of Little St. Hugh." For centuries this church attracted masses of gift-bearing worshippers from all over the country.[14]

In 1232 a Catechumen House was established in London to convert Jews. During the thirteenth century it was often filled to overflowing with unfortunate Jews who had no more inner strength left to withstand all the humiliations and expulsions, all the torture and terror.

In 1254 the king imposed an especially heavy tax on the Jews and assigned the duty of collecting it to his brother Richard. A delegation came to Richard with an appeal that the Jews be permitted to emigrate from England, for which privilege they were ready to abandon their homes and possessions. Their appeal was denied. They were not permitted to leave.[15]

After all the decrees, threats and persecutions, the taxes diminished from year to year; there was no more money left to squeeze out of the Jews of England. In 1262, open rebellion broke out against the king. For more than three years, power rested in the hands of the rebels, a situation which brought more misery to the Jews. In Northamptom, in Lincoln, in Worcester, in other cities, fifteen hundred Jews were murdered. Christian debtors broke into Jewish homes, looting at will, but making sure to destroy the notes of indebtedness, both in the homes of the moneylenders and in the royal treasury. The rebellion was suppressed and the Crown again permitted the Jews to engage in moneylending. But by that time they had very little left to lend.

In 1272 Henry III died and the throne passed to his son Edward, who by then had little hope of ever realizing any taxes from the impoverished Jews in his country. A devout Christian, the new king heeded the warnings of Pope Gregory X, who at the Synod of 1274 had proposed the abolition of all moneylending as a mortal sin. The king therefore banned the business of moneylending in England for both Jews and Christians. The revenue for the need of the government was to come from a per capita tax on the general population. The Jews were given permission to engage in all occupations previously forbidden to them, such as commerce, handicrafts, and even agriculture; they would be able to lease fields (for ten years) and cultivate them.[16]

Had this permission been accompanied by a return to the Jews of their human rights, had it been possible to eradicate or at least diminish the Jew-hatred among the surrounding population, then perhaps, the situation of the Jews could have been normalized, at least in England. But this did not happen. The Church did not cease its Jew-baiting. The urban Christian merchants did not permit the Jews entry to trade. The craft guilds did not accept Jews and did not allow them access to raw materials. To lease land without the right of hiring Christian farmhands, to move into a village and defenselessly expose oneself to hostile peasants—this the Jews did not even attempt. And only a few Jews ventured to engage in commerce.

Most of the Jews remained in dire poverty. Some tried "currency clipping"—melting down coins and reminting them with less silver. Christian moneylenders also engaged in this practice. When the government discovered what was happening it arrested many of the perpetrators. In 1278 almost three hundred Jews were hung for this crime.[17]

The devout King Edward never gave up his hope to convert the

Jews of his kingdom. In 1279 he ordered the Jews to listen to sermons of Dominican monks. In the 1280s the authorities began confiscating all of the large synagogues and turning them into churches. Priests warned the Jews that their children would be taken away from them and placed in monasteries to be brought up as Christians.

In 1287 the king ordered the imprisonment of all heads of Jewish families until they paid a contribution of 12,000 livres. Three years later he ordered all the Jews expelled from England.[18] This decree was issued on 18 July 1290, which happened to be *Tisha B'Av*, a Jewish fast day of national mourning for the destruction of the Holy Temple in Jerusalem. The order specified that Jewish homes, gardens, and storehouses would remain the property of the government and that the Jews would be permitted to take with them only small items of property, or else they could sell these things and take the cash. Jews who were found in England after 1 November 1290 would be executed. Only those Jews in the houses of conversion would be permitted to stay.

More than 16,000 Jews left England and crossed the Channel, most of them settling in France—but not for long. Sixteen years later they were forced to leave France, too, this time with tens of thousands of other Jews who were being expelled from that country.

12

Jews in Central Europe from the Thirteenth Through the Sixteenth Centuries

For a period of twenty-five years after the death of King Frederick II in 1250, there was no central power in Europe to protect the Jews. In many cities the bishops quarreled with the secular authorities over this right, and frequently these conflicts were brought to the pope for arbitration. In 1261, after the archbishop of Magdeburg was given the right by the pope to protect the Jews, he raided the Jewish streets, broke into homes, and helped himself to money and valuables, and then held the wealthier Jews for ransom.[1]

The archbishop then tried to repeat this scenario in Halle, but the burghers of that city, who themselves claimed this right, intervened and stopped him. They even found a nobleman with a company of knights to help them. A battle ensued in which the bishop and his force were victorious, and the Jews remained in his jurisdiction.

It was a time of general unrest and the Jews were often called upon to help defend their city. Many Jews were killed in Koblenz and other Rhine cities in such situations. In one attack on the city of Sinzig, seventy-two Jews were burned alive in a synagogue.[2] However, the usual pretext for such brutalities was the ritual murder charge. In 1270 the Jews in Weisenberg (Alsace) were accused of murdering a Christian child. Seven Jews were tortured to death, two of them converts from Christianity. In Forchheim the body of a little girl was found in a river. A relative of the child "confessed" that she had sold the child to some rich Jews at Easter-time. The people she named were tortured to death.

In 1279 Rudolph of Hapsburg became king of the Roman Empire in Germany. As a result of the long struggle for power, the country was in ruins and the royal treasury was depleted. Therefore, the king began extracting taxes from all his subjects, especially from the Jews. When Jews began to move stealthily out of the area, he threatened them with confiscation of their property and death.

Rabbi Meir of Rothenburg, who wished to settle in Palestine in his old age, made his way under cover to an Italian port city and waited for a ship. Recognized by an informer, he was imprisoned in Alsace. When the Jewish community offered the Emperor payment for the rabbi's release, he demanded a larger sum. From his prison cell Rabbi Meir forbade his fellow Jews to ransom him. It would only lead, he said, to the imprisonment of other rabbis for purposes of ransom. For seven years Rabbi Meir remained a prisoner, until his death. Even for the release of his body the authorities demanded a high price. It was not until fourteen years after his death that Rabbi Meir's remains were ransomed and brought to burial in the city of Worms.[3]

In 1283, as the result of a ritual murder charge, a mob invaded the Jewish quarter of Mainz, killing ten Jews. Around the same time, twenty-six Jews were killed in Bacharach. In 1286, aroused Christian mobs set fire to a crowded synagogue in Munich. None of the Jews escaped.[4]

In 1298 a charge of desecration of the Host was brought against the Jews of Rotingen. A Bavarian noble named Rindfleisch "revealed" that he had been instructed by heaven to avenge this crime. In April of 1298 he and his gang of cutthroats murdered all the Jews of Rotingen. On their way to other Jewish communities they picked up more recruits and in June they massacred hundreds of Jews in Rothenburg, Würzburg, and Nuremberg. In the last-named city a number of Jews locked themselves in a fortress and resisted. Every one of them perished. The number of Jews killed during the Rindfleisch pogroms was almost the same as that in the first crusade. In the course of half a year, from spring to autumn of 1298, Rindfleisch and his gangs destroyed 140 Jewish communities, killing several thousand people.[5] The slaughter did not stop until Albert of Hapsburg became king at the end of that year.

From Bavaria and the Rhine region a stream of emigration flowed eastward to Austria, Hungary, and Poland during the thirteenth century. In Bohemia, after the crusades, the Jews had lived more or less peacefully. The Jewish communities in Prague and other cities in Bohemia grew larger as refugees from Germany, Alsace, Bavaria, and elsewhere came seeking refuge. King Ottokar II, ruler of Austria, Bohemia, and Moravia, was involved in many wars and constantly needed funds. Pleased with the "Jewish taxes" coming into his treasury, he added a few more privileges to the charter which his predecessor had granted the Jews, including the prohibition of the ritual murder charge. For these concessions to the Jews he had received permission from the pope: ". . . in accordance with the statutes of the Pope, we strictly forbid anyone to accuse the Jews who live in our kingdom of using human blood. . . . According to the laws of their religion, Jews are not permitted to use any kind of blood at all."[6] Furious, the bishops convened a synod in 1267 and condemned the charter in the strongest possible terms.

After Ottokar's death in 1276, Austria and all its provinces reverted to the rule of the German emperor Rudolph of Hapsburg. Rudolph allowed the Jews several conditions of Ottokar's charter, but toward the end of the century the persecution began again, including the charges of ritual murder and desecration of the Host. A wafer smeared with blood and tossed on a Jewish doorstep was enough to start a pogrom. Such an incident took place in Korneiburg, Austria. The family who lived in the house was burned at the stake, the Jews were driven out of the city, and their property was confiscated.

In the city of Pelten, Christian debtors seeking to avoid payment of their debts also found a bloodstained wafer near a Jewish home. Again, many Jews were murdered and the rest expelled. The booty was divided among the murderers. This time Duke Albert held the city burghers responsible and punished the guilty. When he died a year later, the Christians hailed it as retribution from God for his defense of the Jews.

Hungary

In the twelfth century Hungary had not yet been deeply indoctrinated in the Christian faith. Jews, Muslims, and Turkish pagans still lived more or less harmoniously among the Christian population. In 1279 a synod of important Chruch leaders took place in Hungary whose purpose was to establish Christianity as the official religion of the country. Plans were made for drawing the pagans closer to Christianity. At the same time, the synod decided that it was time the Jews in Hungary began wearing the yellow patch. King Bratislav, however, vetoed the idea. In fact, he dissolved the synod.[7]

This dynasty, which had treated the Jews so humanely, fell in 1301. During the next century the Jewish communities in Hungary suffered the same tribulations as those in Germany and elsewhere in the Christian world. In some areas of the country, gangs of "Jew-beaters" and *Armleder* (because of a piece of leather they wore as an armband) were running rampant. In 1336 they pillaged Jewish communities around Rothenburg and Nuremberg. In 1337 they almost destroyed the large Jewish community in Frankfurt-am-Main. In Alsace the *Armleder* gangs set out across the land with pickaxes and for a period of two years they robbed and murdered Jews. In 1338 all the Jews in the town of Rupack were killed.[8]

In Regensdorf, a charge of Host desecration led to a murderous riot that spread to other cities in Bavaria, Austria, and Bohemia. The king was supposed to protect the Jews or at least punish the murderers. However, his treasury was enriched by a large portion of the stolen goods. Therefore, he distributed letters of amnesty to his Christian subjects. In one such letter the king wrote:

> Let it be known herewith that the city council and the citizens of Millhausen have come to an amicable agreement with us. They will pay into the royal treasury a thousand pounds (in old Basel coin) for all the claims which we have against them for killing the Jews of Millhausen and for the damage done to the royal treasury by these acts. We forgive the citizens of Millhausen in return for the sum which they have promised to pay us. All the property of the murdered Jews, their homes and gardens, all the pledged articles which had been in their possession, are the property of the king. When the citizens of Millhausen complete the payment of the thousand pounds . . . they will be released from the debts which they owed to the murdered Jews.[9]

The Black Death

In 1348 Europe was stricken by a deadly epidemic that came to be known as the Black Death. It is estimated that in 1348–49 alone one-third to a half of the population in Europe perished from this disease. The fear of a mysterious death which could strike with such suddenness spread through all classes of the population. When rumors began to circulate that the Jews were responsible for the plague, that they were poisoning wells and rivers, the near-hysterical masses accepted it as gospel truth. In many cities of central Europe Jews were arrested and tortured to confess that they had in fact poisoned the wells. Here and there a confession was obtained.

In turn, the stories of Jews confessing to this heinous deed spread even more rapidly than the original rumors. Steeped in Jew-hatred, the ignorant Christian population arose to wreak vengeance upon the "Christ-killers." In dozens of cities Jews were burned alive, tortured, massacred. The pope himself was moved to intervene and declare the Jews innocent, but it did not help.

The worst pogroms occurred in Germany. Inflamed mobs rampaged wherever there were Jewish communities. Emperor Carl IV (1347–78) even threatened his subjects with damages for his murdered *Kammerknecht*, but to no avail. In some cities the Christian authorities tried to rescue the Jews. Help came too late. In Strasbourg the Burgermeister and several officials tried to calm the enraged mobs. Some of the nobles came to the assistance of the authorities. But the citizens would not let themselves be dissuaded. The Strasbourg murderers had in mind the debts which they owed to the Jews, and the valuable chests in the Jewish homes which would now be theirs. All two thousand Jews in the city were driven into the Jewish cemetery and locked into a large wooden barn. It was set afire. A few Jews who converted survived. The Jewish property was divided among the executioners. The debts were cancelled. And the new city council of Strasbourg demanded that Jews be kept out of their city for at least a hundred years.[10]

The example of Strasbourg was followed in other Alsatian cities. In many cities all that remained of the Jews were places called "Jew-ditch" or "Jew-hill" or "*Judenbrand*"—sites of mass Jewish graves. In Sletstadt some of the Jews were killed and some expelled. In Benfeld some Jews were burned and others drowned in a swamp. In Millhausen all the Jews who did not manage to flee in time were put to death.

The large Jewish community in Speyer was destroyed in 1349. In Worms the Jews themselves set their dwellings on fire and perished in the flames. In Mainz the Jews resisted and killed two hundred of their tormentors on the first day. But they were hopelessly outnumbered. On 24 August 1349, six thousand Jews died in the city of Mainz.[11] On the same day, the large Jewish community in Cologne was destroyed. In the summer of 1349 the Jews in Erfurt, Frankfurt-am-Main, and other cities were massacred. In the fall of that year the Jewish communities in Nuremberg and other cities in Bavaria were destroyed. The sole exception was Regensburg, where the city council truly protected the Jews.

In eastern Germany the Jews of Breslau, Königsberg and smaller towns in the Brandenburg area were slaughtered. Gangs bent on killing Jews began roaming through Austria, but here Duke Albert IV stopped them before they could do much damage. In addition to wiping out the leadership of the gangs, he imposed heavy penalties on those cities which had permitted the pogroms. These actions earned him the name "*Judenfreund*" which at that time was a most grievous insult, especially for a Christian monarch.

In those cities where the Jewish population was destroyed, disputes took place between the murderers over the spoils, and between the murderers and the Crown, which demanded damages. Upon part payment, the criminals were pardoned, as in the episode at Millhausen.

Approximately three hundred Jewish communities were destroyed during the two years of the Black Death. The plague itself took its own toll of those Jews who survived. The number of converted Jews was relatively small. Those synagogues that were not burned down were converted into churches. The plague left the cities of central Europe depopulated. Economic and social life was nonexistent. Many of the city councils soon decided to invite the Jews back.

The tragedy of the Black Death was not so easily forgotten by the Jews, however. Most of those who escaped or were expelled and who had managed to settle in Austria, Bohemia, and Poland, refused to return to the scenes of horror. Of those who did return, most left again later, in secret, since Jews were not permitted to move without informing the authorities.

The new Jewish communities in Austria, Bohemia, and Hungary soon drank from the same bitter cup as their cousins in Germany. In 1389, around Passover-time, some Jewish children were throwing sand at each other in a street in Prague. A Catholic priest walked by, carrying church vessels. Something landed in one of them. The priest raised an alarm: Jews had thrown stones at him and at the sacred vessels. A mob gathered, carrying axes, and demanded of the Jews to convert or die.

Several hundred Jews were killed that day in Prague. The rabbi committed suicide. Other Jews followed his example. The synagogue was burned to the ground and the Torah scrolls ripped to shreds.[12] From Prague the gangs marched to other cities nearby and ravaged the Jewish communities there, then divided the spoils with the local duke.

In Strasbourg, a few years after the massacre there, the Jews were invited to return. A small number did so. It was a period when Jews generally had few alternatives and were always hoping for "better times." In 1388 the authorities in Strasbourg again expelled the Jews from the city. This time the expulsion lasted for several centuries.[13]

In the cities along the Danube the authorities adopted a policy of forbidding Jews to emigrate, bleeding them white with excessive taxes, and restricting their human rights. Jews caught leaving illegally were punished and their property confiscated. If they had no property, the Jewish community was penalized with a special tax.

Jews escaped from Hungary to Austria. In 1360 the Hungarian king invited them back, hoping that now it would be easy to convert the downtrodden Jews to Christianity. When the few who returned refused to convert, the king again expelled them. This time the Jews sought refuge in Poland.

The Hussite Wars

In the first half of the fifteenth century the Jews in southeast Germany, Austria, and Bohemia were again victims of a series of pogroms that took place during religious wars between the Catholics and the Hussites. The Hussite heresy was primarily a protest against the corrupt Roman Church. John Huss, father of the movement, was burned at the stake in Koblenz in 1415. His followers, mainly Czechs, fought against the Catholic reactionaries who supported the feudal lords in their suppression of the people.

The Hussite wars worsened the situation of the Jews in those regions. While the Jews had very little to do with the heresy, they were accused by the Church of being its leading agitators. In their campaigns against the Hussite protesters the Catholic zealots attacked many Jewish communities, those closest to the scene of the battles being the hardest hit. In Vienna a rumor spread that the Jews were providing the heretics with food and weapons. The students of the Vienna Theological Seminary invaded Jewish streets in true pogrom style.

In 1420, in the Austrian city of Ehns, a holy wafer disappeared from a church. A Christian woman confessed that she had stolen it and sold it to a rich Jew named Israel. The man and his family were arrested and tortured, along with other Jews of the city. None of them admitted to the "crime." But on the strength of the woman's oath many Jews in Ehns were imprisoned and their property confiscated. The poorer Jews were driven out of the country. The wealthier Jews were kept in prison and tortured. Their younger children were baptized. Some of the imprisoned Jews converted. When a number of them were later caught observing the Jewish Sabbath, they were burned at the stake. Many Jews committed suicide.

The Austrian duke, who was then burning Hussite heretics, took upon himself the task of eradicating the Jews in his area. On 12 March 1421 he ordered the burning of two hundred imprisoned Jews who had refused to convert. All the other Jews in his lands were expelled and their property taken for the duke's coffers.[14]

During the fifteenth century the Jews in central Europe experienced one wave of attacks after another. Dominican and Franciscan monks traveled from one end of Germany to the other hurling fire and brimstone upon heretics and Jews. One such preacher was a monk named Capistrano, an Inquisitor from Italy whom the pope had sent into the heresy-ridden areas to buttress the Catholic faith. To win the trust of the Christians, Capistrano's sermons stressed the "Jewish crimes which have been proven over and over." A fiery orator, he attracted large audiences wherever he went.

In the spring of 1453, the leaders of the Jewish community of Breslau were arrested for the crime of stealing a church vessel containing the Eucharist. Along with the Jews a Christian couple was also seized. Under torture the woman confessed to stealing the vessel and selling its contents to a Jew named Meir. All the Jews of the city, she added, had stabbed the wafers, cut them with knives, and sent them to Jews in other cities to further torment Christ's body.

Capistrano himself conducted the trial of the accused. One Jew who could no longer endure the torture "confessed" to the crime and named others. All the Jews in Breslau were arrested. On 14 July 1453, forty-one Jews were burned to death. The rabbi had taken his own life a day earlier. Several days later another seventeen Jews (ten men and seven women) were burned for the same crime in Schweidnitz. In Lignitz the arrested Jews were burned in the prison, which was set afire during the night. All the other Jews were expelled from the city. Children up to the age of seven were taken from their parents, baptized and brought up as Christians.[15]

The Jewish community of Regensburg had remained intact

throughout the storms of the fourteenth century. Now their enemies fabricated a ritual murder charge which was brought by two converted Jews who had become monks. One of them, Hans Vayol, charged Rabbi Israel Bruna with buying a Christian child from him for ritual purposes. The Christian population of the city was all set for the pogrom. The city council, which apparently did not believe the convert's story, meanwhile held the rabbi in "protective custody." A search was begun for the "crucified" child and its parents. No child was found, nor any parents whose child was missing. When the authorities began to question the convert more closely, he admitted to inventing the whole story. The rabbi was released and his accuser was executed. The population of Regensburg, however, continued to harass the Jews until, in 1519, they achieved their objective: the Jews were expelled from the city.[16]

By the beginning of the sixteenth century very few Jews were left in northern France and central Europe. Much larger Jewish communities were already in existence in Poland, Lithuania, and the Ukraine, which was then under Polish rule.

Jews in Italy

The Jews in Rome, whose community along the Tiber River was a poor one, considered themselves citizens of the Papal City. King Frederick II, ruler over the "old" Roman Empire—Germany, Italy, and Sicily—dealt with the Jews of his Italian provinces in the same way he did with his *Kammerknecht* in Germany. Sometimes he protected them and sometimes he went along with the decrees of the priests. In 1267, in the southern province of Naples, a convert named Manufortes convinced the emperor that the Talmud and the Jewish prayerbooks defamed Jesus and Christianity. The emperor ordered all Talmudic volumes and prayer books confiscated.[17]

During the fourteenth century, when Jews were experiencing terrible calamities in the countries of Europe, Jewish refugees settled in the Italian provinces and Sicily, where the Renaissance had already made a beginning. The Jews here also lived under the pressure of the Catholic Church, and the local rulers also exacted high taxes from them, but they were not subjected to such bloody massacres and expulsions as in the European countries. The Black Death killed many people in Italy, too, but here the lie about Jewish responsibility for the disease was never very effective.

In the seventy years from 1308 to 1378, when the papal court was split between Rome and Avignon in southern France, the Jewish situation stayed about the same. The popes themselves did not treat the Jews too badly and even issued Bulls against false accusations. Their personal physicians were often Jews, who were sometimes able to intercede for Jewish communities that were being persecuted.

In 1419, when the Dominicans began a strong anti-Jewish campaign, the Jews complained to Pope Martin V, who issued a decree against religious coercion. He forbade Christians to interfere with the Jewish observance of their festivals and abolished the yellow patch. In 1429 he made a special appeal to all Christians not to deny the "Christian virtues" to the Jews. This particular Bull cost the Jews a great deal of money, which was collected in the various Jewish communities.

Not all the popes were so well disposed toward the Jews. Most of them spoke tolerantly enough, but their deeds belied their words. Pope Nicholas V, in return for a financial contribution, wrote a Bull granting concessions to the Jews. But this very pope also sent the infamous Capistrano into the Hussite areas. Pope Sixtus IV, who gave his consent to Ferdinand and Isabella for introducing the Inquisition into Spain, allowed refugee Marranos entry into Italy. But Innocent VIII, who succeeded Sixtus, instituted special methods to ferret out "secret Jews" and in 1487 brought the Inquisition to Italy.[18]

The attitude toward Jews in the various Italian provinces was not all cut from the same cloth. It depended on the economic interests of the population, on the whims of the priests, and on the liberal ideas of the rulers. In the port city of Genoa, for example, Jews were not permitted to settle at the demand of the merchants and burghers in the harbor. In Venice, on the other hand, Jews were well-represented in commerce and the handicrafts. This did not mean that the Jews in Venice were citizens with equal rights. The Christian burghers permitted the Jews to live in the city in accordance with a certain contract which they called a *condotta*, for a given number of years. After this period the agreement had to be renewed, which usually meant the Jews had to pay more money. Sometimes the *condotta* was not renewed at all. This contract kept the Jews in a perpetual state of insecurity.

In Padua, life was easier for the Jews than in the port cities. Jews were to be found there in all occupations, including farming. In Ferrara, the situation was comparatively good. When Genoa refused to admit the Jews expelled from Spain in 1492, the duke of Ferrara gladly let them in, granting them access to all occupations. In Florence the Christian burghers invited the Jews in and promised them the right to follow whatever pursuits they wished. However, the *condotta* was part of the arrangement.

Among the most active preachers was an "expert" named Bernard of Siena, who directed his main attack against prosperous Jews. It was obvious, he ranted, that with their wealth the Jews were out to enslave all of Christendom. They had not been able to do so spiritually, so they were endeavoring to do it physically. They kill Christian children. Jewish doctors murder great numbers of Christians. Jewish usurers take outrageous rates of interest. The riches which Jews have accumulated is not theirs, but Christendom's. (Against the fabulously wealthy moneylenders, the Lombards, these pious preachers said not a word.)

Bernard of Feltre preached even more vitriolic sermons. He informed the people that their poverty was the fault of the Jews, and that to be silent in the face of this injustice is a sin. When someone pointed out to him once that there were also Jews who helped Christians, as for instance Doctor Tobias, who treated poor people free, the Inquisitor turned a deaf ear. In his view, the only good Jew was a dead Jew. Even those who appeared to be good were enemies—and he soon had an opportunity to "prove" it.

During Holy Week in 1475, a three-year-old Christian boy named Simon was reported lost in the town of Trent. A few days later a Jew, Samuel, found the boy's body in a stream near his home. He immediately notified the authorities, who promptly arrested him and several other prominent Jews, including Doctor Tobias. The accused contended that the boy's body must have been placed there by a Christian neighbor of Samuel who had lost a court suit to Samuel over a financial matter. It was known that the neighbor had publicly sworn to get even.

These protestations were unheeded. After fifteen days of inhuman torture, the Jews admitted their "guilt." More people were imprisoned. In June, six Jews were burned alive. Two Jews were promised an easier death if they converted—they would be decapitated before they were burned. The property of the Jews was confiscated, but the authorities continued their investigation. The story that Jews had confessed to the ritual murder of a Christian child was spread all across Italy by the priests. A dangerous mood was building up in the land. Jewish leaders pleaded with Pope Sixtus

IV for protection. The pope sent a bishop to investigate. After several months the bishop reported to the pope that enemies of the Jews had "planted" the boy's body in the water and that the imprisoned Jews had confessed after unbearable torture. Furthermore, it was the wealthiest Jews in the town whom the authorities had arrested for the "crime," with the clear intent of confiscating their property.

The pope ordered all further investigation of the Jews of Trent to cease at once; those still being held were to be released. The authorities accused the bishop of having sold out the the Jews. Bernard of Feltre continued his campaign. In December 1475 another four Jews were burned to death.[19] Eventually the priests built a cathedral for Saint Simon, where devout Christians came to pray. (Simon was beatified in 1582 and was venerated until 1965, when the Catholic Church announced that the anti-Jewish accusation had been false and unfounded.)

The center of Jewry in southern Italy at that time was the island of Sicily. As elsewhere, the priests in Sicily compelled Jews to attend church services and listen to missionary sermons. The authorities on the island had levied special taxes on the Jews for protection, but it was of little help. Attacks on Jews became more frequent, particularly at Easter-time. In 1339, Palermo, capital of Sicily, was the scene of a large-scale pogrom. In 1391 the bloodiest pogrom in Spain spilled over into Sicily. Jews were forcibly converted. When they later appealed to the authorities, the bishop of Sicily refused them permission to revert to Judaism.[20]

However, in comparison with other Christian countries, Sicily's Jews lived a relatively peaceful life and the community there continued to grow. By the end of the fifteenth century there were at least thirty separate Jewish communities in Sicily, with an estimated total population of 100,000. At the same time, the governments in Sicily continued to squeeze higher taxes out of the Jews, forbidding them to emigrate.

Since 1282, Sicily had been under the rule of Spain. When the decree was issued on 31 March 1492 expelling the Jews from Spain and its provinces, the tragedy struck the Jews of Sicily as well. The Christian authorities in Sicily, afraid that the expulsion would result in economic ruin for the island, pleaded with the Inquisition to allow the Jews of Sicily to remain, or at least to postpone the expulsion for several years. Torquemada rejected the appeal, postponing the expulsion only until December. At the end of 1492 all 100,000 Jews of Sicily were expelled, taking with them only their personal belongings. All their other property was confiscated by the Spanish Crown.[21]

Many of these Jews went to southern Italy. Several years later that part of Italy also came under the rule of Spain, and in 1505 the Jews there were also expelled. Many then went to northern Italy, others to the Balkan countries, to Constantinople, Salonika, and other cities in Asia Minor. Many of the sick and helpless perished on the way.

During the fifteenth and sixteenth centuries the country of Italy was not a single entity, its various cities and provinces being under different rulers. The Jewish refugees who managed to reach Italian shores were received more or less hospitably. Only a small number of port cities refused Jews permission to settle. The southern province, with its capital, Naples, had a large Jewish community. It fell to Spanish rule in 1503. Seven years later the Jews were driven out of Naples. Thousands of Jewish families who had been there for centuries were forced to leave, together with recent refugees from other places. About two hundred of the wealthier families were allowed to remain, in return for large "contributions."[22] A few years later these Jews were also expelled, leaving southern Italy *Judenrein* until the mid-nineteenth century.

In the northern provinces, several of which were under papal rule, the condition of the Jews depended on who was pope. From 1492 to 1549 the popes in Rome issued no anti-Jewish decrees. In the free cities, the situation was different. In a city where the merchants and artisans guilds had a voice in the government, the Jews were harassed. In Venice, for example, the Jews were forced to live in their own street, known as the "Ghetto."[23]

Around the mid-sixteenth century, when the papacy began its struggle against the Reformation, the situation of the Jews in Italy deteriorated rapidly. In 1553 Pope Julius III ordered the burning of Jewish books. His successor, Paul IV, was one of the worst Jew-baiters ever to occupy the post. As soon as he was made pope in 1555, he issued a decree ordering Jews to pay a certain sum of money which was to be collected from each synagogue in the city. This money was designated for the maintenance of the Catechumen House built by the previous pope in 1543. Under the pontificate of Paul IV such houses for converts were established in other cities with Jewish communities, and all anti-Jewish edicts were strictly enforced.

For a long time the Marranos had lived freely in the papal

provinces, many even returning to the Jewish faith. Pope Paul ordered the backsliders brought before the court of the Inquisition. Those who learned about this in time fled to the free Italian provinces or to Turkey. About a hundred of them were thrown into the dungeons of the Inquisition. In 1556, twenty-four Marranos were burned alive in Rome. In 1559, 12,000 volumes of the Talmud were burned in the city of Cremona, where there was a large yeshiva.[24]

Between 1559 and 1565, under Pope Pius IV, the anti-Jewish edicts were somewhat eased. The ban on the Talmud was lifted, though each edition had to be cleared by a censor before printing, to delete all negative references to the Christian religion. The word "Talmud" itself was replaced at that time by the term *Shisha Sedarim* ("six orders"), abbreviated to *Shass*. For some reason, the word "Talmud" seemed to frighten the Dominican censors.

The next pope, Pius V, a former Inquisitor, revoked all the moderate concessions of his predecessors and returned to the ways of Paul IV. In 1569 he issued a Bull accusing the Jews of defaming the Lord's name, of sorcery, and other sins. All the Jews in his provinces were ordered to convert or be expelled. Most of the Jews prepared for the expulsion, which began in May 1569. The refugees settled in the northern provinces and the free cities like Mantua and Milan.[25] When the pope appealed to these cities to deny the Jews entry, several of them turned the Jews away, and they went on to Turkey.

Pope Gregory XIII continued all the anti-Jewish laws in effect, but did not enforce them very stringently. His main effort lay in conversion. One of his decrees compelled Jews in all Catholic countries to listen to a sermon once a week by a missionary in their synagogues; they were forbidden to challenge or contradict him.

Under Pope Sixtus V most of the anti-Jewish laws were abolished. Forcible conversion was prohibited, but Jews were still required to listen to missionary sermons. Pope Clement VIII reinstituted many of the anti-Jewish laws and the House of Conversion was reactivated. In essence, this was like a prison: easy to get in but very difficult to get out. From 1634 to 1700, 1,195 Jews, men and women, went through the House of Catechumen; from 1700 to 1790, 1,237.[26]

During periods when no Jews entered the House of Conversion of their own free will, the Inquisition would place them there by force. In 1604 the priests compelled the rabbi of the Roman ghetto, with his wife and four young children, to enter the House of Conversion.

After forty days the parents had still not agreed to convert and they were released. Their children, aged two to eight, were taken away from them and baptized. The parents were coolly informed that the children had accepted the teachings of Christian love voluntarily![27]

As life in the Roman ghetto worsened, many Jews emigrated to the free Italian cities and provinces. But here, too, the Jews soon found that they were virtually prisoners in their ghettos. Most Jews were poor and under constant threat of edicts and expulsions. In Verona, where the Jews were forced into a ghetto in 1605, they looked upon it as a blessing in disguise; within the walls of the ghetto they could at least protect themselves from physical attack. And such attacks were growing in frequency in Milan, Padua, and other cities. As a result, masses of Italian Jews emigrated to Turkey and Poland during the first half of the seventeenth century.

13

Jews in Spain and Portugal Through the Expulsion of 1492

Early in the thirteenth century a series of major wars took place between the Christian rulers of Castile and Aragon in northern Spain and the Arab Almohads who ruled the rich central and southern provinces of the Iberian Peninsula. The Jews, who had been persecuted by the Almohads, assisted the Christian armies in the Reconquest.[1] Also helping the Castilian army were "Soldiers of the Cross" from France who, when they entered Toledo, turned their swords against the Jews of that city. The Castilian knights, however, intervened and stopped them.

When the Christians in 1236 captured Seville and Cordoba they invited Jewish refugees from France to settle there. In Seville the king gave the Jews a gift of three Muslim mosques which they converted into synagogues. For the rest of the thirteenth century the Jews in the Christian regions of Spain lived more or less peacefully. However, the priests who came with the Reconquest were opposed to peaceful relations between Christians and other groups in the area, and they demanded the adoption of anti-Jewish measures. The mood among the Christian knights at that time was opposed to special laws against Jews and it took several generations before the hate program of the priests had any serious effect.

The kings, devout Christians themselves, often demonstrated their piety by issuing anti-Jewish laws. Personally they were friendly with their Jewish advisors, physicians, and tax collectors and disregarded their own laws. In 1265 the Catholic king, Alfonso X, issued a legal code containing anti-Jewish provisions, including the old canards that the Jews had crucified Jesus, that they crucify

Christian children, and other "crimes" of that nature.[2] The same monarch disobeyed his own laws by placing Jews in important posts. In time the clergy began to influence him, and in 1280, finding himself in desperate need of money, he arrested many wealthy Jews and demanded outrageous sums from them in exchange for their release.

Concerning the number of Jews in Castile at the end of the thirteenth century there are differences of opinion among historians,[3] but they all agree that the Jewish community there was a significant economic force.

King James I, who ruled over Aragon and Catalonia from 1213 to 1276, and who had played an important role in the Reconquest, now had possession of the Balearic Islands and the rich province of Valencia. He invited Jews from Morocco (many of them refugees from France) to settle in his cities and on the Island of Majorca. In 1258 he granted them a charter in which he promised that Jews would not be mistreated in his kingdom. At the same time, he acceded to the demands of the Dominican monks that the Jews be forced to listen to Christian missionary sermons.

Late in the thirteenth century the merchants and artisans guilds in Madrid and Toledo, the largest cities in Castile, began a campaign against Jewish merchants, artisans, moneylenders, and landowners. The Catholic Church was now pressuring the Crown with complaints and reproaches for not enforcing the anti-Jewish statutes of the synods. The attack by the clergy was two-pronged: pressure on the king, from the top, and stirring up the people, from below. The poison gradually took hold. From around the year 1315, closer attention was paid to preventing evasion of the anti-Jewish regulations.

Around that time a convert, Alfonso of Burgos, accused the Jews of vilifying Christ in their prayers. In a disputation between the apostate and the rabbis, he brought as evidence the words in the *Shemoneh Esreh* prayer, "There shall be no hope for the *minim,*" pointing out that *minim* signifies Christians. The rabbis contended that the word refers to Jewish heretics who change their religion. The king accepted Alfonso's version and forbade the Jews from reciting this prayer on pain of severe punishment.

Jews in the Castilian Civil War

During the reign of Pedro IV (1350-69), his stepbrother, Henry, accused him of utilizing Jewish administrators in his government. With the help of the Catholic Church Henry assembled an army to depose the king. Many Jews joined Pedro's forces and fought loyally in his cause. When the rebels entered Toledo in 1355 they murdered about twelve hundred Jews and seized their property.[4] The insurgents were victorious in the civil war. A wave of violence swept over the Jewish communities of Castile, leaving many Jews dead.[5]

The new king finally ordered a stop to the pogroms, which had further damaged the country, already in ruins as a result of the civil war. With the government treasury empty, King Henry now imposed even higher taxes on those Jews who survived. The priests and the Christian guilds pressed their demand that all the anti-Jewish laws be enforced. The yellow patch was reintroduced. Christian debtors were permitted to cancel a third of their debts to Jews on condition that they pay the other two-thirds, so that Jews could pay their taxes. However, Henry continued to employ Jews in official positions.

After his death in 1379 the Catholic priests exerted an ever-increasing influence on the royal court in Castile. Religious debates were organized in which Jews had no choice but to participate, although Jewish scholars tried to avoid them, knowing that they could be accused of defaming the Christian faith. A number of pamphlets were written at that time by Jewish scholars with suggestions for participants in such debates, ways to better reply to the Christian arguments, advice on how to control one's feelings, how to guard one's words, and so forth, because "Christians, in addition to arguments, also have power and can smother the truth by force."[6]

In 1348, when the Black Death spread through Europe, the Jews in the northeastern provinces of the Iberian Peninsula were accused of poisoning wells and were subjected to fearful pogroms. The plague struck only Aragon and Catalonia, the provinces closer to France, but here too, frenzied Christian masses attacked Jewish communities, seized Jewish property, murdered many Jews, and forcibly converted others. Many smaller communities were utterly destroyed. In Barcelona a pogrom was stopped in time by the king's troops.

In Aragon and Catalonia, Jews were already being forced to display the "badge of shame" on their clothing. The Dominican overseers were keeping close watch on the Marranos, prohibiting them from associating with Jews. Missionaries were preaching sermons in synagogues and the Jews were obliged to answer the preacher's questions and arguments. In the province of Navarra, southern France, the situation was even worse. It was here that the "Shepherds' Crusade" began. Virtually the entire Jewish community of Tudela was destroyed. For several months in 1328 the area was without a government, and as a result, the Jews in many cities were massacred. Six thousand Jews perished that year in Navarra.[7] Philip III, the new king of the province, ordered the arrest of the priests, nobles, and other participants in the killings, but pardoned them soon after. All the property of the victims was transferred to the royal treasury, while the survivors were compelled to pay a special tax for protection.

The kings of Portugal also took part in the Reconquest. Separating itself from the other provinces on the peninsula, Portugal became an independent state in the mid-twelfth century. Up until the end of the thirteenth century the Jews there lived more or less peacefully. By 1325, when Alfonso IV became king, the Catholic priests got the upper hand in the royal court. Decrees were issued ordering Jews not to appear in public places without their "badge." The wealthier Jews were forbidden to leave the country.

Around the mid-fourteenth century the Catholic Church became complete master over most of the provinces on the peninsula and exerted its influence both on the rulers and the ignorant masses. In the court of the Archbishop of Seville, a fanatical priest named Ferrand Martinez waged a virulent anti-Jewish campaign. The king of Castile ordered him to stop inciting to riot and in 1389 relieved him of his title as senior priest. One year later both the king and the Archbishop died. The priests elected Martinez archbishop and there was no one now to block his pogrom incitation.

On 16 March 1391 Martinez preached a sermon in Seville. When he finished, a large army of Christians set out for the Jewish Quarter to put his words into practice. The city police stopped them. Martinez reorganized his followers into a more powerful force and on 6 June, at dawn, they began their attack on the Jewish neighborhoods in Seville, setting fire to homes and murdering whoever they could. Four thousand Jews were slain in Seville on that day alone.[8] Younger Jews were sold as slaves to the Muslims. Many Jews converted. The entire Jewish community of the city, which had numbered around six thousand people, was destroyed.

In Cordoba two thousand Jews were killed. In Burgos and Toledo the Jews were attacked several days later. More than seventy Jewish communities in Castile were destroyed that same year.[9] From Castile the pogroms spread to Aragon. In Valencia, on 9 July 1391, the Jews resisted and killed some of the attackers, but they were soon outnumbered and overpowered.[10] On 15 August two hundred fifty Jews were murdered in Barcelona. Most of the Jews of that city, however, had managed to escape to the prince's fortress. The attackers beseiged the fortress and set fire to the gates. Many of the Jews came forth to battle and were killed. The majority, around 11,000 people, submitted to conversion.[11]

In Palma (Majorca) rampaging mobs destroyed the homes of Christians who were hiding Jewish neighbors. Many Jews fled to Portugal, where the hatred had not yet reached such a fever pitch. In many cities Jews converted in order to escape the gallows and the pyre. Most of them believed that they would shortly be able to return to Judaism. It never occurred to them that they would be handed over to the Inquisition.

The year 1391 has remained in Jewish history as a tragic period when tens of thousands of Jews were massacred and perhaps a hundred thousand converted. The Marranos in Spain were under the authority of the Dominicans from the very beginning. It was the converted Jews of 1391, their children and grandchildren, who became the famous Marranos in the martyr history of the Jews of Spain.

Spain in the Fifteenth Century

During the fifteenth century the last remnants of the Islamic caliphate at the southern tips of the Iberian Peninsula were defeated one after the other. The Catholic rulers began to carry out their dream of establishing a unified Catholic government throughout all of Spain. The only obstacle in their way was the large Jewish population in the Spanish cities. The most important centers in Aragon and Castile had not yet recovered from the pogroms of 1391. For the economic betterment of his province, the king of Castile undertook to restore his *chuderias*, as the Jewish communities were known. He issued strict orders against anti-Jewish incitement and imprisoned Ferrand Martinez, but in order to avoid a confrontation with the Catholic Church, he soon released him.

In 1391 the Church had acquired a fanatical convert named Pablo de Santa Maria, formerly a rabbi of Burgos. An unprincipled careerist, a glory and power seeker, and a capable man, he quickly rose to the rank of bishop. In 1410 the Jews of Segovia were accused of torturing a Host. Several Jews "confessed" under torture. Rabbi Meir Algowitz, the king's physician, was condemned to death. Meir had been friendly with the Bishop Pablo de Santa Maria in his youth. As the royal physician, Rabbi Meir was a prominent and respected figure in aristocratic circles. Apparently the convert felt uncomfortable in his presence.

Bishop Pablo befriended a Cardinal who, during the schism in the papacy, had been recognized in Spain as Pope Benedict XIII (one of three popes at the time). A fanatical Jew-baiter, this cardinal-pope hoped that if he were successful in converting the Jews of Spain, he would be recognized as the most important leader in the Church and become the sole occupant of the papal office. Benedict enlisted Pablo to take charge of the conversion of the Jews.

In 1402, on the advice of Pablo, a series of draconic laws were adopted against the Jews of Spain with the purpose of so degrading, humiliating, and terrorizing them that they would be driven to conversion. Along with these laws there was an intensification of conversion activities by the priests. In 1412 this agitation took on a special form. Pablo's colleague, Vincent Ferrer, a Dominican zealot, assembled a gang of rabid monks who went from city to city breaking into synagogues with wild threats and insults. Ferrer would leap up on the platform with a Torah scroll in one hand and a crucifix in the other, shouting that the only way the Jews could save themselves was to get rid of the Torah and accept the cross. In Toledo, Ferrer and his gang drove the Jews out of their newly built synagogue and proclaimed it a church.

The Jews in the Spanish cities had good reason to remember the massacres of 1391. Terror-stricken and defenseless, masses of Jews began to convert to Catholicism. From Castile the gangs went to Aragon where they drove the Jews to conversion by the same methods. In 1412 more than 20,000 Jews became Christians, most of them out of fear, hoping that the nightmare would be temporary and that they would soon be able to return to their faith.[12]

At the same time, a mass emigration began of people who had remained Jews, as well as those who had converted. Even the threats of slavery and other varieties of punishment could no longer stop the movement to escape from the approaching flames. In 1414 the rulers of the Spanish provinces eased some of the economic thumbscrews on Jews and ordered the Catholic priests to cease their proselytizing activity.

With the assistance of another convert, Pablo then invented still another method of driving Jews to the baptismal font: a religious disputation between apostate priests and rabbis. The debate began in February 1413 and dragged on for almost two years. The Jewish representatives could only defend themselves and attempt to repel the onslaughts of the apostates against the Jewish religion. As the debate drew to a close without a definitive result, the antipope Benedict XIII decreed a ban on the Talmud. Priests began a search of synagogues and Jewish homes.

In 1415 an assembly of Cardinals ended the schism in the papacy by recognizing Martin V as pope. As soon as this was announced, Benedict's own priests deserted him. The new pope annulled the anti-Jewish laws in Spain and forbade the forcible conversion of Jews. However, those who had converted were required to remain Christian.

The Marranos

As a result of the bloody pogroms of 1391 and the terror of 1412, there were tens of thousands of Jewish Christians in Spain in the mid-fifteenth century. The priests called them Marranos—Spanish for "pigs" or "the damned." Many of these Jewish Christians, already of the second and third generation, had become influential citizens, government officials, owners of large etates. Some of the older nobility and the Church leadership looked with envy and suspicion upon the ascendancy of these new families, who were not even true Christians.

In Toledo, in 1449, the Marranos were victims of a vicious attack.[13] The king had imposed a high tax upon the city, but the city council refused to pay it. The Crown ordered the tax collected by force. Most of the tax collectors were Marranos. No sooner had the tax collection gotten under way than a mob attacked the home of one of the collectors and set it afire. The Marranos resisted. Several were killed and their bodies dragged through the streets. The decision of the city council was that New Christians would no longer be permitted to hold public office.

In other cities, too, a movement began against the Marranos, who appealed to the pope for support. The pope ordered the city council of Toledo to revoke its decision. The priests countered with the accusation that the New Christians were in fact secret Jews. Pope Nicholas V then ordered the establishment of a court to investigate the charges. By this time the Marranos were politically influential. In high government circles a struggle was going on between the liberals and the Dominican priests, as well as with those nobles who wished to restrict the rights of the New Christians. The agitation against Jews and Marranos in Spain became increasingly intense.

In 1467 another pogrom was organized against the Marranos in Toledo. A thousand of their homes were burned to the ground. In the fighting, 130 Jewish Christians were killed. The leader of the Marranos was hung.[14] In Cordoba the priests had organized a "Society of Christian Love" whose regulations prohibited the admission of Jewish Christians. During one procession arranged by the Society a rumor spread that Marranos had been insulting them. In the ensuing fighting, many New Christians were killed.[15]

A sizable number of Spanish Jews and Marranos escaped to Portugal, where the Jews were less restricted and where Marranos had even been permitted to rejoin their faith. While Alfonso II (1447–81) was king the Jews there were not molested. He even employed a Jewish financial advisor, Don Isaac Abrabanel, who was a scholar and prominent Jewish leader. After Alfonso's death an accusation was brought against Abrabanel, but he managed to escape to Spain, where he became a leading advisor in the royal court.

Ferdinand and Isabella

In the last quarter of the fifteenth century the two largest provinces of Spain, Castile and Aragon, united to form one kingdom. A united Spain, the priests believed, should be a united Christian country. The rulers agreed, but what was to be done with the Jews? This question had two aspects: there were "open" Jews and there were "secret" Jews. Even most of the second generation of New Christians had remained Jews at heart. When the Catholic priests appealed to the pope in Rome for the introduction of the Inquisition into Spain, he agreed, but he wanted a papal official at its head. Evidently, Rome wished to be master over the confiscated properties of the condemned. The Spanish rulers, however, refused to accept this condition.

Meanwhile the priests made a count of their potential victims and reported to King Ferdinand and Queen Isabella that there were tens of thousands of "false New Christians" in Spain and that a considerable number of them were very wealthy. The royal couple again appealed to Pope Sixtus IV for permission to conduct an Inquisition under their own supervison. In 1478 the pope acceded to their request. For two years influential Marranos bent every effort to prevent the introduction of this cruel institution, but the Dominican priest, Thomas de Torquemada, finally had his way.

In Seville, where the Inquisition was first established in 1480, an obligation was placed upon all Christians, old and new, to inform the Inquisitors about every false Christian they knew. Instructions listing thirty-seven points were distributed, including signs by which to recognize heresy among the Marranos. Should anyone notice the least sign of Jewish custom in a New Christian, even such a small thing as putting on clean linen on Friday evenings or Saturday mornings, he must, as a true Christian, report this to the judge of the Inquisition.

In desperation, a group of Marranos plotted to kill one of the Inquisitors, but their plan was exposed and they were put to death.[16] Many Marranos began to leave Seville, and the authorities put a strict ban on emigration. Those caught leaving were executed. Hundreds of persons were arrested and tortured in the dungeons of the Inquisition to make them confess that they had sinned against their faith. But confession alone was not enough; the victim had to supply names of friends, relatives, neighbors, who also were "false" Christians. Under torture, many did so. The new victims were promptly subjected to the same barbaric process. Most of the accused were burned at the stake and their property confiscated for the royal treasury.

In its first ten months the Inquisition in Seville put three hundred Marranos to death, most of them people of wealth.[17] The royal court saw in the Inquisition a source of substantial income and made plans to open such sources in other Spanish cities as well. When the number of potential victims was exhausted, they announced a "period of grace" for those penitents who would come forward voluntarily and confess their sin; they would be forgiven without punishment. Some Marranos were tricked by this into surrendering to the Inquisition, but after hearing their confession, the Inquisitor demanded that they supply names of others. Those who refused were tortured and burned.

Panic seized the New Christians in Spain. Their cries reached Rome. Sharp protests came from the pope over this torture of Christians on the basis of secret accusations.[18] The Spanish rulers, however, ignored the pope's protest. The wealth pouring into their coffers was more persuasive. The pope then sent a second and sharper protest to Ferdinand and Isabella, accusing them of having in mind not the purity of the Christian faith but rather the extensive property of the victims; furthermore, he complained that the trials of the Inquisition were unjust, that the confessions were obtained under duress and inhuman torture. The royal couple replied in equally blunt language, even hinting that the Marranos had bribed the pope to come to their defense.[19]

The Inquisition was instituted in other cities. In 1483 priestly tribunals were already torturing and burning heretics in Toledo, Cordoba, and Saragossa. As Inquisitor-General the Crown appointed Torquemada, whose name has become a synonym for unspeakable torture. For penitents who accepted their punishment with love, special "penitence processions" were organized. On 12 December 1486 such a procession took place in Toledo. Seven hundred fifty penitents marched through the streets barefoot, half naked, carrying extingushed candles. On 2 April there was another procession of nine hundred penitents. On 16 August the number was even higher. Out of this particular procession twenty-five Marranos were selected to be burned at the stake.

Eventually the priests concluded that the Marranos were not becoming good Christians because the unconverted Jews of Spain exerted too great an influence upon them. They therefore began to consider ways to segregate the Marranos from the Jews. The first step was to encourage informing. Orders were issued to the Jews that if any of them knew a Marrano who habitually associated with Jews, or who carried in his heart a leaning toward Judaism, they must report that person to the Inquisition. Any Jew who knew of such a person and did not report him would be severely punished and his property confiscated. When the rabbi of Seville received this order, he fled to Portugal. Many other Jews followed his example.

The Expulsion

From the mid-1480s until 1491 the united Spanish kingdom was at war with the last remnants of Islam still hanging on in the southern corners of the Iberian Peninsula. In 1487 the Muslim port city of Malaga fell. In 1491 King Ferdinand captured the capital of Granada. Legend relates that Torquemada elicited pledges from the royal couple that the victory over Granada would be celebrated by a decree expelling all the Jews from Spain.

In order to prepare the appropriate social response to such a cruel act as expelling all the old, established Jewish families from their native land—many of them had been there for fifteen hundred years—the authorities staged a blood libel case. One of the imprisoned Marranos, Benito Garcia, was accused of crucifying a Christian child and desecrating a Host. According to the account of the priests who tortured him, Garcia confessed that "he and six other Jews, together with five Marranos, gathered one night in a cave, crucified a Christian child, drained its blood, cut out its heart and used it and the Host to perform their wizardry."[20]

Among the documents of the Inquisition is the confession which Benito Garcia made at the end of his trial:

> I was born a Jew and I converted forty years ago. Recently I came to the correct realization that Christianity was a massive pagan comedy. In my heart I returned to Judaism. I saw the terrible autos-da-fé of the Inquisition and my heart filled with pity for the victims and hatred for the hangmen. I hate Christianity. Yes, a converted Jew is an Antichrist, but an even worse Antichrist is the Inquisitor. The greatest Antichrist is the Inquisitor-General Torquemada.

> I observe Judaism in secret and go to church only when I cannot get out of it. I do not observe any Christian holy days. I eat meat on fast days, go to confession only outwardly. Whenever I see the body of Christ [the Host] I spit on it, because the wafer that is sanctified by the Christians is nothing more than a mixture of flour and water. I obey the Jewish laws. I rest on Saturday. I eat and drink only kosher food. I fast on Jewish fast days, even in prison, and I recite Jewish prayers. I accept my present suffering with humility because I deserve it. It is a punishment for having hurt my father when I accepted the Christian faith and because I took my children to church. Now I have only one request, that my sons should leave this accursed faith and become Jews. If I am released from prison I will go to Palestine and I will try to persuade others to go there too.[21]

The news of this ritual murder trial and the "confession" was spread in all the churches of the land. On 31 March 1492 Ferdinand and Isabella signed the decree announcing that at the end of July of that year all the Jews must leave Spain and never return. That decree reads (in part):

> They must leave our dominion with their sons and daughters. They must never return. They must not live here. They must not even pass through our country and not be here for any purpose. If any Jew is

found in our country after the last date permitted, he will be put to death and all his property confiscated, without a trial. No Christian must hide a Jew in his home, man or woman, under penalty of confiscation of his property.[22]

Don Isaac Abrabanel pleaded with the king either to cancel the decree or postpone the date of the expulsion for several years until the Jews could sell their property and prepare to leave in an organized manner. In return, he promised to collect a large sum of money from the Jewish communities for the royal treasury. One legend says that the sum which Abrabanel mentioned was 30,000 ducats and that the king was about to agree to a revocation of the decree when Torquemada rushed in with a crucifix in his hand and cried out: "Judas Iscariot sold the Savior for thirty pieces of silver, and you want to sell him for thirty thousand? Here, sell him!" and throwing the crucifix on the table, he stormed out of the room.[23]

The senior rabbi of Toledo, with other Jewish leaders, traveled to Portugal and asked King John II to allow the expelled Jews into his country. The king consented, but made it clear that they were not to become permanent residents. He would allow them to stay for eight months in return for an agreed upon sum of money.[24]

Many Jews left Spain even before the date set for the expulsion. The great mass of Jews, estimated at between 200,000 and 300,000, left their homes in late July and early August of 1492 and wandered out into the world hardly knowing their destination.[25] Half went to Portugal. A small group went to the kingdom of Navarra, close to the French border. Many Jews went on to the shores of North Africa, to Italy and Turkey. A sea of adversity came down upon the heads of the wanderers.

At the time the Jews were expelled, another 200,000 Marranos remained in Spain.[26] The Inquisition went about its barbaric job. More New Christians were burned at the stake. Others fled. The Catholic leaders had achieved their objective. Spain was a unified country under the domination of the Church, the Dominican monks, and the Inquisition. The masses of people remained ignorant and backward, superstitious, apathetic. A few centuries later Spain was one of the most backward nations in Europe.[27].

The Expelled Jews in Portugal

Most of the hundred thousand Spanish Jews who fled to Portugal had permission to remain there only eight months. The king had also promised to supply ships for those Jews who would have to leave Portugal, and that the ships would take them wherever they chose to go. At the beginning of 1493 an epidemic struck the Jews who had come from Spain; living in poverty, they were prey to a disease which took thousands of victims. Church and secular authorities began pressing the government to send these accursed people out of the country as quickly as possible. Consequently, a couple of months earlier than scheduled, the king provided ships to take the Jews as far away as possible from Portuguese shores.

In those ports where the ships docked, no one would let the Jews land; for several months they roamed the seas. The captains and ship owners treated the Jews on board as slaves, stealing their property and abusing their wives and daughters. One such ship stopped at the port of Malaga, then under Spanish rule. In accordance with an agreement between the local bishop and the captain, the ship was detained so that priests could be sent aboard to persuade the Jews to be converted and then they would be permitted to land.

The Jews refused. The next step was to cut off their food supply. Every day priests came on board with the same message: whoever wants to stay alive should convert. After several days of starvation—fifty Jews had already died—about a hundred Jews were baptized. The others were released and finally landed in the North African city of Fez.

Those Jews who remained in Portugal were required to pay the Crown a great deal of money at the expiration of the eight months. The great majority were unable to pay, and were declared the personal chattel of the king, who sold them to Portuguese feudal lords. The younger children were taken from their parents and sent to monasteries in the newly discovered St. Thomas Islands. As the children were being taken away, desperate mothers jumped into the sea with their children. Those children who actually were sent to distant lands died of exposure and disease.

When King John II died in 1495, his son Emanuel released the Jews from slavery. The young king had made plans to marry the princess of Spain, and the bride's parents agreed to the match, but only on condition that he first expel the Jews from Portugal. Emanuel conceded, and on 25 December 1496 issued an order that all the Jews must be out of Portugal within ten months or lose their lives and property.

The young king, who did not really want to part with his Jews, many of whom were capable individuals and good taxpayers, tried to persuade them to become Christians and stay in Portugal. When this failed he conceived a plan to achieve the same result by force. He would baptize their children and then the parents would have no choice but to become Christians and stay in the country. Early in 1497 he issued a decree to the effect that at Passover-time the children of Jewish parents, age four to twenty, would be converted. Some Jews who learned about this in time took their children and tried to escape from Portugal. The government intercepted them and attempted to take the children away. A number of parents killed their children and then committed suicide. Mothers leaped into the sea, holding their babies. Others went to the baptismal font along with their children.

When the Marranos in Portugal discovered that the Church was about to establish the Inquisition in that country too, they appealed to the pope to prevent it. The pope granted their request. The king, who was actually pleased with the pope's decision, promised the New Christians that for a period of twenty years he would ask no questions about their piety, but that at the end of that time, heresy would be an offense punishable by confiscation of property. (A number of Marrano families from Spain fled to Portugal during that period.)

In the fall of 1497, when the expulsion was to take place, some 20,000 Jews assembled in Lisbon to wait for ships. The last day of the time limit arrived and no ships had appeared in the harbor. The Jews were informed that since they had not left the country within the prescribed time, they were now all under the jurisdiction of the king. They were herded into a large square outside the city, where priests tried to convert them. When this proved fruitless, an attempt was made to starve them into submission. When this too failed, the Jews were tied with ropes and dragged to churches. Some escaped and leaped to their death from rooftops and cliffs; others began to scream insults at Jesus, hoping to incite the priests to kill them. Many converted and saved their lives. When the king had convinced himself that he was unable to overcome the obstinacy of the Jews, he provided the ships to take them wherever they wished to go.

In 1498 the small kingdom of Navarra fell to Spain and the Jews there were also expelled. The refugees in Italy, North Africa, and the islands had great difficulty finding a place to settle. For months, sometimes for years, they roamed the seas. Some fell into the hands of pirates, who sold them as slaves. Others died of sickness and starvation. The Greek islands were full of Jewish refugees, many of whom reached there by their own efforts; others were brought there by pirates and were ransomed.

Most fortunate of the expelled Jews were those who reached Turkey, then a strong power in Asia Minor. Earlier, Sultan Muhammad II had issued an invitation to Jews to settle in Turkey, guaranteeing them the right to live as they wished. Now, Sultan Bajazet II, realizing that the Jews could revitalize and develop his backward economy, ordered his countrymen to receive the Jewish refugees in a friendly manner. Jewish communities in Turkey ransomed many Jews brought there by pirates.[28]

The Jews throughout the world had looked upon the Spanish Jewish community as the most important segment—the "aristocrats"—of world Jewry. The expulsion was consequently perceived as the Third Destruction in Jewish history. The expulsion of Jews from Germany, which took place around the same time, paled into insignificance before the massive destruction of Spanish and Portuguese Jewry in 1492 and 1497.

14

Germany and Central Europe from the Fifteenth Century to 1648

The Epidemic of Expulsions

Expulsions of Jews had taken place here and there in Christian countries during the twelfth century and earlier. But after the mass expulsion from Spain in 1492, this method of eradicating old Jewish communities was common in all the Germanic lands, especially in places where there had been an influx of Jewish refugees from Spain and Portugal.

Early in the fifteenth century the Jews in Germany, in addition to being subjects of the king, were also under the authority of the local princes, bishops, and city officials, the latter being usually Christian merchants and artisans. The Hanseatic League of merchants and ship owners in the port cities of northwestern Germany barred Jews from international trade. Thus the only occupations left to Jews were petty trade and moneylending.

By that time the western German cities no longer had any large Jewish communities. Most Jews had left of their own volition. With most of the now penniless Jews who remained in those areas, the nobles and city authorities were unable to squeeze any more money out of them. The result was a wave of expulsions that swept through the German cities in the fifteenth and sixteenth centuries.

In 1388 the Jews had been expelled from Strasbourg; in 1394 there was a mass expulsion from France[1]; in 1420 from Austria; in 1424 from Cologne, Freiburg, and Zurich; in 1431 from Saxony; in 1439 from Augsburg; in 1453 from Würzburg; in 1454 from Breslau.

Some of these expulsions lasted two hundred years. In several cities the Jews returned a few years later, only to be expelled again. From Mainz the Jews were expelled four times: in 1420, 1438, 1462, and 1471.[2]

In 1498 the Jews were expelled from Nuremberg, the most important commercial center in Bavaria. In general, after an expulsion, the Jewish property was distributed among the nobles and city burghers. In Nuremberg the Jewish cemetery was levelled and replaced by a street paved with the gravestones.[3] No Jewish community was permitted in that city for the next three hundred years.

The pretexts for carrying out an expulsion were of various kinds. In Nuremberg the main reason given was that the Jews were inviting "foreign" Jews to settle there and that these newcomers were occupying homes needed for Christians. In 1492 the Jews of Mecklenburg in northern Germany were accused of desecrating a Host. Many were arrested and tortured and several "confessed." Twenty-seven Jews were burned at the stake on a hill outside the city. For generations the site was known as Judenbarg.[4] In Sternberg, in honor of the "discovery and punishing" of guilty Jews, a church was erected which attracted many pilgrims. Later, during the Reformation, Jews were expelled from the same area because they were the cause of the obscurantist lie that the Host could work miracles!

In the Brandenburg region of eastern Germany, large Jewish communities arose in Berlin, Spandau, and other cities. In 1510 a Christian blacksmith named Fromm was caught stealing a church vessel containing several wafers. The bishop of Brandenburg seized upon this opportunity to concoct a ritual murder trial. Threatened with torture, the blacksmith confessed that he had sold the wafers to a Jew in Spandau. Under torture the Jew "confessed" that he had made the wafer bleed and had sent pieces of it to rabbis in other cities. Fifty Jews from Spandau, Berlin, and other places were then arrested and tortured. Again, several "confessed" to accusations. Thirty-eight Jews were burned alive in Berlin on 9 July 1510 on this charge.[5]

A few years later the blacksmith confessed to a priest that he had lied because he was afraid of the torture and that the executed Jews had been innocent. This priest subsequently became a Protestant and twenty-three years later the whole lie was exposed. The occasion was a gathering of Protestant nobles in Frankfurt to consider a plan of expelling all the Jews from Germany. Here the priest finally revealed the truth of the Brandenburg libel, whereupon the assembled nobles gave up their plan.[6]

So long as the kings and nobles were not obliged to reckon with their subjects, the protection offered by these rulers was more or less effective. With the growth of cities and the increase in the numbers of people liberated from serfdom, the power of the central authority was weakened, leaving the Jews more vulnerable to attack by the general population.

The Talmud on Trial

Early in the sixteenth century, Jews turned to printing as a means of livelihood, with their first products being the Jewish sacred books. The priests who were concerned with converting Jews realized full well that one of the primary reasons for Jewish steadfastness was the spiritual strength they gained from these works. Thus the Dominican monks in Cologne soon devised a "trial" of the Talmud, using the services of a converted Jew named Johann Joseph Pfefferkorn.

Pfefferkorn, a butcher by trade, had been caught stealing. In prison he was promised his freedom if he became a Christian. In 1504 he was converted and from 1505 to 1509 several anti-Jewish pamphlets appeared under his name attacking the Talmud. Through the Dominicans he approached the king's sister, a nun, and through her, King Maximilian I himself. The emperor, who ruled over Germany and Italy, granted the Dominicans permission to confiscate Jewish holy books and examine them; any books containing anti-Christian expressions were to be burned. However, when prominent Christian humanists and influential Jews appealed to Maximilian, he nullified the decree.

The Dominicans then printed a Latin pamphlet containing accusations against various Jewish books, as well as an appeal to the emperor to reaffirm his original decree. This happened in the spring of 1510, when Brandenburg was in the throes of the hysteria over a desecrated Host. This time Maximilian appointed a commission to investigate the Jewish books and determine once and for all whether or not they blasphemed Christianity or contained any hints concerning the use of Christian blood for ritual purposes. Among the Christian scholars on the commission was the humanist Johann Reuchlin.

A long drawn-out controversy then developed between Reuchlin, on one side, and Pfefferkorn and the Dominicans on the other. In the end, the ban on Jewish books was lifted. In 1520, Daniel Bomberg, a Christian printer in Venice, published the first edition of the Babylonian Talmud.[7]

In the midst of this trouble over Reuchlin's "defense of the Jews," the Catholic Church was suddenly assailed by the much more powerful heresy of Martin Luther, which was spreading like wildfire in many parts of Germany.

The Reformation

A movement against the Catholic Church had begun in many countries much earlier. John Wycliffe in England in the mid-fourteenth century, John Huss in Bohemia early in the fifteenth century, John Calvin and Ulrich Zwingli in Switzerland, among others had already plowed the field and sowed reformist seeds. However, the reform movement which Martin Luther initiated in the first quarter of the sixteenth century found a much more fertile soil.

In addition to being motivated by the moral decline of the Church, Luther and his disciples were also influenced by the Renaissance ideas which had been spreading throughout Christian Europe for a couple of hundred years. In his book, *Jean Christophe*, Romain Rolland wrote: "There had been a time when the universities under the authority of the Church had indeed kept the students isolated from life, had held them behind solid walls and massive gates, far removed from the real world. But the universality within the studies themselves helped to unlock the gates of life and the world."[8]

In the first year of his activity Martin Luther, in his attacks upon Catholicism, came to the defense of the Jews:

> Up until now the corrupt papacy has looked upon the Jews not as human beings but as dogs. It tormented them mercilessly in a most unchristian way and at the same time tried to win them over to Christianity. No wonder the Jews chose not to accept such depravity. Even good Christians who witnessed the crime of the Church against the Jews chose to be Jews and remain righteous, rather than be corrupt Christians. We must use the principle of human love with the Jews, we must show them true friendship, and then they will be convinced that Christianity means the teaching of human love and they will happily accept the Christian faith.[9]

Luther hoped that by reforming Christendom he would achieve what the Fathers of the Holy Church had been unable to achieve by more than a thousand years of missionary agitation, terror, and coercion. A reformed Christendom, he believed, would bring the Jews to the Church of their own free will. Later, disappointed that the Jews had not acted according to his prediction, Luther himself began spitting fire and brimstone upon the "enemies of Jesus . . . this people accursed by God Himself . . . whose suffering is due to their own obstinacy . . . a sinful people which must remain enslaved and unmercifully tormented forever."[10]

In the 1540s, several years before his death, Martin Luther published books filled with vicious Jew-hatred. He gave his blessing to the robbing, beating, and extermination of Jews; he collected all the libels ever invented against Jews and submitted them as evidence of Jewish guilt. To all the crimes of which they were ever accused, he emphasized, the Jews have always "confessed." He charged that Jews were spies for the Turks who were attacking Christian nations in Europe. He urged the burning of synagogues and the expulsion of Jews. Not even the worst popes in medieval Europe had ever descended to such an open call for the mass murder of Jews.

During the wars of the Reformation the Jews were attacked by both sides. The Catholics charged them with responsibility for the Protestant heresy. Catholic soldiers, drenched in Jew-hatred and convinced of Jewish guilt, robbed and murdered Jews whenever and wherever the opportunity presented itself. The Protestant nobles, on their side, accused the Jews of protecting Catholics and of support-ing the king's armies financially. Both sides charged the Jews with assisting the Turks. The knights and foot-soldiers of the Protestant armies were just as anti-Jewish as the Catholics. Luther's permission to do whatever they pleased with the Jews was no secret, neither among the Protestants nor the Catholics.[11]

In 1525, during the Great Peasant Rebellion in Germany, the Jews were in the center of a deadly vortex. The peasants, embittered against their oppressors and filled with anti-Jewish propaganda, made no distinction between the nobles and the Jews. Impoverished city dwellers joined the peasant armies and vented their anger against the Jews. In the Rhine region, where the uprising was strongest, the Jewish population had already dwindled, many having fled.

The Protestant Church had translated the Bible into the vernac-ular, and the art of printing made it widely accessible. Among some

European intellectuals there began to appear a little more respect for the Jewish people which, as the Bible witnesses, had once had its own land and its own language, and prophets who preached social justice. The libels against the Jews continued, however, especially the story that they were helping the Turks. In 1530 a Protestant synod in Augsburg adopted proposals that the Jews be ejected from the southern provinces, which were close to the area occupied by the Turks.

Jews in Frankfurt

In northeast Germany, where Protestantism first established a foothold, the largest Jewish community developed in the city of Frankfurt. Over a long period of time many Jewish refugees had gathered there and together with the older families had formed a sizable community. In the sixteenth century a system of "residence agreements" for Jews similar to the *condotta* treaties in the Italian cities was adopted in Frankfurt. The residence permits had to be renewed every three years, generally at a higher cost, and were restricted to a certain number. A tract of land outside the city was allotted to them for a ghetto, where all the Jews in the city were forced to live.

Jews were restricted also to certain businesses or crafts. They were permitted to sell only things which were left by debtors on unredeemed pledges. Gradually the Jewish merchants introduced other types of merchandise. But though they were permitted to sell shoes and clothing, for example, they were not allowed to buy the raw materials necessary to produce these items.[12]

The narrow, crowded streets of the ghetto held two hundred buildings, many of them four stories and higher, housing approximately four thousand people, with no water or sewage system. On a bridge near the approach to Frankfurt the authorities put up a large painting of Simon, the Christian boy whom the Jews had been accused of "crucifying" and which resulted in the execution or expulsion of the Jews of Tirol in 1475. This painting showed blood running from the child's wounds, with Jews draining it into pots and smacking their lips over it. Near this painting was another one which depicted Jews suckling at the teats of a sow, while others licked the animal's rump. This type of "art" was then popular all over Europe, particularly in Germany.[13]

Early in the seventeenth century a struggle took place in Frankfurt between the poor people and the burghers in the council. The anti-council forces were led by two demagogues, Weitz and Fettmilch, both of them rabid Jew-baiters, whose platform was that the city's problems could be solved by expelling the Jews, but that the king and the rich city councilmen opposed this because they were collecting heavy taxes from the Jews.[14]

In August 1614 Weitz and Fettmilch organized a pogrom against the Jews of Frankfurt, killing many and expelling approximately thirteen hundred. The violence lasted only one day. The burghers of the city council, knowing that it could easily spill over into their streets, dispersed the mobs with the help of the police. The king's troops arrived in the city to punish the guilty. Weitz and Fettmilch were beheaded; many of their followers were imprisoned. The expelled Jews, who had stayed for eight months in neighboring Jewish communities, were permitted to return.[15]

When the Thirty Years' War broke out in 1618, the Jews of Frankfurt were still recovering from the pogrom they had suffered in 1614. An agreement had been reached between the king and the city council that no more than five hundred Jews could reside in the ghetto. In order to maintain this number, a maximum of twelve marriages were permitted in the ghetto each year.[16] Outside the confines of the ghetto, Jews were permitted to appear in the center of town only in the daytime on business. They could not bid against Christian for products in the marketplace until the Christian had finished their buying. Jews were not even permitted to touch the bread or fruit they wished to purchase.

Jews in Hamburg

For centuries Jews had been barred from the free city of Hamburg, center of the Hanseatic League. It was not until the end of the sixteenth century that a Jewish community began to develop there "through the back door." Jews were still forbidden to enter the city. A group of wealthy Portuguese Marranos, however, settled in Hamburg as Christians. Hamburg was a Protestant city, with no fear of a Catholic Inquisition. The Marranos, converts of the second, third, fourth, and even fifth generation, gradually began to return to the religion of their grandparents. They established a *minyan*, the required group of ten men, in a private home to worship as a congregation. Their Protestant neighbors, who had never seen a Jew and did not know what a Jewish religious service was, suspected them of being secret Catholics and wanted to expel them from the city. When the true situation was revealed to them, the expulsion was prevented. These Marranos remained as a Jewish kernel in Hamburg.[17]

At that time Hamburg was a center of world trade. Jewish merchants from Amsterdam and other German states began arriving there, first for business purposes and later to make their homes. When the Thirty Years' War erupted, the Jewish community of Hamburg was large and well established. By 1648–49, when many refugees from the Chmielnicki massacres in Poland settled in Hamburg, the clergy was able to convince the city council to expel the "foreign" Jews.

By the mid-seventeenth century the religious base of Jew-hatred in Germany, among both Catholics and Protestant, had already been weakened and diluted. However, the prejudice itself remained deeprooted and continued to express itself in violence. Jewish rightlessness was firmly established, and the "crime" of moneylending continued high among the anti-Jewish charges. From the fourteenth to the seventeenth centuries large numbers of Jews voluntarily left their old established communities and moved eastward to Austria, Bohemia, Poland, and Lithuania.

Jews in Austria, Bohemia, and Hungary until 1648

Expulsion of Jews became the practice also in Austria, Bohemia, and Silesia, the countries east of Germany, where Jews had come as refugees from persecution in other Germanic areas. In Vienna, as in all of Austria, Jews had been barred since 1421 and the days of the Hussite heresy.

In Bohemia there had been large Jewish communities for several centuries. In 1501, when a rumor spread that the Jews were to be expelled, they appealed to King Vladislav, who assured them he would not permit it so long as they continued to pay their taxes punctually. But three years later, in Pilsen, the Jews were charged with desecrating a Host and the king promptly acceded to the mayor's request that the Jews be expelled. The same process was repeated in Budweis, where two Jews were burned at the stake.[18] In 1508 the city council of Prague also obtained permission to expel the Jews, but they were allowed a year's time to prepare. In the interim the king revoked his consent and even forbade the emigration of those Jews who wished to leave voluntarily.

In the 1540s the Turks defeated the Hungarians in a number of battles. Reports spread that the Jews had helped them. In 1541 the king ordered the expulsion of all the Jews except those who converted. One month's time was allowed the Jews to prepare for the expulsion. When pogroms occurred in several cities, the king punished the guilty and postponed the expulsion for an additional few months. Early in 1542 many Jews left Prague and migrated to Turkey and Poland. It was not long before the king realized that he was depleting his own income and again revoked the expulsion order.

However, Jew-baiters kept pressing King Vladislav to restrict the rights of Jews or to expel them from his domain altogether. In return, they promised to pay whatever losses the royal treasury would suffer. When this plea proved ineffectual, they staged a blood libel. Such frame-ups resulted in the destruction of many Jewish communities in Austria, Bohemia, and Silesia during the sixteenth century.

In Vienna, where a large "illegal" Jewish community had developed, the city council forced the "temporary residents" to wear an identifying mark. In 1551 the king broadened this decree to include all Jews in his lands. In 1556, when Pope Paul IV ordered all Jews in the papal provinces to be confined to ghettos, the rulers of Austria, Bohemia, Hungary, and Silesia faithfully carried out his wishes.

In 1557 King Ferdinand informed the Jews of Prague that he would no longer grant them residence permits and that as soon as their current terms expired, all the Jews in Austria, Bohemia, and Silesia would be expelled. The Jews sent emissaries to the court and the effective date of the expulsion was postponed for one year and renewed twice, but in 1561 the king refused to consider any further delays. Mordecai Zemach, an influential "court Jew," hurried to Rome to intercede with Pope Pius IV. His mission was successful and the expulsion from Prague was stayed.[19]

In 1572 the Jews of Vienna were expelled, but only a few years later a number of Jews settled there illegally. By 1599 there were about thirty Jewish families in Vienna who had been granted residence permits. Many other "illegal" families lived there openly, built synagogues, and paid inordinate taxes. In 1600 some of the poorer Jewish families were expelled. But other Jews continued to come to Vienna. While the mayor and the priests prodded the king about expelling the Jews, Rudolph II and his successor, Matthias, ignored their suggestions. However, whenever Jews failed to pay a tax promptly they were threatened with expulsion and often went deeply into debt to raise the money.

During the Thirty Years' War, with the royal treasury a bottomless pit, there was no limit to the taxes on Jews. The king, however, did attempt to protect them from physical harm, but in order to mollify the priests he consented to other kinds of restrictions on Jews.

Jews in Hungary

In 1526 Turkish armies captured a stretch of territory in the Balkans. The area was inhabited by Hungarians, and in many of the cities there were Jewish communities. Rumors spread in other parts of Hungary that the Jews had spied for the Turks. Angered and frustrated by their defeat, Christian princes expelled the Jews from Edenburg, Pressburg, and other cities where they had lived for a long time. The Turks ruled their part of Hungary for one hundred fifty years, and under their reign the Jews were free of persecution.

In 1529 a Christian boy was found dead in a field outside the city of Posen. All the Jews of that city were arrested and confessions were wrung from several of them. On 21 May 1529 thirty Jews were burned to death for this "crime."[20] The surviving Jews were driven from the city and all their property confiscated. The Jews of nearby Marburg were also arrested, but the king ordered them released. Around the same time, the Jews were expelled from Pressburg and Sidnoy among other towns in the area.

In 1572 the Hungarian parliament ordered Jews to pay twice as much in taxes as did Christians. In addition to this general tax there were special "assessments" which so impoverished the Jewish population that many families moved secretly from the Christian to the Turkish part of the country.

The war between the Christians and the Turks was renewed every couple of years. When in 1601 a Christian army recaptured the city of Stuhl-Weisenberg, the conquerors wreaked vengeance first on the Jews. Many of the older Jews were murdered; the younger ones were sold as slaves. Jewish communities in Germany, Italy, and Turkey ransomed most of them.

The Christian rulers and the clergy continued to enforce the exceptional laws against the Jews of Hungary. By the middle of the seventeenth century the Jewish communities there had greatly declined as migrations took place to Turkey, Poland, and Lithuania.

15

Jews in Poland and Lithuania

Exactly when Jews first settled in Poland is not clear. We know that as early as the ninth century, Jewish merchants from western European lands were trading with the East. We know also that in the tenth and eleventh centuries there were Jewish minters and other officials in Poland.[1] After the first two crusades in 1096 and 1146, masses of Jews from the west settled there. Although Christianity was not as deep-rooted in Poland as it was in the west, stories of Jewish sorcery and perniciousness could be found in abundance in the Catholic sacred texts, and the Jews in those regions felt the whip of hatred from the very beginning. In 1173 Prince Mieczyslav III of Posen and Kalish ordered the students of the seminaries to stop attacking Jews, which is the best evidence that attacks upon Jews had already taken place.

In 1241 the Tatars invaded Poland and left many communities and estates in ruin. After these attacks the rulers of Poland invited merchants and artisans from Germany, including Jews, to help rebuild the devastated economy. As the immigrants streamed into the country, the Polish cities gradually revived. Germans and Jews both engaged in the same trades and crafts, but the long-standing Jew-hatred among the Germans expressed itself immediately. In 1264, Boleslav, ruler of "Greater Poland," granted the Jews a Charter of Privileges, one of which was a guarantee of protection from physical harm.

The clergy was hardly pleased with this development, and in 1267 a synod of Polish priests appealed to the Crown to annul the charter and introduce the anti-Jewish laws that were then in force in other

Christian countries. Their request was denied and Jewish immigration continued unabated, especially during the years of the Black
Death, when entire Jewish communities migrated eastward.

A new and much broader charter was granted the Jews by King
Casimir the Great (1333–70). Jews continued to arrive in Poland and
settle in the cities. Industry and trade expanded. The Germans in the
cities organized themselves into separate communities, guilds and
craft associations, as did the Jews. The Polish nobility, some of
whom had pledged their estates to Jewish moneylenders, attempted
to limit the rights of Jews to own land. To their aid came the priests,
utilizing every anti-Jewish manifestation that came their way.

During the Black Death, several of the western Polish provinces
were also hit by the disease, and with the plague came the familiar lie
that Jews had poisoned the wells. Major pogroms took place in
Silesia, which bordered on Germany. Masses of Jews fled from the
western lands to Poland and Lithuania. By the mid-fourteenth
century there were larger Jewish communities in Posen, Krakow,
Lwow, Volhynia, and other areas.

Late in the fourteenth century the Lithuanian Grand Duke
Jagiello married the Polish Queen Jadwiga, joining the two countries together. One of the conditions of the union was that Lithuania
and its royal court would adopt the Catholic religion. Jagiello ruled
this united kingdom for half a century (1334–86). Following the
urging of the priests, he did not renew the Jewish charters, but
neither did he accede to all the anti-Jewish laws they were proposing.

The priests did not give up. In 1399 they spread a rumor in Posen
that the Jews had desecrated a Host. The local bishop arrested the
rabbi and thirteen prominent Jews. After a trial by torture, they
were burned at the stake.[2] In 1407 a priest announced in a sermon in
Krakow that Jews had crucified a local Christian child and used its
blood for ritual purposes. That same day an infuriated mob invaded
the Jewish quarter, looting and murdering.[3] The king later fined the
Krakow city officials for not stopping the pogrom.

For a long time there had been a tolerant attitude toward Jews in
Lithuania. Masses of Jews had settled there, engaging in all sorts of
occupations. From the end of the fourteenth century there are
records of established Jewish communities in all the larger cities in
Lithuania and Volhynia. Jews were settled in large numbers in
Brisk, Grodno, Luczk, and Ludmir. Kiev, too, already had a Jewish
community. Eventually Jagiello did renew the charters, adding
important privileges.

In the mid-fifteenth century Poland was at war with a German military order and suffered a defeat. The priests blamed King Jagiello: God was punishing the Polish people for his friendliness to the Jews. Several members of the nobility joined this opposition with demands that the king abolish the Jewish privileges or else they would withdraw their forces from the war. In 1454 Jagiello cancelled many of the provisions in the Charter.

Despite these restrictions, the Jewish population of Poland and Lithuania increased manyfold. Masses of Jews were then running for their lives from Germany and the Danube region. The anti-Jewish laws in Poland were not strictly enforced. Jews leased estates and worked as artisans and handicraftsmen. Jewish toil and trade helped to develop the country. At the same time, there was occasional violence against Jews as a result of the hate propaganda.

In 1464 there was a campaign in Poland for a crusade against the Turks, who had just captured the holy city of Constantinople. On their way to do battle with the Turks, the "volunteers" attacked Jewish communities in Galicia, beseiged the capital, Lwow, and demanded that the Jews be handed over to them. The city council refused. On being given a sum of money, the mob left.

The city council of Krakow, on the other hand, opened their gates to the crusaders, who pillaged stores and homes and murdered thirty Jews.[4] The *kehillah* ("congregation") of Krakow complained to King Casimir, who imposed a large fine upon the city. In the same year a savage pogrom took place in Posen, on the pretext that Jews were responsible for a serious fire in the city. The German burghers in the cities were constantly trying to create a pretext for a pogrom. In cities where they were dominant, the local authorities began to place restrictions on Jewish businesses and occupations.

In Warsaw, by the mid-fifteenth century, there was already a well-established Jewish community that had grown up together with the new city. At the time of the Capistrano agitation in 1454, there were riots against the Jews in the city, and in 1483 they were expelled. Three years later they were permitted to return. In 1527 they were again expelled and kept out for two hundred fifty years afterward.

In 1495 the grand duke of Lithuania, under pressure by people who owed money to Jews, expelled the Jews from his country, thus cancelling all the debts at one stroke. Most of these Jews settled in the Polish cities. Some went to the Crimea, where there was a large Jewish community in the port city of Feodosia. Eight years later the Jews were invited back to Lithuania. Their homes and estates were returned to them, as were their synagogues and cemeteries.

In Posen, Krakow, and Lwow, which had large German populations, the Jews suffered continual physical attacks, libels, restrictions, and an occasional pogrom.

During the reign of Sigismund I (1506–48), many Jewish refugees arrived from Germany, Austria, and Bohemia. The mayors of the cities made the usual complaints to the king: the Jews were taking away space, homes, livelihoods from Christians. In 1532 Sigismund limited Jewish immigration into some cities. One exception was Krakow, where the king resided. Many refugees from Bohemia and Silesia settled in Krakow at that time. When the Jews in other cities complained to the king that they were being harassed, he threatened the offenders with the death penalty.

The Polish *szliachta*, the so-called nobility, maintained its traditional right to convene periodically in assemblies which became known as the *Sejm* (Parliament). As time went on, the clergy and the city councils (mostly inimical to Jews) took an increasing part in these deliberations. In the *Sejm* of 1538 the Jew-haters succeeded in proposing strong anti-Jewish recommendations to the king.[5] Sigismund and the nobility were then feuding over the rights to the taxes on Jews. In 1539 the king granted this right to many of the nobles.

During this period the Catholic clergy increased its influence. The Reformation in neighboring Germany had badly frightened the priests in Poland. Signs of the heresy were beginning to appear in their country, too, In 1539, for example, when the priests discovered an elderly Christian woman preparing to convert to Judaism, they burned her at the stake.[6] Rumors spread among the Catholics in Poland that many Christians intended to convert, that Christians were being circumcised and spirited away to Turkey. ("Turkey" was then the favorite bugbear.)

King Sigismund ordered the arrest of prominent Jewish leaders of Krakow and Posen. When an investigation revealed that the rumors of conversion were completely without foundation, the arrested Jews were released and Sigismund reinstituted the Charter of Privileges *in toto*.[7] The pressure of the clergy, however, grew more and more insistent, and in 1543 the king prohibited any further Jewish immigration into Krakow.

Under his successor, Sigismund II, the situation of the Jews grew no worse, at least officially. With the Reformation in ascendency in central and western Europe, the Polish priests stepped up their campaign against non-believers, especially Jews. In 1556 they arrested three Jews and a Christian servant-girl in Suchaczew. The girl was accused of stealing a wafer from a church and giving it to her

Jewish employer. The three Jews were charged with stabbing the Host until it bled. None of the accused, even under torture, confessed to the crime, but a court consisting of priests and an emissary of Pope Paul IV sentenced them to death. When the bishop applied to the Crown for confirmation of the sentence, Sigismund II postponed his decision. The priests then took matters into their own hands and executed two of the Jews. The third man escaped. In 1557 the king ordered all such charges taken out of the hands of the priests; henceforth they were to be heard by the *Sejm* in the presence of the king and the nobles.[8]

In 1564 a Jew was sentenced to death in Bielsk (Lithuania) for draining the blood of a Christian child. Similar accusations were made in other cities. The king issued strict orders that these charges were not to be prosecuted unless they were verified by seven witnesses, four Christians and three Jews.

In the meantime, the *Sejm* was accepting more of the proposals that came from the synods. Gradually the Jews were made to wear identification, restrictions were placed on their occupations, and various privileges were taken away. After Sigismund II died in 1572, the *Sejm* annulled the right of that dynasty to rule; thereafter, the kings of Poland were to be selected by the *Sejm* itself.

King Stefan Batory (1576–86) continued a moderate policy toward the Jews, but they were unceasingly harassed by the priests and the guilds. In February 1577, in a pogrom in Posen, several Jews were murdered and much property destroyed under the pretext that the Jews had insulted a convert. With the support of King Batory, the Jesuit Order in Poland strengthened their influence. Like the Dominicans in Rome, the Jesuits began a campaign to imbue the younger generation with the Jesuit spirit. All over Poland they opened schools for children and youth, and along with the theological foundations of Catholicism they filled their students with an unreasoning hatred of Jews.

By the mid-seventeenth century this hatred was widespread in Poland, with physical attacks on Jews taking place in almost every part of the country. In Vilna there was a pogrom as early as 1492. In Posen, assaults on individual Jews were a daily occurrence. Many Germans who had settled there had been in the Fettmilch gangs in Frankfurt.[9] Students from the Jesuit academies, out for a "little fun," would attack Jews on the street or break into Jewish homes. In an attempt to put a stop to this, Jews brought gifts to the Jesuit school, and eventually these gifts evolved into regular taxes.

In Krakow a Jew-hater named Miczinski published a book in 1618 called *The Great Wrongs which Poland is Suffering at the Hands of the Jews.* Basically it was a list of all the ritual "crimes" ever committed by Jews. Priests drew from this text for their sermons. Demands for expulsion became more frequent. A Christian doctor accused his Jewish "colleagues" of killing Christian patients. Ritual trials multiplied and Jews were tortured to death in attempts to make them confess. In 1579 a Jesuit priest compiled and published a list of Christian children "martyred" by Jews, with the names of the Jews who had "confessed" to the crimes.

In 1597 several Jews, arrested in Poltusk for desecrating a Host, were burned at the stake. The following year, in a village near Lublin, the body of a Christian boy was found. Three Jews were tortured and executed after they "confessed" to using the child's blood in the baking of matzos.

In 1598 a Jesuit priest named Moyeczki published a book listing the best known ritual murder and Host desecration charges against Jews in Germany, Bohemia, Austria, and Poland. In 1602 Bishop Hubiczki in Krakow issued his *Jewish Cruelties Against the Holy Sacrament and Christian Children.* In 1604 a trial over a desecrated Host took place in Bochnia (near Krakow) and Hubiczki's book was offered in evidence. All the Jews of the town were expelled.

In 1628 the Jews of Przemysl were victims of a pogrom. When the king ordered the leaders of the mob punished and demanded damages for the losses he had suffered, a ritual murder case was cooked up. None of the three accused Jews confessed. One of them died under torture. But no expulsion took place.

In 1635 Pyotr Jurkevicz, a Christian, was caught stealing silver vessels from a church in Krakow. The city council promised to release him if he confessed that along with the vessels he had also stolen a wafer and sold it to a Jew. Jurkevicz agreed and told his well-rehearsed story, but he was not freed. The authorities started a search for the Jew—a tailor in Krakow—whom Jurkevicz had named. The tailor, who had apparently gotten wind of the frameup, disappeared. The conspirators then demanded that the Jewish community surrender the accused. When that failed, another Jew was taken hostage.

In an effort to strengthen their case, the authorities sentenced the Christian, Jurkevicz, to death. Before his execution he confessed that he had lied and he revealed the whole plot, including the part played by the city council. Jurkevitz was burned at the stake, but the search for the missing tailor went on. At this juncture the king intervened. The Jews of Krakow insisted they knew nothing about the tailor's whereabouts and were cleared of suspicion. But the matter did not end there. A story spread that the Jews had placed Jurkevicz under a spell, which was the reason he had absolved the Jews from guilt. On 6 May 1637 a pogrom broke out in Krakow. Several Jews were thrown into the Vistula and were drowned. Others were released after they promised to convert.[10]

In 1639 a ritual murder trial took place in Leneczyca, where two trustees of a synagogue had been accused of murdering a Christian child. Although torture did not yield the desired confession, the wounds on the child were taken as clear proof that the Jews must be guilty. They were hacked to pieces and their dismembered bodies displayed at crossroads. The remains of the child were placed in the Leneczyca church inside a coffin. On the wall a mural was painted depicting Jews as they drained the blood of a Christian child.

Early in the seventeenth century masses of Jews from the larger cities in western Poland moved to the smaller towns in Galicia and Volhynia and the Kiev area in the Ukraine. This stream of emigration grew especially strong during the reign of Vladislav IV from 1632 to 1648.

The Chmielnicki Massacres

The area of Byelorussia, Kiev, Volhynia, Podolia, and Ruthenia, which the Polish kings ruled in the fifteenth and sixteenth centuries, were inhabited by peasants who had accepted the Greek-Orthodox faith. The nobles considered the peasants as less than human and exploited them in any way they chose. Not surprisingly, the hatred of these Ukrainian peasants for the "Polacks," as they called them, knew no bounds. Aside from the brutal way they treated their subjects, the Polish nobles were Roman Catholics who spent most of their time in the big cities or in foreign countries, leaving their estates to be managed by overseers.

Among the Jews who had moved into these eastern areas of Poland were artisans, innkeepers, and some leaseholders of estates. The nobles kept raising the rent on their properties. To meet the payments, the Jewish leaseholders kept raising the prices on whatever resources they had on the estates—firewood from the forest, use of pasture land, fishing rights, among other things. It did not take long before the object of the peasants' resentment was the Jewish leaseholder rather than the Polish nobleman, whom they very rarely saw. The Jewish middleman was both visible and vulnerable, and the priests never tired of recounting the stories of "Jewish crimes." A great reservoir of Jew-hatred thus accumulated in the hearts of the peasants.

In the rebellion of 1637 in Poltawa, two hundred Jews were murdered when the estates and Catholic churches were set to the torch.[11] For punishment, many peasants, along with their leader, were whipped to death. The Ukrainian masses seethed in fury. The air grew heavy with the clouds of a terrible storm. In the southern part of the Ukraine a group of peasant villages had organized themselves to repel the Tatars who used to ride in from the Crimea and make off with livestock and even young people (whom they sold to the Turks). In the same area, at the mouth of the Dnieper near the Black Sea, there was a settlement of peasants who had escaped from serfdom and who called themselves "Cossacks," which signifies free men. Together with the Ukrainian peasants, the Cossacks were easily able to drive off the Tatars, and in time they took the offensive against their villages. The Polish government soon saw the military value of the Cossacks, supplied them with arms and recognized their right to select their own elder or hetman.

In the spring of 1648, however, the Cossacks joined forces with the Tatars against the Poles. Under the leadership of their new hetman, Bogdan Chomil (or Chmielnicki, as the Poles called him) the Cossacks and Tatars attacked some smaller Polish army units and defeated them. The victory acted as a signal. In hundreds of villages throughout the Ukraine the peasants rose up against their oppressors. Members of the nobility, along with their estate managers and servants, were slain without mercy.

Hardest hit were the Jews. As soon as the uprising broke out, most of the Jews in the smaller towns fled to the cities, but here there were hardly any forces able to withstand the hordes of Cossacks, Tatars, and inflamed peasants. Those Jews who stayed in the villages and small towns were massacred. Only the few who agreed to convert to Greek Orthodoxy were spared.[12]

After finishing with the estates of the nobility, armies of marauders set upon the larger cities. East of the Dnieper, in the province of Poltava, in the cities of Peryeslav, Piriatin, Lokhvitza, and Lubnu, thousands of Jews were brutally murdered and their property stolen. From here the bands moved to the western shores of the Dnieper. In the Kiev area, the Jews of Porobischa, Czivotov, and other smaller towns were slaughtered. The Cossacks and Tatars surrounded the city of Kiev, where several thousand Jews had fled for safety. Since the Cossack and Tatar armies were on separate sides of the city, many Jews surrendered to the Tatars, who sold them as slaves in Turkey and Crimea. Most of the Jews in Kiev perished at the hands of the Cossacks. Almost all the Jews who were sold by the Tatars were ransomed in Feodosia and Constantinople.

In the fortress city of Nemirov, where some six thousand Jews had gathered from nearby towns, the Cossacks tried to storm the walls, but failed. They then marched to the fortress carrying Polish flags, and the Jews, who had been expecting help from the Polish army, threw open the gates. On 10 July 1648 the Cossacks slaughtered the six thousand Jews in cold blood and pillaged the city.[13]

The same fate met the Jews who had fled to Tulczyn. Here, too, the attackers resorted to a ruse, promising the Poles that no harm would come to them if they would surrender the Jews. Somehow the Poles got the Jews to lay down their weapons, then they let the mobs enter the city. When the Cossacks finally left, fifteen hundred Jews and six hundred Poles were dead.[14] In the Podolian city of Bar, again, both Jews and Poles were massacred.

From Podolia, Chmielnicki's armies moved on to the cities of Volhynia. Some 12,000 Jews had fled to the fortified city of Polonnoye. The fortress was well-constructed and well-manned, but some of the nobleman's people opened the gates. Those Poles who had horses were able to escape. Those who did not were killed together with the Jews of Polonnoye, Miropol, Lubar, Ostropol, Baranovka, and other places nearby.[15]

The Cossack hordes then went on to Zaslav, Ostroh, Mezricz, and Old Constantine. Nathan Hanover, who survived the massacre and left a chronicle, related that in Ostroh and Mezricz alone, ten thousand families perished. In Old Constantine, several thousand Jews were killed.[16] Other bands moved north toward Byelorussia and Lithuania. In July and August 1648 the Jews of Minsk, Chernigov, Staradub, Homel, and many other cities and towns in those areas were slaughtered. In Mogilev and Smolensk some two thousand Jews were slain.

Chmielnicki himself turned southward to Galicia and beseiged the fortified capital of Lwow. Again they tried to trick the Poles into believing they were only after the Jews, but this time it did not work. Chmielnicki finally agreed to retreat, for a price. All the money in the city was surrendered to him and he pulled out his Cossacks.

Moving toward Zamoscz and Lublin, they destroyed many smaller towns on the way, such as Nahrev, Tomashev, and Sheberezin.

In the first half of 1649 tens of thousands of Jews were killed in Poland. After a major battle in Sbarez, peace was finally negotiated. Chmielnicki was declared ruler over the Ukraine, but under the authority of Poland. His demand that Poles and Jews be forbidden to settle in the Ukraine was granted.[17] A year and a half later the fighting began again. The Tatars broke their alliance with Chmielnicki and the Cossacks were defeated by a Polish army on 1 July 1651 near the town of Beresteczko. In the new peace that was signed in Byela-Tserkov in October 1651, Chmielnicki accepted a provision permitting Poles and Jews to settle in the Ukraine.

At the same time, Chmielnicki began secret negotiations with Russia, and in 1654 Russian troops and Ukrainian Cossacks invaded Lithuania and Byelorussia. Again Jews were the victims, although in much smaller numbers than before simply because there were not too many Jews left there. In Mogilev the Jews prepared and put up strong resistance. Finally they were offered safe conduct to the headquarters of the Polish General Raziwil, who had promised to help them. Weary and starving, the Jews accepted the offer. But no sooner were they out in the open than the Russian troops cut them down, sparing only those who agreed to convert to Greek Orthodoxy. King Casimir later granted all the converts the right to return to Judaism.

At the same time as the Russian invasion, Sweden launched an attack on Poland. Because the Swedes did not make the Jews their special target, a rumor spread among the Polish troops that the Jews were sympathetic to the enemy. Many Polish army detachments, especially those under General Czarnicki, began a pogrom of Jewish communities. Pozna, Kalish, Krakow, and Pyetrkow suffered most severely.[18]

The number of Jews who perished at the hands of the Chmielnicki Cossacks in 1648 and 1656 is not known. Estimates range from 100,000 to 500,000.[19] By Jewish scholars it was assessed as the worst catastrophe since the destruction of the Second Temple in 70 C.E.

Among many Jewish communities throughout the world a new hope arose that the terrible afflictions of their time could only be the promised prelude to the coming of the Messiah. Thus, when the false messiah, Shabbatai Zvi, appeared in the East, masses of Jews seized upon this hope and put their faith in the new Redeemer.

16

Jews in Poland After the Massacres of 1648–49

The wars against the Russians and the Cossacks left Poland in economic ruin. Demoralized by the Chmielnicki massacres, the Jews returned gradually to the Polish towns, where the taxes levied upon them by the various authorities continued to multiply. Attempting to escape persecution and poverty, many Jewish artisans settled in the villages and smaller towns. Jews again turned to leaseholding, petty trade, and tavern-keeping. (The nobles, with a monopoly on whiskey production, leased the distributing rights to Jews.)

With the conquest of large sections of Lithuania by the Russian army in 1658, the Jews were again expelled from Vilna. In the Byelorussian city of Bikhov, three hundred Jews were murdered by Russian soldiers in the winter of 1659.[1] In 1660 the Jewish community of Pinsk was destroyed. The then king of Poland, Jan Casimir (1648–68) issued decrees aimed at easing the plight of the Jews, but they were not always effective. The Church not only continued its agitation, but constantly pressured the monarch for new anti-Jewish legislation.

In 1657, in the Lithuanian town of Roczenoi, the battered body of a Christian child was "found" in a Jewish courtyard. All the Jews of the town were charged with the murder. In a trial that lasted two years, no evidence or witnesses were produced, but two prominent Jews of the town were beheaded anyway. Many other attempts were made in Poland to stir up ritual murder cases. In 1663 a Jewish apothecary in Krakow was brutally murdered after a charge that he had profaned the names of Jesus and Mary. When the Jews of

Krakow appealed to Rome, complaining that leading Catholics in Poland were fabricating lies and murdering innocent Jews, the pope ordered the Polish clergy to put a stop to the practice, but they paid no attention.

Reared in a Jesuitical spirit, young Polish hoodlums frequently started riots in the Jewish quarters of the cities. In 1664, when such a pogrom was organized in a suburb of Lwow, the Jews there resisted. Reinforced by drunken rowdies and armed members of the city militia, the mob soon overpowered the defenders, leaving a hundred Jews dead or wounded. The survivors fled to Lwow. As rumors of another pogrom spread, the Jews there armed themselves and prepared to resist. On 12 July 1664 the churchbells in Lwow clanged insistently, summoning the Christian population to battle. Again the Jewish forces were outnumbered. Some two hundred Jews were killed in the two pogroms. All Jewish property was seized by the authorities.

Lwow was not an isolated instance. Attacks on Jews took place in all parts of Poland. In 1664 King Casimir called upon his subjects to stop the killing and plundering of Jews. A few years later King Vishnievetski again appealed to his people to maintain order, a sure sign that the attacks on Jews had not ceased. In 1671, a mob in the town of Novarodok burned two Jewish women on the charge of witchcraft.[2] In 1682, during an attempt by a gang of hoodlums to break into Jewish homes in Krakow, one of the gang was shot. A mob formed and vandalized Jewish stores. When the Jews complained to King Jan Sobeski, one of the offenders was sentenced to death. The Jews pleaded with the king not to carry out the sentence. The king agreed, but ordered all the stolen goods returned.

In 1681, Jew-haters in Vilna announced that a census was being taken and that everyone had been ordered to go to a certain field outside the city to be counted. Those Jews who appeared at the site were beaten with clubs. In 1687 pogroms took place in Vilna and Posen. In the latter city laws were passed limiting the birth-rate of Jews. No more than four or five Jewish marriages a year were permitted. At Hanukkah-time a mob assaulting the ghetto was met by armed Jewish resistance. After a three-day battle the attackers retreated, leaving several dead behind them. A number of attempts were made in Posen to instigate ritual murder trials, but not all of them succeeded.

In 1690 an infant was found dead in Vilna. Apparently the "nanny" had been negligent and an accident had resulted. After hiding the body in a field, she concocted a story about Jews having taken the child from her by force. Since the guilty persons were not known, three prominent Jews of the city were beheaded. These ritual murder libels became more frequent. Hardly a Passover eve in Poland went by without an anti-Jewish accusation in some city or village.

During the long war with Sweden (1700–21), Poland joined an alliance with the Russian czar Peter I. Russian, Polish, and Swedish armies moved across the countryside, and Jews suffered at the hands of each one. After the Swedes captured Lwow they placed a steep tax on the Jews there. When the Jewish community declared it was unable to pay it, the Swedes hung two of its leaders.[3] Russian army units, led by Cossacks, persecuted Jews with no provocation at all. During 1702–1704 the *Haidamaki* ("brigands") rampaged through the Ukraine attacking Jewish communities in the Kiev area, in Volhynia, Podolia, and Galicia. Hardest hit were the cities of Bar, Nemirov, Zaslow, and many smaller towns. The various city councils continually harassed the Jews, restricting their rights in Lwow, Grodno, Krakow, Lublin, and Vilna. Polish priests copied the anti-Jewish libels of the thirteenth and fourteenth century Catholic synods. Five hundred years later they were still able to get a law passed by the king forcing Jews to listen to Christian sermons. From 1740 to 1752 a Bishop Kobelski delivered such sermons in synagogues in Luczk, Brod, and other cities, even inviting leading rabbis to debate with him, an honor which they all refused.

In 1726, several rabbis and community leaders in Lwow were arrested on the charge of persuading a convert to return to Judaism. When the convert was confronted with several people and asked to identify the individuals he had accused, he pointed to the head of the yeshiva, Rabbi Chaim Rayzes, and his brother Joshua. A court of priests sentenced the two men to a horrible death—their tongues were to be pulled out, their arms broken, their bodies dismembered. Joshua hung himself. The sentence on Rabbi Rayzes was carried out in all particulars.[4]

In Dubno two Christian women converts to Judaism were arrested. Even under torture, one of them refused to renounce her new faith. After her body had been cut to ribbons by 186 lashes, she was burned at the stake. The second woman, together with her Jewish husband, was beheaded. Several Jews who had attended the wedding were whipped. The entire Jewish community of Dubno was fined.

In the spring of 1698 the body of an unidentified child was discovered in the church morgue in Tzusmir. Upon investigation it was learned that a poor woman, who had no money for baptizing the child or for burying it, had left the dead child in the church. The local court sentenced her to several days in jail for not having baptized the child. The local priest, Zhukowski, overruled the sentence and ordered the woman tortured until she confessed the "truth"—that she had sold the child to a Jew.

In due course the woman did "confess" to selling her son to the head of the Jewish community, a man named Berek, and that the child's body had been returned to her covered with wounds. When she was confronted with the man face-to-face she recanted her confession. After another period of torture she again confessed that her original story was true. Berek, even under torture, refused to corroborate her story. The explanation that the Jesuits gave of the man's heroism was that he had smeared a magic salve on his body which deadened the pain! The priest Zhukowski, an "expert" on Jewish magic, recommended that they torture the Jew's shadow, because Jewish sorcery can render a person insensitive to pain, but cannot do this for the shadow. Berek continued to maintain his innocence.

Meanwhile the Jews of Tsuzmir appealed to the king, who ordered the trial delayed until he could be present himself. The priests thereupon speeded up the trial, sentenced Berek to death, and carried out the verdict. He was quartered and beheaded and his dismembered body was displayed at crossroads in the area. The excuse given to the king was that his message had arrived too late.

Another trial took place in Tsuzmir in 1710, in which Zhukowski's chief witness was a demented young Jew who had escaped from confinement and gone to a church to be converted. The priests renamed him Neophyte. He told them that he was a rabbi and knew for a fact that Jews used blood in their magic, that Jewish brides and grooms eat an egg mixed with Christian blood at the wedding ceremony, and that Jews use Christian blood in the Passover *afikomen* custom.

Jewish leaders asked that they be permitted to confront Neophyte. The debate was arranged for May 1712 in Warsaw, but the convert did not appear. Nevertheless, on the previous "testimony" of this insane "expert" three prominent Jews of Tsuzmir were found guilty and executed. Furthermore, on recommendation of the priests, King Augustus II expelled all the Jews from the city on the charge of murdering Christian children.

In 1739, when the ruler of Austria expelled the Jews from Breslau and other cities in Silesia, King Augustus III ordered the Jewish refugees kept out of Poland. In Kameniec-Podolsk, which Poland had just retaken from the Turks, there had been an old Jewish community ever since the fourteenth century. Many Jews had fled there after the Chmielnicki massacres while it was in Turkish hands. Now the priests demanded that the Jewish tradesmen and artisans be expelled because "Jews are friends of the Turks and enemies of the Christians." The king ordered most of the Jews expelled, with the exception of leaseholders and whiskey dealers, who were needed by the nobles.

Following the Chmielnicki catastrophe of 1648–49 a powerful belief took hold among many Jews that a Kabbalist named Shabbatai Zvi was the messiah. Even after Shabbatai had converted to Islam in 1666, secret groups of disciples persisted in their belief. These sects, some of which lasted into the twentieth century, were shunned by the rest of Jewry. In the mid-eighteenth century this belief had a rebirth in the person of Jacob Frank. When it became known (in a feudal Podolian town called Laskrynin) that the new messiah was a disguised disciple of Shabbatai Zvi and was conducting orgies with his followers and their wives, the rabbis excommunicated him. The "messiah" challenged them to a debate. Before a panel of Catholic priests Frank "proved" that the Talmud denigrates Christians. Public book-burnings were organized in Kameniec in October 1757 where hundreds of Jewish books were destroyed. Two years later Jacob Frank "proved" that Jews use Christian blood in baking matzos.[5]

In 1736, several score Jews were arrested in Posen on a charge of ritual murder. Two of the accused died under torture, but none of the Jews confessed to any criminal act. Five others were beheaded and burned. The bodies of the two men who had been tortured to death were exhumed and also burned. In addition, the Jewish community in Posen was fined exorbitantly. After four more horror-filled years in the dungeons, the rest of the accused were freed in 1740 by royal decree, but in order to assuage the priests, the king appended a number of anti-Jewish provisions to be inforced against the Jews of Posen.

In the spring of 1747, when the snows melted, the body of a Christian was found in a field in Zaslow. The local priests seized the opportunity. A Jewish leaseholder was celebrating the circumcision of his new son. All the guests were arrested and tortured. Several confessed. All of them were put to death in unspeakably brutal ways.

On Passover eve in 1753, the corpse of a three-year-old Christian child was discovered in Zhitomir. A Jewish leaseholder in the neighborhood was charged with the murder, and all the other Jewish leaseholders in the area were arrested. Bishop Soltik of Kiev, an "expert" in ritual murder trials, boasted in a letter to the Bishop of Lwow that he had already apprehended thirty-three Jews on this one charge. When not even one of the Jews confessed under torture, the priests obtained a sworn statement from the child's father accusing the Jews of the murder. On the basis of that "evidence" thirteen Jews from the towns of Pavoloch and Chodorkov were put to death on 26 May 1753.[6]

In Yampole the central Jewish community organization appealed to the pope and the king against a ritual murder charge. Two years later a statement came from Rome declaring that ritual murder charges against Jews are generally false and must be substantiated by thorough investigation. From King Augustus III came an order releasing the accused. The blood libel epidemic was halted for several years.

In 1761 the Jesuit priest Pikulski published his *Jewish Iniquity*, a collection of ritual murder charges. This book was studied in all Jesuit schools in Poland. (Even today, in the last quarter of the twentieth century, it is an important text in Polish church seminaries.[7]) Based on the "evidence" in Pikulski's book the *Sejm* in Lwow ordered all Jewish books burned, all Jewish schools shut down. Jews were forbidden to speak Hebrew or Yiddish. Even in prayers, only Polish or Latin was permitted, and priests were to be assigned to Jewish services to enforce these laws. The Jews resisted this decree by special "gifts" to local overseers, and it was never enforced.

The Haidamaki

In the summer of 1734 the Haidamaki—organized bands of brigands in the Ukraine—attacked Jewish towns in the areas of Kiev, Podolia, and Volhynia. Terrible slaughters took place in Shargorod, Kremenetz, Miedzibicz, Chmelnik, and Polonnoye. For a brief period, King Augustus III was able to stop the massacres, but two years later the pogroms began again. This time the Jews in Corsun, Prohobisht, Raczkov, and Granov were the target. After another brief respite, the Haidamaki ran amok again, leaving many Jews dead in Amchislav, Kryschev, Bichov, and places around Mohilev in

Byelorussia. In 1744 Polish troops together with Jewish volunteers drove the gangs from Amchislav. In 1750 the Haidamaki again wreaked havoc in the Kiev area and Volhynia—in Vinitza, Latichev, Sarna, Fastov, Uman, Radomysl, as well as in Chernobyl and Loyev in Byelorussia. After these massacres the Haidamaki were quiet until 1768.[8]

In 1764 the Polish nobles, after a bitter conflict among them-selves, selected as their king Stanislaw Poniatkowsky, a protégé of Czarina Catherine II. Many of the nobility were opposed to him and a struggle ensued in which the Catholic clergy expressed strong opposition to any "fraternizing" with Russian Orthodoxy. Among the nobles in favor of Poniatkowsky were several who were ready to abolish the privileges of the Catholic clergy. During this bitter struggle the Jews were not forgotten by the *Sejm*. In their deliber-ations they decided that each individual Jew over the age of one year must pay the per capita tax directly, not through the *Kehillah* as before. (Apparently this was done because the Jewish community organization had been deducting part of the taxes for its own budgetary needs.) A little later that year the *Sejm* abolished the central *Kehillah* body altogether.[9] In 1768 the *Sejm* voted to transfer to the councils in the larger cities the function of regulating the rights of the Jews. Taking advantage of this new law, the guilds adopted further restrictions on Jewish tradesmen and artisans. They even taxed Jews for the expense of administering the new regulations in Krakow and most cities of Poland.

During the last third of the eighteenth century, when the Czarist government was preparing to annex part of Poland, it organized bands of Haidamaki to raid Polish cities along the borders. In the spring of 1768 Russian Orthodox priests spread a forged letter from the Czarina among the Cossacks and peasants of the Ukraine ordering the Haidamaki to invade Poland and destroy all the "Zhids and Polacks." In April the Haidamaki attacked Smila, Cherkass, Corsun, Tetyev, and nearby villages. Along the way, other Ukrain-ian bandits joined them and together they plunged into a murderous orgy, killing Jews and Poles indiscriminately and burning down synagogues and Catholic churches. Thousands of Jews and Poles sought refuge in the fortified city of Uman.

Uman at that time was the property of Baron Pototski, who had his own army there to defend his city. The soldiers were mainly Cossack mercenaries. One commander by the name of Gonte betrayed his superiors and joined the Haidamaki. The officer in charge of the defense of Uman, a Pole, was secretly negotiating with the Haidamaki, who assured him they had only the Jews in mind and would not touch the Polish nobles. When the murderers were permitted to enter the city they did indeed turn first on the Jews. Gonte informed the Jewish leaders that if they brought him the money which they had hidden, he would stop the killing. They brought him as much as they could collect, but the killing went on. After the Haidamaki finished with the Jews they turned on the Poles. Some ten thousand Jews and Poles were slaughtered in Uman, and the city became one huge cemetery.[10]

On the eve of the partition of Poland the largest collective Jewish community in the world was then in that country, settled mostly in small towns and villages. Jews could live wherever they chose, with the exception of a few larger cities, one of which was Warsaw. Jews were permitted to enter Warsaw only on business, for a period of no more than two weeks. Those who were in the middle of business dealings would leave the city by one gate and, after some money changed hands, come in again through another, receiving a permit for another two weeks. When hundreds of so-called temporary Jewish residents accumulated in Warsaw, the city council raised a demand for their expulsion. In May 1775 this demand was granted, but soon Jews reappeared in Warsaw. In 1784 and 1790 they were expelled once more.

When the "Jewish Problem" came to the fore in Poland in the 1780s, various solutions were proposed. Jews should be permitted to live only in villages and small towns and should be allowed to enter the forbidden cities only temporarily on business. Jews must assimilate and stop speaking their *zhargon* (i.e., Yiddish), or printing books in that language. Jews must not be innkeepers or tavernkeepers, but must engage only in "honest" work—handicrafts or farming. None of these proposals were taken seriously. Poland was on the verge of disintegration; the very existence of the Polish state hung by a hair. The entire population of Poland was then around 8.8 million. The census of 1788 showed 617,000 Jews in Poland and Lithuania, though the real total was closer to 900,000.

The *Sejm* of 1789 had many serious problems on its agenda, yet the Jewish Problem kept reappearing in the deliberations. In the street the problem was acute. On the one hand, the Jews were demanding more humane treatment; on the other hand, the city councils and the Catholic priests were continually pressuring for more restrictions on Jews, including expulsion. Pamphlets for and against were disseminated widely. The liberals argued that in order to make useful citizens of the Jews it was necessary to take a more tolerant approach. The reactionaries favored forcible methods and police repression. Whenever the subject came up in the *Sejm* there was an unbridgeable difference of opinion and the matter was tabled.

Early in 1790 a pogrom was instigated in Warsaw by Christian merchants and artisans who wanted to be rid of Jewish competition. By that time there were several thousand Jews in the city, most of them petty tradesmen and handicraftsmen. In March 1790 the Christian tailors' guild demonstrated at the Warsaw city hall, demanding the expulsion of the Jewish tailors from the city; otherwise, they threatened to kill all the Jews in Warsaw. The *Sejm* sent two deputies to hear out their complaints. After the hearing the deputies promised the Christian tailors that their demands would be met. The next day the city authorities expelled all the Jewish artisans from Warsaw. After a few days some of the Jews, having nowhere else to go, stole back into the city and went about their business.

On 16 May 1790 a Christian tailor confronted a Jewish tailor in the street and tried to tear a piece of work out of his hands. After a scuffle the Jew managed to escape, still in possession of his goods. The tailors' guild raised an alarm. Crowds gathered. A Jew had killed a Pole, was the rumor. There were cries of revenge. A riot began. Jews resisted. The police attempted to disperse the mobs, who then turned on the police. It took a detachment of troops to restore order.

After 28 September 1791, when the news came that the Jews in Paris had been granted full citizenship rights, the liberals in the *Sejm* raised the issue again. Unable to oppose the idea openly, the Jew-haters found another excuse. Since many Jewish communities in Poland were deeply in debt, the new rights and privileges would not be granted to them until they paid their debts.

At the end of May 1792 the Russian army invaded Poland from the east. From the west came the Prussians. The war ended with the Second Partition in 1793. Russia annexed Volhynia, Podolia, and large sections of the Kiev and Minsk areas. Prussia took Kalish, Plock, Danzig, among other cities. All the areas severed from Poland at that time contained large Jewish populations.

In 1794 Thaddeus Kosciuszko issued a call to all Polish patriots to drive out the invader. Among the volunteers who responded were many Jews, who were organized into a regiment under Berek

Joselewicz. Among the Polish soldiers killed in battle were several hundred Jews.

The uprising was crushed, and as soon as the Russians entered Warsaw the Polish members of the city council appealed to their commander for permission to expel the Jews from the city. The commanding general refused, but imposed a special tax on Jews for the right to reside in Warsaw. Soon afterward he abolished this tax and permitted Jews full residence privileges in the city.[11]

In 1795 Poland was partitioned for the third time. Warsaw and Bialystok fell under the authority of Prussia. Russia annexed Lithuania and the province of Grodno. Austria took Krakow and western Galicia. The territory annexed by East Prussia was heavily populated by Jews. Any Jew who was unable to prove that he was a resident of Warsaw for a given period of time, or who could not show evidence of a specific occupation, was expelled. The "privileged" Jews received special "letters of protection."

This situation did not last very long. In 1807, when Napoleon conquered Prussia and Austria, he annexed parts of Poland and created the Grand Duchy of Warsaw with that city as the capital. The entire Grand Duchy had a Jewish population of about 400,000. Napoleon's new constitution guaranteed full equality for all persons. The local rulers, however, did not extend these rights to Jews. Appeals to Napoleon were ignored. To the Jews who asked why they were being deprived of the protection of the constitution, the rulers of the Grand Duchy replied on 17 October 1809 that this was being done for only ten years, "in the hope that during this interval they may eradicate those characteristics which make them distinct from the rest of the population."

When Jewish representatives petitioned for their human rights as citizens of Poland, the reply was: "We can not grant you equal rights because of your dishonest occupations. Your way of life is strange and harmful to society. . . . Jews will have to reform themselves in order to achieve equal rights with everyone else."[12] When Berek Joselewicz, then a colonel in the Polish army, was killed in the war between the Grand Duchy and Austria, the Polish leaders declared him a hero, but left his wife and children destitute. Finally, she was permitted to reside in Warsaw and open a tavern.

One of the laws which worked a special hardship on the Jews was compulsory military service. All Polish males between the ages of twenty-one and twenty-eight were required to serve in the armed forces. At that age, however, most Jewish males were already heads of families. For observant Jews, military service was particularly punitive, since they were obliged to do various things forbidden by their religion. Masses of Hassidim simply did not report for duty. They inundated the authorities with petitions, and they offered to pay a recruit tax in lieu of service. Those who were already in the army refused to eat non-kosher food or work on the Sabbath. Finally the Ministry of War grew tired of the game and stopped recruiting Jews. A steep tax was imposed instead.

In 1812 all of former Poland was involved in Napoleon's disastrous war with Russia. The march of the French armies to Russia and then the movement of both armies the other way, left the country devastated. Jews were robbed, starved, and left homeless. Even during this grim war the rulers of Poland found time to issue new laws against Jews.

After the defeat of Napoleon, the largest part of the Warsaw Grand Duchy remained in the possession of Russia. Most of the Jewish population now became Russian-Polish Jewry. Since then and up until relatively recently, the largest Jewish community in the world was within Russian borders.

17

Jews in Austria and Germany, 1648–1789

In the second half of the seventeenth century and through the eighteenth, when commerce and industry in western and central Europe were coming into their own, the established religions lost much of their influence over the life of the peoples. Among European intellectuals appeared a new spirit of freedom which to some degree limited the mistreatment of Jews. In Austria and eastern Europe, however, medieval Jew-hatred was still too well entrenched. The Chmielnicki massacres, the wars and persecutions in Poland, had driven many Jews westward again. Jewish refugees from the expulsions in Germany and the Thirty Years' War had settled in Vienna, Prague, and other cities in Austria and Bohemia even before the catastrophe in the east. After the Chmielnicki massacres, still larger masses of Jews fled there from the scenes of carnage.

In Austria, which had become a citadel of Catholic reaction after the Reformation, the clergy barely tolerated the Jews. Barred from the center of Vienna, the Jewish community had developed in one of the suburbs and by the mid-1600s consisted of some eight hundred families. The new stream of Jewish immigrants so alarmed the Jew-haters in Vienna and other cities that they urged Frederick III (1627–57) to limit Jewish immigration or better still, to expel all the Jews from his country. He ignored their counsel.

His successor, Leopold I, considered the toleration of Jews in his kingdom to be a cardinal sin. In 1669 a royal commission of priests investigated the Jewish problem and turned up the "information" that the Jews had been expelled from Spain because of their enmity to Christendom; that the Jews were to blame for the rebellion of the Cossacks against the Poles; that Jews insult Jesus in their syna-gogues; that Jews have sexual relations with Christian women; that Jews are friendly with the Turks; that Jews were driving Christian merchants and artisans out of business.

The Vienna City Council corroborated all' the "evidence," espe-cially the last point, and in the summer of 1669 the king ordered the Jews to leave the city and its environs. The expulsion was to take place in two stages. In the first two weeks all the poor Jews were to be expelled, that is, those who had not paid their taxes, including rabbis and other religious functionaries. The wealthier Jews were allowed time to settle their debts and wind up their business. The date for their expulsion was set for the first day in March.

All their frantic efforts to stave off the expulsion were unsuc-cessful, and in the summer of 1670 Vienna became *Judenrein*. Some time before the actual expulsion the police took sixteen prominent Jews as hostages, lest the other Jews poison the wells or set fire to the city. The Vienna synagogue was converted into a church. One cornerstone of the new church contained an inscription saying that a temple of God now stood on the site where formerly there had been a "nest of murderers."

Many of the poorer refugees found a haven in Hungary and the Bohemian cities. Fifty of the richest families were invited to settle in Berlin,[1] which had been closed to Jews since 1510. Soon other Jews, most of them merchants, began migrating to Berlin and nearby cities in Brandenburg. As their enterprises grew, so did their taxes.

In 1673, three years after the expulsion from Vienna, requests began to reach the government for a readmission of Jews into the city. King Leopold acceded, and by the early part of the eighteenth century the Jewish community in Vienna totaled around four thousand, the same number as before the expulsion.[2]

Once more, the Catholic priests began their attempts to limit the Jewish population. Between 1718 and 1723 new anti-Jewish legis-lation permitted only one marriage in each Jewish family; other family members who wished to marry had to leave Austria. Wives and children of employees of the Jews were not permitted to live in the center of Vienna. All Jews had to wear special clothing for identification.

In Prague, Nickelsburg, and other cities the Jewish communities continued to grow. As soon as masses of Jewish refugees began arriving there, the priests in Bohemia and Moravia passed laws against the new immigrants. In 1670, when Jewish refugees came from Vienna, accusations and repressive decrees multiplied rapidly. In 1689 almost all the Jewish homes in Prague were destroyed by fire. The Christians refused to allow the homeless Jews to live near them. For several years the Jews lived in caves outside the city until new homes could be built.

On Yom Kippur Eve in 1722, a Catholic priest entered a Prague synagogue to preach a sermon. He was requested to leave. When he refused, he was forcibly ejected. In retaliation, the synagogue was destroyed and the Jews were forbidden to rebuild it. The three trustees of the synagogue were branded on their foreheads and expelled from the city. One of them, an old man, was sentenced to hard labor in the construction of a new church.[3]

In Silesia, then part of Bohemia, Jewish communities were permitted in the smaller towns; in Breslau, a larger city, Jews could stay only for one day at a time. This period was gradually extended to two days and more, and in time, Breslau contained a sizable Jewish community.

In the Turkish part of Hungary Jews were free of harassment. In 1686, in a war between Austria and the Turks, a Christian army besieged Budapest (then in Turkish hands) and Jews helped in the defense of the city. When the Christians recaptured Budapest, many Jews were killed in a pogrom. Others escaped to Turkey. King Leopold then forbade all Jewish residence in Budapest, but they were allowed to reside in other cities.

During the reign of Maria Theresa over Austria, Bohemia, and Hungary from 1740 to 1780 the situation of the Jews deteriorated further. The empire was embroiled in several protracted wars and Jews were continually being accused of aiding the enemy. In 1744, when Prussian soldiers invaded Prague, the Jews suffered both at the hands of "their own" army and at the hands of the invaders. When the Prussians accidently missed the Jewish quarter, a rumor arose that the Jews had a secret pact with them. When the Prussians were driven off, Austrian and Hungarian soldiers, together with the city population, organized a bloody pogrom. The queen, insisting that the pogrom was too lenient a punishment, ordered the Jews expelled from Prague in the dead of winter, giving them one month's time to prepare.[4] Panic-stricken, the Jews tried to delay the expulsion until after winter, but at the end of February 1745 most of them were forced to leave the city. Some two thousand Jews who owed taxes to the government were permitted to remain for another month. For two and a half years these refugees wandered in vain from place to place seeking a home.

Inside and outside the country protests were raised against the cruel behavior of the queen. In 1748 permission was granted for Jews to reside in Prague, but for no longer than ten years. Maria Theresa kept close watch on the number of Jews in her provinces. She ordered the keeping of accurate records of Jewish merchants arriving in Vienna or Prague, who were not permitted to remain in the city for more than four days. Unwittingly, however, she herself added a couple of hundred thousand Jews to her population at one stroke. As a result of the partition of Poland in 1772, Austria received the large province of Ruthenia (Galicia) with its large Jewish population.[5]

Maria Theresa's son, Joseph, became king in 1765, ruled together with his mother until her death in 1780, and by himself from 1780 to 1790. In the spirit of liberalism then sweeping western Europe, the enlightened king attempted to introduce reforms into his dominions. The Jews in Galicia in 1772 constituted a very important problem for him; his solution was to integrate them into society by reforming Jewish life.

One year after he ascended the throne he announced his "Patent of Tolerance." The Jews were to be educated, not in Yiddish or Hebrew, but in German. Jewish rights to engage in business or the handicrafts were broadened. Jews were given the right to own and cultivate land. They no longer had to wear distinctive clothing. Their children could attend German schools, even the Christian religious schools. In 1787 he further decreed that Jews would be subject to compulsory military service.

Joseph II's "Patent of Tolerance" sounded socially positive and progressive. However, in the environment in which it was attempted, and the police methods by which it was carried out, the masses of Jews preceived it as anti-Jewish. Living amid a general population of around eleven million in Austria, Bohemia, and Hungary, the 400,000 Jews in Austria were culturally isolated. In Galicia the great mass of Jews were devoutly observant and had no contact with the speech, culture, or even the alphabet of the German language. They spoke Yiddish, conducted their business affairs in Yiddish, kept their accounts in Yiddish, and settled their differences in a Jewish court. In addition to all the various kinds of work they did in the smaller towns, they earned their living by trading, leasing mills, forests or rivers, distilling whiskey, and running taverns.

Declaring that these "Jewish occupations" were not honorable enough, Joseph II decreed that Jews could no longer lease forests, mills or ferries, keep taverns, or live in the villages. Overnight, a hundred thousand Jews were deprived of their livelihood.[6] When the city councils questioned the king about Jewish access to trades, government positions, equal rights, the king assured them he had nothing like that in mind; it was not his intent to help Jews multiply in his lands. In fact, he would do everything in his power to keep their number from increasing.[7]

Jewish rightlessness, even with the Patent of Tolerance, remained the same as it had been almost everywhere else. Jews could not live in Vienna or in any of the other places from which they had been banned before. In Lwow, the Jews were permitted to live only in certain quarters of the city. In Krakow, the Jews were restricted to a ghetto. Wherever the laws limiting Jewish marriages and births had been in effect before, they were now renewed. Rabbis could perform marriages or divorces only by special permission of the government. Again, compulsory military service proved to be the harshest decree of all.[8]

Only a small number of Jews perceived the Patent of Tolerance to be their salvation and spoke in favor of it. The *maskilim* ("followers of the Enlightenment") and the wealthier families, to whom the Patent granted additional rights of trade, who long tended to assimilate, welcomed the opportunity to send their children to government schools.

Jewish "equalization" did not end with the economic ruin of the hundred thousand Jews who were driven out of the villages. The enlightened monarch also undertook to "humanize"—that is, Germanize—the Jews culturally and make them worthy of being tolerated. The Patent of Tolerance was not designed for any humanitarian purpose, but with the aim of benefitting the government, of making the Jews into citizens who would be useful to the state. Like Frederick the Great, Joseph II regarded the Jews as useless and harmful.[9]

For the reeducation of the Jewish masses, the king established compulsory "normal schools" for Jewish children. No Jews, men or women, could receive permission to marry unless they had graduated from a normal school. The masses of Jews in the Galician cities and towns were ultraorthadox, fanatical Hasidim. For them "Enlightenment" was tantamount to heresy, a bridge to apostasy;

they saw the normal schools as no different from the old Houses of Conversion.

To supervise this reeducation of the Jews, the monarch appointed one of the Berlin *maskilim* named Herz Homberg. A bitter foe of the pious Jewish way of life, Homberg viewed it as a system of superstition which must be eradicated. His task was to open the normal schools in the Jewish towns. Appealing to the rabbis for help, he warned them that if they refused, he would report them to the authorities. Like most Jews, the rabbis immediately stamped him as an informer and a "destroyer of Israel."

Unconscious of the history which led the Jewish masses to cling so stubbornly to their traditional customs, Homberg accepted uncritically the approach of the enlightened ruler, an approach which consisted of truncating Jewish tradition suddenly and violently. Homberg opened approximately one hundred normal schools in the Jewish towns. He was short of teachers, and the number of children who enrolled was even smaller than the faculty. When he realized that the rabbis, rather than helping, were actively opposing him, he denounced them to the king in the following language:

> The Jews are infected with a tremendous national and religious arrogance which must be eradicated. . . . Very harmful for the Jews is the spiritual power of the rabbis. . . . They are to blame for the moral barbarism of the Jewish masses. . . . All the yeshivas must be closed. The Hebrew language is also superfluous; the Yiddish-German hodgepodge is a total disgrace and must be banned. . . ."[10]

Homberg also compiled a list of Jewish religious books which, in his opinion, were full of superstitions and "poisonous hatred of other peoples." All these books, he recommended, should be subjected to an auto-da-fé.

The Jews sent letters to the king denouncing Homberg as an "enemy of the Jews" and forced him to leave Lwow, the center of Jewish Galicia. A total failure, the normal schools were closed down in 1806. In Vienna, where Homberg settled, he wrote a textbook whose purpose was to "bring Jewish youth closer to German culture." He persuaded the authorities to make this book compulsory reading for Jewish youth. A decree was issued which provided that no Jews would be granted a marriage license unless and until they passed an examination on this book.

A measure of tolerance was granted by the new ruler, Francis II, to a very small number of Jews in Vienna and several larger cities; for the masses of Jews in Galicia, Hungary, Bohemia, and Moravia a whole series of new edicts went into effect. In Vienna a residence quota of one hundred Jewish families was in force. Upon payment of a special tax, Jewish merchants from abroad or from other Austrian cities could stay for two weeks to two months. In 1789 there were an estimated seventy-five hundred Jews in Vienna illegally, with the local guardians of the law often bribed to look the other way. To rid the city of these illegal residents, the government set up a special commission. The police took to harassing Jews in a variety of ways, including midnight raids on homes. Two generations of Austrian Jews went through this kind of persecution, which was not stopped until 1848.[11]

The wealthier Jews in Vienna did not have too many "privileges" either. In 1792–93 they submitted a petition to the government requesting the abolition of certain restrictive decrees. They asked for permission to build or buy homes in Vienna. They requested the abolition of the Jewish wedding tax and the regulation that a police inspector must be present at the ceremony. They asked that the bridegroom be permitted to recite his vows in Hebrew, not German. They asked that government notices sent to them be addressed to "Herr So-and-so," and not "The Jew So-and-so." The authorities irately rejected the petition.

The tolerated Jews also suffered from the general anti-Jewish restrictions. They could not deal in wheat, salt, or food products. Jewish physicians were not permitted to treat non-Jewish patients. It was not until 1811 that Jews won the privilege of building a school for children. Permission to construct a synagogue was not granted until much later.

In 1806, when Napoleon convened an assembly of Jewish deputies, and a bit later the Sanhedrin, in Paris, the ruling circles in Vienna became alarmed. Viewing it as a typical Napoleonic move to win the sympathy of Jews for the French and against Austria, they reinforced police surveillance in Vienna, Prague, and the larger cities in Galicia and Hungary to prevent the dissemination of pro-French propaganda among the Jews. After Napoleon's defeat and during the Congress of Vienna in 1815, all Jewish privileges were abolished in Austria and everywhere else in Europe.[12]

At the turn of the nineteenth century, the Jews of Bohemia and Moravia were as bereft of rights as they had been in the Middle Ages. The number of Jews in those countries was strictly controlled, with various laws against increasing their population. Restrictions on Jewish occupations were similar to those in Austria. Other restrictions stemmed from Herz Homberg's proposals on enlightening the Jews. Rabbis were required to complete courses in philosophy and ethics in an Austrian university, Jewish books had to be cleared by the censor, and so on. Military service was as oppressive here as it was in Austria. A request by Jews to substitute a recruit tax for military service was denied. Not many Jews served in the military; many hid from the police for years, living like criminals. Many newborn Jewish males simply were not registered by their parents.

At the beginning of the nineteenth century there were approximately a hundred thousand Jews in Hungary. Most of them eked out a living by petty trade and peddling. The Christian tradesmen did their utmost to make life unbearable for their Jewish competitors, and their pressure on the authorities eventually resulted in a heavy tax on Jewish peddlers.

In 1789 compulsory military service was ordered for Hungarian Jews, but the parliament decided the Jews had not yet earned the honor of serving in the Hungarian army. Instead, a steep recruit tax was imposed. During the period of the Napoleonic victories, the Jews in Hungary offered to serve in the armed forces if they were granted equal rights and if the persecution of Jewish tradesmen were stopped. The parliament granted several privileges and allowed Jews to serve in the military, but the laws against the peddlers were not repealed. The recruit tax was in force until 1848.

Jews in Prussia

King Frederick William the Great had permitted fifty wealthy Jewish refugee families from Vienna to settle in Berlin for a twenty-year period, which ended in 1688, the year that he died. His successor, Frederick I, extended the contract, which continued the previous ban on increasing the number of Jews in Berlin and other cities.

The harassment of Jews on the basis of charges by informants sometimes led to bizarre results. One informer accused the Jews of vilifying Jesus in the *aleynu* prayer, where worshippers were reportedly spitting at the mention of his name. At the same time, a Hebrew booklet called *Maaseh Toluy* ("*The Story of the Crucified*") that circulated among Jews was charged with slandering Mary. The king summoned the rabbis to swear that the charge was false. With regard to the *aleynu* prayer, he decreed that it be chanted aloud and that the congregation neither whisper nor spit while it was being çhanted even though such activities were really not a part of the recitation of the prayer.[13] A Christian overseer, paid for by the congregation, was assigned to the synagogue to watch for violations.

A new set of decrees was issued by Frederick II (1714–1770). The limit on Jewish families in Berlin was fixed at 120, with new residence privileges to be issued only in return for substantial payments. Only one marriage per Jewish family was permitted, but for 2,000 marks an exception would be made in the case of second and third members of the family. Despite these regulations, the number of Jewish families continued to increase. The census of 1728 showed 180 Jewish families in Berlin and more than 1,200 in other Prussian towns and cities. In 1730 the king ordered the number of Jews in Berlin decreased to 100 families, with the Jewish population in the provinces to remain the same. The Jews tried by every means to have these decrees annulled, but were unsuccessful. In 1737 the poorer Jewish families left Berlin.[14]

During the reign of William I of Prussia, and with his support, a work was re-published which has contributed significantly to Jew-hatred in Germany and throughout the world. In 1694, Johann Andreas Eisenmenger, a Protestant, had published his *Entdecktes Judentum* (*"Judiasm Exposed"*). In the forward he wrote:

> This book is a complete account of true facts showing how the Jews heinously insult, defame and denigrate the Christian trinity, how they degrade Christ's mother Mary, how they mock the New Testament of the Apostles. . . . It also contains facts about the corrupt Jewish faith and the strange and comical customs of their religion. Everything in this volume is proven from their own Jewish books.[15]

Eisenmenger was a teacher of Hebrew at Heidelberg University. In 1680, while he was living in Amsterdam, three Christians converted to Judaism. Apparently this disturbed him deeply. A student of Hebrew, he gained the trust of some Jewish scholars with a story that he was thinking of converting to Judaism and therefore wished to familiarize himself with Jewish theology. For nineteen years he studied the Talmud and Hebrew mythology and became well versed in Jewish law. In his researches he copied out every reference he found that could be interpreted as maligning Christianity or that put Judaism in a bad light. His *Entdecktes Judentum* was a compendium of all the passages he had collected. None of them were quoted in context, and in most cases he distorted or falsified even these isolated quotations.

Most of these passages were no longer even news in anti-Jewish circles, but what Eisenmenger did was to match up these half-truths with all the fabricated slanders that had been made against Jews during the Middle Ages. All the lies over which tens of thousands of Jews had been murdered were listed in his book as "facts." He "proved," for example, that according to Jewish law, a Jew sins when he saves the life of a Christian; that rabbinic literature is full of commands to kill and destroy Christians; that the only thing a Jewish doctor will do for a Christian patient is shorten his life; that Jews had poisoned wells in the fourteenth century and caused the Black Death. (The blood libel in Trent, over which almost all the Jews of that Italian city were killed, is described as an incontrovertible fact.)

The Jews of Frankfurt appealed to the banker, Oppenheim, an influential Jew in Austria, to urge the king to stop publication of Eisenmenger's book. Fortunately the book also contained a few anti-Catholic comments, and King Leopold, a devout Catholic, ordered the edition of two thousand copies sequestered. In 1704, Eisenmenger died. For the next forty years the two thousand volumes stayed under royal lock and key while his heirs moved heaven and earth to get them released or at least to get permission to print another edition. In 1740 Frederick II, on his own authority, granted permission for a second printing of *Entdecktes Judentum*.[16]

Two generations later, when the cry for Jewish emancipation went up in all the countries of Europe, Jew-haters made use of Eisenmenger's book to show why Jews should not be granted equal citizenship rights. Anti-Semites from the mid-nineteenth century down to the present have used Eisenmenger's "proof" to show why Jews are not worthy of sympathy.[17]

King Frederick II of Prussia, who authorized the reprinting of Eisenmenger's book, admitted that he hated Jews. Count Mirabeau, the French liberal, characterized the Jewish regulations of Frederick II as stemming from "a cannibalistic attitude toward Jews." According to these regulations, only a few selected wealthy Jews were "protected" Jews of the first category. An even smaller number were in the second category. A third category consisted of physicians and employees of the wealthy Jews. They had no privileges. To this category belonged the philosopher Moses Mendelssohn, who was assigned to a certain manufacturer as a bookkeeper.

In several cities in Prussia, Jews were confined to their ghettos as if they were prisoners, and for this right of "residence" they had to pay a special head tax. In addition, there were a protection tax, a recruit tax, a silver tax, a tax every three years for the community trustees, a fire-fighter tax, various stamp taxes, a wedding tax, a tax on remarriage after a divorce, and a tax for registering the birth of a child.

A particularly insidious and bizarre tax was the so-called porcelain tax which was imposed on the Jews of Prussia in 1769. At the marriage of the first son, the parents—in addition to the wedding tax—had to buy a complete set of porcelain dishes at an exorbitant price. This was true not only on the occasion of a marriage, but also when registering the birth of a child, buying or selling a house, recording a civil document. For all these things Jews were forced to buy a set of porcelain dishes. The porcelain factory, of course, belonged to the king. Since the individual Jewish family did not need all these dishes, the owner had a "right" to sell them abroad, but at a price less than half of what he had paid for them. The porcelain tax was not abolished until 1788, two years after Frederick II's death.

In 1742, after a war with Austria, Prussia annexed the region of Silesia, in which there were large Jewish communities, notably in Breslau. In 1744 Frederick decreed that only twelve Jewish families (the wealthiest ones) could remain in Breslau; the others were to be expelled. Jewish tradesmen and artisans throughout Silesia were severely restricted. Buying or building a home in any Prussian city was forbidden to even the wealthiest Jews.

At one point, a census revealed that in Berlin there were three hundred fifty Jewish families and in other Prussian cities more than two thousand. Although King Frederick received a great deal of revenue from these families, he ordered the number of Jews in Berlin and elsewhere sharply reduced. In Berlin, the marriages of second and third children in a family were no longer permitted. During the Seven Years' War from 1756 to 1763, in desperate need of funds, Frederick permitted the marriage of second and third children, but only upon payment of 70,000 marks.

Like Maria Theresa in Austria, King Frederick II also dreamed of reducing the number of Jews in his dominions. And again, it turned out precisely the opposite. In 1772, after the partition of Poland, Prussia annexed the province of Pomerania, with its city of Posen. Large and well-established Jewish communities existed not only in

Posen but in nearby towns. The king thereupon established a Pale of Settlement; wherever Jews lived at the time of the annexation, they could remain, but deeper into Prussia they could not go.

Germany then was comprised of three hundred small duchies. Communication between one political unit and another—especially for Jews—was very difficult. At each border of a duchy a Jew had to pay a tax equivalent to that for crossing a cow over that border. When the German Jewish philosopher Moses Mendelssohn, who was already internationally known, came to Dresden in 1776, he was stopped and required to pay the same tax as was due for bringing in a Polish ox.[18]

Jews in Dresden did not have the right to buy or build a home, but had to rent from Christians. They could not engage in any handicrafts, but were permitted to deal in old clothes, rags, or money. Close police surveillance was kept on Jews with residence permits to prevent them from hiding visiting Jews. The rulers of Prussia and the other German provinces made no attempt to conceal their hatred of Jews. They made it absolutely clear that they did not wish the number of Jews in their lands to increase since Jews were an "ugly and pernicious race."

There were other reasons for limiting Jewish rights. A ruler of the Baden government, for example, explained that, "With their abilities the Jews would soon become much better masters of the trades . . . and would out-compete our artisans. . . ."[19]

In Frankfurt, where a Jewish Quarter had been in existence for several centuries, the maximum number of families permitted was five hundred. The area of the ghetto was never enlarged. From time to time searches were conducted to count the number of residents. After the conflagration in 1711, when the Jewish Quarter was almost completely destroyed and Jews had to survive somehow in Christian barns and stables for several years, the city added a small area to the ghetto. Jews were permitted out of the ghetto only during the day and had to be back inside at sundown, when the gates were locked from the outside.

At the beginning of the seventeenth century there were very few Jews in the smaller German provinces, most cities having expelled the Jews during the Middle Ages and later. The new mercantilism, an expanding world trade, and emerging new industries forced the Protestant and Catholic rulers of the Germanic lands to overlook the strict laws and let the Jews return. In Saxony, for example, the Jews had been expelled "forever" during the first half of the sixteenth century. When the famous fairs were introduced into

Leipzig, Jewish merchants were permitted to take part, at first for several days only. The same process took place in Dresden.

After a few wealthy Jews received permission to settle permanently in Leipzig, a Jewish community gradually developed in both those cities. In 1705 the Dresden city council, suddenly realizing that there were fifteen Jewish families living in the city permanently, protested to the ruler of the province. However, he would not permit any of the Jews to be expelled. He prohibited them from building a synagogue and instructed them to keep their religious services in their homes quiet and unobtrusive. By the time of the Seven Years' War (1756–63), Dresden's Jewish community numbered almost a thousand. In 1777, when the Jew-haters in the city tried to expel the Jews, Moses Mendelssohn, who was friendly with one of the leading Christian merchants in the city, intervened and succeeded in having the decree withdrawn.[20] Not until the beginning of the nineteenth century, after the Napoleonic emancipation, were Jews officially permitted to reside in Dresden and build a synagogue. The same thing happened in other provinces from which Jews had been expelled "forever" a century earlier.

In the Protestant cities and provinces the anti-Jewish laws were enforced more strictly than in the Catholic towns. When Jews returned to those areas from Poland and the Ukraine, demands were raised that they be restricted. Times had changed, however. It was an era of enlightenment, and the request for anti-Jewish legislation was ignored.

Catholic Bavaria was no exception. In Stuttgart, capital of Baden province, there had been a substantial Jewish community at the beginning of the eighteenth century. In 1738, after a Court Jew named Suess was hanged on charges of embezzling, all the Jews of the city were expelled. Stuttgart was *Judenrein* until the beginning of the next century, when Jews all over western Europe were struggling for emancipation.

In 1781 Christian Wilhelm von Dohm, a German liberal, wrote a work defending civil rights for Jews in which he pointed out that the 200,000 Jews in Prussia and the other German states were being sorely oppressed. His account, cited by the historian Simon Dubnow, is worthy of note:

There are principalities where Jews are not permitted to live at all. Only travelers may stop there, if they pay for the privilege, and then usually for not longer than one night. In many other states a small

number of Jews is permitted to settle, but only in certain neighborhoods and at a very high price. In many places only Jews with a
certain amount of capital are permitted to settle. Large masses of
impoverished Jews stand outside the locked gates of our cities and are
driven from border to border. . . .

If a Jew has several sons he can transfer his right of residence—in the
land where they were born—only to one son. The other sons must be
sent away to other countries to live. If he has daughters, then it is a
matter of chance if they can find husbands among the few Jewish
families in the area. Therefore one rarely sees a Jewish head-of-family
who lives together with his children and grandchildren.

When a Jew finally does receive the right to live in a principality, he
must repurchase this same right every year for a substantial sum of
money. A Jewish young man cannot marry without special permission—which not everyone receives—and for this permission he
must, of course, pay. If a child is born, he brings with him another set
of taxes. No matter how much a Jew pays for various privileges, he is
still extremely restricted. A Jew cannot serve the state in either the
civil or military field. Almost nowhere is he permitted to own real
property. An artisans' guild would consider it dishonorable to accept
a Jew into membership. Jews are everywhere eliminated from various
occupations.

Only a small section of them—the most capable—have displayed the
hardihood to overcome all the persecutions and achieve higher levels
of learning and art. Even those few who are an honor to humanity are
not forgiven for the "crime of their Jewish origin." No matter what
talents they have, it is of little help to them.

The Jew who is not allowed to work, who is not allowed to develop his
abilities, has no other choice but to turn to trade. And even in trade he
is subject to edicts and a mountain of taxes. There are very few Jews
who own enough capital to open their own business. Most of them
must begin by engaging in petty trade—or lending out their money at
interest.[21]

As a consequence of Dohm's book, the subject of Jewish civil
rights was widely discussed. During the latter half of the eighteenth
century, in the upper circles of the European intelligentsia, a positive
attitude became apparent toward the degraded and the wronged.
Jewish emancipation was definitely on the agenda. It could not be
fulfilled, however, in the stifling atmosphere of monarchist Europe,
but became possible only after the revolutions in France and
America at the end of the eighteenth century.

18

Jews in France from the Expulsion to the Dreyfus Affair

After the great expulsion in 1394 France remained *Judenrein* for three centuries, but Jew-hatred in that country continued to deepen as the priests persisted in their preachments about the "crimes" of the Jews. From 1690 to 1720, the Abbé Fleury published a twenty-volume ecclesiastical history in which he repeated most of these "crimes" recorded in Church chronicles over a period of fifteen hundred years. Some of the material is presented in the form of a catechism:

Q. Did Jesus have enemies:
A. Certainly: the sinful Jews.
Q. How much did they hate Jesus?
A. Very much. They murdered him.
Q. Who betrayed him?
A. Judas Iscariot.
Q. Why was Jerusalem destroyed?
A. Because the Savior was murdered there.
Q. What happened to the Jews?
A. They were dispersed over the world and enslaved.
Q. What has happened to them since then?
A. They are still dispersed and enslaved.
Q. For how long?
A. For the last 1700 years and forever after.

A Church tract written in the fifteenth century gives this account of how the Jews treated Jesus:

They insulted him, slandered him. . . . They slapped his face . . . spit at him. . . . They beat him over the head with clubs, then placed a crown of thorns on his head, pushing the needles in until the blood ran down his face. . . . Pilate wanted to take him out and show him to the multitude, but the murderers screamed, "Take him away! Crucify him!"[1]

During the centuries when France was *Judenrein* there were some small colonies of Marranos mostly in the south in Rouen, Nantes, Bordeaux and a few other cities. Their Christian neighbors called them "Portuguese" because they had come to France from Portugal, having escaped the claws of the Inquisition which, in the sixteenth century, was burning Marranos at the stake.

The religious wars in France between the Catholics and the Huguenots were extremely bloody. In one twenty-four-hour period—the infamous Saint Bartholomew's Day massacre of 24 August 1572—the Catholics murdered 30,000 men, women, and children. It has been estimated that close to a hundred thousand Huguenots were killed over a forty-day period as the Catholic priests accused the Huguenots of being Jewish heretics and disguised Jews.

While France officially had no Jewish population during that time, a small number of Jews did manage to survive there. Aside from Jewish physicians who were invited by rulers, some Jewish merchants came into the port cities on business for specified periods. A small number of Jews stole into the country and stayed illegally with the help of a few bribes in the right places. In Bordeaux the Portuguese Marranos gradually began to return to the practice of Judaism.

In 1615 an expulsion of Jews was decreed, with violations punishable by death and confiscation of property. It is not known how many people left at that time, but no further expulsions took place from France. Jews began to return in small numbers. In the reign of Louis XIV (1643–1715) Jewish communities existed in several cities. When the French Revolution broke out in 1789 there were probably no more than ten thousand Jews in all of France.

In Avignon, during the eighteenth century, Jews were required to attend church services once a week and listen to slanderous sermons against Judaism. These sermons produced no converts to Christianity, but the missionaries there had other, more effective, means of doing that. They could baptize Jewish children against their will and not return them to the parents unless they too converted. It was enough for a Christian neighbor or a convert to inform the Church that this or that Jewish child "wished to be converted" and the child would be dragged to the baptismal font.[2] Jews began leaving Avignon and settling in other areas of France. In Provence the Jews at first settled as Christian Marranos, until they felt it safe to reveal their identity. Late in the seventeenth century denunciations were sent to Paris charging that Marranos in Marseilles were worshipping as Jews and circumcising their male children. In 1682 an order came from Paris expelling all the Jews from Provence.

Early in the eighteenth century the Marranos in Avignon began to discard their Christian guise and observe the Jewish way of life. Gradually German Jews from Alsace added to their number. In 1722, after denunciations to the authorities, a decree was issued in Paris confiscating the property of the "Portuguese" for the benefit of the royal treasury. The Jews proffered a gift of 100,000 livres and the decree was withdrawn.

Several years later came another expulsion decree. The "Portuguese," who considered themselves superior to the German Jews, appealed to the Crown, maintaining that they were valuable to the country. Their appeal, accompanied by a sizable gift, was granted. The poorer Alsatian Jews were expelled from Bordeaux and the entire province.[3]

In Paris itself, from which Jews had been barred for several centuries, there were about eight hundred Jews in 1789, most of them merchants and recent immigrants. In southern France— Bordeaux, Marseilles, Breton and a few other cities—the Jews were descendants of the Portuguese Marranos, mostly culturally assimilated.

To the north, Jews were settled in Alsace, which was part German, and in the city of Metz in Lorraine. Strasbourg, capital of Alsace, had banished Jews in the mid-fourteenth century, when almost two thousand Jews there were killed on the charge of poisoning the wells. Alsace was annexed by France from Austria in 1648, after the Thirty Years' War. Strasbourg was taken in 1681, during the reign of Louis XIV. With Alsace came several thousand Jews. The government responded to the "Jewish problem" by setting up a Pale of Settlement where Jews were permitted to reside as "tolerated" taxpayers.[4]

As is well known in the history of France, the decadent royal court was fast draining the resources of the country. The Jews of Alsace, most of them poor, were taxed to the bone and severely limited in the occupations they could pursue. The Alsatian governor, a Jew-baiter, accused the Jews of cheating Christian debtors, and recommended to the government that all the Jews be expelled from the province. The Jews appealed to Moses Mendelssohn for help. In turn, Mendelssohn asked his friend Wilhelm von Dohm to write to the king, which he did.[5] The king ordered an investigation and the lie was exposed. The governor was dismissed and the Jews were permitted to remain in Alsace. By the eve of the Revolution, the Jewish population in Alsace had grown to thirty thousand.

Strasbourg was still *Judenrein.* In Metz the Jews paid for the right of domicile, with their total number closely regulated. In 1718, for example, their number was 480 families, restricted to a ghetto. In addition to the general taxes, they were required to support various church institutions. In Nancy the number of Jews permitted was 180 families. The local police would frequently raid the ghetto and deport any Jews above that number.

Various regulations were adopted to decrease the number of Jews in Alsace. Marriages were forbidden among Jews without special permission and the presence of a government inspector. Violation of this law was punishable by confiscation of property and expulsion.

In Paris only the leading Jewish merchants were permitted to reside. These were mostly from among the Portuguese, with a few scattered German Jewish families. At the beginning of the Revolution there were about one hundred fifty Jewish families in the city, totaling about a thousand people.

Early in the eighteenth century, with the ideas of the Enlightenment in the ascendancy, French philosophers were doing battle with various kinds of injustice. None of them strove as mightily against religious fanaticism as did Voltaire. Yet even Voltaire believed that the Jewish Bible was responsible for the religious stagnation of the Middle Ages. Diderot, Holbach, and other philosophers also maintained that the Jews, because of their religion, could never become enlightened and equal participants in a free human society. The Jews, they asserted, could never become complete human beings until they ceased to be Jews. This negative image of the Jew coincided closely with the views which the Church had been espousing for centuries.

When the delegates of the French provinces met on 5 May 1789 in Paris to participate in the *Etats-Généraux,* there were no Jews among them, since Jews were not entitled to representation. (In the National Guard, which stormed the Bastille on 14 July, there were several Jewish volunteers, who were given a friendly reception.) From all over France came petitions and proposals to the National Assembly. The petitions from the Jews requested an end to anti-Jewish decrees. Conversely, many petitions from the Alsatian Christians requested a return to the anti-Jewish laws of the Middle Ages. From Strasbourg came a petition to maintain the anti-Jewish prohibitions which had been in effect there since the days of the Black Death.[6]

At the time the Bastille was being stormed, peasant uprisings were taking place against the nobility in Alsace. In the process, Jewish homes were pillaged and burned. More than a thousand Jews ran for their lives to the Swiss city of Basel. In the National Assembly protests were raised against these pogroms. Most of the delegates responded sympathetically to the speakers who demanded humane treatment for the persecuted Jews. In the first month of the Revolution, the Assembly began its debates on the "Jewish problem." Two opposing sides gradually crystallized. The reactionaries used all sorts of political tricks to further their cause. On the liberal side were several leaders of the Revolution, who fought untiringly for equal rights for the Jews of France. Such were the Catholic priest Abbé Grégoire, the statesman Mirabeau, the Protestant minister Saint-Étienne, Clermont Tonner, and several others. Later they were joined by members of the Third Estate, such as Robespierre. The liberals were predictably apologetic in their arguments. "Give the Jews freedom of worship," Saint-Étienne told the Assembly, "and they will become more human."[7]

On 14 October the Assembly heard a representative of the Alsatian Jewish community appeal for equal rights. When the President promised the Jews safety and equality, there was prolonged applause in the chamber. However, the actual granting of equal rights was postponed again and again. On 21 December 1789 the Assembly debated the issue of active rights of citizens, that is, who was eligible to vote and run for office. When the liberal deputy Clermont Tonner expressed the opinion that Jews who obey the law should be considered active citizens, there was an uproar in the chamber and the meeting was adjourned.

A separate appeal was sent to Abbé Grégoire by the Portuguese Jews asserting that they were better than the Jews from Alsace; in fact, they were virtually Frenchmen, and to lump them together with the poor Jews from Alsace was wrong. The others did not even want civil rights; all they wanted was to maintain their community rights.

The Portuguese requested that they be considered separately, therefore, and granted equal rights. Their demand was approved. On 28 January 1790 the National Assembly granted them equal civil rights, and the matter of equal rights for the Jews of Alsace was tabled.

To the Revolutionary Administration in Paris (the Paris Commune) came Jewish volunteers in the National Guard requesting that it urge the National Assembly to grant full civil rights to all Jews immediately. The Paris Commune was now playing an increasingly important role in pushing the Assembly further to the Left. The struggle for Jewish emancipation undertaken by the Paris Commune broke the resistance of the anti-Jewish forces. After several more debates and postponements, the National Assembly on 27 September 1791 voted full civil rights to the Jews of France. The resolution was signed by the king on 15 November 1791.[8]

After many centuries of rightlessness, the Jews of France had attained equal citizenship in the law. In practice, Jew-hatred did not dry up and blow away. Among the Jews the Declaration was greeted enthusiastically. The Alsatian Jewish representative who had made the plea for emancipation delivered an address to the Assembly in which he expressed thanks to the Almighty and to the governing body of the people for its beneficence, "so that now we Jews are recognized as citizens and Frenchmen." Indeed, the French Jews did become fierce patriots of their country. Many threw themselves body and soul into political life. They regarded the Jew-hatred among their neighbors as a sickness which would eventually be cured and disappear.

In the days of the revolutionary "Committees of Public Safety" (1793–94), when terror ruled France, and when the new "Religion of Reason" took the place of the old "foolish religion," some Jews must have been heartbroken as they watched sacred commandments being broken, holy texts ripped apart, traditions defiled—and much of this being done by Jews themselves. Many Jews probably baked matzos and conducted their seders in secret, as the Marranos had done in Spain and Portugal.

The hardwon civic freedoms resounded across the borders of France into neighboring lands. With the victory of the French armies in the German provinces and in areas of Switzerland and the Netherlands, Jews in those countries began to migrate to France. In 1806, fifteen years after the granting of equal rights, the number of Jews in Paris tripled from one to three thousand. In Strasbourg, which was completely free of Jews up to 1789, a large Jewish community developed. In all of France the number of Jews rose to approximately 135,000.[9]

Coming into the French cities during those turbulent times, unhindered by the Church or by anti-Jewish political rulers, young Jews soon began to assimilate. The environment was not completely free of Jew-hatred, however. In 1806, Isaac Berr, Alsatian fighter for emancipation, wrote to Abbé Grégoire:

> Yes, certainly they granted us equal rights at that time. But those rights remained only on paper. The hatred toward us did not vanish when Emancipation arrived. The guilds still do not allow a Jew access to any craft. . . . They are still insulting us, they are still mocking us, just as they did before.[10]

Napoleon Bonaparte, who became absolute ruler over France, was not too staunch a friend of the Jews. Viewing the Jews with suspicion, he began to find fault with them. The continuing wars had destroyed a large portion of France's resources. There was a scarcity of the necessities of life. Popular discontent was rampant. The French anti-Semites did what enemies of the Jews had done on many occasions before—they blamed the Jews for all the country's ills. Returning from his great victory over Austria and Germany in 1806, Napoleon spent some time in Strasbourg, with its rabid anti-Semites, and as soon as he returned to Paris he ordered the Jewish problem placed on the agenda of various government councils.

At the first session of the National Assembly, the reactionary Count Louis-Mathieu Môle delivered a report on the Jewish problem and proposed that "exceptional" laws be applied to the Jews. Most members of the Assembly protested. At a second session, which Napoleon attended, a liberal member replied to Môle, stating that exceptional laws against the Jews would be tantamount to a battle lost on the field of justice. He was applauded by most of the delegates present, but not by Napoleon, who delivered a strongly anti-Jewish speech, listing all the slanders he had heard in Strasbourg.

> We cannot remain indifferent when members of a nation that was oppressed for so many centuries take over two important Districts in Alsace. With these people you cannot employ civil principles. They must be treated politically. We can not permit the Jews to take real property as security for loans. They have taken possession of entire villages.[11]

Napoleon, convinced that the Jews needed to be reformed, decided to call together an Assembly of Jewish Notables (the "better" Jews) and listen to whatever proposals they themselves would make. On 30 May 1806 he issued two decrees: (1) To declare a moratorium of one year on all Jewish judgments for debt; (2) To convene an assembly on 15 July 1806 of prominent Jews who lived in France or in the lands ruled by France. One hundred Jews must attend. He wished to ask them certain questions and get their replies.

When the Jews of France and the occupied countries heard that the emperor, their liberator, was convening a Jewish assembly, they were overjoyed and full of hope. The representatives who came to Paris were not actually chosen by their fellow Jews; most of them were appointed by the prefects of the districts. A total of 112 religious and lay leaders attended this Jewish assembly. Napoleon appointed three members of the French governing council to conduct the meeting. For some reason (perhaps deliberate) they chose to open the proceedings on a Sabbath, the twenty-ninth of June. The Jews conferred: Should they request a postponement of the opening session? The mood was: Jews must show the government that they were ready to obey the rules. The decision was to do as they had been asked.

The first speech on the program, explaining the nature of the meeting and what the emperor expected of the Jews, was delivered by the same Count Môle who, a few months earlier, had advised the National Assembly to adopt exceptional laws against the Jews. He reminded his audience that they were Frenchmen. "His Majesty the Emperor requires of you that you remain Frenchmen. . . . It is up to you whether you keep or lose the right to call yourselves Frenchmen. If you are not worthy of it, you will lose that right. . . ."[12] After this warning the count intoned a list of twelve questions which the emperor had prepared and to which he wanted answers. Several of the questions were "delicate": What is the relationship of Jewish laws to the laws of the kingdom? How far does Jewish patriotism go? What is the attitude of Jews to their non-Jewish neighbors? Did the Jews strictly forbid mixed marriages? Could a Jew lend money at interest only to a non-Jew?

After listening to the opening address and the list of questions, the mood of the Jews at the meeting must have plummeted. If they did not answer the way the emperor wished them to, they would no longer be considered Frenchmen. Some of the questions dealt with fundamental and difficult issues of concern to Jewish survival.

There were no easy answers, especially when the asker is a ruler who apparently has something in mind that bodes the Jews ill.

Several of the leading delegates (the "good Jews") kept close tabs on their fellow delegates; the devout Jews here were capable of acting rebelliously and ruining them all.

Finally the "Notables" formulated compromise answers to Napoleon's questions. As to whether a divorce is valid without the sanction of the secular court, they replied that a religious divorce by a rabbi becomes valid only when confirmed by the court of the land. Regarding mixed marriages they replied that such marriages are recognized by Jews as civil, not religious marriages, and that the Catholic Church also recognizes such marriages but does not sanctify them. In all such matters the Jewish religion always places the government above Jewish religious law.

Concerning the patriotic questions, there were no doubts or ambiguities. During the reading of the questions, when Môle asked whether the Jews considered France their home and whether they were ready to defend it, the delegates arose and responded as one: "Yes! Unto death!"

Apparently satisfied with the replies, Napoleon decided to give them the sanction of an authoritative body. The title he chose for that body was "Sanhedrin," after the ancient court which had created Jewish law during the time of the Second Commonwealth. At a meeting of the Jewish assembly on 17 September, it was announced that Napoleon would convene a Sanhedrin of seventy-one Jewish scholars to discuss and decide upon new Jewish laws, and that these laws would be as binding as the laws of the Talmud.

The assembly prepared an agenda for the Sanhedrin and early in October 1806 a call went out to the Jews of Europe to select delegates to the new Sanhedrin in Paris. The effect on the Jews of the Diaspora was electrifying. The title Sanhedrin itself, plus the fact that it was being called by the emperor, the "Liberator," uplifted the spirits of Jews wherever the call was read. The Sanhedrin was opened on 19 February 1807, with seventy-one delegates present, including forty-five rabbis from France, Alsace, the German provinces, and Italy. In addition, there were twenty-six Jewish laymen who had conducted the Jewish assembly a year before.

The sessions were public and lasted a full month. Several of the delegates, acting as a sort of plenum, then followed up the work, but it was no longer of any importance. The whole business of the Sanhedrin, as soon as the initial ceremonies were over, lost all significance. There was no authoritative body to carry out the "laws" that had been adopted.

At the end of the moratorium year on Jewish debts, it was extended indefinitely on Napoleon's order. Jewish creditors began to protest. When the emperor heard about the protests, he issued a decree stipulating that a debt on which a Jewish lender had taken interest in advance—even if only for the first week or month—was to be cancelled forthwith. Christian moneylenders who practiced the same system were not affected by this decree.

Napoleon's next decree prohibited Jewish merchants from doing business without a license, which they had to obtain from the city authorities. To get such a license, the merchant had to supply proof of his honesty and good conduct. Christian merchants needed no such license. The only way a Jew could get such permission was by bribing some official, as had been the practice before the Revolution.[13]

Napoleon also prohibited newly arriving Jews from settling in the regions of the upper and lower Rhine, on the pretext that the Germans there had demanded of him that he not "flood" their area with Jews. He also prohibited Jewish conscripts from providing substitutes, as everyone else in the country had a right to do. All these prejudicial regulations were supposed to be enforced only in districts where Christian citizens were complaining about their Jewish neighbors.

Jewish protests came from many districts. From Paris, for example, the authorities reported to the emperor that out of almost three thousand Jews in the city, only four were moneylenders, and about one hundred sixty were soldiers in the French army. The Jews were asking: "Why are we being punished with these anti-Jewish decrees?"

Napoleon's edicts were to go into effect in sixty-eight districts with Jewish populations. In twenty-four of these, the decrees were gradually lifted. In forty-four districts in France, Germany, and Italy, the Jews were to be penalized. Several years later, after Napoleon's defeat, the decree was withdrawn in the rest of the districts. Ironically, to the previous regime fell the task of reinstituting the old Jewish rights which Napoleon, the defender of the French Revolution, had abolished.

After Napoleon, in the France that was left within its former borders, there were between fifty and sixty thousand Jews, most of them in Alsace. The reactionary restoration which followed in

Europe in 1814 did not abolish equal rights for Jews in France. The Jews of Alsace remained without civil rights, which had been taken away from them by Napoleon. His decree had fixed a period of ten years in which the Jews of Alsace were to become "honorable." In 1818, at the end of this period, strong agitation against Jewish emancipation began in France, particularly in Alsace. However, the French parliament, by a large majority, adopted legislation granting the Jews full civil rights.

As an urban element, the Jews in France participated in the commercial and industrial awakening then taking place; they engaged in the professions, became manufacturers, or government officials, and were to be found in both the army and intellectual circles. With increased assimilation into French society, conversion among French Jews was common. Characteristic is a request from a subscriber to a French-Jewish newspaper, *Archives Israélites*, that his copy of the paper be sent to him in a wrapper, so that the superintendent of his building would not know he was Jewish. The wife of the communal leader Cremieux, without his knowledge, converted their two children to Catholicism.[14]

The Dreyfus Affair

In 1870, with the Jewish community of Alsace-Lorraine now under German rule, there remained in France approximately a hundred thousand Jews, spread out among the most important cities in the country, the majority being in Paris. Jew-hatred, which had diminished after the Revolution, was on the rise at the end of the century. In addition to the anti-Semitic influences coming from Germany, there were internal factors in France which brought this about.

The Third French Republic, established in 1871, had restricted the privileges of the Church. Among the liberals in the government who voted against the Church were several prominent Jews. Having some scores to settle, the Church intensified its anti-Jewish agitation. In addition, the defeat which their country had suffered at the hands of the Prussians in 1870 still rankled the French. The French historian Hippolyte-Adolphe Taine, for example, suggested that the Republicans were not even Frenchmen or Catholics.[15] A close alliance developed among the Monarchists, the aristocracy, and the Catholic hierarchy. They directed their efforts against democracy, the liberals, the *sansculottes*, and the "foreigners" (that is, the Jews).

Aside from all the other causes of anti-Semitism in France, there was still the need for a scapegoat on whom to blame the failures of government, the poverty of the people, and whatever else was wrong, including the military defeat of 1870. The growth of modern anti-Semitism in Germany in the last third of the nineteenth century was easily transported to France, where the successful banking house of Rothschild was known to everyone. When the bank of the Catholic monarchists, *Union Générale*, became entangled in speculations and went bankrupt, the blame was placed on the Rothschilds.[16]

Jew-hatred was equally prevalent in leftwing circles in France. Early in the century the noted Utopian, Charles Fourier, had agitated against the Jews who were, as he termed them, "swindlers and thieves." The words "Jew . . . merchant . . . swindler," he said, were synonymous. Jews were people without conscience, he insisted—moneylenders, parasites, criminals. All Jews are merchants and all merchants are swindlers; and Jews become merchants precisely for the reason that they are swindlers.[17]

Fourier's disciple, Tousinel, published a work in the 1840s with the title, *Les Juifs rois d'époque* (*"Epoch of Jewish Domination"*), which is replete with the age-old anti-Semitic slanders.[18] The most rabid anti-Semite in France at that time, Edouard Drumont, in 1886 published his book, *La France Juive*, in which he announced that the Jews had occupied France back in the Middle Ages, and that ever since then the French nation had been struggling to liberate itself. He even ascribed the Revolutionary Terror to the Jews. The Revolution of 1789, which granted the Jews civil rights, was the source of all of France's troubles. The Jews, he asserted, had been ruling France since then with the help of Rothschild's millions.

Drumont's book was reprinted in many editions before the end of the century. In France itself more than 100,000 copies were in circulation. Translated into German, tens of thousands of copies were distributed in Germany and Austria. Influenced by Drumont's book, a National League of Anti-Semites was organized in France. In 1892, *La Libre Parole* (*"The Free Word"*), began publication in Paris under Drumont's editorship. As late as 1891, several anti-Semitic deputies in the French Chamber introduced legislation to expel the Jews from France.[19]

At the end of 1889, a company which had been formed to build the Panama Canal went bankrupt. Almost half a million people lost their money. A great uproar went up in France. Among those accused in the scandal were a number of Jews. And louder than all the protesting voices was Drumont's *La Libre Parole*, which placed all the blame for the bankruptcy on "the Jews" who had swindled honest Frenchmen. After a few days, however, the agitation suddenly stopped. It had turned out that several important figures in the anti-Semitic campaign were the real guilty parties in the bankruptcy.[20]

In 1894 the anti-Semites in France got the opportunity they had been seeking. Under the influence of the propaganda of Drumont and others like him, the Dreyfus affair was conceived and utilized to inflame French public opinion. Ever since the defeat in 1870, a revanchist mood against Germany had been growing in France, accompanied by a spy phobia. In September 1894 a French counter-espionage agent stole from the German embassy in Paris a document which a high French military officer, spying for Germany, had delivered there. The existence of such a document was a political scandal of the first magnitude. Inspired by the prevalent "Jews are spies" mood, an investigative committee checked for similarities of the document's handwriting with that of a Jewish captain in the French army named Alfred Dreyfus. Handwriting experts detected no similarity, but the French General Staff charged Dreyfus with espionage.

Captain Alfred Dreyfus had achieved a high rank in the army by virtue of his ability and devotion to the country. The moment suspicion fell on him of being a German spy, the anti-Semites in and out of Drumont's newspaper accepted it as proven fact. Agitation against the "Jew Dreyfus" began in the shrillest possible tones. The military court did not dare entertain the slightest doubt of Dreyfus's guilt, although there was no evidence to prove it.

During the court-martial the judges were handed another secret document which allegedly eliminated every doubt of Dreyfus's involvement. The decision of the judges was unanimous: guilty. Sentenced to twenty years' imprisonment, Dreyfus was publicly degraded in a Paris park while thousands of enraged French citizens outside the iron fence screamed "Death to the Jews!"[21] Dreyfus continued to insist he was innocent, but nobody listened any longer. The "spy" was sent to Devil's Island in French Guiana to expiate his guilt.

Among the officers on the French General Staff was a lieutenant colonel Henri Picquart, who in 1896 was appointed head of the Bureau of Army Intelligence. An honest man, he decided to look into the Dreyfus affair himself. Examining the documents, he noticed a forgery in the "secret paper" which had convinced the military court of Dreyfus's guilt. Continuing his investigation, Picquart grew more certain that there was no real evidence to prove Dreyfus guilty. He also managed to intercept a suspicious communication from the German ambassador to a certain Major Esterhazy. He proved to his own satisfaction that the handwriting on the espionage document was quite similar to that of Major Esterhazy.

Picquart revealed his discoveries to his assistant, Lieutenant Colonel Henri, who happened to be a close friend of Esterhazy, and who, unknown to Picquart, had provided the secret document to the court. Soon afterward an order came down from the General Staff transferring Picquart to a post on a remote island. To close friends he communicated his secret: there was no real evidence of Dreyfus's guilt, but there was evidence against the prominent and influential Major Esterhazy.

Eventually this secret information reached the French public, and a well-known Jewish journalist, Bernard Lazare, wrote a pamphlet proving the captain's innocence. At the same time, details of Picquart's discoveries were made known to the Chamber of Deputies, which began a debate on the Dreyfus affair. Esterhazy was tried in open military court which, to uphold the unassailability of the French army, cleared him of the charge.

In the Chamber, in the press, and throughout French society, a bitter struggle went on between the Dreyfusards (those who considered him innocent) and the anti-Semites who insisted it was unthinkable to reopen his case. On 13 January 1898 the novelist Émile Zola released his now famous letter to the press, "J'accuse," in which he laid bare the corruption of the French General Staff. The letter had a tremendous effect in France and throughout the world.[22] For this grave "insult" to the honor of the French army, Zola was sentenced to a year in prison, but he escaped to England and from there continued to hammer away at the real criminals. The entire War Ministry was involved in the scandal, he charged.

Meanwhile, Colonel Picquart wrote letters to the premier offering to prove that the espionage document was written not by Dreyfus but by someone else, and that the same was true of the so-called secret document. This time Picquart was arrested. But at this point something happened which broke the back of the anti-Dreyfus forces. Lieutenant Colonel Henri, who had supplied the document, admitted to his superior that he had forged it in order to protect the honor of the army. Arrested, he committed suicide. Major Ester-hazy fled to Austria.[23]

When they realized the game was up, the anti-Semites organized demonstrations against Zola and began a frenzied agitation which led to physical attacks upon Jews. In the elections to the French parliament in 1898 they demanded of candidates that they prevent a review of the Dreyfus case. But after Henri's suicide and Esterhazy's flight, the government had no choice but to order a retrial. In September 1899, Dreyfus was brought back from Devil's Island for a new trial. The judges, although they were persuaded of his innocence, were so terrorized by the existent anti-Jewish furor, that they issued a very peculiar decision: "Dreyfus is guilty. Under the circumstances, however, we cannot sentence him to twenty years, but only to ten, to be served not at Devil's Island but in a prison." In the next breath the court appealed to the president of France to pardon Captain Dreyfus.[24] Against the advice of his family and his lawyers, Dreyfus accepted the pardon.

The furor, however, did not subside with his release. In 1903, Socialist Deputy Zhores reported to the Chamber that new forgeries by the General Staff had been uncovered. The new Minister of War agreed to another investigation of the Dreyfus affair. This investigation took two years, and in 1906 a court completely cleared Dreyfus of any guilt.

Reverberations of the Dreyfus case were felt also by the Jews in Algeria, which had been conquered by France in 1830. At the urging of the *Alliance Israélite* in Paris the French government had declared the Jews in Algeria to be French citizens. The anti-Jewish propaganda which was spread in Algeria found fertile ground. From Paris came Edouard Drumont himself. During the Dreyfus affair, anti-Semitic groups were organized and Jew-baiting material was widely distributed. In the larger cities, Jews were the victims of violence. In these anti-Jewish activities, French, Italian, Arab, and Spanish inhabitants of Algeria joined together to vandalize Jewish homes, stores, and synagogues.

19

Jews in the Smaller Centers up to the End of the Nineteenth Century

Spain and Portugal. After some 200,000 Jews were expelled from Spain in 1492, an equal number of baptized Jews still remained, most of them Crypto-Jews or Marranos, thousands of whom were burned later by the Inquisition. Tens of thousands fled the country. Several centuries later there were still tens of thousands of Marranos in Spain, descendants of the original converts. One Marrano who escaped to Amsterdam gave this account of the secret Jews in Spain and Portugal:

> In these countries the monasteries and convents are full of Marranos. Many priests, Inquisitors and bishops are descended from Jews. Many still carry their Jewish origin in their hearts, while publicly they wear the mask of Christianity for the sake of worldly wellbeing. . . . Here in Amsterdam and other cities there are former monks, Franciscans, Dominicans, who have rejected idolatry. . . . In Spain there are still bishops and priests whose parents, brothers and other family members migrated to Holland in order to be Jews openly.[1]

The auto-da-fé became part of the national culture of Spain, just as the gladiatorial contests did in ancient Rome. King Charles II of Spain (1680–1700), a mentally unbalanced individual, organized a "spectacular" mass auto-da-fé in Madrid to entertain the guests at his wedding. For these "games," eighty-six condemned heretics were brought to Madrid straight from the Inquisition's dungeons in

Toledo, Seville, and other places. In the main square of the city a platform was constructed for the guests, with a special amphitheater for the royal family. On the day of the wedding the condemned were led out to the square, barefoot and wearing "penitential" shirts and paper hats decorated with representations of the devil. In their hands they carried burning candles. Priests carried crucifixes and pictures of condemned Marranos who had fled Spain. The king was given the honor of lighting the fire as he swore an oath to continue his loyal cooperation with the Inquisition. Sixteen victims were burned that day. Each time a new one was set ablaze the multitude cheered.[2]

When the French Bourbons took over the Spanish throne, the Marranos expected the Inquisition to be abolished, as it had been in France. Some of the Marranos who let their guard down soon discovered their mistake. In Madrid at that time a concealed synagogue was discovered with a congregation of twenty families and their own rabbi. From 1720 to 1730 at least one hundred autos-da-fé were conducted in various Spanish cities; several hundred Marranos were burned to death, many others managed to escape from the country. In the second half of the eighteenth century the new spirit of enlightenment penetrated the Iberian Peninsula, but the fires of the Inquisition were not extinguished until 1820.

Holland. Up to around 1650 the Jewish community in Holland consisted almost entirely of former Marranos from Spain who had returned to the faith of their ancestors. In the mid-seventeenth century Jewish refugees from the Ukraine, Poland, Austria, and Bohemia streamed into Holland. Dutch merchants visited Spain and Portugal to transact business. Suspicious that some of these people were former "Jewish Christians," the Inquisition spied upon them. Several former Marranos did in fact fall into the trap of the Inquisition, as spies were sent into Amsterdam. The Inquisition also intercepted personal correspondence between former Marranos in Holland and their old friends and family who had stayed behind in Spain and Portugal, and the insatiable fires of the auto-da-fé were kept ablaze.

As the number of Jews increased in Holland, Christian merchants began demanding government restrictions on Jewish trading privileges. In 1632 the Amsterdam city council abrogated the right of Jews to join commercial and craft guilds.[3]

When Holland was proclaimed as the Batavian Republic in 1795, the Jews were emancipated as individuals, but not as a national group. As in France, anti-Jewish hostility did not disappear with the granting of equal rights. In one respect, however, the history of the Jewish community in Holland was different, for after Napoleon's defeat in 1815, the rights of the Jews were not revoked. Not many Jews came to settle in Holland during the nineteenth century. Emigration from Germany, Russia, Rumania, and Galicia went mostly to America. The largest Jewish community in Holland developed in Amsterdam. In 1881 there were 82,000 Jews in Holland; in 1900, 104,000.[4] Anti-Jewish prejudices in that country remained minimal; the Dutch were influenced very little by the "modern anti-Semitism" which swept up most European countries in the late nineteenth century.

England. England became a republic in 1649. Oliver Cromwell, leading spirit of the revolution in that country, was tolerant of other beliefs and willing to annul the law of 1290 which prohibited Jewish immigration into England. Parliament, however, was not ready for that drastic step. Marranos, who had been settling in England as Christians for almost a century, virtually discarded their public masks during the period of the upheaval and were permitted to live as Jews in London and other cities.

In the second half of the seventeenth century the Jewish communities in England were augmented by other Marranos from Spain and Portugal. Gradually, Jewish merchants from Germany also began to settle in England. With the growth of the Jewish communities came Christian petitions to the Crown to stop any further immigration into England and to restrict the rights of Jews already living there.

In 1673, on the basis of strict Anglican Church laws and the agitation by Christian merchants, the leaders of the Jewish communities were charged with having adopted another religion without permission of the Church. The Jews responded that if they were not permitted to worship God as they chose, they would prefer to leave the country. The government then decreed that the charges be withdrawn and that the Jews must be allowed to live in peace.[5]

During the late seventeenth century more Jews came to settle in England and again the Christian guilds protested. In 1677 all Jewish immigration was stopped. Jews could not buy land or houses because of an oath which required the purchaser to say, "I swear by my faith as a Christian. . . ." Jews were not citizens in England. Even those who were born in the country were taxed as aliens. A number of British intellectuals—Locke, Pelham, Toland—argued for Jewish emancipation, and in 1753 a law was adopted by both Houses of Parliament naturalizing the Jews of England. Riots erupted all over the country. Insults were hurled at members of Parliament. In November of the same year, the law was abrogated.[6]

When the nineteenth century began there were approximately 30,000 Jews in all of England, most of them in business or the professions. A wave of conversions developed as the only way open for them to the upper levels of English society. As Jews they enjoyed equal rights in all respects except those of voting and running for public office.

In 1829 Parliament emancipated the Catholics in England. Supported by several leading Christian liberals, the Jews raised a demand for full emancipation. Tens of thousands of signatures were collected on petitions to change the election oath so as to include Jews as voters or candidates. On a number of occasions the House of Commons adopted resolutions changing the form of the oath, but these were struck down by the House of Lords. Finally, in 1866, both Houses adopted legislation changing the oath so as to exclude no Catholics, atheists, or Jews.

By the early 1870s there were 63,000 Jews in England. At the end of the century, Great Britain was influenced by the rampant anti-Semitism in France and other European countries. Several times Prime Minister Gladstone expressed unmistakable anti-Jewish sentiments, going so far as to question the loyalty of the Jews to England.[7] In 1881–83 the historian Goldwyn Smith published anti-Jewish articles in leading British journals. However, no government in Europe permitted such sharp protests against the Russian pogroms and the Dreyfus affair as did the British. When Adolph Stöcker, leader of the German anti-Semites, came to London in 1883 to deliver an address on the occasion of Luther's quarter-centenary, the Lord Mayor refused to permit him to speak.

In that same decade many Jews came to England as refugees from the pogroms and persecution in Russia, Galicia, and Rumania. Most of them planned to go on to America, but lack of funds kept them "temporarily" in London. Thus a sizable Jewish community grew up in Whitechapel, the poor district of the city. In 1881 there were 65,000 Jews in England; by the end of the century the number had risen to 200,000.[8]

Belgium. The archives reveal a decree expelling the Jews from Brussels, Louvain, and nearby towns as early as 1261. Some of the

Jews expelled from France in 1306 settled in Belgium; three years later most of them were killed during a local crusade. In 1311 a small Jewish community again appeared in Louvain. During the Black Death in 1348–49 most of the two hundred Jewish families in the Belgian cities were either massacred or expelled. In 1370 several Jewish families in Brussels and Louvain were burned at the stake after a Host desecration charge. Nothing further is heard about any Jews in Belgium until the sixteenth century. When Napoleon conquered the country, the Jewish community there consisted of some eight hundred people.[9]

By the end of the nineteenth century there were still only around two thousand Jews in Belgium. Jew-hatred was widespread. In 1898 Catholic priests in the Belgian Senate tried to pass a law against Jewish peddlers, arguing that all the peddlers in Belgium were Jews. In a speech to the Senate, the Jewish senator Hirsch exposed this as a lie, since there were 19,000 peddlers in the entire country and only two thousand Jewish families, many of whom were artisans and merchants. The law proposed by the priests was defeated by a large majority.

That same year, in a thinly disguised anti-Jewish demonstration, Catholic priests marched through Brussels in their sacerdotal robes, carrying pictures of the saints, as all the church bells in the city tolled. Leaflets were distributed announcing that the Church was celebrating a great anniversary, "the miracle of the Host," which five hundred years earlier had bled when the "Jew Jonathan" tortured it with knives and spears.[10]

The lie of that "miracle" was a particularly brazen and provocative one. The legend of a Host desecration by a Jew named Jonathan in Paris in 1390 was re-created in Brussels seventy-nine years later in every detail, including the blood streaming out of the Jew's house into the street. The Jew in Brussels was also burned to death outside his house with a volume of the Talmud in his hands. In Paris the Temple du Billet had been constructed on the site of the "miracle," while in Brussels it was the St. Gedil Church.[11] The demonstration in Brussels was really an "act of solidarity" with the ugly anti-Jewish agitation then emanating from Catholic France around the Dreyfus affair and with the bestial anti-Semitism rising in Germany, Austria, and Russia.

Switzerland. After the time of the Black Death, when the Jews in the Swiss cities were murdered or expelled, there were almost no

Jews there for two hundred years. In the sixteenth century some Marranos settled in a few cities. In the seventeenth century the grandchildren of these Marranos began appearing publicly as Jews. At that time more Jewish families settled in Switzerland, refugees from expulsions in the German provinces. Rights of domicile were sold to them at a high price in two towns in Baden province, Engyngen and Lengau, where they were required to sign an agreement not to increase their number.

In 1792 these two hundred families renewed the agreement.[12] Only the eldest son in a family was permitted to marry, and this only upon payment of a large sum on money. Proof was required of the new husband's honesty, sobriety—and property. No foreign Jews were permitted to enter the Swiss provinces except on business and for a day or two at the most. Upon crossing the Swiss border in or out, a Jew had to pay the "cattle tax."[13]

In 1798 Switzerland, now governed by France, became the Helvetian Republic. The Jews of Baden province then petitioned the government for equal rights. The issue was debated in Parliament, with the opposition trotting out all the old canards. At a subsequent session the legislators arrived at a compromise: they would emancipate only those Jews who could prove they were conducting themselves in an exemplary manner, who pledged to obey the constitution of the country, and who rejected their national distinctiveness. Questionnaires were sent to Jewish leaders asking if they could accept Swiss citizenship under those conditions. Several of the respondents replied that the Jewish faith instructs Jews to obey the laws of the land in which they live; conversely, nowhere do Jewish teachings prohibit obedience of the law of the land. (This meant that the Jews intended to remain true to their faith.) Based on these replies, the Swiss parliament on 16 March 1799 narrowly defeated the proposal for Jewish emancipation. In September 1802, mobs staged a pogrom of the Jews of Endyngen and Lengau. The Jews of Switzerland remained with no civil rights.

The constitution adopted by Switzerland in 1848 specified that all the rights therein applied only to Christians. When the Jews attempted to attend the fairs in the prohibited towns of Zurich and Basel, they were driven away. On 15 May 1862 the Lengau lawmakers emancipated the Jews by a vote of one hundred thirteen to two. Immediately a protest movement began, leading to new elections. Most of the liberals who had voted for emancipation were reelected. The question of equal rights for Jews was then submitted to a referendum, with the result that the law giving Jews equal rights was abrogated.[14] The Jews then appealed to the Swiss Bundesrat, which ordered the Lengau municipal government to cease restricting Jewish rights. The Jews in the province of Baden were emancipated. In the other Swiss states they remained rightless.

Finally, for the sake of international trade agreements, the Swiss national government was compelled to grant Jews equal rights. As early as 1835 France had broken off trade relations with Switzerland and was on the verge of breaking all relations, because that country was not admitting French citizens (Jews) to its markets. For similar reasons the United States refused to sign a trade agreement with Switzerland in 1850. In 1854, England—and in 1863, Holland—did the same.[15]

In 1866 most of the anti-Jewish restrictions in Switzerland were abolished. By 1874 the Jews there were completely emancipated. In 1880 the Jews were admitted to all Swiss cities, including Zurich, Berne, and Basel. There were at that time about seventy-five hundred Jews in Switzerland, and Jews from other countries were beginning to settle there without interference. Toward the end of the century, Jewish ritual slaughter of animals was prohibited after a referendum. (During the Hitler terror, Switzerland sealed its borders and refused to admit Jewish refugees.)

Italy. The ghetto in Rome had been in existence for many centuries. According to the description of one Dutch traveler in 1724, it consisted of two main streets and six smaller ones. Some three thousand Jewish families (about 15,000 people) lived there in subhuman conditions, with no running water or sewage system. The gates of the ghetto were locked every night from the outside. Jews in business were severely restricted. Aside from small food stores, most of the Jewish merchants dealt in old clothes. Special taxes of an insulting nature were imposed upon the Jews. For example, they had to pay for the ghetto watch, that is, they paid their own jailers. They were forced to support the missionaries who came to preach to them every week and the Houses of Conversion, as well. A Jew held "unsuccessfully" in one of these Houses had to pay forty days' board and lodging before he was released.

The Carnival tax was a remnant of the Middle Ages when Jews were forced to race each other until they collapsed. In order to buy their way out of this medieval "game" the Jews had to pay a tax. In addition, the priests devised a humiliating procedure for collecting this tax. The Jewish representative of the ghetto was required to appear before the Senate with the money in his hand, kneel before his Christian masters, say a few formulized words, and promise to be a good and obedient servant. The leader of the Senate would put his foot on the Jew's back, take the money, and call out *Andate!* ("Get out!"). In the street, a crowd waited to mock the Jew and shout after him, *Andate, Andate.*[16]

On the stage, Jews were grotesquely caricatured. In public, Jewish men had to wear a yellow hat; the women, a yellow kerchief. Violations of this regulation were punishable by flogging. Every Saturday afternoon the papal police would come into the ghetto and force Jews to attend church services to "hear the Lord's word." Jews were prohibited from "imitating" Christian customs. Thus, recitation of psalms at funerals was forbidden to Jews, because it had become a Christian custom. Jews could not light candles in memory of a deceased person or set up gravestones, for the same reason. Jews were prohibited from walking near a church where converts were being "educated." Any Jew who allowed a fugitive candidate for conversion into his home was put into the stocks. For persuading such a convert to remain a Jew the punishment was imprisonment, confiscation of property, and a sentence as a galley slave.

Leaders of the ghetto community were particularly vulnerable. In cases where the Christian overseers could not find a Jew who had been accused of a crime, they arrested either the rabbi or a trustee of the synagogue or some other prominent member of the community as a hostage.

Monks in Rome would stand on platforms near churches and preach to passersby about the "crimes" of the Jews and their terrible religion. This agitation frequently resulted in violence against individual Jews.

Worst of all was the practice of forcible conversion. Converts were recruited from among Jews who expressed the slightest doubt about Judaism. Such individuals would never again be left in peace by the missionaries. Converts were also recruited from among Jews who got into trouble with the law. Young children were an especially good target. Missionaries would seize a Jewish child, baptize it, and then give the distraught parents a "choice"—convert or lose the child.[17]

In the summer of 1787, an impoverished Jew in Rome volunteered to be converted. In a Catechumen House he told the priests that there were two orphaned boys in the ghetto, related to him, who were also ready to convert. The police could not find the boys and rounded up eighty Jewish children as hostages. The leaders of the Jewish community were arrested, flogged, and forced to give up the two boys, who were dragged to the Catechumen House against their will. In addition, the community was forced to pay a huge fine for the crime of hiding the two boys who "wanted to be converted."[18]

In Padua and Livorno the Jews had to renew their residence rights every ten or twelve years, but they were not treated as brutally as in the papal cities. When Jew-baiters in Venice erected a large painting on a bridge showing Jews slaughtering a Christian child, the Senate there ordered the painting taken down. In 1684 Venetian troops beseiged the city of Budapest, then ruled by the Turks. The Jews there helped the Turks defend the city against the invaders. Enraged by this news, a mob broke into the ghetto of Padua on 20 August 1684, but was dispersed by a detachment of troops from Venice.[19]

Attitudes toward Jews varied from city to city. In Florence, Genoa, and other cities in the north, Jews were treated much more liberally than in Venice or Padua and certainly more so than in the papal cities.

During the eighteenth century, large sections of Italy fell under Austrian rule and the new rulers invited Jews to come and settle. Very few Jews responded. In 1740 Jews were invited to settle in any city or town in Sicily, with permission to engage in whatever occupation they chose, including farming. A number of Jews accepted the invitation. An anti-Jewish campaign began immediately, including death threats to any Jews who dared settle in Sicily. The campaign was so virulent that King Charles III of Austria was forced to withdraw his invitation and advise those Jews who had already arrived in Sicily to leave.

For a brief period of six years, from 1769 to 1775, during the papacy of Clement XIV, the situation of the Jews in Rome changed for the better, with many of the oppressive decrees being abrogated. This interlude, however, was followed by twenty-three black years under Pius VI (1775–98), who revived all the old regulations and appointed the Inquisition to supervise the ghetto. He also established Catechumen Houses in other cities.

The revolution in France had some repercussions in Italy. An unsuccessful rebellion in Rome in 1793 resulted in a strong counter-attack by the Catholic hierarchy, during which the Vatican accused the Jews of preparing several thousand tricolor hats for the revolutionaries. With the failure of the uprising, a mob attacked the ghetto in Rome. The rabbis and other Jewish leaders were arrested and subjected to large fines. In retaliation for the beheading of Louis XVI, the Jewish Quarter in Rome was vandalized; when Paris abolished the authority of the Catholic Church, priests in Rome kidnapped Jewish children and forcibly converted them.[20] Obviously, the clergy were taking out their resentment on the closest and most defenseless victims.

In 1797 the French army under Napoleon occupied the largest cities and provinces in Italy. On 15 February 1798 Italian freedom fighters deposed the pope. The ghetto walls came down. Jews ripped the "mark of shame" from their hats. One of the first acts of the new government was to proclaim the emancipation of the Jews. But this freedom did not last very long. In the fall of 1799, when Napoleon withdrew his army from Italy, a Neapolitan Catholic force took over the government in Rome, abrogated Jewish rights, and ordered the Jews back into the ghetto.

In turn, this situation also proved to be short-lived. In 1808 Napoleon's army again occupied Rome and other Italian cities. Jewish rights were restored, but this time Napoleon also brought along his Jewish exceptional laws.[21] After Napoleon's defeats in 1812–13, the Jews again were placed under the heel of reaction. For another half century the 30,000 Jews of Italy remained without rights. In the political reaction which followed, the priests conducted a hate campaign against "the Jacobins and the Jews." Jews were driven back into the ghetto. Jewish students were expelled from the universities. Any Jew who wished to travel to another city was required to obtain an affidavit from a priest certifying to his honesty; then he had to show this document to a priest at his place of destination and bring back still another attestation when he returned.

In 1830, when another uprising broke out in Paris, the people in the Italian cities also took to the streets, demanding liberty and equality. Among the Italian freedom fighters were many Jews, as Jewish hopes soared again. The rebellion, however, was crushed by the Austrian army. The papal lieutenants reintroduced "order." The Jews in Italy returned to their medieval status.

During the pontificate of Pius IX (1846–78) the movement for national unification gained strength throughout Italy. Even the pope spoke out in favor of liberal reforms. In the spring of 1848 he ordered the walls of the Jewish ghetto demolished. In November of the same year, during a revolutionary upheaval, he fled from Rome as Giuseppe Mazzini assumed power. Jews were well represented in the camp of liberty and Mazzini agreed to full Jewish emancipation.[22]

Again the rebellion was defeated, this time by the French, who invaded Italy and reinstalled the pope and his Jesuit cardinals. Again the Church was quick to settle accounts with the Jews. What the pope resented particularly was the fact that the Jews had slighted his beneficence in breaking down the ghetto walls. As punishment he drove them back into the ghetto and reinstated all the former anti-Jewish laws, including those having to do with forcible conversion.

In June 1858 the papal police broke into the home of a Jewish family named Mortara, in Bologna, and removed their six-year-old son Edgar. The Vatican "explained" that the child had been secretly baptized by a Christian servant in the Mortara household. This scandalous affair was picked up by the world press, and from all quarters came demands that the child be returned to his parents. Moses Montefiore in London, Cremieux in France, and other influential Jews throughout the world appealed to the pope. The rulers of Austria and France warned His Holiness that such a drastic step would bring nothing but harm to the Catholic Church. Pope Pius IX rejected all these protests and appeals. The boy was raised in a monastery and grew up to be a Christian missionary and a Jew-baiter.

In 1870, during the Franco-Prussian War, the army of King Victor Emanuel of Sardinia entered Rome. The Italian cities and provinces became one nation and the pope's secular authority was abolished. The unification of Italy brought full emancipation to the 35,000 Jews of that country.[23] The Jewish community of Italy remained relatively small as Jewish families emigrated to America along with masses of other impoverished Italians.

Rumania. In the second quarter of the nineteenth century many Jews from the Ukrainian provinces, especially Podolia, fled from the czar's malicious decrees to Moldavia and Wallachia, which were partially under Turkish rule. They earned their livelihood in handicrafts, petty trade, and leaseholding. The Boyars (the local landowners) regarded the Jews there, both the native-born and the refugees, as permanent aliens.

In 1848 the "spirit of liberty" reached the land of the Danube and in several cities the people clashed with government troops in the streets. The rebellion was crushed by Russian and Turkish troops.

After the Russo-Turkish war of 1854–56, the two provinces of

Moldavia and Wallachia, with the blessing of the European governments, united to form one country to be known as Rumania. At the Paris peace conference between Russia and Turkey, European diplomats inserted a point into the constitution of the new country stipulating that the Jewish population in Rumania must be given equal rights.[24]

In 1859 the political leadership of Rumania was in the hands of Colonel Couza, a liberal who favored the emancipation of the Jews. The Boyars were strongly opposed to this step, however, and Couza was forced to retreat. In 1866 the Jewish problem surfaced again, with the liberals insisting that not all the Jews in the country could be considered "foreigners." Those Jews who were born in the country must be emancipated immediately. Not so, argued the Jew-haters; all Jews are foreigners and must never be granted equal rights with Christians. The Boyars then began inciting the general population against civil rights for Jews.

On 28 July 1866, when the issue was to be voted on, mobs broke into the parliament building and terrorized those legislators who had advocated Jewish rights. The deputies fled from the building. The mob made its way to the Jewish Quarter, vandalized homes, and burned down the synagogue.

Later the same year Ion Bratianu, an anti-Semite, became premier of Rumania. He began by expelling the Jews from the villages. One group of Jews were driven across the Danube to the Turkish border. The Turks refused them entry. On Bratianu's order the Rumanian police shot or drowned several hundred of the refugees.[25] This barbarous act aroused such indignation all over Europe that Bratianu resigned. Two years later he was back in office. In October of 1868, two months after his appointment, a pogrom took place in Galacz.[26] From 1870 to 1873 there was a series of pogroms in various Rumanian cities.

In 1878, at the peace congress in Berlin, Rumania was again on the agenda, with a number of European governments demanding that it emancipate the Jews within its borders. The Rumanian government thereupon emancipated some eight hundred Jews who had served in armed forces. The rest of the Jews would be emancipated individually, the government promised. The process never took place. Two hundred thousand Rumanian Jews remained without rights, victims of continuing persecution and pogroms.

The same peace congress also obtained equal rights for the Jews in Serbia and Bulgaria, two smaller Balkan states liberated from

Turkey. Serbia had a Jewish population of around 5,000; Bulgaria, 10,000. During the Russo-Turkish war of 1877 the Jews in Serbia and Bulgaria were victims of pogroms by both armies.

The Near East. In the mid-thirteenth century the Near East was conquered by Mongolian invaders who plundered the cities and the countryside and laid waste the whole area. Around 1250 a Turkish tribe known as the Mamelukes drove the Mongols out of the region. Syria and Palestine remained in a devastated condition for several centuries. The caliphs, whom the Islamic Mamelukes appointed to govern the provinces, were zealots for their faith and enforced all the Omar Laws against non-believers. The Jewish community in Palestine during the sixteenth, seventeenth, and eighteenth centuries remained small. The destitute Arab Muslims considered the Jews to be their enemies. The few Sephardic Jews who had returned to Palestine from Turkey were at least able to establish some rapport with the Arabs; the Ashkenazic, or western, Jews could not.

The Turkish viziers demanded exorbitant taxes from the Jews. Every Passover eve the tax collectors would descend upon the Jewish community, apprehend people in the streets, and hold them in prison for ransom. If a Jew was too poor to pay, relatives or neighbors would have to raise the money for his release.

Up to the eighteenth century, small Jewish communities existed in Egypt and Syria, most of them with a long history. Although the situation of the Jews there was not particularly good, it was still better than in Palestine.

In Morocco, during the seventeenth and eighteenth centuries, the government was in the hands of fanatical Muslims. The Jews who came to Morocco from Spain and Portugal merely exchanged one set of persecutors for another. The Berber population in the country was divided into castes of various gradations. The Jews were considered lower than the lowest caste and were the most oppressed.[27]

Many Jewish refugees who fled Spain and Portugal in 1492 reached the shores of Turkey, where they were received humanely. Jews settled in Constantinople, Salonika, Smyrna, and some smaller cities. However, the Christian blood libel soon caught up with them in Islam. In 1532 the Jews in a small town in Asia Minor were thus accused and the sultan ordered an investigation. As it turned out, the slanderers themselves were exposed and punished.

Under the Ottoman Turks the Jews lived in relative peace. Joseph

HaNasi, a royal advisor and a Jew, even undertook the task of rebuilding Tiberias in Palestine. Jews in the Christian lands were invited to come and help rebuild their old country. At that time Pope Paul IV and his successor, Paul V, waged a relentless anti-Jewish campaign. Two ships carrying Jews set sail for Palestine from Italian ports, but were intercepted by pirates. Most of the Jews on board were sold into slavery.

When the Austrian army occupied Belgrade (now in Yugoslavia), Queen Maria Theresa considered the possibility of expelling the Jews from there, as she had done in Vienna. The Turkish sultan, when he discovered this, informed her that his country was ready to admit all the Jews she would expel. In 1749 the queen announced that the rumor of the expulsion was completely unfounded.[28]

At the start of the nineteenth century, France had an eye on the undeveloped countries in the Near East—Egypt, Syria, and Palestine—which for several generations had been ruled by a backward and enfeebled Turkey. In 1832, Mehemet Ali, the viceroy of Egypt, rebelled against Turkey and proclaimed Egypt an independent state. Mehemet Ali also took over Palestine and Syria.

The Blood Libel of 1840

On 5 February 1840 a Franciscan monk, Brother Thomas de Camangiano, disappeared in Damascus. It was known that a Turkish mule dealer had threatened to kill him. Thomas's monastery brothers, however, spread the story that the Jews had murdered him for ritual purposes. On the advice of the French consul the local sharif arrested several Jews. One of them confessed under torture that he had been involved in the "crime" and named other Jews who had helped him. These people were also arrested and tortured. Joseph Lanado, an older man, died on the rack. Another converted to Islam. Several "confessed."

Three rabbis in Damascus were picked up. Accused of blood libel, family groups were imprisoned. Sixty young children were held by the police without food, waiting for their mothers to "confess" so they could get their children back. A few converted to Islam, but none of them confessed. When it was learned that one of the rabbis was an Austrian, the ambassador of the country obtained his release. Upon the rabbi's release, a large mob of Muslims gathered, demanding that the rabbi be handed back to the authorities. The ambassador refused to do so.

The French consul in Damascus then disseminated a pamphlet

describing how Jews use the blood of murdered Christian and Muslim children for ritual purposes. To Paris he sent anti-Jewish reports and called for friendship with the Syrian rulers. With his eye on the political stakes, he moved heaven and earth to justify the ritual murder charges in Damascus.[29] The 20,000 Jews in that city were now in fear of their lives. Hundreds fled.

In the meantime, Jew-baiters on the island of Rhodes invented their own blood libel. Finding a murdered Greek boy, they circulated a rumor that the Jews had killed him. One Jew was arrested and "confessed" under torture. Pogroms followed in Smyrna, Beirut, and other cities. The Turkish government stepped in and subdued the disturbances. The trial of the Jew in Rhodes was transferred to Constantinople, where he was found innocent and released.

News of the Damascus blood libel spread throughout the world. In Rome the Franciscans had already erected a monument to the new martyr, St. Thomas, "whom the Jews had murdered." Jewish leaders in Europe appealed to their governments for help. Adolphe Cremieux pleaded with the appropriate officials in France to deny the libels concocted by their consul in Damascus. The result was nothing but excuses and evasions. In London, Vienna, and the United States large demonstrations took place against the perpetrators of the blood libel and their French partners. A delegation of prominent Jews from England traveled to Alexandria in Egypt to demand justice for the Jewish victims in Damascus. Cremieux obtained the signatures of all the European consuls in Alexandria on a petition to release the accused. When Mehemet Ali learned that the consuls of Europe were about to issue a united protest against the injustices of his government, he ordered the release of the arrested Jews. Nine of them were freed. Four had perished in the prisons under torture.

The sharif was brought to Alexandria in chains, tried, and beheaded. This was of little help fo Mehemet Ali, however. In October of the same year the united European governments returned Syria to Turkish rule. Nevertheless, almost every year at Passover time the blood libel was dredged up in Turkish and Greek cities and the government would squelch the disturbances before they got out of hand. In 1842 several Greeks in Smyrna tried to instigate a pogrom when the body of a boy was found on a beach with cuts in the skull. Despite a block by the police, a mob set fire to several Jewish homes.

The same year, a ritual murder charge was made against Jews in

Constantinople, again over the mutilated body of a drowned child. The local anti-Semitic newspaper printed a sensational story whipping up a foreboding atmosphere. The police were unable to stop the resultant violence before serious damage had been done to the Jews of that city. When a coroner's report disclosed that the wounds on the child's head had been inflicted several days after death, the Greek editor of the newspaper was sentenced to prison.[30]

In 1860 Jewish leaders in Europe formed an international assistance organization known as the *Alliance Israélite Universelle* to assist Jews who were being persecuted in Christian and Muslim lands. The initiator of the *Alliance* was Adolphe Cremieux. In 1861, when news came of the anti-Jewish campaign in Morocco, the *Alliance* sent a representative to make an on-the-spot investigation. The report he brought back was that the Jews in Morocco were virtual slaves of the local sultan and the feudal landowners. The Jews were impoverished and lived in a dirty ghetto under constant threat of expulsion from the country.[31] The *Alliance* appealed to the governments of Europe for help in correcting this situation. From several capitals came warnings to the sultan of Morocco that if this lawlessness toward Jews was not corrected, relations with his country would be in jeopardy. As a result, the situation improved somewhat in the port cities most frequently visited by foreigners, but in the interior of the country nothing really changed.

Persia. Early in the seventeenth century, Shah Abbas I, informed by a convert that the books of the Kabbalah contain magical verses harmful to the ruler, ordered all Jewish books destroyed. He further decreed that all the Jews in his country must convert to Islam or face expulsion. Many Jews formally converted, hoping for better times when they would be free to return to their faith. Thus, in the seventeenth century, there were many Muslim "Marranos" in Persia.

In the reign of Shah Abbas II (1642–66), the pressure on the Jews to convert was intensified. All the older synagogues were shut down; the newer ones were turned into mosques. Not only were the Jews required to recite the verse, "Allah is God and Muhammad is His prophet," but they also had to study the Koran and take an oath of loyalty to Islam. Anyone caught observing Jewish customs was severely punished.[32] In 1865 the *Alliance Israélite* received a plea from the Persian Jews for help against attacks and oppressive decrees. At the request of the *Alliance*, the British Parliament made inquiries of Teheran and the Shah promised to improve the situation.

The Americas (1654-1789). Along with merchants and other settlers who fled religious persecution in Europe came Marranos, in mortal fear of the Inquisition in their countries. They hoped that in the Spanish colonies they would be able to live a normal life. In 1514 the Spanish government decreed that any new Christians who were suspected of heresy would be forbidden to leave Spain or settle in the colonies. Many of the wealthier Marranos found ways to escape the claws of the Inquisition and eventually got to the colonies. Generally, they settled in Central America.

Before long, however, the Inquisition caught up with them. As soon as a community of Marranos settled in a colony and grew careless about their Christian piety, the murderers in black cloaks appeared on the scene looking for victims. Thus the Inquisition was introduced into Cuba, Puerto Rico, Mexico, and other Spanish and Portuguese colonies where free spirits had come to settle. Worst of all was Peru, where a large number of wealthy, long-established Marrano families were burned at the stake.[33] The property of the victims, in accordance with Church law, was taken by the priests and the local rulers of the colonies.

When Portuguese colonies were founded in the area now known as Brazil, many prominent Marranos from the home country went to settle there. Here too, the Inquisition was close behind. In 1624 the Dutch, who had founded some of the colonies in North America, set out to conquer Brazil. In the battle for Rio de Janeiro the Marranos fought on the side of the Dutch. The Portuguese were defeated, but in 1645 they recaptured the territory and a few years later expelled the Jews from Brazil. Some Jews went to Holland, others to British and French islands. One ship carrying Jewish refugees was captured by pirates. A French ship came to their rescue and brought twenty-three Marranos into New Amsterdam, a Dutch port.

The then governor of the port, Peter Stuyvesant, at first refused to admit the twenty-three new immigrants. In a letter to the Dutch West India Company in Amsterdam, he referred to Jews as "that deceitful race . . . hateful enemies and blasphemers of the name of Christ" and requested permission to send them away.[34] The West India Company, however, insisted that the Jews be permitted to settle in New Amsterdam, although not as equal citizens with the

Christians. They could not build a synagogue, they had to live in a separate part of town, and they would not be permitted to hold public office.

To this small group were added more Jews, mostly grandchildren of the Marranos who had returned to the Jewish faith and no longer needed to disguise themselves as Christians. In other respects, they were still without rights. They could not trade in goods of their choice; they could not buy a home or land to farm; they could not bear arms or stand watch, as other citizens did. When the port of New Amsterdam was taken over by the British, the situation changed for the better. New Amsterdam became New York.

Like all other Christians in those days, the English had their own anti-Jewish prejudices. However, it was enough for the Jews that they were permitted to live freely as Jews, without fear of the Inquisition. Gradually they established themselves in the new country. They did not expect too many social or political rights, nor did they receive them.

In the second half of the seventeenth century more Jews arrived in the North American ports from Europe and South and Central America. In time they won additional rights and democratic freedoms. They planted roots and were integrated into American life. Jewish communities appeared in Guiana, Jamaica, Barbados, and other islands. In Paramaribo, capital of Surinam, there were approximately eighteen hundred Jews in the mid-eighteenth century, who were mostly of Spanish and Portuguese origin.

Christian merchants in the island soon began to complain about Jewish competition. The English rulers, however, were concerned primarily with economic development and rejected these complaints. Not much different was the situation of the Jews who settled in the French colony of Martinique in the seventeenth century. King Louis XIV even issued a decree giving the Jews on that island equal rights. In 1685, however, they were expelled.[35] Most of them went to the British and Dutch colonies.

On the North American continent the Jews settled mainly in the port cities. Five Jewish communities arose in the late 1600s and early 1700s: Newport, Rhode Island, New York City, Philadelphia, Charlestown, South Carolina, and Savannah, Georgia. In addition, Jews were scattered in other ports along the Atlantic coast, such as Boston and Reading. The census of 1790 shows a population in North America of approximately four million (including a half million blacks). It is estimated that the number of Jews was between three and five thousand.[36]

The attitude of the Christians in the United States toward the Jews was a tolerant one. The Puritans revered the Jewish Scriptures and regarded the Jews as God's chosen people. They selected biblical names for their children, as well as for many of their settlements. The immigrants from France, Germany, and other European countries had certainly not forgotten that the "Jews crucified Jesus." On the soil of the new country, however, these same Christians, who generally were seeking a new life, behaved more humanely toward Jews.

In the colonies there was often a shortage of artisans, traders, and various types of middlemen, and these needs could often be met by Jewish immigrants. The Jewish peddler who followed the covered wagons and brought a variety of useful articles to the farflung communities was most welcome. The Jewish merchants played an important role in the growing economy of the country. In such an atmosphere the Jews did not feel superfluous and began to enjoy a certain sense of security. Jews considered themselves the equal of everyone else in many ways, although socially and politically, prior to 1776, they were still far from having equal rights.

Sweden. Up until the last quarter of the eighteenth century Jews were not permitted to enter Sweden unless they first became Lutherans. In 1774 a Prussian Jew named Aaron Isaacs, by trade an engraver, came to Stockholm. Because of his craft he was welcomed by King Gustave III (1771–92), who permitted him and his family to stay in the country as Jews. When this became public knowledge, people followed the "strange Jews" in the street, pointing and shouting insults. Complaints were registered with the king for permitting Jews to defile Sweden's soil by their presence.[37]

However, as the people gradually became accustomed to the presence of Jews, King Gustave permitted Isaacs to bring in some of his friends. Only one condition was attached to the invitation—the Jews who came must be honest. The city council of Stockholm stipulated a number of other conditions for Jewish residence in that city: they must reside in a separate quarter; they must wear a yellow band on their hats in public; they could not deal in any goods except old clothing; they could not engage in any craft which had a Christian guild. The king rejected all these conditions and permitted Jews to live in Sweden virtually as free citizens. They were even permitted to build a synagogue, on condition that their services would be conducted with decorum.[38] In 1803 the Jewish community in Stockholm consisted of sixty-nine families.

Finland and Denmark. In the wars with Sweden in 1721 and 1743, Russia annexed Finland. The Swedish system of government was left intact, but Jews were prohibited from entering the country. Not until the early nineteenth century was permssion given for several Jewish families to settle in Finland.

In Denmark at the end of the nineteenth century there were some three thousand Jews, most of them former Marranos from Portugal. Although not severely restricted, they were nevertheless considered foreigners.

20

Struggle for Emancipation in Germany After 1789

During the late eighteenth century the Prussian authorities, influenced by the liberal ideas current in Europe, were already debating the question of Jewish emancipation. As early as 1787 King Frederick Wilhelm had summoned Jewish leaders and listened to their request for the abolition of the "Jewish regulations" of 1750. For two years a government commission studied the matter and in 1789 submitted an "improved" program which did not touch the basis of the old regulations, namely, the division of the Jews into "Privileged" and "Tolerated" classes. The permission granted to Jews to engage in handicrafts was a mockery, because it contained a proviso that Jews were not to engage in tailoring, shoemaking, or carpentry. After the point permitting Jews to buy land for farming, comes a note that this refers only to land which has never been worked before. Most of the taxes on Jews remained in effect, as well as the responsibility of the *Kehillah* for paying those taxes. The Jewish leaders therefore rejected the "new" program. Frederick Wilhelm later commented that he was concerned for all his subjects, including the Jews, and would gladly grant them equal rights, but that obstacles to this stemmed from the religious customs of the Jews themselves.[1]

Four months after Jewish emancipation was proclaimed in France (September 1791) the Prussian monarch ordered his cabinet to prepare a plan to improve the situation of the Jews in his lands. Early in 1792 a French army invaded the Rhine region. The king postponed the Jewish reforms. Immediately following the war came the second and third partitions of Poland in 1793 and 1795. Prussia annexed the Polish provinces which were densely settled by Jews. For these newly added Jews in Poland the Prussian king also issued regulations concerning their rights and duties.

Those who had lived in the annexed provinces for a long time were granted domiciliary rights, provided they were engaged in secure businesses or professions. Those who were recent settlers, or who had no assured income, were required to leave the cities and provinces. The Jews who stayed were taxed more heavily in return for "protection." They were also required to pay for permission to marry, a privilege which was granted only to men over the age of twenty-five with an assured income.[2]

Around the turn of the century, a strong anti-Jewish agitation began among the Christian population, because too many Jews were "becoming Germans" and entering German high society. In 1803 a minor court official named Grattenauer published a virulent pamphlet in which he castigated Germans for fraternizing with Jews. Many high-placed citizens were associating with Jews in the "salons of culture," which were sponsored mostly by wealthy Jewish women who had converted to Christianity.[3] Grattenauer warned Germany's social leaders not to be deceived by odious Jewish "swindlers and defamers of Christ." There is an unbridgeable chasm between the Jews and true Germans, he insisted. The Jews bear the mark of Cain. They should again be compelled to wear the yellow patch. Germans should keep away from Jews as from a plague.[4]

In 1792, when the French occupied the Rhine cities of Mainz, Worms, and Speyer, the Jews there became emancipated. In Frankfurt-am-Main the battles between the French and Austrian armies had resulted in vast destruction, with the Jewish quarter virtually demolished. When the French emerged triumphant in 1806, the Jews were permitted to leave their medieval ghetto. A year later Prussia was also defeated by Napoleon's armies. The peace treaty removed various territories from Prussian rule. Out of the Polish territories which Napoleon took from Prussia he created the Duchy of Warsaw.[5]

In 1808 the Jews in Prussia renewed their struggle for equality. Again the king ordered one of his ministries to prepare a proposal. The resultant document proposed that the Jews be granted limited rights on condition that they renounce their national culture, because the Jewish people are a "harmful element within the nation." Judaism should permit intermarriage with Christians. This would not necessitate changing religion, but the offspring of mixed marriages must be brought up as Christians. Separate schools for Jewish children should be abolished; they should attend the same general schools with German children.

For almost a year this proposal was studied by various ministries. Opinions differed, but there was general agreement that the Jews were a harmful and corrupting factor in society and must be "reformed." In March 1812, after the proposal had been reviewed several times, the king issued his "Edict Concerning the Jewish Civil Situation." The special Jewish taxes were abolished, as were the exceptional laws. Jews were given access to academic and government positions and were admitted into the armed services. The Jews in Prussia greeted the news with great joy.

In an anonymously published pamphlet, David Friedländer, a disciple of Moses Mendelssohn, advocated the reform of Jewish religious services as a mark of gratitude. His recommendations included a revision of the prayerbook to excise antiquated and irrelevant passages, such as laments over the destruction of the Temple of Jerusalem. Jews were no longer in exile, Friedländer contended, they were now emancipated Prussian citizens whose Fatherland is Germany.[6]

Just around that time war broke out between Russia and France. As an ally of Russia, Prussia joined the battle against Napoleon's domination of Europe. The German Jews threw themselves zealously into the war on the side of their Fatherland and fought in all the battles between 1812 and 1815. Many were decorated for bravery. But neither the dilution of the prayerbook nor Jewish patriotic heroism could extinguish or even dampen the fires of Jew-hatred in Prussia. The Congress of Vienna in 1815 reinstituted the old system in Europe. Jew-baiters in the German cities and provinces viewed Jewish emancipation as a product of Napoleonism which had to be eradicated.

Westphalia. In the six years that Napoleon ruled Europe (1806–12) the Jews in several countries were emancipated. Over the Kingdom of Westphalia which Napoleon created out of several provinces in central Germany, he crowned his brother, Jerome Bonaparte, king. In 1808 Jerome abolished restrictions on all citizens, including "our subjects who believe in the Torah of Moses." A Jewish deputation came personally to greet and thank the king, whom they called "The

Liberator." Jerome responded to their praise with compliments of his own and promised the Jews equality with all other citizens.

When Napoleon read a report of this friendly reception in a Westphalian newspaper, he wrote his brother an irate letter upbraiding him for being too friendly with the Jews. Among other things, he pointed out:

> I have gone to the trouble of making the Jews more human, but I have never desired to narrow the distance between us. Moreover, I have always avoided doing anything which could be interpreted as meaning that I respect these most contemptible of people.[7]

As soon as Napoleon was defeated, Jewish emancipation in Westphalia crumbled. After six years of existence, the rights of the Jews—whose number had been increasing—were abruptly revoked.

In Frankfurt-am-Main Jewish emancipation did not even last that long. This was the last city in Germany to keep the Jews locked in a ghetto. In 1806 the city joined the Rhine Federation which Napoleon had created. But neither the Liberator King nor the new government in Frankfurt rushed to emancipate the Jews. The local authorities ruled that for such an important step it was necessary to get the consent of the citizenry of Frankfurt. Several privileges were granted, however. While the ghetto was not abolished, permission was given to enlarge it in order to ease the crowded conditions. All occupational restrictions were retained. A new regulation provided that the rabbi of the ghetto, in addition to his Jewish scholarly qualifications, must also have a diploma in philosophy.[8] All previous taxes remained in force.

The leaders of the Westphalian Jewish community now protested this degradation of the Frankfurt Jews. Among the protesters was a young man, a child of the ghetto named Leyb Baruch, who later converted and became famous as Ludwig Berne, one of the pillars of German literature. At that time Berne wrote a penetrating, satirical essay about the reactionary leaders of Frankfurt. Unable to get it printed, he circulated it in manuscript. Among the opponents of Jewish emancipation was the poet Goethe, who mocked and pilloried the Jews of Frankfurt for objecting to the new constitution so generously offered them by the city fathers.[9]

In 1810 Frankfurt became part of the Rhine Region. Jewish rights were again the order of the day. The city authorities demanded a price of 440,000 gulden from the Jews to cover the revenue they would lose over the next twenty years by granting them civil rights. The Jews of Frankfurt paid this tremendous sum and bought their own emancipation. Three years later the allied armies opposing Napoleon entered Frankfurt. Jewish rights were promptly revoked. The 440,000 gulden were never returned.

In Hamburg the emancipation of the Jews was of brief duration also. Napoleon's army entered that city in 1810 and the Jews were immediately granted equal rights, but the German victory over Napoleon again destroyed everything for them. In March 1813, Russian troops entered Hamburg and reestablished the old order.

The same process took place in the other cities of the former Hanseatic League. From Lubeck and Bremen, Jews were expelled entirely. Important cities in Saxony, such as Leipzig and Dresden, had not abrogated their anti-Jewish laws at all during the period of Napoleon's rule. The "cattle tax" on foreign Jews was not abolished there until after the combined Prussian-Russian armies drove out the French.

When the Rhine Federation was established and Jews were being emancipated in nearby cities, the Duke of Mecklenburg was forced to grant the Jews in his area certain privileges. However, he did not want a fight with the city council over this. The Diet therefore proposed a number of conditions for the emancipation of the Jews of Mecklenburg: they must give up their Sabbath, their dietary laws, and their marriage laws; they must send their children only to German schools; Jewish parents would be permitted to have only one son working with them in a business (the other sons must become handicraftsmen, farmers, or artists). The Jews rejected the offer.

In 1812 the Duke of Mecklenburg, influenced by the emancipation in Prussia, was prepared to offer the Jews certain privileges. They would be admitted to military service and government positions, provided they gave up their own *Beth Din* (court for internal matters) and their marriage laws. Intermarriage would be permitted, provided that the wedding be held in a church and with the understanding that the children would be raised as Christians. The anti-Semites in the Diet, however, refused to approve either the privileges or the conditions.

In Bavaria, early in the nineteenth century, the Jews waged an unsuccessful struggle for equality. On 10 June 1813 the Bavarian government proclaimed certain "Privileges to the Israelites" which actually were only the old degrading restrictions. The Jews were granted residence rights, but they remained "protected Jews" and had to pay for that privilege. Only one son in a family was permitted to inherit the father's residence right. The regulation frankly admits that the government's purpose is to reduce the Jewish population in the province. The king did agree to admit a certain number of Jews into his country, but only if they were artisans, manufacturers or farmers. This Bavarian "constitution" remained in force until 1848.

In Baden, which is not far from the French border, the Jews were granted several privileges, but the Grand Duke decreed that they would be fully emancipated only when they could prove they were trying to become equal to Christians in their political and moral behavior and in their occupations.

The issue of Jewish emancipation was also debated by the Congress of Vienna. It was impossible, after Jews had fought in wars to free their countries of foreign domination, to openly deprive them of their human rights. So a semantic subterfuge was devised. A moderate resolution was adopted. It stipulated that those Jews who had been granted civil rights by cities and provinces would remain emancipated, but that this did not apply to other Jews. The trick was that in most cities and provinces in Germany and Austria the Jews had not been granted their rights by those local authorities but by a foreign power—Napoleon—and their emancipation was therefore null and void.[10]

After Napoleon's defeat, the mood in the German lands became increasingly nationalistic and reactionary. This mood combined with a hatred of all foreigners, especially the French and the Jews, who had always been and remained alien in Germany. Hostility to Jews became even more pronounced during the Restoration. Anti-Jewish pamphlets full of exaggerated stories about Jewish wealth appeared in the cities. In 1817 a brochure by Fredrick Ruhs, "Concerning Jewish Pretensions to German Citizenship," became very popular. Ruhs's message was that a nation consists of a single people with a common language, a common religion, and common national feelings, and that Jews are foreigners in each of these aspects. In addition, Jews believe only in business and the accumulation of wealth, not in productive labor. They should be compelled to wear the yellow patch just as they did in the Middle Ages. There is only one path for Jews to become German citizens, said Ruhs, and that was conversion.[11]

On music hall stages comedians ridiculed the Jews, mimicked their language and lied about their wealth and their "disgusting

habits." The German audiences laughed, absorbed the Jew-hatred—
and enjoyed themselves. Jews, and some non-Jews, tried to reply to
the attacks. The replies, however, were apologetic and feeble.
Hardly anyone in the country dared say a good word about Jews.
When Pastor Teremin, a German poet, translated Byron's *Hebrew
Melodies*, he found it necessary to defend himself for even touching
the word "Hebrew." In the forward to the translation he wrote: "I
hope that with this translation I am not committing any wrong to
Christendom . . . and that I will not be suspected of being a friend of
the Jews."[12]

Literary circles idealized the old folk heroes and the old folk spirit.
The romantic folklore contained much of the medieval attitude
toward Jews. All this was part of the ancient, romanticized *Volksgeist* of Germany. The general reactionary mood eventually affected
the students. Professors combined their nostalgia for the *Volksgeist*
with theories about Germany's punishment for tolerating Jews. In
August 1816 a pogrom broke out in Würzburg, Bavaria; another
followed during the following months in Bamberg and other cities.[13]

In Frankfurt-am-Main the Jews continued to demand the rights
which they had bought at such a high price; emancipation was their
due according to the Congress of Vienna. On 10 August 1819 a mob
of students and workers attacked the ghetto. The heaviest damage
was done to the home of the banker Rothschild, a fact which
alarmed the city council. Should Rothschild move his bank from the
city, it would mean great financial loss. The pogrom was stopped.
During this time, similar riots took place in Leipzig, Dresden,
Darmstadt, Mannheim, Pforzheim, and other cities in Baden. In
Prussia only the Jews in Danzig were attacked.

At the end of 1819 a certain Gund-Radkowski published a
pamphlet containing undisguised pogrom incitement. He urged that
Jewish males be deported to remote islands to work on the
plantations, and that the women be placed in houses of prostitution.
The remaining Jews should be liquidated. Apparently this was too
much even for the Prussian government. The publication was
sequestered, after many copies had already been distributed and
were being read and declaimed wherever people gathered.[14]

In 1816 there were around 25,000 Jewish families in Prussia. The
Jews here had not received their rights from any foreign power but
from the Prussian government itself. After the victory over Napoleon, Prussia had annexed new provinces both from the former
Duchy of Warsaw and from the smaller kingdoms created by

Napoleon. For the Jews in these areas, where new constitutions had been written, the Prussian emancipation did not apply.

In the original Prussian lands, government officials also sought ways to restrict Jewish rights. One minister drafted a document "proving" that Jews have opprobrious customs; that all Jews are swindlers; that Germany would be committing a sin by emancipating such people. Another minister supported these conclusions, but added that only Jews who convert should be granted equal rights and that the conversion efforts should therefore be stepped up.[15] The emancipation of the Jews was not officially revoked, but it was gradually dissolved. Jews were not permitted to hold government posts. Jewish lawyers and physicians were not allowed to practice. Jewish teachers were not given employment. Official correspondence to Jews no longer carried the salutation "Herr" but "The Jew So-and-so." The title "Israelite" was changed to the derogatory "*Jude.*"

In the 1820s the Prussian king forbade the reforming of Jewish prayer services for the purpose of making them similar to Protestant services. Thus Jews were forbidden to change the language of their prayers and ceremonies. The Reform temples were shut down. Rabbis were forbidden to preach in German. Jews were welcome to convert, but to retain the Jewish faith or adapt Jewish worship to the Christian—that was *verboten.*

In the early 1830s, a number of courageous fighters for Jewish rights emerged. One of them was Gabriel Riesser (1806–63) who, as a Jew, was refused permission to practice his profession of law. In 1830 and 1831 he published two books in which he described the situation of the Jews in Germany, condemned the rash of conversions, and called for a struggle for Jewish emancipation. This would be a struggle for liberty and justice, he said. The Jewish problem is only a question of religious freedom. Jews must be free to follow their own religion and not be compelled to put on the mask of another faith in order to enjoy civic equality. Riesser polemicized with those who denied Jews their rights on the pretext that Jews are a separate nation.

Do German Jews have another Fatherland except Germany? When a Jew is driven out of Germany, can he go and settle in his "own" country? He has no other country! The German Fatherland should and must demand of the Jew whatever it demands of all its other citizens. The Jews will gladly obey. They will sacrifice everything— except their faith and their conscience.[16]

In 1847 a conference of the provincial Diets was convened in Berlin to consider a plan for solving the Jewish problem in Germany. After deliberating for several months, a law was passed to "integrate" the Jews: they must be given equal duties along with equal rights, but with certain exceptions: Jews would be eligible only for those government positions not connected with judicial, police, or administrative functions; Jews could be professors in universities if this did not conflict with the statutes of the given institution; Jews would not be permitted in the academic senates of the universities; contrary to Frederick William IV's decree of 1840, Jews could serve in the army, but not as officers; Jews had no voting rights in the municipal Diets.[17] Jewish children could study religious subjects only in schools supported by the Jews themselves; for general education they must attend the Christian schools. In addition to all this, Jews were divided into "naturalized" citizens (Prussia) and non-naturalized citizens (Posen). The law was in effect for only a few months. The March revolution in the fateful year of 1848 changed the situation for the better.

In the province of Bavaria in the 1830s and 1840s, there were about 60,000 Jews, living in two areas where the laws concerning Jews were not alike. In Old Bavaria the medieval exceptional laws were still in force. In the second area, comprising the Rhine provinces where Jews had been emancipated by Napoleon, the laws had been partially amended. In both areas the Jews had no voting rights. During the pogrom violence in 1819 in the neighboring areas, the Jews in Bavaria also suffered. In 1831 the Jews petitioned the Bavarian government once more. During the ensuing debate in the Diet a proposal was made to grant the Jews certain rights on condition that they renounce the Talmud and observe their Sabbath on Sunday. The proposal was defeated.

Early in 1836 the government summoned 400 Jewish representatives from the most important cities in Bavaria and handed them questions concerning their views on various Jewish beliefs. The questions dealt with the basic tenets of Judaism, such as the belief in a messiah, the return to Zion, Jewish prayers. The Orthodox and the Reform Jews differed sharply in their replies. The government's decision was that since these replies were so different from each other, the Jews would have to wait still longer for equality.[18] Jewish communities in Bavaria continued to submit petitions for emancipation until 1848, when the March revolution granted their plea.

In Baden the revolution found the Jewish problem not completely solved. In Saxony, Hanover, Mecklenburg, Brunswick, and Hesse the question of Jewish rights was at the same stage as in Bavaria and Baden. By and large, however, German Jewry in the first half of the nineteenth century had made progress. The privileges which Jews received, first under Napoleon and then by their own struggles, elevated them economically and culturally, and to some extent socially. The number of Jews in the German provinces increased. At the beginning of the century there were about 250,000 Jews throughout the German lands. By 1848 their number had grown to 400,000.[19]

Meir Anshel Rothschild (1744–1812), a moneylender of Frankfurt, who in the last quarter of the eighteenth century was a financial agent for a German baron, had been involved in important transactions with Napoleon. After Meir's death his five sons became major bankers in the largest cities of Europe. The Rothschild name was used as a handy symbol of "pernicious Jewish wealth" by Jew-baiters everywhere in the world. This practice has continued into our own time. And it is given equal emphasis by right-wing reactionaries, on the one hand, and left-wing socialists and communists, on the other hand, all in the name of "justice and progress."

Germany of 1848. The revolution which began in the early months of 1848 in Paris had its effect also in Germany, Austria, and Italy. Liberal forces got the upper hand, but only temporarily. Equally temporary was the emancipation of the Jews in Germany. Political upheavals took place in Bavaria, Baden, Saxony, Württemberg, Hanover, Hesse and Prussia, and in some provinces attacks on Jews accompanied the revolutionary turbulence. In Baden, peasants pillaged the estates of the nobility and, while they were at it, also the property of Jews. In Heidelberg, Mannheim, and other cities the people demonstrated against the rich, the government, and the Jews, who were the easiest target. In retaliation for the struggle of the Bavarian Jews for civic equality, mobs rioted in the streets, demanding "Death to the Jews!"[20] When the news came that the Revolution had triumphed in Berlin and Vienna, the anti-Jewish agitation gradually subsided.

At the "People's Parliament" on 29 August 1848, Gabriel Riesser delivered an address attacking those who were blocking full civic equality for Jews. He was greeted with stormy applause. The legislators voted not only for emancipation for Jews but for everyone in the provinces regardless of religious belief. The same proposal was made at the Diet in Prussia.

By the end of 1848, however, reaction was again in the saddle in Germany. On 5 December the kaiser dissolved the founding assembly but retained Point 12 of the constitution, which provided for general emancipation. Conflicts continued with the government for a few decades over this point, which begins, "Freedom of religion is guaranteed to everyone. . . ." Point 4 of the constitution reads, "Government positions may be filled by anyone who qualifies."[21]

Despite the political advances of 1848, the Jews were still not, in fact, granted civil rights. The liberal declarations everywhere remained only paper promises. In several provinces (for example, Bavaria), Jews did not even get these rights on paper. In the 1850s, reaction was dominant in almost all the German provinces. In 1856 a bill to revoke Point 12 of the constitution was introduced into the Prussian parliament. The proposal was rejected. After continued pressure, the reactionaries succeeded in adding Point 14, which emphasized the Christian foundations of German society. On the basis of this point, Jews were prohibited from serving as judges, professors, or school teachers. Jewish attorneys were not permitted to practice. The government explained that while the constitution prohibited the limiting of Jewish rights, the director of an institution could not be compelled to hire or not to hire an applicant, especially where it involved a leadership position.

In Bavaria the authorities rejected the emancipation proposal of the Diet with the excuse that although the Jews now deserved to be emancipated, the Christian population of the province was not yet ready for it. A great many Jews left Bavaria at that time, most of them emigrating to America.[22] In Saxony, the Christian merchants of Leipzig and Dresden convinced the government that Jewish rights must be restricted. In Baden the old anti-Jewish laws remained in the constitution along with the new ones granting them rights. The same happened in other provinces.

In the late 1850s the need to unite the German provinces into one single state weakened the reactionary feudal lords who had fought against this every step of the way. The liberal forces in all the provinces gained new strength. Two Jewish deputies were elected to the Prussian parliament in 1859. When the minister of justice "explained" that Jew could not be judge because of the Christian nature of the oath of office, a struggle ensued to abolish the oath, with a majority voting for the liberal position.

Victorious over Austria in 1866, Prussia annexed several provinces with large Jewish communities; the number of Jews in Prussia rose overnight to 300,000.[23] The same year, the Confederation of

German States was organized under the hegemony of Prussia. Four hundred Jewish communities in the area of the Confederation submitted petitions for full emancipation. On 3 July 1869 the first full emancipation of Jews in Germany was signed by Kaiser Wilhelm and Chancellor Bismarck.[24]

Germany was then dominated by a strong spirit of nationalism. The wars that it had waged and won—in 1866 against Austria, in 1870 against France—contributed to the chauvinistic Pan-Germanism which was then beginning to manifest itself. Together with this nationalism appeared a new phenomenon, modern anti-Semitism, that was more evil than the pervasive Jew-hatred of the Middle Ages.

Struggle for Jewish Emancipation in Austria and Hungary.

When the Congress of Vienna met in 1814 to establish order in Europe, Jews from Vienna, Prague, and other cities in Austria petitioned the assembly for emancipation. The Congress, however, where King Francis I of Austria was an important leader, decided that the situation in all the countries of the Confederation would remain in the status quo. Two years later the Jews of Vienna appealed to the king directly, who turned the matter over to his ministers. The reply was negative. The government then proposed certain reforms to "make the Jews worthy of equality." Jewish religious books, including the prayer book, should be translated into German. Jewish children should attend the general Christian schools. To the Ultraorthodox Jews in the Austrian provinces (Galicia, Bohemia, Moravia, Hungary), these recommendations were tantamount to apostasy. Their opposition was so vehement that the government withdrew its proposal.

In the years between 1815 and 1820, there were around two thousand Jewish families living in Vienna, a total of some 12,000 people, and in no other city in the world were Jews so deprived of rights. Only two hundred of those families—the "tolerated" Jews—were living there legally. The other Jews in Vienna had a right to be there only two weeks, and only on business, a situation which they dealt with by various maneuvers, including bribery. Many Jews lived in Vienna completely illegally, that is, they either paid the police nothing, or paid in part and owed the balance. Midnight searches by the police in homes and inns were common. Police would raid synagogues during Sabbath or holiday services, looking for "illegals." The Jews of Vienna suffered a great deal of general harassment at the hands of the local police.[25]

Occupations of the Jews were severely restricted, even those of the "tolerated." They were not permitted to own retail businesses or apothecaries; Jewish physicians could not treat Christian patients; Jewish lawyers could not practice. In Vienna a Jewish intelligentsia arose who could only practice their professions if they converted to Christianity. This group was already sufficiently assimilated to take such a step and in the 1820s and 1830s there was a veritable epidemic of conversions.

In the Viennese courts Jews were subject to an oath-taking procedure in which the judge warned them not to rely on the fact that their religion permits Jews to swear falsely in a Christian court. This degrading oath was not abolished until 1846.[26]

In the Austrian provinces of Bohemia, Moravia, Galicia, and Hungary the situation for Jews was no better than in Vienna. Apart from their rightlessness, the Galician Jews were sunk in poverty. The number of Jews in Bohemia and Moravia was strictly limited; they were taxed beyond reason and restricted as to where they could live. In Prague the Jews lived in a locked ghetto. Many cities permitted Jews to enter only for the purpose of participating in the fairs, and only on condition that they sleep in an inn outside the city limits. The list of taxes was endless—on property, on marriages, on births, on burials. For kosher meat they had to pay twice as much as for the non-kosher variety. As a result, poor Jews rarely ate meat. The price of candles was tripled or quadrupled. Sabbath and mourning candles were an absolute necessity for Jews; the Jewish tax collectors grew wealthy at the expense of their impecunious "co-religionists."

The 300,000 Jews in Galicia were the poorest of the Jews in Austria. Most of them had been expelled from the villages by the Patent of Tolerance.[27] Many went into debt in order to pay their taxes. Their marriages were almost all illegal. Out of 50,000 Jewish families, a total of 137 marriages were registered officially in the year 1825; in 1830 only 119. This was probably ten percent of all the marriages that actually took place. Many tragedies resulted from these secret marriages. If they were discovered, the young couples were compelled to pay twice as much in marriage taxes, or face imprisonment. Couples who married under such circumstances lived in a constant state of fear, as did their families.

At this time the Jews of Galicia and the other Austrian provinces were subject to compulsory military service. In Bukovina this law had not yet been adopted, so Jews began to move to that province. The government soon put a stop to it.

The city of Krakow and environs had been declared a "free republic" under Austrian authority. The Jews there were restricted to a ghetto, except for merchants, manufacturers, and professionals.

In an election to the Hungarian Parliament in 1839 the deputies were given many liberal mandates, among which were proposals for Jewish emancipation. Representatives of Jewish communities in Hungary submitted petitions for civic equality. The lower house of the parliament approved the petitions. The upper house voted against full emancipation, but recommended certain privileges: the Tolerance Tax should be abolished; the Jews should be permitted to leave the ghetto; they should be allowed to engage in the professions, to purchase land, to build homes. These recommendations were submitted to the central government in Vienna, which ruled that the Jews would be permitted to leave the ghetto, but would not be exempt from the Tolerance Tax.[28]

In 1842, when several Jews of Pressburg moved into Christian streets, their new neighbors protested. Even more effective was the fear of the artisans' guilds of Jewish competition. While the parliament again voted to recommend the abolition of the Tolerance Tax, this was accompanied by another recommendation that the Jews reform their customs and change certain of their laws which separate them from Christians and prevent them from mingling with their neighbors.

The Orthodox Jews, who made up the greatest majority of the Jewish community, were outraged by these proposals, seeing in them the hand of Jewish "heretics" who were even ready to pay the price of conversion in return for equal rights. Therefore, they sent a message to the legislators: "The Jews do not wish to be emancipated or to mingle with their Christian neighbors. The Jewish homeland is Eretz Israel, not Hungary."[29] The leaders of the parliament obliged them and withdrew the recommendation for Jewish rights, commenting that the time was not yet ripe for Jewish emancipation.

In March 1848 mass demonstrations took place in Austria demanding the abolition of the autocracy. Troops fired upon the demonstrators. The king promised to convene an assembly of popular representatives to adopt a constitution. But instead of calling together the people's representatives to draft a constitution, the king himself, in April 1848, made public his own constitution.

Regarding the Jewish question he recommended that it be tabled until it could be taken up by the new Reichstag. In the middle of May elections were held and in July the "Founding Reichstag" met, with several Jewish representatives taking part in the deliberations. Among the items on the agenda was Jewish rights. Proposals were made to table the matter. Rabbi Isaac Mannheimer, in a powerful oration, demanded the abolition of the shameful Tolerance Tax and the taxes on kosher meat and candles. His proposal was adopted by a large majority.[30]

On 14 March 1849 Francis Joseph I, the new king of Austria, proclaimed a liberal constitution which contained the following point:

> I, Francis Joseph I, declare that everyone is entitled to his own beliefs and religious customs. Civil and political rights are not dependent on religion. Civic duties, however, must not be obstructed by religious customs.[31]

As soon as the constitution was made public, Jews began to move out of the ghetto into homes on Christian streets. They bought plots of land in the villages. Jewish attorneys began to use their professional skills. Jews obtained positions in the schools and aspired to university professorships. However, the multinational character of Austria turned out to be a blow to these hopes. In Bohemia, the Czechs and the Germans were in conflict. The Jewish intellectuals were caught in a dilemma. Educated in the German language, they leaned toward the Germans. This so enraged the Czech patriots that they attacked Jews in Prague. The same process was repeated in Hungary and in the former Polish and other Slavic areas. The hotter the fight between the nationalities, the more dangerous it became for Jews to take sides.

In Galicia the Jews, who fifty years earlier had been Polish citizens, felt closer to the Poles. They could not forget that Austria had expelled tens of thousands of Jews from the villages. The Orthodox rabbi of Krakow, Dov Berish Meisels, was a Polish patriot who belonged to the most radical Polish group. A current joke had it that when he was asked why an Orthodox rabbi would join the "Lefts," he replied that it was because Jews had no "Rights."[32]

In Hungary the Jews fared worse during the stormy year of 1848, although many Jews then joined the National Guard. Hungarian merchants and artisans were opposed to letting the Jews out of the ghetto and into the Christian streets. On 19–20 March 1848, mobs attacked Jewish homes and stores and levelled the synagogue while the police and the army stood by. When the Jews demanded protection they were informed by the city council that it would be forthcoming if the Jews moved out of the Christian streets "to calm the anger of the people." The Jews agreed to do so.[33]

Pogroms followed in other Hungarian cities, especially where Jews had bought homes in Christian neighborhoods. The epidemic reached Pest, where on 19 April a demonstration took place demanding the expulsion of all Jews who had settled there after 1840. Another demand was that Jews be expelled from the National Guard.

As the Hungarian separatist movement continued to gain strength, the parliament proclaimed Hungary's independence from Austria. Expecting Austria to send an army into Pest, the Hungarians mobilized. Jews were ordered to join the army and help defend their country. Masses of Jews, hoping this would result in their emancipation, volunteered. Jewish communities contributed large sums of money for the defense of Hungarian independence.[34]

On 18 August 1849 the Austrian army dispersed the Hungarian parliament. Hungarian Jews were compelled to pay a large fine. Shortly thereafter this money was used to open German schools for Jews in Hungary as a way to counter the Magyar influence. The effect, however, of having Jewish children studying German in the Hungarian cities was only to incite anti-Semitism.

As in the rest of Europe, reaction was the order of the day in Austria. Jew-haters raised a demand for cutting back the rights of Jews, particularly their right to reside among Christians. In 1853 a law was passed in Vienna prohibiting Jews from buying land in areas which had been barred to them previously. Demands were raised again for controlling the size of the Jewish population. Jewish physicians and lawyers were prohibited from practicing. Jewish teachers were dismissed from their posts. Jewish emancipation was in limbo.

In 1859 Austria lost a war to Italy and France. One month after the defeat the Austrian government announced that it was preparing a reform of its laws concerning Jews. In February 1860 a law was passed permitting Jews to buy land and homes in the previously forbidden cities and provinces, and permitting them to live anywhere they chose. In 1866 Austria was again defeated, this time by Prussia. In 1867 Austria made peace with Hungary. The result was the formation of Austria-Hungary. All the national minorities in the empire, including the Jews, were emancipated.[35]

At the same time, the exclusive right of Catholic monks to be teachers in elementary and high schools was abolished. Many Jews then became teachers, lawyers, physicians, journalists. Although they had the right to vote, Jews could still not hold public office. The reason here was not directly related to anti-Semitism. Austrian deputies were elected by nationality. The Germans, Hungarians, and Czechs elected their representatives according to the number of voters who spoke those national languages. Jews who lived in Vienna spoke German and voted for Germans; Hungarian Jews for Hungarians, and so on. The Germans did not nominate any Jews, nor did the Poles. Jews themselves called their language (Yiddish) a "jargon," not a "true" language. They did not speak Hebrew. The few Jews who were elected to the parliament were recorded there as Germans, Poles, or Hungarians.

This situation was one of the chief reasons Nathan Birenbaum undertook to raise the status of Yiddish to a national language by calling the Czernowitz Conference in 1908.[36]

21

Modern Anti-Semitism at the End of the Nineteenth Century

Germany. Modern anti-Semitism is a new version of the old Jew-hatred which was widespread among the nations for many centuries. What was new in the modern version was (1) that all the old charges against the Jews, which had mostly been based on blind fanaticism, were now a matter of pseudoscientific "truths" and (2) while the old Jew-hatred demanded of the Jew that he give up his Jewishness and convert, the new version did not allow the Jew any way to do this, either by total assimilation or by conversion.

The four volumes of Arthur de Gobineau's pseudoscientific race theory were not immediately translated from the French into German, but they nevertheless became quite popular in Germany. His race theory fit right into the ideologies then prevalent in Germany: the Aryan race is the noblest, and the Germans are its best representatives. The Semitic race, conversely, is the lowest and the most pernicious.

During the nineteenth century rapid industrial growth took place in the more developed European countries, including Germany, with a corresponding urban expansion as the village population streamed into the cities. Jews, too, moved from the smaller towns to the larger centers. In 1816 there were only three thousand Jews in Berlin (more were not permitted to enter).[1] By 1854 there were already 54,000 Jews in Berlin; in 1910, 144,000.[2]

The Jews had shed their long gabardines, shaved their beards, assimilated linguistically, and reformed their manner of worship.

The emancipated German Jews were already "Germans of the Mosaic persuasion" and did not expect Jew-hatred ever to return, much less to increase. They were certain that with the spread of knowledge and education, the false and dangerous hostility to Jews would vanish.[3] All the Jewish "shortcomings" were fast disappearing. Jews no longer spoke the "corrupt Judaeo-German"; their German was perfect. All the anti-Semites would soon see that Jews are good, loyal German citizens, not foreigners, not "unproductive," and certainly not enemies of the Fatherland.

Heinrich Graetz, the noted Jewish historian, declared in the foreword to the last volume of his *History of the Jews*, written in German: "I can say with satisfaction that I am happier than many of my predecessors. In the civilized world we Jews have finally achieved rights and recognition."[4] Graetz and many other Jews of his generation deluded themselves. In the third quarter of the nineteenth century, not only had Jew-hatred not disappeared from Germany, but it was actually on the increase.

Generations of Germans had maintained the stereotyped concept of the Jew as a criminal element, a crafty swindler, a thieving bloodsucker, a virtually subhuman species, a tool of Satan. Many German intellectuals considered the Jews to be worthless, in accordance with the oft-quoted comments of Voltaire or the other anti-Semites of the Enlightenment. Malcolm Hay quotes Voltaire: "Jews are an ignorant and barbarous people who for a long time have combined the most unworthy avarice with the most detestable superstition."[5]

Their German neighbors observed very well that the Jew, as soon as he was emancipated, accomplished a great deal. In one generation the despised *Jude* had attained a prominent economic and cultural position. Obviously the "cunning Jew" had achieved this not by honest means, diligence, and ability, but by swindling and shady deals. The preachments of the Church and the anti-Semite of the Right and the Left that Jewish wealth was the result of chicanery was accepted by the people as unquestioned truth. The notion was widely current that big business, capitalism, the banks, the stock market, all were Jewish inventions.

The wars in central Europe in the mid-nineteenth century had promised victory and prosperity, but failed to bring either. Under the leadership of the Iron Chancellor Bismarck the separate dukedoms were transformed into a strong nation which united the ethnic German people under a state ruled by the Prussian Junkers.

Nationalism grew rapidly among all the European peoples during this period, but in Germany there was super-nationalism. Everywhere the foreigner was looked upon with suspicion, but in Germany he was met with hatred.

Among the new ideologies which raised the temperature of hatred during the nineteenth century was the Romanticism then current among the German intelligentsia. Romanticism taught that the highest "aristocrat" in the land was the people itself. A people is one family, with one language. The folk language and the folklore are the repository of wisdom and all the other national values. The great courage of the people is symbolized in the ancient folk heroes who fought for the people's cause. Along with all this, the medieval folk hatred of Jews returned to Germany. All the old libels were revived: the Jews are deadly enemies of Christ, they crucify Christian children, they poison wells and do the work of the devil.

The nineteenth century also saw the rise of the scientific theories of Herbert Spencer and Charles Darwin, which led to the cynical deprecation and condemnation of the weak and the lowly in society. In his *Origin of the Species* Darwin showed that the "unfit" of all the species perish, that only the strong survive—the stronger animals, the stronger plants, and similarly the stronger peoples; it is a law of nature. In 1881 Darwin warned: "The lower races which, in the uncivilized world, would be eliminated, will in the near future inundate the world. . . ."[6]

In 1873 Germany was hit by a severe economic crisis which resulted in an extremely dangerous anti-Semitic storm. The expanding industry which had brought masses of people from the countryside into the cities left them there to "sink or swim." They had no trade unions, no social security arrangements of any kind. The working day was twelve to sixteen hours; the wages were abominable; child labor was commonplace. As long as there was work and some hope of improving one's lot, people were patient. They grumbled, but it did not go much further than than. Even if the factory owner was a Jew, it did not matter too much. Working conditions in the Jew's factory were no worse than in other places; sometimes they were even a little better.

During the crisis, however, when masses of workers were unceremoniously left hungry and without a roof over their heads, the "culprit" was immediately spotlighted: the enemy was the foreigner, none other than the *Jude*. This singling out of the Jews as the main cause of all the trouble became the practice of both Right and Left.[7] Among the anti-Semites of the political Right were the impoverished feudal lords who blamed the moneyed aristocracy for their social, economic, and governmental decline, and the symbol of that aristocracy was the Jew. On the Right was also the Church, both Catholic and Protestant, which had never ceased its dissemination of Jew-hatred. With the advent of capitalism, however, the Church lost its birthright. When Bismarck found that he could not safeguard the absolutism of the German state, because of the influence of the Roman pope upon Catholics in Germany, he obtained the help of the liberals in the country and waged a *Kulturkampf*, greatly reducing the pope's influence in Germany. Among these liberals were several prominent Jews, German patriots. As a result, Catholic hostility toward the Jews mounted. In general, the declining Church saw the emancipated Jew in the ascendancy; in the anti-Jewish chorus, the voice of the Church was among the loudest. The most strident voice on the Right, however, was that of the German ultranationalists, who accused the Jews of bringing French socialist, anarchist, and democratic ideas into Germany.

From the Left the anti-Jewish clamor was equally effective, as it is evident in the words of Proudhon:

> The Jews poison everything they touch. . . . The Jew was and remains a misanthrope. . . . This race must be sent back to Asia or assimilated by force. If not, expel them or destroy them utterly by fire. This is our duty. In the Middle Ages the people did this instinctively; we must do it consciously.[8]

The anarchist leader Bakunin wrote:

> The Jews are parasites, leeches which suck the blood of the nations. . . . Jews support Marx, on the one hand, and Rothschild on the other.[9]

In his writings and speeches Bakunin always coupled Marx with Rothschild as a sort of twin.

Eugen Dühring, one of the Left's leading spokesmen in Germany, stated in his *Die Judenfrage*:

> The Jewish people is the worst branch of the Semitic race. . . . The aim of the Jews is to rule the world, exploit the peoples. . . . The government should remove Jews from public positions, from the press; it should not permit them to be teachers and merchants. We must not permit mixed marriages, so that our blood not be mixed with Jewish blood. . . ."[10]

The socialist and pseudo-socialist writings during the 1880s in Germany, Austria, France, and Russia do not lack anti-Semitic propaganda.[11]

The difference between the old anti-Jewish charges and those in the latter part of the nineteenth century was that now they were made not only on Sundays in church, but seven days a week in many places. Jews were mocked and insulted at mass meetings, in theaters, in taverns, on the street, in the newspapers. Special anti-Jewish organizations were founded. Anti-Semitic congresses were convened. The Jews were denounced as the "internal enemy." Heinrich von Treitschke, a German historian, coined the slogan, "Jews are our misfortune."[12] William Marr warned the Germans that the Jews were planning to destroy Germany: "Let us bow our heads and say, '*Finis Germania*.'"[13] Demands were raised to drive the Jews back into ghettos or expel them from the country.[14] In 1890, five deputies were elected to the Reichstag on an anti-Semitic program; by 1893 there were already sixteen.

The Jewish community in Berlin several times suggested to the Prussian government that anti-Semitic agitation was a threat to public peace, as well as a danger to the Jews. Their recommendations were ignored. In an attempt to counter the anti-Semitic propaganda, Jewish leaders issued apologetic tracts showing that Jews are loyal German citizens, that they are not a separate nation but Germans of the Mosaic persuasion, that they should be regarded in the same light as Catholics and Protestants.

Against this apologia Treitschke wrote a series of articles for the prestigious Prussian journal, *Jahrbücher*, in which he "demonstrated scientifically" that the Catholics and Protestants are branches of one Christian tree, and that they are German by origin. Jews, however, belong to another religion and another race, as proven by the Jewish historian Graetz. Jews are a separate nation, united with the Jews of the whole world; they are not Germans.[15]

Anti-Jewish incitement in Germany had its logical outcome. In the early 1880s physical attacks on Jews occurred in public places, with students prominent in the mobs. In the name of patriotism the anti-Semitic press, supported by the Conservative Party with the tacit approval of Bismarck, printed diatribes against Jews. A three-pronged petition was submitted to Bismarck by the organized anti-Semites: (1) All immigration of Jews into Germany must be stopped at once; (2) Jews must be dismissed from public positions and not permitted to serve as judges, attorneys, and such; (3) Jewish teachers must be dismissed from public schools and a law passed that only Christians may teach in German schools. These proposals were already being implemented quietly in Germany. By 1887 all Polish, Galician and Hungarian Jews had been expelled from German cities.[16] In March 1881, anti-Semitic petitions bearing a quarter million signatures were presented to Chancellor Bismarck.

On 12 November 1880 seventy-six prominent liberal leaders in Berlin published a protest against the government for permitting anti-Semitic agitation and physical attacks against Jews. In the Reichstag, debates on the Jewish Question began. No decisions were reached and the hate propaganda was not stopped. In 1881 organized anti-Semitic groups appeared in Germany bearing the innocent title of "Reform Societies." By 1885 there were fifty-two such groups; by 1890, one hundred thirty-six.[17] In Neu-Stetin, anti-Semites had burned down a new synagogue in February 1881; several months later pogroms took place there and in other provincial towns and cities. Concerned lest Germany acquire a reputation as a land of pogroms (like Russia), the government sent word down that pogrom incitement would be severely punished. The attacks stopped.

In 1882 an international congress of anti-Semites in Dresden adopted a series of anti-Jewish resolutions. Delegates were present from Russia and Hungary, as well as from Germany and Austria. The Congress called for the formation of an international organization of anti-Semites. After all, did not the Jews have their own *Alliance Israélite Universelle*? One delegate, who considered the program too moderate, insisted that the Jewish problem could be solved only by expulsions. When asked where the Jews would go, he replied: "That's *their* worry."

The German anti-Semitic activists generally were not ignorant street ruffians. In addition to Treitschke, other well-known cultural leaders such as the philosophers Eduard von Hartmann and Johann Scher were busy spreading Jew-hatred all over the world. The composer Richard Wagner (1813–83), who was Hitler's teacher and prophet, was constantly warning the German people against the racial degeneration that would result from mixing with the Jews.[18] In 1885 a Congress of German anti-Semites took place in Bochum, a large industrial city in the southern Rhine region. This meeting was already run by extremists who advocated that the German working class must be mobilized by means of anti-Semitic actions.

In 1884, in a village in Pomerania, the body of a fourteen-year-old

Christian boy was found in a river. Anti-Semites accused Jews of the murder. A farmworker testified that on the day the boy disappeared he saw the Jew, Josephson, near the bridge. Josephson and two other Jews (a father and son) were arrested. In their cellar, police found a pot of blood which, upon analysis, turned out to be ox blood. The witness changed his story. He had not actually seen Josephson near the bridge; it was the Catholic woodcutter, Berent, who had paid him to say he had seen the Jew. Berent was arrested and tried in Danzig before a jury of six Protestants and six Catholics. The trial ended in a hung jury; the Protestants found Berent guilty, the Catholics were not convinced. The Jews and Berent were freed.

In 1891, in a town called Ksanton, the body of a five-year-old Christian child was found with his throat cut. The Jewish *schochet* ("butcher") Bushoff was arrested. No evidence being presented against him, he was released. Protest meetings were organized demanding that the investigation be reopened. Bushoff was re-arrested. His trial took place in Cleves, a large city, and after eleven days of testimony, he was acquitted. The anti-Jewish agitation, however, continued until Bushoff and several other Jews moved out of the town.

The final decade of the nineteenth century saw an intensification of reaction and anti-Semitism in Germany. In 1891 an anti-Semitic candidate for the Reichstag, Alvardt, published a pamphlet, "The Hopeless Fight of the Aryans Against the Jews," in which he openly called for pogroms. The Prussian police confiscated the pamphlet and imprisoned Alvardt for a theft he had committed. In the elections to the Reichstag in 1893 the anti-Semitic party drew a quarter million votes and elected sixteen deputies, among whom was Alvardt.[19]

Anti-Semitic agitation in Germany generally increased during holiday seasons. As customers streamed into the stores, anti-Semites stood outside with leaflets calling for a boycott of Jewish businesses. Students demonstrated for the exclusion of Russian Jews who had been coming to Germany to study.[20] In 1890 prominent liberals—Christians and Jews—founded the "Society against Anti-Semitism" and attracted several thousand German citizens as members. In 1891 the Society published a book, *The Mirror for Anti-Semites*, in an effort to counter the anti-Semitic "Catechism." It was not very effective; the "Catechism" was circulated in hundreds of thousands of copies, the *Mirror* only in ten thousand.

The Social Democratic Party, which by 1890 had a strong fraction in the Reichstag, began a counterattack against anti-Semitism in Germany. August Bebel, in the name of the Social Democrats, published his "Anti-Semitism and Social Democracy" in which he condemned the anti-Semites. In general, however, the Social Democrats failed to recognize the national rights of the Jews. Like everyone else, they did not consider the Jews a separate nationality; a nation without a land was inconceivable to them. This principle remained rooted in the socialist programs of almost all the workers' parties in the world.

Houston Stewart Chamberlain, a particularly dangerous anti-Semite, was born in England, brought up in France, fell in love with the Germans, and settled in Berlin. Married to Richard Wagner's daughter, he became a popularizer of Wagner's "cultural" anti-Semitism. In 1898 he published *Grundlagen* (*Foundations of the Nineteenth Century*), a book replete with fantastic race theories. He "proved" that throughout the entire nineteenth century there had been a continuing struggle between the best, most honorable representatives of the "noble" Aryan race, the Germans, and the worst representatives of the Semitic race, the Jews. He also "proved" that the most important figures in Jewish history are, in reality, descended from the Aryan race. King David, the prophets, Jesus, all were Aryans, not Jews, who have never produced anyone that contributed anything useful to humanity. To permit the Jews to go on existing is, therefore, a crime.[21] Wilhelm II recommended *Foundations* as a textbook in the public schools. Up until 1945 this work was printed in more than a hundred editions. Chamberlain lived until 1927 and in his later years became friendly with Adolf Hitler.

On Passover eve of 1900, the dismembered body of a German high school student was discovered in Konitz. Suspicion fell on a German woodcutter named Hoffman, who had accused the student of having sexual relations with his daughter. At the instigation of local anti-Semitic newspapers, a Jewish woodcutter, Israelski, was also arrested on suspicion of ritual murder. After a thorough investigation both men were released for lack of evidence. The effect, however, was to stir up a fresh wave of Jew-hatred.

Austria-Hungary. The anti-Semitism which flourished in Germany in the last two decades of the nineteenth century crossed over into Austria-Hungary and quickly found fertile soil. Anti-Semitism in Austria-Hungary was both traditionally Catholic and "modern."

Among the many nationalities there the Germans were most numerous. In Vienna, where the number of Jews had been limited before, the Jewish population had greatly increased since the emancipation in 1867, and the anti-Semites began complaining that Vienna was "full of Jews." (The census of 1869 shows 40,000 Jews in that city with residence rights; by 1900 there were 147,000.)[22]

In 1873, when the economic crisis hit Vienna, as it did many other European centers, the Jew-hatred which had been lurking in dark corners came out into the open. In 1871 August Rohling (1839–1931), a professor at Prague University and a Catholic theologian, published his *Talmud Jude*, in which he repeated all the anti-Jewish slanders that had appeared in Eisenmenger's *Judaism Revealed* in the seventeenth century.[23] The book was directly responsible for a rise in anti-Semitic agitation wherever it was read. In 1880 a German Protestant theologian, Franz Delitch, analyzed the work and showed that it was full of lies, that the translation from the original Talmudic texts was incorrect, and that Rohling's commentary was false, that he did not even begin to understand the Talmud.

In the early 1880s, organized anti-Semitic groups made their appearance in Austria. Georg Schönerer, an outspoken anti-Semite of the Left, and a Reichsrat deputy, was very influential in Vienna. An advocate of Pan-Germanism, he maintained that Austria must ally itself with Germany and create a Greater Germany.[24] He accused the Austrian Jews of weakening German national feelings, of "Polonizing" and "Magyarizing" the pure German culture. Jews are friendly to Poland, Hungary, Czechoslovakia, and are, therefore, enemies of Germany.

When news of a ritual murder in Hungary spread in 1882, Rohling published another brochure entitled, "Human Sacrifices of the Rabbis," in which he "proved" that Jews use Christian blood for ritual purposes. When it became known that Rohling was going to testify as an "expert witness" at the trial in Hungary, the Jewish Reichsrat deputy, Rabbi Joseph Bloch, accused him of intending to commit perjury. Rohling brought the rabbi into court. Both sides proposed to bring experts to testify on their behalf. Bloch's witnesses were to be outstanding Christian theologians and Talmudic authorities. Rohling proposed a convert named Justus, who had become a Protestant and then a Catholic. As soon as the trial began and Rohling realized that he would be exposed, he withdrew his charge against the rabbi and asked the court to stop the trial.[25] Rohling's effectiveness was thus impaired, but he continued to hurl accusations against the Jews. His writings have remained source books for anti-Semites until today.

In 1891 the anti-Semites elected thirteen deputies to the Austrian Reichsrat, and among them was Schönerer. Joining the thirteen was a Viennese lawyer, Karl Lueger, a skilled orator and a powerful demagogue. From year to year the number of anti-Semitic deputies in the Reichsrat increased. In 1895 the anti-Semites elected Lueger mayor of Vienna. Emperor Franz Joseph, however, refused to confirm Lueger for the post, on the ground that he would cause disturbances in the city. After street demonstrations demanded that Lueger be confirmed, the Vienna City Council again elected him. Again the emperor refused to confirm him. After the third time, Lueger took office. Jews were immediately dismissed from positions in the city government. Jewish merchants were not given orders for municipal supplies. Jewish students in public schools were required to pay tuition.

In 1893 a Catholic priest named Deckert published an article in the newspaper, *Fatherland*, charging Jews with killing Christian children for ritual purposes. Rabbi Bloch thereupon wrote an article for the influential *Austrian Weekly* ridiculing the priest and his accusations. Deckert had relied on a letter from a convert, Paul Meyer, who reported that as a child he had participated in such a ritual murder in his native city of Ostroh, near Lublin. Meyer named several Jews who allegedly had been involved in the crime. Bloch and other Jewish leaders brought Deckert into court. At the trial, the convert denied that he had ever written such a letter or ever participated in such a murder.

In Vienna, as in Berlin, the Jews organized a defense society and were successful in stopping several blood libels. The society was hardly a match, however, for the avalanche of anti-Jewish propaganda coming from all sides. No non-Jews appeared as allies to help the Jews combat the ugly campaign. The Social Democratic Party in Vienna, under the leadership of Victor Adler (who later converted to Christianity), ignored the rising tide of anti-Semitism. At the Socialist Congress in Brussels in 1891 Adler opposed any involvement with the Jewish problem.[26] In a private conversation he explained that anti-Semitism is not such a bad thing, because it awakens the working class and the middle class against the capitalists, and this is good for socialism. In other words, anti-Semitism is a useful tool that helps pave the way for socialism. The *Narodnaya Volyo* in Russia at that time was also pleased that Jews were supplying the "bloody lubricant" to grease the wheels of the revolution.[27]

In March 1882, in a village near Krakow, the body of a pregnant Christian woman, who was apparently murdered, was found near a Jewish home. The Jew, Riesser, and his wife were arrested, along with a Pole, Zochlinski, an uncle of the victim. A witness testified that the uncle had had sexual relations with his niece. After an investigation, Zochlinski confessed to the crime, but added that Riesser had helped him commit it. The court sentenced Zochlinski, Riesser and his wife to death. The high court in Vienna overturned the decision. These legalities dragged on for four years, during which time Zochlinski died in prison. It was not until 1886 that the higher court finally released the Jewish couple.

In the cities and villages in Galicia an atmosphere for a pogrom was building among the Poles. One anti-Semitic priest, Stoyalovski, announced his candidacy for the Reichsrat in western Galicia. In a campaign characterized by pogrom incitement, he directed his demagogy at "Jewish exploiters" who grow rich at the expense of the peasants. The result was that during his campaign in July 1898, pogroms actually took place in thirty towns in his district.[28]

In Bohemia the nationalism of the Czechs was no less active than that of the Poles. Hostility toward the small number of Jews in Czechoslovakia (2 percent of the population) emanated from both Czechs and Germans. In 1897 the government in Vienna granted equal status to the Czech language. The Germans demonstrated in the Reichsrat. In Prague, Czechs took to the streets, attacking Germans and Jewish-owned businesses whose names sounded German. Stores were vandalized, homes burned, synagogues destroyed. However, this did not prevent German anti-Semites from demonstrating against and even abusing Jews in Czechoslovakia.

In 1899 the anti-Semites on both sides united to create a ritual murder frameup. Around Passover time, the body of a Czech girl was found in a woods near a Czech town. Witnesses testified that on the day of the murder they had seen a young Jew near the woods, one Leopold Hilsner, accompanied by two other unidentified Jews. Hilsner denied any complicity in the matter. Anti-Semitic newspapers, both Czech and German, reported it as a ritual murder. Hilsner was tried, found guilty, and sentenced to death.

Attacks began on Jews in Prague and other cities. Speaking out against the decision of the court, Tomáš Masaryk, later president of the Czech Republic, published a pamphlet, "The Need to Review the

Trial in the Town of Polne." Analyzing all the details of the case, he showed that the trial had been so influenced by the anti-Semitic atmosphere that the result was "a Czech version of the Dreyfus case in Paris."[29] The pamphlet was confiscated by the government. Debates took place in the Reichsrat over the conduct of the trial. One Democratic deputy used the opportunity to read Masaryk's brochure into the record. The newspapers reprinted it as a parliamentary report which, according to law, was not subject to censorship. Masaryk was charged with contempt of court. Censured students organized anti-Masaryk demonstrations.

The Jewish population in Hungary was a significant minority. In 1880 it numbered three-quarters of a million, and by 1900 it had grown to 900,000. The nationalists in the country were eager to "Magyarize" their minorities, particularly the Jews, who had no "Jewish-land" anywhere to defend their interests. For many generations the Jews in Hungary had listed German as their first language when they registered as citizens. Resenting this the Magyars accused the Jews of "Germanizing" Hungary. In the next registration, three-quarters of the Jews listed Hungarian as their mother tongue. In actuality, 90 percent of the Jews spoke Yiddish.

The Magyarization of the Hungarian Jews did not protect them from anti-Semitic insults and attacks. Anti-Jewish pamphlets were distributed in Hungary just as they were in Germany and Austria. Petitions were circulated among the people asking the government not to permit Jewish refugees from the Russian pogroms to settle in Hungarian cities. The Austrian parliament, however, rejected these demands, declaring: "We must not drive away from our gates persecuted people seeking a place of refuge."

On 1 April 1882, in the village of Tisza-Eszlar, a fourteen-year-old girl disappeared while on an errand. Rumors of a ritual murder spread throughout the village, in which there were about two hundred Jews. Two months later the body of a girl was pulled out of the Danube, the face badly mutilated; she was wearing a dress that had belonged to the missing girl. The mother insisted it was not her daughter.

Anti-Semites then spread the story that the Jews had purposely dressed the body in the girl's clothing to confuse the situation. Since the girl would have had to pass the synagogue on her errand, the caretaker, Joseph Sharf, was arrested, along with several leading Jews of the community. Some Christian boys who had been playing with the Sharf children related that they heard from the caretaker's six-year-old son that his father had killed a little girl. The child was interrogated and said he had heard the story from his fourteen-year-old brother Moritz. Upon interrogation, Moritz said he had heard the story from the children in the street, and that he had told his brother their father was being accused of murdering the Christian girl.

The interrogators kept after the boy until they extracted a "confession"—he had watched through a keyhole in the synagogue and seen his father and two other Jews kill the girl and drain her blood into a pot. On the basis of this confession, fifteen Jews in the village were arrested. The boy was taken away to a neighboring town, placed in the home of a wealthy Christian family, and promised all sorts of rewards if he would convert and testify against his father and the other Jews. The Tisza-Eszlar murder case was sensationalized all over the country. On 28-29 September 1882 a pogrom took place in Pressburg while the police stood by. Government troops were sent in to quell the riots as martial law was declared in the area.

Meanwhile the chief prosecutor began a review of the "Jewish" crime" and ordered the trial moved to another city. Leading attorneys in the country, Christians and Jews, participated in the defense. The fourteen-year-old Moritz, witness against his own father, had been well-rehearsed, but became so entangled in his studied answers that his testimony was thrown out. The court discovered how the "investigators" had distorted the facts. Experts showed that the body in the river was that of someone the same age as the missing girl. The most important attack on the blood libel was made by the prosecutor, who reduced the entire trial to what it really was—a frameup against Jews. "The investigation as conducted by the anti-Semites is a disgrace to Hungarian justice. . . . Anti-Semitism was imported into our country from foreign lands—Russia and Germany." The arrested Jews were released.[30]

In response, the Jew-baiters spread rumors that the Jews had bribed the court. They threatened revenge. In several villages there were attacks upon Jews. The government punished the attackers severely. In 1884, two years after the Tisza-Eszler case, the anti-Semites elected seventeen deputies to the parliament. As the years went by, however, they continued to lose ground. The Jews of Hungary soon became true Hungarian patriots. By the turn of the century the atmosphere of hate in Austria-Hungary had cooled off, but only on the surface. Deeper down, Jew-hatred remained strongly rooted and unshakable.

In a census taken at the end of the century there were approximately 2.2 million Jews in Austria, living as a minority among the various peoples in the country.[31] With the exception of those in Galicia and Bukovina, the Jews were linguistically assimilated. The large majority of Jews spoke Yiddish, but they themselves considered Yiddish not a legitimate language, but a jargon. In Budapest the Hungarians wanted the Jews to become Magyars. In Prague the Jews were expected to become Czechs. The Poles of Krakow and Lwow expected the Jews there to be Polish patriots. None of the national groups regarded the Jews as a separate people with its own national rights.

Because of their historical proximity to Germany, and especially under the influence of the dominant German culture in Central Europe, the Jews in most Austro-Hungarian cities felt closest to the German language and culture. The Magyars of Budapest, like the Czechs of Prague, therefore saw the Jews as their enemies who had "Germanized" their countries. The nationlists among both these peoples thus had another reason for their old Judophobia—Jews were foreigners everywhere.

At the turn of the century there were many anti-Semitic parties and groups in Austria. The Christian-Socialists, the Pan-Germans, the German Radical Party, the National Socialists—these are the best known. In addition, there were anti-Semitic student groups in most universities. All these groups had the support of the Catholic Church. Anti-Semitic tirades in the press were forbidden, except for speeches made in the Reichsrat, and the anti-Jewish newspapers made full use of this privilege.

In 1905 the Austrian government decided to democratize the parliament in Vienna and institute proportional representation for the nationalities in the country. Justifiably, the basic identifying mark of a nationality was taken to be the language spoken by the people. Elections were held in the spring of 1907. Eight of the larger nationalities were eligible to comprise the Reichsrat. The Jews, fifth according to their number, were not among those eight. Neither the government nor any of the other national groups recognized the Jews as a separate people. The Jews themselves were sharply divided over this issue. Jewish assimilationists insisted that Yiddish was not a language, that Jews are Germans of the Mosaic faith, or Poles of the Mosaic faith. Some Jewish nationalists maintained that the Jewish language was Hebrew, a language which very few Jews at that time understood and still fewer could speak. The assimilationists also insisted that if Jews had any national language at all it was Hebrew; certainly not the "hybrid and corrupted German jargon" spoken by the Galician Jews.

The Germans, Poles, Czechs, and other groups, who were interested in increasing the number of their deputies, wanted the Jews to vote for them. To their aid came the Jewish assimilationists who argued that the Jews in Vienna should register as Germans, in Prague as Czechs, in Krakow and Lwow as Poles. They warned the Hasidim in the backward Galician towns that if they registered as Jews and listed Yiddish as their language, it would not help them anyway, and the Poles would only punish them for having done so.[32] Jewish national leaders such as Nathan Birenbaum propagandized for recognition of the Jews as a people, with Yiddish as their national language. Petitions to that effect were submitted to the Reichsrat. The Ukrainians of Galicia, anxious to weaken the position of the Poles, supported these petitions. The Polish anti-Semites, however, declared categorically that they would not permit a third nationality in "their" Galicia. The Jews are not a nation, they insisted. Even the Polish Socialist Party, which at that time wielded considerable influence, refused to recognize the Jews as a separate people.[33]

This furor around the elections served to raise Jewish national consciousness. Yiddish began functioning as a language which could elect more Jews to the Reichsrat and help the Jews in Austria achieve political rights, fight against anti-Semitism, and generally improve the Jewish situation.

In the Galician city of Drohobicz, the struggle between Jewish nationalists and assimilationists resulted in a bloody tragedy. In the elections for the Reichsrat in 1911, the Poles nominated an assimilated Jew named Levenstein as a Polish candidate. The Jewish *Folkisten* and other organizations nominated a nationalist Jew. By manipulating the balloting. the Poles declared Levenstein the winner. On 8 June 1911 the outraged Jews in Drohobicz organized a demonstration in the streets. They were dispersed by the militia, who shot into the crowd, killing twenty people and wounding many others.[34]

Polish anti-Semitism in Austria early in the twentieth century was on the rise. The Poles themselves were not the political masters in their own cities and villages, but they found ways to persecute the Jews. They organized consumer cooperatives to boycott Jewish merchants. Jewish artisans and handicraftsmen were similarly boycotted.

Linguistic assimilation in Hungary was well advanced, with the Hungarian language virtually forced upon everyone. Even the Orthodox Jews (the largest majority) adopted Hungarian. Still suffering from the anti-Jewish excesses of the 1880s, the Jews were wary about raising nationalist issues.

Before World War I there were about 2.25 million Jews in Austria-Hungary, and the number remained almost unchanged as the natural increase in population emigrated, mostly to America. The first battles of World War I took place in Galicia, and the Jews fled deeper into the country. When the Russians later retreated from Galicia they evacuated many of the remaining Jews into the Russian hinterland.

22

Jews in Russia Until the End of the Eighteenth and the Beginning of the Nineteenth Centuries

For many centuries before Russian rule extended over that country's southern provinces and the Crimean Peninsula, Jewish communities had already existed there. Records exist of such communities in Crimea as early as the days of the Roman Empire. In the fourteenth and fifteenth centuries, when the attacks on Jews in Christian countries in central and western Europe were intensified, many Jewish refugees found a haven in southern Russia, Crimea, and the Caucasus.

In 1475 Turkey conquered the Crimean Peninsula, and the Sephardic Jewish communities in Turkey were able to communicate with the Jews in Kiev, Volhynia, Poland, and Lithuania. When the Jews were expelled from Lithuania in 1495, many of them found a home in Crimea. The vast territories of Muscovy were then already closed to Jews, the Russian Boyars, rulers of the country in the fifteenth and sixteenth centuries, having prohibited Jewish settlement there. Jews were looked upon as harmful sorcerers, and many of the western Jew-baiting slanders made their way into Russia, where they found ready ears.

Czar Ivan the Terrible (1547–84) was strongly opposed to admitting Jews into his country; he was simply afraid of them, considering them tools of Satan. In 1550, when Jewish merchants came from Poland to Russia with goods, the czar ordered them put into prison and their property confiscated. When Sigismund II, king of Poland, appealed to Ivan to release the merchants, who were Polish citizens, Ivan replied that he would never allow Jews into his country; that Jews brought nothing but evil everywhere and it was his duty to protect his people.[1]

From time to time hostilities broke out between Russian and Polish armies. In February 1563, when the Russians occupied the Polish city of Polotsk, Ivan ordered the Jews of that city thrown into the Dvina River. Russian troops chopped holes in the ice over the frozen river and drowned many Jews,[2] sparing only those who converted to the Greek Orthodox faith. Several years later, when Polotsk reverted to Poland, Jews settled there again.

When the Russian Boyars, seeking a permanent czar for their country, were negotiating with King Sigismund III of Poland about placing his son on the throne, one of the conditions they proposed was that Jews must not be permitted to migrate from Poland into Russia. In 1638 a Polish king again appealed to Czar Michael Romanov to permit Jewish merchants into Muscovy. The request was denied. Polish merchants, replied the czar, were always welcome in his country, but Jews, never.

Jews were also unwelcome in Riga, capital of Latvia. The local merchants, together with the priests, were adamant about not admitting Jews into their city.

In the second half of the seventeenth century, when Russia conquered certain Polish territories, the priests drove out of Kiev, which was conquered in 1667, those Jews who had settled there after the Chmielnicki massacres. In 1702 in the town of Horodnya, province of Tchernigov, the priests invented a blood libel around a drunken brawl which had resulted in the death of one man. The actual murderer reported that some Jews had killed his friend. The Jewish tavern-keeper and several other Jews were arrested and tortured, and a confession was extracted from them. How the matter ended is not known, except that it reached the attention of the czar.[3]

During a war which Peter I waged against the Swedes, the Russian troops, many of them Cossacks, marched through Jewish towns in Byelorussia robbing and killing *Zhids* in the tradition of Chmielnicki. A Jewish archive of Amchislav has a record of a pogrom of local Jews begun by a Cossack detachment. Czar Peter, who happened to be there, stopped the pogrom and punished the ringleaders.[4]

When the Russian army wrested the city of Smolensk from the Poles, the Greek Orthodox priests appealed to their synod in St. Petersburg for permission to expel the Jews and destroy the synagogue. Their request was granted. Expulsion also was decreed upon the Jews of the Ukraine, east of the Dnieper River.

In the interim between Czar Peter's death and the ascension of Catherine II in 1762, centralized authority in the country was shaky, and several changes in power occurred, but no matter who the ruler was, no Jews were permitted to enter the country. When merchants from the border areas appealed to the Czarina Elizabeth to permit Jewish merchants to bring in goods, she replied that "from the enemies of Christ she wanted no profits."[5]

In 1727 Catherine expelled the remaining Jews from Russian territories. The decree reads: "Male and female *Zhids* who live in the Ukraine and other Russian cities shall immediately be driven across the border and never again be allowed on Russian soil."[6] A few years after the expulsion, when the nobles realized that merchants from the west of the Dnieper were no longer coming into their area, they appealed to the Boyars to permit Jews to settle again. Their request was granted, but under condition that Jewish merchants must sell their goods wholesale, not retail. The priests, however, were afraid that the *Zhids* would exert an undesirable influence on Christians.

It happened that in 1737 there was a controversy regarding a Christian who converted to Judaism. A Russian named Vosnitsian, a religious man who was "seeking God," had a Jewish friend, Baruch Lebov, who translated the Old Testament for him. The Jew had been among those expelled from Smolensk. Later he had been permitted to return there with goods. The Russian crossed the Polish border with his Jewish friend where he was converted to Judaism and circumcised. Later he returned with his friend to Smolensk. Vosnitsian's wife informed the authorities and both men were arrested. The trial was carried out with the knowledge and approval of the czarina, who was extremely interested in the matter. The two "criminals" were sentenced to death and burned at the stake.[7]

The decree to expel the Jews, which was renewed every few years, provided that anyone who would agree to convert would be allowed to remain. It is not known whether even one conversion resulted from these promises.

In 1710 Latvia went from Swedish to Russian rule and the Jews, who had been there for several centuries, were expelled. A request by Latvia to allow Jewish merchants into the country at least on a temporary basis was rejected by the czarina in 1743.

As a result of the three partitions of Poland in 1772, 1793, and 1795, Russia annexed a territory densely settled by Jews. In 1791 Catherine II instituted the Pale of Settlement. Jews could stay where they were, but were not permitted to move deeper into the interior.[8] Thus the Jewish population was basically to be found in the following provinces: Minsk, Mogilev, Vitebsk, Podolia, Kiev, Poltawa, Tchernigov, Yekaterinoslav, and Crimea. The number of Jews in the Pale of Settlement at that time, according to all estimates, was around 800,000.[9]

Jews who lived in the cities were designated *mestchany* (city dwellers) and were taxed twice as heavily as the non-Jewish city population. Jews also had to pay a "recruit tax" in lieu of military service, since they were not conscripted. Groups of Karaite Jews in Minsk and Crimea were exempt from this double tax. The governors of the provinces were informed that it would be "advisable" to separate the Jews from the peasant population, that they should be expelled from the villages and turned into city dwellers.

In 1797 the province of Minsk suffered a famine. The central government summoned the landowners and requested an explanation. Among the reasons they offered for the famine was that the Jews were selling whiskey to the peasants on credit, thereby reducing their productivity. That the landowners were selling the grain abroad, or that they were using it for making the whiskey, was of course not mentioned.

Similar reports came to the government from the nobility in Volhynia, Podolia, and, later, Lithuania. The Lithuanian governor added a suggestion: in the new territories, the Jews must be expelled from the villages and settled in the cities; also, the Jewish religious sects must be abolished.[10] The government assigned Senator Gabriel Dyerzhavin to tour those provinces, investigate the causes of the peasant impoverishment, and submit a project to correct the situation. Dyerzhavin also turned to the landowners for information, and then reported that all the problems in the provinces were being caused by the Jews. When Czar Alexander I created a "Committee for the Organization of the Jews," Dyerzhavin was among its members.

Word soon reached the Jews in the Pale that certain decrees were in preparation. Rabbis declared fast days. Influential Jews were sent to the government with petitions. But in 1804 the new project was announced. The Pale of Settlement was to remain, but Jews were forbidden to live in the villages or to engage in leaseholding, tavern-keeping, innkeeping, or the sale of spirits. Jewish artisans, manufacturers, and larger merchants would be permitted to move deeper into Russia. The decree was to go into effect on 1 January 1807 in the Ukraine and a year later in Byelorussia and Lithuania.

In 1806, as soon as the announcement was made about the expulsion of Jews from the villages, groups of Jews from the province of Mogilev appealed to their governor for farmland in southern Russia. The governor sent the requests to St. Petersburg. The minister responsible for this project appealed to the governor of the Kherson area to distribute land to these Jews, and advised the Jews to prepare for the journey to Kherson. When this news spread, petitions for land arrived in St. Petersburg from many other Jewish groups. Kherson, however, did not have all that free land to distribute.

In the meantime, the deadline was approaching for the expulsion of the Jews from the villages. The Jews grew uneasy as 60,000 families tottered on the brink of ruin. They sent petitions to St. Petersburg. At this point, partial help came from an unexpected source. In 1806 reports arrived that Napoleon was convening a Sanhedrin in Paris. Russian and Austrian government circles viewed this as a maneuver to win over the populous Jewish centers of eastern Europe to the side of France against their host countries. The Russian government thereupon sent inquiries to the larger Jewish communities to learn what the Jews would suggest as the best way to implement the legislative project of 1804.

The Jews replied that those laws must be repealed altogether. Several weeks later the situation had changed. In 1807 the Tilsit peace treaty between Napoleon and Prussia was signed and the fear of a French invasion of Russia was dispelled. St. Petersburg decided not to abolish the project of 1804, but to amend it. Instead of expelling all the Jews from the villages at one time, the process was to be spread out over a three-year period.

In the summer of 1808 the authorities in the province of Vitebsk began expelling Jews from the villages and from their occupations. Hundreds of Jewish families were brutally herded into cities and towns and left to shift for themselves. Jews began migrating toward Kherson to settle on the land. Some sent petitions to the capital.

Most moved southward without even waiting for permission. The journey took weeks. People beseiged the offices of the bureaus that were supposed to administer the distribution of the land. There was nothing to eat and nowhere to sleep. Families started back north on foot. Many died on the way. Only a few actually received any land.

In 1810 an order was issued to stop settling Jews on the land.[11] Only three hundred Jewish families (two thousand people) had managed to settle in Kherson as farmers.

In St. Petersburg a new committee was set up to consider ways and means to accomplish "the organization of the Jews." After three years of study, the decisions of the new committee were published:

> It is obvious that the root of the drinking evil is not to be found with the tavern-keepers but in the right of distilling, which constitutes the prerogative of the squires and their main source of income. Let us suppose the 60,000 Jewish tavern-keepers to be turned out of the villages. The result will be that 60,000 Russian peasants will take their place, tens of thousands of efficient farm-hands will be lost to the soil, while the Jews cannot be expected to be transformed into capable farmers at a moment's notice. . . . It is not true that the village Jew enriches himself at the expense of the peasant. On the contrary, he is generally poor and ekes out a scanty living from the goods they need. . . . The Committee . . . deems it necessary to put a resolute end to the now prevailing methods of interference and allow the Jews to remain in their former abodes.[12]

After considering the report of the committee, the government revoked the decrees.

In 1812 Napoleon attacked Russia. At that time, Jews were not conscripted, but the "war theater" was in zones with populous Jewish communities and the Jews there were hard hit. Except for the fact of the Pale of Settlement, the Jews in Russia did not suffer from any special anti-Jewish legislation, as did the Jews in western Germany. Czar Alexander I himself had a rather tolerant attitude toward Jews. In Grodno, for example, the Russians turned the police power over to the Jews. Most Jews were therefore pro-Russian and anti-Napoleon.

In 1802 Czar Alexander had recommended that the Jewish city-dwellers be admitted to the city councils. The Polish citizens in Vilna protested. "Jews," they objected, "are immoral." Jews earned their living by swindling non-Jews. From Kovno came even stronger protests. "In our courts there is a crucifix with the sacred figure of

Christ. A Jew will not look at Jesus, much less swear by Him. His oath will be utterly worthless."[13] The czar withdrew his proposal.

After 1815, when the largest part of the Duchy of Warsaw was taken over by Russia, there were already two million Jews living in that territory.[14] Late in 1817 a proposal was adopted to call together Jewish representatives for a discussion of what to do with the Jews. Governors of the provinces with large Jewish communities ordered them to select two representatives for each province. The "Jewish deputation" gathered in St. Petersburg and, over a period of seven years, worked out various plans to "ameliorate" the Jewish situation. Each plan was rejected by the government. Finally, having achieved nothing, the group was dissolved.

While the Jewish deputies were gathering, the czar had ordered the establishment of a "Society of Israelite Christians," that is, of converted Jews. They were promised all sorts of benefits as the czar dreamt of a steady stream of converts. They were offered free land in the southern provinces, or wherever else they wished to go. They were promised civil rights and special tax privileges. The government set aside large tracts of land in Yekaterinoslav and appointed overseers to organize the expected flow of converts. But "nobody came to the party." The project remained on the books until 1833, when Nicholas I abolished it.

During this period, however, a widespread movement of Greek Orthodox "Sabbatarians" arose in several provinces of central Russia. The Sabbatarians were a Christian sect who observed the Sabbath on Saturday, circumcised their male children, and believed in the Jewish Bible. Since there were no Jews in those far-off provinces, the government began an intensive search for the originators and leaders of this movement and came up with a few elderly peasants, one of whom reported that he had had an excellent teacher—the Jewish Torah.[15]

From St. Petersburg came an order to pick up all the leaders of the sect, conscript the younger men, and send the older ones to Siberia. All the members of the sect of "*Zhids*" were to be punished. Troops were sent into the area, entire villages were laid waste, thousands of Sabbatarians were banished. Children were taken away from their parents to be raised as good Orthodox Christians.

In 1821 famine and starvation struck the Byelorussian provinces. On 11 April 1823 a ukase came from the capital to the governors of Mogilev and Vitebsk to expel all the Jews from the villages. The order was accompanied by verbal instructions from the czar himself that before the expulsions were to be carried out, the authorities must make provision for the shelter and livelihood of the Jews who were to be moved. He also proposed that arable land be made available to them. This part of the czar's order was not carried out. But early in 1824 the Jews in the villages of the two Byelorussian provinces, more than 20,000 families, were expelled. Many of the destitute were taken into Jewish homes in the towns. A few families joined the Jewish colonies in Kherson. Most were left stranded.[16]

In 1827 the new czar, Nicholas I, proposed that in order to "render the Jews harmless" they be conscripted into the military for at least twenty-five years starting from the age of eighteen. They would be sent deep into the interior of Russia where there were no Jews. In time they would forget they were Jews. To make absolutely sure, he would take the Jewish boys away from their families when they were twelve years old and send them to live with Christians until they reached the age of eighteen, when they would begin their twenty-five-year service, at the end of which they would undoubtedly be true Russians.

Furthermore, the government placed upon the *Kahal* (the organization of the Jewish community) the responsibility for providing a given number of recruits each year. Leaders of Jewish communities that failed to meet their "quota" would be severely punished. These leaders were usually the wealthier and well-established Jews. To fill the quotas they conscripted the children of the poor. When parents resisted, they hired *Khappers* ("snatchers") to pick up young children in the street (or even in their homes) and turn them over to the armed "recruiting sergeants" who then marched the new recruits under guard to their distant destinations.

It consequently happened that Jewish boys of eight or nine, conscripted into "Nikolai's army," were sent into the interior of Russia on marches that took weeks and months. Many died on the way. Those who survived were placed in Russian homes where they were supposed to be "freed" of their Jewishness. Here they were taught about "Christian love" by means of various punishments for refusing baptism, for refusing to eat pig, for not crossing themselves.[17]

From the beginning, when the recruiting decree was issued, there was a law on the books that Jewish young men who were already married were exempt from military service. Therefore, when the decree was issued, Jewish families hastened to get their ten- and twelve-year-old sons married. The government soon amended this law. The minimum marriage age for Jewish children was set at eighteen for boys, sixteen for girls. Furthermore, marriage was no longer grounds for exemption from military service. The recruiting decree remained in effect during all of Nicholas's reign, from 1827 to 1855, when Alexander II revoked it.[18]

In 1827, the same year that the decree went into effect, another order was issued expelling the Jews from the city of Kiev. In 1830 the Jews were expelled from the villages throughout the whole province. The same year the Jews were expelled from the cities on the shores of the Baltic Sea, from Courland to Latvia; soon afterward they were expelled from the southern cities of Sevastopol and Nikolayev.

In 1834 government circles came to the realization that the expulsion from the villages had achieved nothing. The Jews had been ruined, but the lot of the peasants was no easier. Russia was getting nowhere with its "Jewish problem." The Jews had remained Jews. The army recruiting was not accomplishing its purpose. The Jewish population was multiplying. New methods were called for. In 1835 a new regulation was issued. Jewish community leaders must learn how to speak, read, and write Russian. Public documents must be in Russian, Polish, or German, not Yiddish or Hebrew. The *Kahal* remained the recruiting and tax collection agency. In 1836 censorship of the Talmud, prayerbooks, and other sacred Jewish works was instituted; every book was required to carry the censor's stamp on the title page. All books published in a foreign country must be presented to the police, who would take them to a censor. In the police headquarters of many towns heaps of Jewish books accumulated. Under guard, wagonloads of books dotted the highways of the Pale.[19]

These regulations, and others like them, certainly embittered the lives of the Jews, but they did not lead to conversion. In 1840 the government again concluded that its methods of "transforming" the Jews were getting nowhere, and that what was basically at fault was Jewish education. Jewish children, starting at a very early age, were taught not only their religion, but also the Talmud, which was, to the government, the root of all evil in Jewish life. The government council therefore adopted a number of important measures which were intended to abolish the traditional Jewish *heder* and establish new schools. A committee was set up to "reform Jewish life in Russia." Minister of Education Uvarov, a member of the committee, proposed that in all Jewish towns and cities elementary schools be opened by the government where Jewish children would study the Russian language and other secular subjects, as well as the Bible. The Talmud was not in the curriculum at all.

In order to prepare the Jews to accept this new educational system, the government would have to send ahead a prominent Jewish orator to popularize the plan. The minister had someone in mind for the job, a rabbi named Max Lilienthal who preached in German in a Reform Temple in Riga. Lilienthal accepted the task and began a tour of Jewish communities to propagandize for the opening of the government schools. He traveled widely and strove mightily to implement the plan; he even managed to open a few schools. But when he finally realized that the true intent of the Russian government was to convert Jewish children, he stopped in the middle of his work and went home.

The few elementary schools that had been opened were empty; the two rabbinical seminaries in Vilna and Zhitomir were also in difficulty. To cover the costs of these institutions new taxes were imposed on kosher meat and candles. The collection of taxes was contracted out to Jews who made the lives of the ordinary Jews in the small towns miserable for many years.

In April 1843 a new decree was issued, expelling all Jews from the cities and towns within fifty miles of the western borders. This decree would have affected thousands of Jewish families in the Ukraine, Lithuania, and Poland, but it was never implemented. The order, however, remained on the books.

Then came a new government plan whereupon instructions were issued to the governors and police in the towns to "encourage" Jews to turn to "productive" work; but the police did not know how to carry out these instructions. The government documents had also mentioned Jewish dress and the beards and earlocks of the men, so the police in the small towns began a drive to shave off Jewish beards, shorten the gabardines, and prohibit new wives from cutting off their hair. Generally, the Jews did not observe these edicts, but followed the dictates of their religion and humane behavior. The Hasidic masses were ready to give their lives for their traditional customs.[20]

In addition to official government harassment, the Jews found themselves subjected to a revival of the blood libels. In 1816 the body of a murdered four-year-old Christian child was found in Grodno. Sholem Lapin, a neightbor of the child's family, was arrested, although no evidence was found to connect him with the murder. A convert appeared, however, who testified that Jews need Christian blood at Passover time to smear on their doorposts. The case reached St. Petersburg and in February 1817 the government ordered the inquiry halted, the Jew released, and an investigation begun to find the real murderer.

A more serious incident occurred in the town of Velizh in the province of Vitebsk. In 1823 the badly battered body of a three-year-old Christian boy was found in a swamp. Two "witnesses" came forward, one a prostitute named Terentiava, the other a demented woman named Yeremiava, who "proved" to the parents that their child had been murdered by Jews. Specifically they accused two prominent Jews of Velizh. The chief judge of Vitebsk listened to the story of the accusers, examined the accused, and released them for lack of evidence. Terentiava was rebuked by the court for bearing false witness and the case was listed as unsolved.

Two years later, Terentiava sent a letter to Czar Alexander explaining that the murdered child had been her own, that she knew the Jew who had killed the child, and that apparently the court had been bribed by the Jews to squelch the case. The czar ordered the investigation reopened. Two domestics were found with similar stories, and on the basis of this "testimony" many Jews in Velizh were arrested and interrogated. By that time, Nicholas I had become czar. When he received the report of the investigation, he ordered the guilty Jews punished and their synagogue shut down. At the trial, the entire Jewish population of the town was in the prisoner's dock. The number of Christian children "murdered by the Jews of Velizh" kept rising. The trial became too large for the local court and was transferred to the Senate.

For four years that legislative body studied the case and then turned it over to the highest court of the land—the government council. Finally, an old official named Mordvinov managed to get to the bottom of the story. The Jews were acquitted and released. The false witnesses were exiled to Siberia. In signing the release, however, the czar commented that he was doing so only because there was not proof of guilt, but that actually he was not convinced that all the Jews of Velizh were innocent, most likely there was a Jewish sect which did practice these barbaric rites.[21]

In 1852 a ritual murder charge was made against the Jews of Saratawe province, although the entire Jewish population there consisted of a few score families. The police arrested a number of Jews, among them Yankl Yushkevitch and his son, an apostate. None of those arrested admitted to the crime. In July 1854, in the middle of the Crimean War, Nicholas created a commission to investigate the matter of the blood libel and determine once and for all whether there were really Jewish sects that used human blood in their ritual. The commission worked for two years, during which time the Jews arrested in Saratawe languished in prison. The commission concluded that there was not a grain of truth in the story and reported their findings to the government. The prisoners, however, were not released. The Saratawe court remembered the czar's comment in the Velizh case, that probably there are secret Jewish sects that use human blood. On this basis the arrested Jews were sentenced to life imprisonment. The sentence was affirmed by Alexander II in May 1860. Not until 1867, when the czar was in Paris and Crémieux was able to speak with him, did he release the elder Yushkevitch, but not the son.[22]

The oppressive political atmosphere in Russia was conducive to the appearance of Jewish informers who blackmailed their own communities by threatening to "expose" Jewish secrets which were inventions to begin with. In one town in Podolia two such informers were killed, resulting in a trial in which the entire Jewish community stood accused. Eighty Jews were arrested, among them two rabbis. Twenty people were found guilty and flogged with steel whips; several died, the rest were exiled. Rabbi Israel Friedman of Ruzhin managed to escape to Austria.

In 1815, when Russia annexed the greater part of the Duchy of Warsaw, with its half million Jews, the status of Jewish rights remained unchanged.[23] The leaders of autonomous Poland, wishing to emulate Prussia and its "reformed and respectable" Jews, asked the reformer David Friedländer to advise them. Friedländer, who considered it an honor that a government should seek his help, came to Warsaw, familiarized himself with Jewish life there, and offered his solution.

The Polish Jews, he suggested, are extremely backward culturally in comparison with the Prussian Jews, mainly because of the influence of the Talmud and the Hasidic movement. The Jews must be exposed to Polish culture; they must learn to speak Polish and give up their Yiddish. They must reform their religious practices. In this way, they would become assimilated and respectable and would then be in a better position to ask for equal rights.

A few score *Maskilim* among the wealthier and assimilated Jews, in view of the fact that they were already "respectable," petitioned the Polish authorities for immediate emancipation, separately from the rest of the Jews. They were informed that they would have to wait until all the other Jews were ready.

Meanwhile, anti-Jewish agitation in the country was increasing. In Warsaw, Jews were driven out of homes where they had lived for years. Newly arrived Jews were subject to a special tax; the period of time they could legally stay in the city was sharply curtailed. The 1818 *Sejm* again debated the Jewish question. A proposal to give more rights to wealthier Jews and to those engaged in more "acceptable" occupations was met with the argument that it was impossible to reform the Jews and that they must therefore be restricted, their numbers reduced, and eventually they must all be expelled from Poland. Among the masses in the villages, Jew-baiting was stepped up by the local priests. Blood libels cropped up repeatedly. Innocent Jews were arrested and tortured. When word came from the capital that false witnesses in ritual murder trials would be prosecuted, the charges subsided for a while.

In 1830, during the revolt in Warsaw against Russian rule, several assimilated young Jews appealed to the rebels for permission to form a Jewish regiment and join the fight for Polish independence. The reply from the commander was that Jews were not wanted in the Polish army. The minister of war improved upon that answer: He would not allow Jewish blood to mingle with Polish blood on the battlefield.[24] Despite this, the Warsaw Jewish community contributed a great deal of money to the struggle for Poland's freedom. A number of Jewish volunteers were accepted by local Polish leaders, but were organized into a separate detachment. The rebellion failed. After 1833 Poland was ruled by Russian overseers. No change took place in the Jewish situation until 1843, when the Czarist government introduced the conscription system and all other anti-Jewish laws into Poland.

Jews in Russia, 1848–75

In 1848 the Russian government began to divide Jews into "productive" and "unproductive" categories. The latter were completely without rights. The recruits into the army came only from that class, which included anyone without a trade, without property, or without an insured income. It also included those who had been expelled from the villages. The "productive" category comprised the larger merchants, the farmers, artisans, and urban shopkeepers. All the "productive" Jews were required to submit documents to the police before April 1851 proving their economic status. Those failing to submit these documents in time would automatically be placed in the "unproductive" category. Many Jews did not even know how to obtain such documents. Even after the government extended the prescribed period until autumn of 1852, many Jews still remained without the necessary papers.

The worst plague of all was still the recruiting of young boys into the army. Jews tried to evade this edict by any means possible. They maimed themselves. Many hid; others fled the country. When the recruiting began, most of the Jewish candidates before the draft boards were either cripples or midgets. With the Jewish quotas of conscripts not being met, leaders of the Jewish community were reprimanded, fined and sometimes even taken as recruits them- selves. During the Crimean War, however, a large number of Jewish soldiers gave their lives in defense of a country which treated them as second-class citizens or even criminals.

In 1852 the war with Turkey took place. After the defeat at Sevastopol and the peace conference in Paris, Alexander II (1855–81) became the new czar. Among the reforms which he instituted in 1861 to emancipate the Russian peasants from serfdom, Jewish rights were not mentioned. The recruiting law, which had been revoked as soon as he became czar in 1856, was replaced by a law that provided that Jews must be recruited in the same manner and in the same proportion as the rest of the population. Conscrip- tion of children was abolished, as was the responsibility of the *Kahal* to supply the recruits.

But the Russification of the Jews remained as important a task to the new czar as it had been to his father. Civil rights for Jews were not on the agenda, the Russian bureaucracy being more inclined to their restriction. In June 1865 permission to reside outside the Pale was granted to Jewish artisans, mechanics, and even apprentices in certain trades. As a result, many Jews without skills streamed toward that area seeking employment. The police were already keeping a watchful eye on the "legitimacy" of these immigrants. When the question arose as to whether Jewish army veterans were among those permitted to live outside the Pale, the czar ruled in the negative. Several years later this permission was also granted.

The government schools which had been opened during the reign of Nicholas I had a very small enrollment. In 1855 Alexander II set a twenty-year period at the end of which the Hebrew schools and yeshivas were to be shut down and the government schools were to take over the education of Jewish children. At the end of the twenty years the government schools were almost completely empty. The period was not extended. The rabbinical seminars in Vilna and Zhitomir were closed in 1873.

In the Polish rebellion of 1861–63, Berish Meisels, a Warsaw rabbi, issued a call to the Polish Jews to support the fight for Polish freedom. The call contained promises of peace and happiness in a liberated Poland. Many Jewish volunteers responded. After the rebellion the situation of the Jews deteriorated markedly as the Russian government began an intensive program of Russification of both Poles and Jews.

In 1860 a certain Jacob Brafman, furious with the Jewish community leaders of Minsk because they had tried to turn him over to the Russian army as a recruit, became an apostate and found a way to even scores with them. Having gained access to the archives of the Minsk *Kehillah*, he translated some of the entries into Russian and added his own fabrications. Linking the *Kehillah* with the *Alliance Israélite* of Paris, he constructed a whole chain of crimes which the Jewish community was supposed to have committed against the Russian government.

Brafman submitted this material to General Muravyov, who had been assigned the task of Russifying the Polish provinces after the unsuccessful rebellion of 1863. A zealot for Russification, and an anti-Semite, Muravyov printed Brafman's pamphlet and sent copies to all the police headquarters in cities and towns with large Jewish communities. In St. Petersburg the pamphlet was greeted as an important and authentic document about Jews, whom Russian rulers had long viewed as an "internal enemy."

In his travels across Poland in 1870 the czar had seen masses of Hasidim in their "peculiar" manner of dress, which he considered an affront to his efforts to correct Jewish backwardness. He ordered the overseers of the Polish provinces to begin implementing his father's twenty-year-old decree against Jewish dress. The police carried out their orders with enthusiasm.[25] Along with this a commission was set up to draft plans for weakening Jewish solidarity, eliminating the *Kahal*, and breaking down the traditional Jewish customs.

In 1871 Greek merchants in Odessa, attempting to eliminate their competition, spread rumors that the Jews had robbed a church and stolen a crucifix. Mobs rampaged through Jewish neighborhoods while the police stood idly by. Not until the fourth day of the pogrom did army troops stop the violence. Government investigators were advised that this was a popular protest, an outpouring of the people's wrath against Jewish exploiters. The czar accepted this "explanation" as the unchallengeable truth. In the government commission another point was noted: the problem of "Jewish exploitation" of the Russian masses.

At the same time, the governor of Kiev province, who had read Brafman's pamphlet, submitted to Czar Alexander a memorandum on the Jews. He contended that the Jewish problem was the most important problem facing the government. In the Ukrainian provinces the Jews were growing richer and richer, everything was in their hands—the estates of the nobility, the factories, the lumber mills, the distilleries. In the provinces of Kiev, Volhynia, and Podolia "Jewish exploiters" owned twenty-seven sugar factories out of one hundred five, all the breweries and almost all the mills. In addition, the Jews continued to maintain their *Kehillah* which was in close touch with their main center in Paris.[26]

From the Polish provinces it was reported to St. Petersburg that the Jews there were not being Russified; on the contrary, they were Polish patriots and were aiding and abetting Polish separatism. All these charges were discussed by the commission, which reached the decision (1) that the *Kahal* must be dissolved, and (2) that the Jews must not be allowed to move out of the Pale of Settlement, lest they become the economic masters of the whole country. As the mood in Russia under Alexander II became more reactionary, it also became more anti-Jewish.

In 1877 the Russo-Turkish war began. Russia's rallying cry was Pan-Slavism—the liberation of the Balkans from Turkish rule. Many Jews shed their blood in this war. At the Congress of Berlin in 1878, which discussed the question of the liberated peoples, the representatives of England, France, Germany, Austria, and Italy voted to emancipate the Jews who lived in Rumania, Serbia, and Bulgaria. Only the Russians voted against this proposal. How could they vote for equal rights for Jews in other countries when the Jews in Russia still had no such rights? After much persuasion, the Russian representatives agreed to the emancipation of the Jews in the Balkan countries, but not in Russia.[27]

Following the 1870s, Jew-hatred began to appear more prominently among the Russian people, as well as among government officials. In 1878 a ritual murder trial took place in Kutais in the Caucasus. On Passover eve a little Georgian girl had disappeared. The local Jews were arrested and charged with the murder. The

Jews, however, turned out this time to have ardent defenders, among them Daniel Chvolson, a well known apostate, and they were acquitted. Chvolson, a professor in the St. Petersburg seminary, published a pamphlet, "Do Jews Use Christian Blood?" in which he showed the falsity of this charge.[28]

In the second half of the nineteenth century, larger industrial enterprises arose in Russia, leading to the development of an urban working class which was inhumanly exploited. At that time a new spirit of protest and rebellion appeared in Russia, a movement which attracted substantial sections of the Jewish intellectuals.

23

Anti-Semitism in Russia at the Turn of the Century

With the growth of industry in Russia in the mid-nineteenth century and with the minimal rights granted to them by Alexander II, Jews in that region began to participate in various aspects of the economy. The Russian merchants soon protested. When Alexander III became czar in 1881, the deepening of political reaction was accompanied by a rise in the anti-Semitic temper of the country. Involved with the terrorists who had assassinated the previous czar was a Jewish young woman. (She had not participated in the actual killing.) This gave the anti-Semites an excuse to put the blame for the assassination on the Jews and to incite the ignorant masses to stage pogroms.[1]

Jew-hatred in Russia, however, did not begin with the assassination of the czar. Organized groups of anti-Semites began surfacing in Russia in the last quarter of the nineteenth century. Anti-Semitic newspapers appeared—*Novoye Vremya* in St. Petersburg, *Kievlianin* in Kiev, and several other sheets in Lithuania and southern Russia. On its front page *Novoye Vremya* reprinted a translation of William Marr's "Triumph of Jewry over the German People,"[2] and added editorially, "This will be our fate, too."

Alexander III had been educated by a professor of law named Constantin Pobedonostsev, a Greek Orthodox by faith, a confirmed Russian chauvinist, and a committed anti-Semite. When Alexander became czar he appointed Pobedonostsev as his chief advisor.

In the first few days after the assassination of Alexander II, *Novoye Vremya* wrote that Jews had been involved in the murder. Several days later the phrase "Jews had been involved" became "Jews were the leaders of the plot." By the middle of March, secret agents from Moscow and St. Petersburg had arranged with the police chiefs in the cities of the Pale that "when the people rise up to take revenge on the *Zhids*," the police were not to intervene.

Early in April 1881 a rumor spread in Elisavetgrad (southern Russia) that a pogrom was being prepared. The 15,000 Jews in the city appealed to the police to prevent it. Troops were sent from a nearby garrison. While the troops were in the city, the situation stayed calm. On 15 April the soldiers were recalled. As though that were a signal, the pogrom began. The police did nothing. The next day the violence was repeated on a larger scale. Again the police stood by. In the evening, peasants came in from the villages to joint the pogromchiks. On 17 April, a detachment of troops entered the city and ordered the mobs to disperse. They refused. Several shots were fired by the soldiers, killing and wounding a number of people.[3]

The result: scores of Jews dead and seriously wounded, a thousand Jewish homes and stores gutted, damage in the millions of rubles. Several days later the scene was repeated in some thirty towns and villages near Elisavetgrad. During the latter part of April, pogroms took place in fifty towns and villages in the provinces of Kiev and Volhynia. A gang of thugs arrived by train in Berditchev, but waiting for them at the station was the *Samo-oborona*, a Jewish self-defense group, which had been given permission to organize. (The police chief had to be paid for the privilege.) The pogromchiks were not permitted to leave the train and the Jews of Berditchev were spared.

The peasants in the villages believed that it was the czar himself who had ordered the Jews beaten and robbed. In the province of Tchernigov a local village leader persuaded the people not to attack the few Jews who lived there. The peasants demanded, and received, a document from him that they would not be punished for disobeying the czar's order.[4] In some villages, where the priests explained that the czar had really not ordered a pogrom, the Jews were left in peace.

A particularly vicious three-day pogrom took place in Odessa, which had a Jewish population of 100,000. On the third day the police dispersed the mobs. The Jews in Odessa had a well-organized self-defense group, led by students. The police there arrested eight hundred people, including one hundred fifty Jews, who were punished along with their attackers.

In mid-July pogroms took place in the provinces of Poltava, Byelorussia, and Lithuania. In many places, Jewish streets were put to the torch. A delegation of prominent Jews in St. Petersburg pleaded with the czar to declare the pogroms against the law and order them stopped. He refused, accusing the Jews of having provoked the peasants to violence by exploiting them. Another Jewish delegation appealed to Minister Ignatiev to stop the pogroms; he gave them the same lecture as the czar. When the Jews replied that most of the Jews were impoverished themselves, and that this was due to their lack of rights, he advised them to emigrate to the West. He said that the borders were open and the Jews could leave Russia whenever they pleased.[5] The government refused to help the victims of the pogroms in any way. The Jews of St. Petersburg were even forbidden to collect funds for that purpose.

Panic seized the Jews of Russia. Flight to America was the best way out, but that required funds, which they did not have. Rumors spread that certain Jewish philanthropists in England and France had agreed to pay the travel costs of any Jews who could get to Austria. Tens of thousands of Jews reached Brod in Eastern Galicia, where they then spent several months, hungry and sick. Only eight thousand finally managed to sail to America. Many others returned to their ruined homes. Some remained in Austria, or made their way to London.

In August 1881 the czar created a special commission to investigate which Jewish occupations were "harmful" to the Christian population and how those occupations could be eliminated. The commission gave the czar the answers he was looking for. The governor of Kiev recommended that the emigration of Jews from Russia be speeded up. The anti-Semitic press also joined the hue and cry. *Novoye Vremya* printed a parody on Hamlet's soliloquy. In Russian the words for "To be or not to be" are "*bit ili nie bit*," which is a pun on "to beat or not to beat." The editor of the Slavophile paper, *Russ*, proved that Jews are enemies of Christian civilization and that those Russians who destroyed Jewish homes were expressing their justified wrath.

Some of the *Narodniki*, the Russian revolutionaries, who believed that the peasantry should govern the country, considered the pogroms to be "the beginning of the long-awaited political change" in Russia and circulated handbills which began, "Arise, workers and peasants, take revenge on the landowners, rob the Jews, kill the authorities. . . ."[6]

Christmas Eve 1881, in a crowded Catholic Church in Warsaw, someone shouted fire. Twenty-nine people were trampled to death. There had actually been no fire. Rumors spread that two Jews had been inside the church. Riots began. On the second day, the violence mounted. On the third day the governor of Warsaw ordered the pogrom stopped. Twenty-four Jews had been seriously injured, forty-five hundred Jewish homes and a number of synagogues destroyed, with property damage running into millions of rubles. Each year, from 1882 until 1884 the pogroms were repeated, but on a smaller scale. In two hundred cities there were large scale pogroms; in six hundred towns and villages, smaller pogroms took place. Several thousand Jews were killed, many more injured. Thousands of Jewish women were raped. Most of the Jews in Russia were left destitute.

The Jews in Russia did not have the right to protest, but protest meetings did take place in London and New York. Voices were raised in England urging that official protests be lodged with the Russian rulers. On 1 February 1882 a large protest meeting was held in the London city hall, with the lord mayor presiding. Speeches were made by members of Parliament, by bishops and professors. A particularly vigorous address was delivered by the Catholic Cardinal Manning. A moderate resolution was adopted and presented to Prime Minister Gladstone, who replied that the British government could not submit such a statement directly to a friendly government, but that at the right opportunity the matter would be raised informally and personally.

In Russia even this was taken as an affront. The official government newspaper responded:

> There are rumors that a British intervention is being prepared regarding the Jews in Russia. Any interference by a foreign government on behalf of the Jewish nation in Russia would only call forth displeasure among broad sections of our population, which in turn would lead only to negative repercussions on the Jewish situation in Russia.[7]

The journal of the Russian Foreign Ministry fumed:

> What do the English Judophiles want—to start a quarrel between the British and Russian governments? Do they wish to disrupt the good

relations between the two governments—good relations that were barely established after Lory Beaconsfield's cabinet was replaced by Gladstone's?[8]

In New York City a large protest meeting was held in February 1882 where Supreme Court Justice Davis said,

If there is no improvement in the situation of the Russian Jews, then we in America, in addition to good advice, also have enough dollars to bring all three million persecuted Jewish citizens of Russia over to this country.[9]

Among the Jews in the Russian towns and cities, "immigration" and "America" became household words. Had there been money available for the journey, hundreds of thousands of Jews would have emigrated. In Kharkov and other cities the BILU movement was formed to settle young people in Palestine. (BILU is an acrostic from the Hebrew words which mean "House of Jacob, get thee out.") Another group, *Am Olam* ("Eternal People"), emigrated to America to build a communal life based on a just social order.

In mid-March 1882 the Jews of Balta (Podolia), having heard rumors of a pogrom, appealed to the chief of police for protection. They received an evasive reply. The Jewish population of Balta was three times larger than the Christian. Young Jews asked for permission to create a self-defense group and were turned down, but went ahead secretly with their plans. On 29 March, Easter Sunday, a mob set out to pillage Jewish stores. They were met by Jews carrying clubs, were driven back, and hid in the building of a fire company. When police and militia appeared on the scene the pogromchiks emerged from their hiding place. Instead of dispersing them, the police attacked the Jews, and then the police chief himself led the growing mob into the populous Jewish streets. Members of the self-defense group were jailed. Several of the mob also were arrested, but were released immediately.

The pogrom lasted fully two days. On the third day the governor arrived and stopped the violence, which had resulted in the death or injury of forty Jews, one hundred seventy with lesser injuries, and many Jewish women raped. All twelve hundred and fifty Jewish homes in the city were damaged and the synagogues vandalized. The Jewish community of forty-five hundred was left destitute. Not a word about this pogrom appeared in the Russian press. The news did not reach the foreign press until several days later.

On 3 May 1882, leaders of the Russian government, influenced by reports of the provincial commissions which had been studying the "harmfulness of the Jews," issued a new series of laws. These May Laws, as they were called, forbade Jews from living in the villages, restricted their residence to towns and cities within the Pale, prohibited them from buying or renting property in the villages, and from doing business on Sundays or Christian holidays.[10] (The law was subsequently amended so that only new Jewish settlers would be barred from the villages; old-time settlers could remain.)

Because Ignatiev's pogrom policies had disgraced Russia in world opinion, he was removed. The new minister of the interior, Dmitri Tolstoy, was no less an anti-Semite, but he issued orders holding the guardians of public order strictly responsible for any violence that might take place. This order was only partially effective. In many places there were "disturbances" until mid-1884.

Driving out long-time villagers was not part of the program, but anti-Semites found an old ordinance that permitted the village to expel "abnormal" elements. A properly authorized official would arrive, get a few of the peasants drunk, and have them sign a document that they did not want such and such a person in their village, for such and such reasons. This was sufficient to get a Jew expelled.

On 10 April 1882 the Russian army released an order reducing the number of Jewish physicians in the military service, because "Jewish doctors do not carry out their duties conscientiously," thereby endangering the health of the men. For this insult to their professional competence many Jewish doctors resigned from the service. A Doctor Yaroshevski declared that so long as this insult remained on the books it was beneath Jewish dignity to serve in the military. He was brought into court.[11]

On 10 May 1883, a few days prior to the coronation of Alexander III, a hundred Jewish homes and stores in Rostov-on-Don were destroyed during a pogrom. On 20 July a major pogrom took place in Yekaterinoslav, with the mob having to be dispersed at gunpoint. A few days later the violence was repeated in smaller towns in the area. In Novomoskovsk the pogrom was particularly savage. On 7 June 1884, in a pogrom in Nizhni-Novgorod, a city outside the Pale of Settlement, seven Jews were murdered; two of the more seriously injured died a few days later. Several of the mob were tried and exiled to Siberia.

During the coronation the government announced a series of privileges for the general population, but for the Jews, only new restrictive decrees. The governor general of Odessa at that time declared that there were so many Jewish children in the government schools that there was no place left for the Christians. Therefore, he proposed a quota system for Jews in high schools and universities. The czar, delighted with the idea, ordered the system put into effect as soon as possible. Within the Pale, 10 percent of the school population were permitted to be Jewish, outside the Pale, only 5 percent, and in the universities, only 3 percent. The *numerus clausus* was introduced in July 1887.[12]

In the villages, the Jews were constantly harassed. If, for instance, a Jewish family were to leave for a few days, perhaps to visit relatives in the city, it would return to find itself in trouble. Jews were also forbidden to move from one village to another. The "productive" Jews who had been permitted to reside outside the Pale of Settlement during the reign of Alexander II were allowed to retain Jewish house servants such as tutors or bookkeepers. Many Jews, therefore, were registered in Moscow, St. Petersburg, and other large cities as servants in the "privileged" Jewish homes. In the 1880s the police set about correcting this situation. Raids on Jewish homes disclosed people who may have been living and working for as long as ten years in a city without legal documents. More than 20,000 Jews were expelled from Kiev during this period.[13]

In 1883 the czar established a commission to study the effect of the May Laws. After five years of work the commission issued its report. Having made its study rather objectively, the commission reported that the restrictions on Jews had not resulted in a solution to the Jewish problem; they had only made it worse. In addition to the hardship to the victims, it had also hampered the economic growth of the country. A majority of the commission members favored the enactment of liberal reforms and the abrogation of many of the restrictive decrees. A majority of the Council of State concurred. The report was promptly squelched by Alexander III.

The anti-Semitic temperature soared. A British journalist who visited Russia in 1890 reported that when one of the czar's intimates advised the ruler to ease up on the Jews, the czar had retorted: "We must not forget that it was the Jews who crucified our Lord and spilled his precious blood."[14] Several Russian authors, opponents of the rising reaction in the country, wrote a statement protesting against the proposed new decrees. More than a hundred writers signed the statement, among them V. Korolenko and Leo Tolstoy. The government paid no attention. The newspapers in Russia were forbidden to print the text. It did appear, however, in Berlin,

London, Vienna, and other cities abroad.[15]

On 10 December 1890, at a large protest meeting in London, a resolution was adopted asking the czar, in a friendly tone, to be merciful to his Jewish subjects. No newspaper in Russia published this appeal. No response came from the czar. The anti-Semitic press, however, did comment: "What do they want, those Semites? They never lived as well as they are now living in Russia. No matter how much you give them, they always want more. . . ."[16]

In the winter of 1890-91 it was announced in the press that Jewish handicraftsmen and mechanics living in Moscow must gradually move to those provinces which had been assigned to them. First the police began a search for "illegal" Jews who had been living in the city for some time. Those who were apprehended were led out of the city like common criminals. Then came the order that all the artisans and handicraftsmen must prepare to leave Moscow in a few weeks. In the fall the expulsion began, despite the dropping temperature outdoors. In January an order came from the governor general postponing the expulsion until the end of winter, but the order arrived too late. Twenty thousand Jews had already been forcibly driven out of Moscow in the dead of winter.[17]

The pogroms had enabled the Russian government to carry out its objective of getting the Jews out of the country. In the 1880s around 15,000 Jews left Russia each year of the decade. After 1890 the number doubled. The more relatives there were who had already reached American shores, the more "ship tickets" arrived at Jewish homes in Russia and the more Jews left. In the year of the expulsion from Moscow, 118,000 Jewish families left Russia. Only around 40,000 of them reached America. The rest were stranded in Brod and Berlin, Hamburg and London, Antwerp and elsewhere.

Baron Maurice de Hirsch, Jewish financier and philanthropist, had bought land in Argentina and proposed to organize the emigration of a large number of Russian Jews each year, but the actual emigration to Argentina turned out to be rather limited. From 1892 to 1894 only some six thousand Jews settled in that country. In later years the number increased.

After the expulsion of the Jewish handicraftsmen from Moscow in 1891, only the merchants of the "first class" remained, and they paid a special annual tax of at least one thousand rubles for the privilege of residing in the city. The same year, a new building for a synagogue (under construction for ten years) was completed. The building had a cupola with a Star of David at the top. The authorities ordered the cupola removed, and closed the synagogue pending a permit. When the permit did not arrive, the rabbi and the president of the congregation sent a petition to St. Petersburg. A reply came immediately: (1) the rabbi and the president were ordered to leave Moscow, and (2) the building must be converted for some other use than a house of worship, otherwise it must be sold. If these were not done before 1 January 1893, the government would sell it at auction.[18] The Jewish community managed to convert the building into a vocational school.

In 1894 Alexander III died. Nicholas II, the new czar, surrounded himself with people recommended to him by the anti-Semite Pobedonostsov, whom he appointed as his leading advisor and chief deputy. It was Pobedonostsov who worked out the formula for ridding Russia of its Jews: one-third must be forced to emigrate, one-third to die (of starvation) and one-third to assimilate (that is, to become Christians).[19]

In 1898 no new Jewish merchants of the first guild were permitted to enter Moscow. Anti-Semitic newspapers reported that the government intended to rid the entire Moscow province of Jews. When the government opened its own liquor stores, which could be operated only by Christians, the Jews lost that means of livelihood, too. The result of all the anti-Jewish laws was economic ruin for the Jews. Studies by the Russian economist, Subotin, showed that from 1894 to 1896 the number of needy Jewish families increased by 27 percent. The number of destitute Jews who asked for charity at Passover time reached 40 to 50 percent of the Jewish population in many places.[20]

When a number of wealthy Jews offered to help their impoverished brothers and sisters, the government interfered. Israel Brodski, a Jewish financier in Kiev, proposed to open a bank where Jewish workers could get interest-free loans. For this purpose he offered to contribute 120,000 rubles. The government agreed, but only on condition that the managers of the bank must be Christians appointed by the government. Brodski replied: "I am a Jew myself and I can not permit an institution established with my money, and bearing my name, to discriminate against Jews."[21] He withdrew his offer, which was precisely what the government wanted.

The quota of 3 percent for Jewish students in the larger universities was reduced to 2 percent. Jewish students who attended schools in other countries, when they returned with their diplomas, had no right to use the knowledge they had acquired. Many of these young people threw themselves into the revolutionary movement.

The country was growing progressively uneasy. In the anti-

Semitic press Jews were blamed for all the troubles of Russia. On 21 April 1899 a pogrom took place in the port city of Nikolayev. For three days several thousand looters pillaged, killed, and raped as the police and Cossacks stood by.

By the end of the century the revolutionary movement in Russia had reached a significant presence. Masses of Jewish youth joined the movement to free Russia of its ultrareactionary pogrom-prone regime, and to liberate the Jews as well. Hundreds of young Jews, inspired by the dream of freedom, were arrested and languished in prison or Siberian exile. It appears that these punishments frightened no one. It was a "generation that had lost its fear," wrote the journalist Moshe Katz years later.[22]

Around 1897 a Russified Moldavian named Krushevan began issuing an anti-Semitic newspaper called *Bessarabetz*, in which all the material was copied from *Novoye Vremya*. The *Bessarabetz* accused Jews of exploiting Christians, of being socialists, of preparing a Godless revolution, and of crucifying Jesus. The government permitted no other newspapers to be issued in southern Russia.

The minister of internal affairs, Wenzel von Plehve, a former gendarme, devised a scheme which he laconically referred to as a plan to "drown the revolution in Jewish blood."[23] To start, they selected the city of Kishinev in Bessarabia, with a population of 110,000, almost half of which were Jews. On Passover Eve the Jews of Kishinev learned from handbills distributed throughout the city that "by order of the czar" it would be permissable to beat Jews during the three days of Easter.

Unable to obtain legal sanction to organize a self-defense group, the Jews began underground preparations. Sunday, 6 April 1903, the first day of Easter, at noon, all the church bells in the city began ringing at once. Thousands of Christians from all walks of life began looting Jewish homes located in Christian neighborhoods. Armed with axes and knives, the mobs then advanced on the Jewish quarter, screaming *"Bey Zhidov!"* ("Beat the Jews!"). When the Jewish self-defense group in certain streets resisted, the police intervened, disarming and arresting them.

The following day the pogrom was renewed, with the addition of thousands of peasants who had come into the city from nearby villages. Unspeakable barbarities were committed. When a Jewish delegation managed to get to the Bessarabian governor to ask for help, he replied that he was waiting for instructions from St. Petersburg. Toward evening an order came from Von Plehve to stop the pogrom. Armed troops appeared immediately on the streets. On 8 April, early in the morning, as the mobs started gathering again, the police and troops barred their way. Incredulous, many of the mob advanced and were arrested. This pogrom resulted in forty-five Jews dead, eighty-six injured seriously, five hundred with minor wounds, fifteen hundred homes and stores gutted, and two pogromchiks dead.

The lamentations from Kishinev reached the Jews of Russia and the world. From all civilized countries came protests to the Russian rulers. Minister Von Plehve's news release said that on Passover the Jews of Kishinev had started a fight and the Christians defended themselves.

Most of the newspapers in Russia printed the "official" news, but abroad, the truth of the Kishinev pogrom was reported in detail. The foreign press also published a secret letter from Von Plehve to the Bessarabian governor two weeks before the pogrom advising him that if there were any disturbances they were not to be stopped, and that no weapons were to be used. Soon after the Kishinev pogrom, young Jews began organizing self-defense groups in many towns and cities.

In St. Petersburg a Jewish student lunged at the journalist Krushevan with a knife, but only scratched him. The student was exiled to Siberia. The strong feelings among Jewish youth led, on the one hand, to their increased activity in the revolutioary movement, and on the other hand, to a strong national awakening. A world Zionist movement had crystallized in 1897 and many young Jews now became interested in its ideas.[24] Von Plehve, of course, ordered the governors and chiefs of police to ban Zionist meetings and all activities having to do with Jewish nationalism.[25]

On 29 August 1903 the Jewish self-defense group in Gomel, attempting to stop some drunken hoodlums who were robbing Jewish stores, killed one of the vandals. In the pogrom that following, twelve Jews were left dead or seriously hurt, eight pogromchiks were killed or injured, and two hundred fifty Jewish homes and stores were destroyed. The press reported that the Jews of Gomel had attacked Christians, including the police, who had been forced to use their rifles.

The Russo-Japanese War

In the Russian army that fought against Japan in 1904–1905 there were many Jews. The number of Jews who fought were greater in proportion to those in the army in general, because the recruits from the Ukraine were sent to the Far East, while the eastern recruits went to the western regions. During the war, the anti-Jewish laws on the mainland remained in effect. For example, families of Jewish doctors and reservists who had been sent to the front were expelled from Moscow, because the husbands were no longer there and without them the residence rights were not valid.

The victories of the Japanese armies sent the Russian leaders into a panic. The defeat was totally unexpected. There could be no explanation for it other than that the Japanese must be connected with the worst enemies of Russia—the Jews. The czar began to refer to the Japanese as *Zhidy*, and anti-Semitic newspapers accused the Jews of secretly helping the enemies of Russia.

On 28 July 1904 Von Plehve was assassinated. In his place the czar appointed the Vilna governor, Mirski, who was considered a liberal. When the Jews appealed to him to prevent any more pogroms, he promised to do so. In the fall of 1904 the Russian army called up its reserves for active duty on the Japanese front. Angered by this, the peasants vented their feelings on the Jews; in many places it was the reservists who started the pogroms which took place in the provinces of Mogilev, Byelorussia, Kiev, Podolia, and Volhynia. The police did not interfere.

The war in Japan gave rise to a great deal of unrest in Russia. Together with the reactionary agitation against "the Jewish internal enemy" there was an increase in the number of strikes and terrorist acts against government leaders. The recommendation of the liberal Minister Mirski was that the government offer the people some concessions. On 25 December 1904 Czar Nicholas proclaimed a program of new reforms. On 9 January 1905 a crowd of workers marched to the Winter Palace with a petition to the czar for help against exploitation by the factory owners. The procession, led by Father Gapon, carried crucifixes and portraits of the czar. The priest had promised the workers that he would win the concessions for them in a peaceful way. The procession was stopped by the Royal Guard which, without any warning, began firing into the crowd, killing and wounding many. The marchers were dispersed.

A revolutionary storm broke over the country. Anti-Jewish agitation increased markedly, with the anti-Semites spreading propaganda that Jews were leaders of the anarchy rampant in the land. A national patriotic organization against reforms, The Union of the Russian People (*Soyuz*), became active. From the war fronts came news of decisive Japanese victories. The czar grew more alarmed. On 8 February 1905 he issued a new declaration in which he would permit the election of people's representatives and discuss with them the drafting of a constitution giving the people more rights.

The reactionary cricles were also preparing, organizing pogrom groups in many cities as they called upon the populace to "Beat the revolutionaries and the Jews." Some of their other "teachings" were that the slogan "Down with the Autocracy" was a Jewish invention, and that "the *Zhids* are our worst enemies, they betrayed Russia to Japan." "Down with the Jew Constitution!" they mocked.[26]

Early in 1905 pogroms took place in Bialystok, in Lithuanian towns, and in the province of Kovno. In Simferopol a pogrom resulted from a rumor that a Jewish boy had thrown a holy Christian picture into an outhouse.

In most places the pogromchiks were met by organized Jewish defense groups, which were often assisted by Russian revolutionaries. One group was gathered in an open field outside Zhitomir, learning to use their weapons, when a rumor spread that they were firing at a portrait of the czar. The pogrom, which started during Easter, lasted three days. Several Christians who had joined the Jewish self-defense group were killed by the mob. A group of young Jews from Chudnov, having heard about the pogrom in Zhitomir, armed themselves and started out for that city. On the way they were attacked by a mob and beaten so severely that ten of the fourteen Jews died.[27]

In the summer of 1905, when it became known that a Russian fleet had been sunk in the Far East, the revolutionary movement took a great leap forward. In every city there were strikes and demonstrations. The czarist government replied with more agitation and violence mainly against Jews. In Lodz, troops fired into a demonstration of Jews and Poles. In Bialystok troops suddenly attacked a crowd of Jews in the street, killing fifty people. In Kerch the police fired on a demonstration, mostly of Russians, killing ten and wounding many others.[28]

Throughout the country the storm raged. In October 1905 the revolutionists called a general strike. The czar responded with a manifesto promising the people full citizenship rights, freedom of speech, press, and assembly, and a parliament (the Duma). Russia would be a constitutional monarchy. Along with the czar's manifesto came a bloodbath of Jews. From 18 to 25 October, in the largest cities, wherever there was a branch of the Union of the Russian People, pogroms took place. There were at least six hundred pogroms in one week![29] All the pogroms that took place during that frightful week were carried out in the same manner. The demonstrations of the people celebrating their promised freedom were met by patriotic counterdemonstrations. Clashes took place between the two groups. The police fired at the revolutionists. In the confusion, the "patriots" started a pogrom against Jews. During the violence in Odessa, the Jewish self-defense group fought bravely, but was no match for the well-armed police. More than three hundred Jews were killed; thousands were wounded. More than fourteen thousand Jewish and Russian homes were destroyed.[30]

In the first months of 1906, when the elections to the Duma began, a state of war existed in many places due to the existing anarchy. Polish anti-Semites were furious with Jews who wanted to elect Jewish, rather than Polish, representatives from Warsaw. Nevertheless, twelve Jews from Russia and Poland were elected to the Duma, among them Maxim M. Vinaver, a noted attorney from St. Petersburg, the Zionist leader Shmarya Levin, and the historian Simon Dubnow.

The Duma convened on 27 April, dominated by the Constitutional Democrats (Cadets), who intended to introduce a democratic system of government and restrict the rights of the czar and his henchmen. The important point that arose immediately was agrarian reform to pacify the peasantry. A question was raised about the involvement of the government in the October pogroms. Minister of the Interior Stolypin promised a reply in a month. On 1 June 1906, at the time the Duma began discussing these problems, a pogrom broke out in Bialystok, the third within a year. Police and militia assisted the murderers. Eighty Jews were killed, hundreds wounded.[31]

News of the pogrom reached the Duma the next day. Jews and non-Jews protested vehemently. Radishlav, a Cadet deputy, spoke out sharply against a government that permitted such crimes. A delegation of three deputies was immediately sent to Bialystok to investigate the matter on the spot. They reported that according to all the evidence the massacre had been organized by the Union of the Russian People and the bands of ruffians called the Black Hundreds. At the same time, a debate began in the Duma over the report on the October pogroms, which turned out to be a whitewash of the government. Prince Ussarov, a liberal deputy, and governor of

Bessarabia, disclosed that in the central police department at St. Petersburg there was a printing shop that had printed all the pogrom proclamations. He demanded a change in the system of government in Russia.

On 7 July the Duma adopted a resolution to depose the Council of Ministers, which was to blame for the massacres. Two days later, when the deputies arrived at the Duma, they found the building locked and the way barred by armed soldiers. On the door was a proclamation from the czar himself. The Duma was being dissolved for interfering in matters that were not in its jurisdiction.

After the dissolution of the Duma the anarchy and terror increased. In the course of five months, from September 1906 to January 1907, more than five thousand political "criminals" were executed, many of them Jews. Several thousand "politicals" were exiled to Siberia. Pogroms broke out in more than fifty cities. In Shedlitz thirty Jews were killed, and one hundred fifty were wounded. Stolypin, meanwhile, tried to convince the czar to grant the Jews some concessions. Nicholas II's reply was: "As long as I am Czar, the *Zhidy* of Russia shall not have equal rights."[32]

The elections to the Second Duma in February 1907 took place under the pressure of the reactionary government. Though Jews were threatened with pogroms if they elected Jewish deputies, three Jews were elected. However, the Second Duma was also dissolved, this time with the excuse that it was preparing an uprising against the czar.

On 3 June 1907 the voting system was changed in such a way that very few liberals and revolutionaries could be elected to the Duma. Therefore, the Third Duma was comprised almost entirely of landowners and priests, the same classes that had been ruling Russia for several centuries. These same groups were instrumental, at the beginning of this century, in creating the *Protocols of the Elders of Zion*, which became, and remains, the most important tool in the hands of Jew-haters throughout the world.

24

Intensification of Jew-Hatred in Russia: The Protocols of the Elders of Zion

As a result of the defeat inflicted upon Russia by Japan, and the upsurge of revolutionary unrest in the country, the Black Hundreds intensified their anti-Semitic agitation. In order to persuade the frightened czar to approve the use of extreme terror, the Russian Secret Service in 1905 published a second edition of the *Protocols of the Elders of Zion* which supposedly contain irrefutable proof that the Jews were to blame for the crisis in Russia.

The *Protocols* had been printed in the winter of 1902–1903 by Sergey Nilus, a fanatical mystic, under the title of *The Antichrist as an Imminent Political Possibility: Protocols of the Meetings of the Zionist Sages*. The 1905 edition, printed in *Tsarskoe Selo*, the czar's residence, was entitled *The Great in the Small: Antichrist as an Imminent Political Possibility*. The *Protocols* were not invented by Nilus; he merely translated them from the French. Their history is complex and has several origins which are not connected with each other. We shall present them *seriatim*.

Origin 1. "A Dialogue in Hell" ("*Dialogue aux Enfers*"). In 1864, Maurice Joly, a liberal French lawyer, wrote a little book called "A Dialogue in Hell between Montesquieu and Machiavelli," in which he satirized Napoleon III of France, who was a cynical opportunist and a swindler and who tried to buttress his power by a variety of dishonest methods. Joly introduced the spirits of two famous philosophers engaged in calm discussion. One was the very popular Italian, Niccolò Machiavelli, who died in 1527. His writings, which became a guide for all the world's dictators, deal with the problem of how a ruler can maintain his power. William Ebenstein in his book *Great Political Thinkers* wrote:

> A ruler must try to make himself beloved of his subjects. This is necessary in order to keep his power. But if a ruler is faced with the choice of being "good" and well-liked or of frightening and terrorizing his people, then the latter is a much better course of action, because it is more effective.[1]

According to Machiavelli, the greatest sin a ruler commits is not in being inhuman but in losing his power. Machiavelli's fellow discussant is another famous philosopher, the French encyclopedist, Montesquieu, who died in 1755. Also a student of the problems associated with power, he believed that "power corrupts." Rulers must not be given too much power. Of course, in order to govern, a ruler does need a certain amount of power, but this power must be controlled by law. The people, said Montesquieu, elect their representatives to a parliament, which creates the laws, and the ruler must govern in accordance with those laws.

In the "Dialogue," Machiavelli has the most to say about the way a ruler should govern. Montesquieu offers comments on and questions the morality and legality of means used to attain his end. Machiavelli replies that he is not afraid of the people for he would control all the news services and the press and confuse them, raise false issues, and deceive them. "But won't the people catch on?" Montesquieu insists. Machiavelli replies that he would terrorize the people and put several of their leaders in prison, guillotine a few, and the rest will tremble for their lives.[2]

Joly's book was printed in Belgium anonymously. After a number of copies had been sold, the police caught on to the content of the text and it was not difficult for them to find the author. In 1865 Joly was arrested, fined, and sentenced to fifteen months in prison.

Origin 2. Hermann Goedsche, a German anti-Semite, who had lost his position in the postal service over some forged signatures, wrote several short stories under the pseudonym of Sir John Retcliffe. His specialty was the sensational story, into which he often wove lies about Jews. When he came upon Joly's "Dialogue," he wrote a tale about a midnight meeting of twelve rabbis in the Old Prague Cemetery. Each rabbi came from a different Christian country and they reported on their progress in gaining more power in the Christian countries.

Goedsche's story was translated and published in Russia in 1872 under the title, "The Jewish Cemetery in Prague: A Meeting of the Representatives of the Twelve Tribes of Israel." The most important passages in the story were copied straight from Joly's "Dialogue." In this version, the chief rabbi makes a speech in which he recommends that the Jews seize power and terrorize the *goyim*. Each representative reports on what the Jews are doing in his country in the effort to dominate the Christians more rapidly and completely. One reports that the Jews in his country have concentrated all the national wealth in their own hands. A second reports that the Jews accept as surety only forests and fields, with the intent of taking over the whole country. A third reports that the Jews in his country are gradually gaining control of the railroads, the mines, the dwellings, the cities. Another reports that the Jews are beginning to take over leading government posts, the better to control the Christians politically.[3] Still another rabbi boasts that the Jews in his country have already taken over the press and all the news media and can now report only what they wish the *goyim* to know. A rabbi from an industrial country boasts that the Jews there have become masters of commerce and industry. Another reports that the Jews in his country are the leading attorneys and legislators; and another states that the Jews are preparing to disrupt the Christian religion and take away the Church's right to educate Christian children. Yet another rabbi claims that the Jews in his country are manufacturing new deadly weapons with which the *goyim* can kill each other off in the wars the Jews are planning. All the reports thus had the style and content of Machiavelli's program. In 1891, when the czarist government was fanning the anti-Semitic flames in Russia, G. V. Butmi, a Black Hundreds leader, reprinted Goedsche's horror story.

Origin 3. Around 1860 a converted Jew, Jacob Brafman, reported to the police that the organization of the Jewish community was working against the government. The document remained in the files of the St. Petersburg police.

Origin 4. Somewhere around the middle of the 1890s a police official in St. Petersburg, Pyotr Rachkovski, went to Paris to look for a connection between the Jewish *Kahal* and the *Alliance Israélite*. He brought back a document in French, which was evidently a copy of the original *Protocols*.[4]

In the tumultuous year of 1905, when the *Protocols* were reprinted, they also appeared in the czarist newspaper *Znamye*, whose editor was then P. A. Krushevan, organizer of the 1903 pogrom in Kishinev.[5]

In the 1905 edition Nilus included the speech of the chief rabbi at the meeting in the Prague Cemetery (invented by Goedsche). The rabbi says:

It is already 1800 years that we Jews . . . have been waging a war against the Cross. . . . They persecuted us, degraded us, made us suffer horrible deaths, but our people have survived and are spread throughout the world . . . because the whole world belongs to us and we shall inherit it.[6]

In 1907 the *Protocols* were published in a new edition. It is interesting that in the forewords to the various editions, other sources are listed as origins of the *Protocols*. In the 1905 edition, Nilus relates that he received them from a woman, who stole it from a leading Freemason in France. The foreword of the 1907 edition says that the *Protocols* were stolen from an important Zionist leader in France. This foreword is different from the others in another significant way. It says:

The statement made in a previous edition that the name "Elders of Zion" should not be confused with the Zionists is not correct. The *Protocols* are actually Zionist documents. Zionism was originated by the Jewish prince, Dr. Herzl, in 1896 and is widespread among Jewish intellectuals. . . . The truth is that the Jews maintain Zionism only as a pretext. In actuality the Zionist institutions are a revolutionary organization which is secretly led by the Jewish Labor Bund.[7]

In a new edition in 1911, Nilus declares that the documents reveal the Jewish program for dealing with the *goyim*. The *Protocols*, Nilus falsely asserts, are the speeches which Theodore Herzl made at the Zionist Congress in Basel in 1897.

In 1918 the White Guard general Denikin published the *Protocols* in Novocherkask, the site of his headquarters, and spread them among his troops and the civilian population. Afterward, the *Protocols* were published in Rostov-on-Don by the White Guard general Wrangel, whose officers distributed the books among the people in all the surrounding cities and villages. When these officers later scattered throughout the world, they "favored" the peoples of Western Europe and America with copies of the poisonous documents.

In France several anti-Semitic groups were active at that time, most of them led by the Catholic Church, which was resentful because a number of Jewish deputies in parliament had voted with the liberals to abolish the exclusive right of Catholic monks and nuns to teach in the public schools. In addition, the more serious newspapers in France played up the "Jewish Protocols," reproducing entire paragraphs. From France the *Protocols* were picked up and published in Arabic in Beirut, Damascus, and Cairo.[8]

In Germany, Count Ernst Reventlow, who later became one of the leaders of the Nazi Party, published the *Protocols* in several editions. The former Kaiser Wilhelm, who had lost his throne, greeted the *Protocols*, as he had the anti-Semitic "Foundations of the Nineteenth Century" by Chamberlain.[9] General Ludendorff, who together with Hitler carried out the Munich putsch in 1923, also endorsed the *Protocols*.

In 1923 two more editions of the *Protocols* were published in Germany, this time by Alfred Rosenberg, who later became Hitler's close co-worker. In the foreword Rosenberg accused the Jews of having started the First World War and of selling Germany out to her enemies.

In England an anti-Semitic group known as "The Britons" published the *Protocols* in 1920. In addition, major newspapers such as the *London Times* and *The Spectator* took these absurd forgeries seriously, quoting lengthy passages and printing articles about them under banner headlines. The *Morning Post* used the headline "Cause of World Unrest." These articles were then reprinted in the United States by Henry Ford in a book called *The Jewish Peril*. The *Protocols* themselves were published by Henry Ford in his *Dearborn Independent*. This newspaper at that time had no more than 20,000 readers, but the sensation of the *Protocols* soon brought the number up to around 300,000. In 1927 Henry Ford recanted and forbade the use of his name in connection with this material.[10]

Several million copies of the *Protocols* were printed and distributed in the United States from 1919 to 1923. The quota system which

Congress adopted in 1921 to limit Jewish immigration was, aside from the fear of bolshevism, also influenced by these forgeries.

The Protocols Exposed

In 1920 the European correspondent for the *New York Times*, Herman Bernstein, made a study of Goedsche's sensational story about the rabbis at the Prague Cemetery and recognized the motif of the *Protocols*. In a brochure, "The Story of a Lie," he showed that the "reports" of the rabbis were almost verbatim copies of the words which the *Protocols* put into the mouth of a rabbi or of Theodore Herzl. The brochure was printed in February 1921. Six months later the *London Times* printed a full expose of the forgeries by its correspondent in Constantinople, Philip Graves.[11] His friend, Count Radichev, the former liberal deputy in the Duma, now an emigrant in Turkey, had been in southern Russia in 1918-19, in the area conquered by General Denikin. He had read the *Protocols* and they had struck him as pure fabrications. How and when the forgeries had been invented, he did not know.

In 1919 Radichev bought an old library that belonged to a former officer of the Okhrana (Russian Secret Police). Among the books, he found one in French, with a torn title page on which the word *"Enfers"* and the date, 1865, were still legible. Reading the book out of curiosity, he recognized both the style and the language as similar to the *Protocols*. Entire passages of the forgeries were copied from this book.

Despite frequent exposure as forgeries, the *Protocols* were continuously reprinted. In Germany, ten million copies were issued during the Hitler years; in 1935 they were assigned as compulsory reading in the public schools. Hitler's *Mein Kampf* and the *Protocols* were displayed prominently in every household.[12] In the Arab countries today the *Protocols* are still very popular. King Faisal of Saudi Arabia used to present his guests with copies, translated into many languages.[13]

In brief, the content of these forgeries is as follows: The Jews are planning to conquer and rule the non-Jewish world. The Jews are a small people, but very powerful: they control all the gold and all the banks in the world. They own the press and the news media and deliberately disseminate false news in order to create chaos and confusion. It is the Jews who bring about economic crises and unemployment, discontent, and rebellion among the people. In this way they are really the instigators of revolution. Their policies lead the nations to wage continuous warfare and kill each other off. Mercy is foreign to Jews. Nothing is forbidden to them and they commit every crime known to man. Their main objective is to destroy all the *goyim* and rule the world.

Below are a few brief excerpts from the twenty-four *Protocols*.

1) We [the Jews] are now the most powerful force in the world because we are invisible. We are concealed, but we are here and we are continually adding to our strength, until eventually we shall become so powerful that the *goyim* will never again be able to conquer us.[14]

2) The governments of the world use a very important method of maintaining their power: they control the thoughts of their peoples through the press. Freedom of the press has become sacrosanct. The *goyim*, however, do not know how to make use of this means. Today we are the masters of the press everywhere; through the press we rule. We have also acquired complete control of all the gold in the world; while it has cost us oceans of blood and tears, it was worth it. We have suffered many casualties, but every one of our casualties is worth a thousand *goyim* in the eyes of God.[15]

3) The nations have a problem with their workers. So we come to the enslaved proletariat and propose that they become socialists, anarchists, communists. . . . We support all these groups, as we preach in our Masonic lodges. . . . In reality, we are interested . . . in the killing of the *goyim*.[16]

4) In order that our accumulated wealth may work to our best advantage, it is necessary to create industrial and commercial monopolies. . . . To ruin their industries we shall infect the *goyim* with a hunger for luxuries which will swallow up all their wealth and bankrupt them. . . .[17]

Following is a comparison of Joly's "Dialogue" with the *Protocols*:[18]

Dialogue	*Protocols*
Has politics anything to do with morals?	The Political has nothing in common with the moral.
This word "justice" itself, by the way, do you not see that it is infinitely vague?	The word "right" is an abstract thought and proved by nothing.

I am less preoccupied by what is good and moral than by what is useful and necessary.	Let us, however, in our plans, direct our attention not so much to what is good and moral as to what is necessary and useful.
What forms of government would you apply to societies in which corruption has stolen everywhere, in which morality has no guarantee?	What form of administration rule can be given to communities in which corruption has penetrated everywhere?
Machiavelli: . . . Who makes the sovereigns? Montesquieu: The people. Machiavelli: It is written: Per Me regnat. Which means literally: God makes kings [Through Me kings reign].	Per Me reges regnat. "It is through me that Kings reign." And it was said by the prophets that we were chosen by God Himself to rule over the whole earth.
To all internal agitation, he must be able to respond with a foreign war; to any imminent revolution, with a general war.	We must be in a position to respond to every act of opposition by war with the neighbors of that country which dares to oppose us.
What is essential is the use against one's enemies of all the arms they could employ against you.	We must arm ourselves with all the weapons which our opponents might employ against us.
I would institute . . . huge financial monopolies, reservoirs of the public wealth, on which depends so closely the fate of all the private fortunes that they would be swallowed up with the credit of State the day after any political catastrophe.	We shall soon begin to establish huge monopolies, reservoirs of colossal riches, upon which even large fortunes of the goyim will depend to such an extent that they will go to the bottom together with the credit of the States on the day after the political smash.

The Jewish historian, A. Tcherikower, who gathered material about the role of the *Protocols* in the Ukraine during the Civil War of 1918–21, reports that from the early part of the century, when the *Protocols* first appeared, until 1918, the forgeries were barely known there. It was not until the civil war following the Bolshevik revolution that they were widely disseminated and led to attacks on Jews.[19]

With the pogroms of 1905–1906 a period of reaction set in, its tone provided by the *Soyuz* (Union of the Russian People) and its shock troops the gangs of thugs organized by the Black Hundreds. In

1906–1907 the courts of the land were busy with trials of the murderers who had killed and maimed thousands of Jews during the pogroms. Most of the accused were acquitted "for lack of evidence." The constitution which Czar Nicholas had promised was soon watered down and forgotten. In the Third Duma (1907), anti-Semitic laws were pushed through the chamber. The numerous clauses in educational institutions was made even more restrictive. When the liberal candidate Radichev warned that these laws were unconstitutional, he was hooted down with cries of "Jew-lover."[20]

The Mendel Beilis Trial

In the spring of 1911 the body of a murdered twelve-year-old boy was discovered near a brickyard outside of Kiev. Suspicion fell upon a woman who was the leader of a gang of theives. However, the *Soyuz* had resolved to make this into a ritual murder case. Anti-Semitic newspapers sensationalized the news: a Christian child had been murdered by Jews for ritual purposes. By some sleight-of-hand the suspicion was removed from the gang leader and a campaign began to involve Jews in the murder. The brickyard belonged to a Jew; the overseer of the place was a Jew named Mendel Beilis. A witness soon came forward to swear that he had seen the victim playing with other children near the brickyard when the Jew had dragged him inside. The police arrested Beilis. He was beaten but refused to admit any guilt. For months he was held incommunicado, not even permitted to speak to an attorney.

Hundreds of people attended the funeral of the murdered boy where they were handed leaflets accusing the Jews of the crime. "Beat the Jews and Save Russia" again became the slogan of the hour. The blood libel caught the attention of the entire civilized world. From everywhere came protests against this medieval frame-up. The trial began in October 1913 before a jury of twelve simple peasants. Prominent attorneys from Moscow and St. Petersburg came to defend Beilis and the Jews. The *Soyuz* provided a Catholic priest names Parnaytis, a "specialist in the rules of Jewish ritual murder," who undertook to prove that Jews had committed the murder for ritual purposes.

During cross examination the leading witness for the prosecution, a lamplighter, admitted that certain answers had been drilled into him by the police. After a few hours of deliberation the jury acquitted the defendant. The government thereupon sued the liberal newspapers and the lawyers for the defense.

The Jews in Poland Before World War I

During the years prior to World War I the National Democratic Party was active in the Polish part of Russia. The Endeks, as they were known, did intensive anti-Jewish work among the Poles and Russians, agitating against Jewish economic positions and proposing restrictions of Jewish rights in commerce and industry. They were supported by the *Soyuz*. The leader of the Endeks in the Third Duma was Roman Dmowski, who became notorious as a Jew-hater in Poland between the two World Wars.

In the 1912 elections to the Fourth Duma the Poles demanded of the Jews that they not put forward their own candidates, but vote for the candidate nominated by the Poles. The Jewish organizations agreed, but on condition that the Polish candidate not be an anti-Semite. The Poles in Warsaw, however, put forward an anti-Semitic candidate. The Jews in Warsaw consequently voted for the Polish Socialist candidate, who was in fact elected with the help of the Jewish vote. For this "betrayal" the anti-Semites heated up their hate campaign during the Mendel Beilis trial. In the press, in the streets, in the theaters, Jews were taunted with the name "Beilis." In general, the influence of the Endeks continued to deepen among the Polish people in the interbellum period when Poland was already an independent state.

Jews in World War I

All of the most important countries in Europe which fought in World War I contained Jewish communities. In the German army there were 100,000 Jews, a disproportionately large number when compared with their percentage of the population. In France, England, and Austria, Jews took second place to no one in fulfilling their patriotic duty. Thus it happened that Jewish soldiers in the Allied armies fought against Jewish soldiers of the Axis powers. It has been estimated that more than 200,000 young Jews were either killed or disabled on the battlefields of Europe.[21] Jews who lived in the war zones suffered especial hardship.

The czarist generals, fearing that the Jews would fraternize with the Germans as the Russian troops retreated, drove the Jews out of the forward positions deeper into the hinterland. Tens of thousands of Jews in Poland, Lithuania, and Galicia were thus ejected from their homes during 1915, the year of the great Russian defeats. Hundreds and thousands of hungry and homeless Jews wandered through strange lands. In many places the Russians permitted the Jews to remain where they were, but took hostages as insurance against the Jews becoming too friendly with the enemy.[22]

With most of the able-bodied men in the army, many farms in Russia were left unattended. The railroads, which were in poor condition before the war, were almost totally ruined by the war. Food supplies grew scarce, especially bread. The people began to protest. In the spring of 1917, two-and-a-half years after the start of this senseless war, the second revolution erupted in Russia. In February 1917 the autocracy fell. A few weeks later the Provisional Government abolished all restrictions against Jews. The Jewish population was given recognition not as a religious minority but as a national minority, with all nationality rights. The October Revolution did not revoke this equal status, but the resulting civil war from 1918 to 1921 gave rise to a thousand deadly pogroms all over Russia. Tens of thousands of Jews were killed or crippled. Masses of Jewish women were raped. Almost a thousand Jewish communities were burned, pillaged, and destroyed.[23]

The worst pogroms took place in the Ukraine. The majority of the Ukrainian population—the peasantry—had little or no political or national awareness. There was, however, a small class of intellectuals, with an old tradition of struggle for Ukrainian independence, who gloried in Chmielnicki's rebellion against the Polish lords in the seventeenth century and honored the Ukrainian poet Shevchenko, whom the czarist government had exiled in the nineteenth century as a nationalist. Soon after the fall of the czar a national Ukrainian council was formed whose objective was to sever the Ukraine from Russia and create an independent state. At the end of 1917 the various Ukrainian groups and parties put together a government and as military leader chose the representative of the Sitcheviki regiment, Semyon Petlura.[24] In April 1918, soon after the Bolsheviks signed the peace treaty with the Germans in Brest-Litovsk, the German army marched into the Ukraine, occupied Kiev, and halted at the Dnieper.

With the Germans confiscating much bread and other foodstuffs, the anger of the people reached the boiling point. In 1918, this anger exploded in a rebellion led by Semyon Petlura, when news arrived about a revolution in Germany, and it became clear that the German army would have to leave the Ukraine. The Germans were defeated, but it was not easy for them to retreat. German and Austrian soldiers sold their weapons to the peasants in exchange for bread or to the ataman for safe conduct to Germany. The Ukrainians thus acquired a great store of arms. In January, reports of pogroms came from Berditchev, Ovruch, Zhitomir, and many other places.[25]

When the Germans left in February 1919, the Bolsheviks entered Kiev. The Jews were caught in the vortex of a civil war. To whip up the Ukrainians against the Bolsheviks, the hetmans gave their troops freedom to attack the Jews in the towns. The name of Leon Trotsky, leader of the Red Army, and the names of several other prominent Jewish leaders of the Communist Party in Moscow or Petrograd, were the best proof that "the Jews were Bolsheviks." The Ukrainian army began living off the pogroms and Jewish bloodshed.

As the Russians entered Kiev, the directorate of the Ukrainian National Council fled the city. Petlura's staff settled in Kameniec-Podolsk. On 15 February 1919 Petlura sent the Ataman Semosenko to the city of Proskurov with several hundred drunken Cossacks. With no advance time to prepare their self-defense group, the 20,000 Jews of Proskurov were subjected to a pogrom whose bestiality exceeded anything that had gone before. No fewer than fifteen hundred Jews were left dead.[26]

The battles between the Bolsheviks and the Ukrainians spread across a large area of the Pale, especially in the Podolia, Volhynia and Kiev provinces. Wherever the Petlura forces entered they organized pogroms. The Bolsheviks would then attack and drive them out. The Jews in the towns began to look upon the Red Army as their redeemers. Here and there reports came of Red Army men who also robbed Jews, but it was common knowledge that such offenders were punished by their officers. Most important, the Jews were well aware that anti-pogrom education was being carried out among the Red Army units.[27]

During May and June of 1919, after grave defeats at the hands of the Bolsheviks, the Petlura armies retreated. As soon as a town remained without a ruler, which happened quite frequently, local "rebels" appeared who started their own pogroms. In mid-summer 1919 a new army of White Guardists entered the Ukraine from southern Russia, led by the czarist General Denikin. Armed by the Western powers, they captured Kiev and occupied large sections of the Ukrainian provinces. Most of Denikin's officers were members of the *Soyuz* whose slogan, "Beat the Jews and Save Russia," was well suited to the mood of the embittered peasants. Pogroms were instigated by the Denikin forces just as they had been by the Petlura gangs. Many peasants in the Ukrainian army deserted to Denikin.

Out of the defeated Petlura units many bandit gangs were formed who also took part in the massacre of thousands of Jews in the Ukraine. The cruelties of the local hetmans—Angel, Zelioni, Gregoryev, Machno, Struk, Sokolovski—are well-documented.[28]

In the same summer of 1919 other enemies arose against the Bolsheviks. In Byelorussia, General Bulak-Balachovitch, who was also subsidized by the Western powers, organized pogroms that were no less savage than those of Petlura and Denikin. Soon after Denikin's defeat, General Wrangel began his march up from the south. His officers, too, were disseminators of the *Protocols* and his troops also bathed in Jewish blood. Fortunately, they were defeated before they could get deeper into the country.

There were several Soviet regiments, composed of rebel groups in the Ukraine, that also engaged in pogrom activity—the Taraschaner Division, the Bokun regiment, the Sixth and Eighth regiments. But the political commissars in the Red Army conducted intensive educational programs, and several pogrom instigators were shot. As a result, many Red Army soldiers in the Ukrainian regiments deserted the Bolsheviks. Here and there a Red Army detachment deserted to the Petluras, killing the Jews, the Commissar, and other Communists in their units. By 1920 the Red Army had succeeded in eliminating many of the bandit armies.

In the spring of 1919, Polish army units, subsidized by the Western powers, penetrated the Ukraine, Byelorussia, and certain areas of Lithuania and captured Kiev. In their march, as they went through a town or city, they shot people just to terrorize the population. When the Poles entered Pinsk on 15 April 1919, a Polish officer ordered thirty-five young Jews shot because they had attended a meeting to consider how best to distribute the relief funds given by the Joint Distribution Committee. In the city of Lida, thirty-nine Jews were shot. In Vilna the Poles executed fifteen Jews, among them the Yiddish writer A. Veiter. In August the Poles shot thirty-one Jews in Minsk. When the Jewish deputies in the *Sejm* protested, the Polish government offered one excuse—the Polish army was fighting against Bolshevism and shot only Communists.

When the Bolsheviks sent the Polish army reeling out of Kiev toward Warsaw, Polish soldiers again led a pogrom of the Jewish communities along the line of retreat. In the counterattack, the Poles repeated the pogroms. This carnage continued until the signing of the peace agreement in Riga in the fall of 1921.[29] For the Jews in the Ukraine, 1919 was a year of atrocities no less barbaric than those of Chmielnicki in 1648–49 or of the Haidamaki in 1768. One hundred thousand Jews were murdered or maimed during 1919.

By the hundreds of thousands, by the millions, the Jews strove desperately to save themselves. The best place of refuge was America, but there they began closing the gates to Jewish immigration in 1921. By 1924 those gates were already sealed. The millions of Jews in Eastern Europe remained exposed in the hellish nightmare of Polish anti-Semitism and Soviet social and economic experiments, and later, Soviet forced assimilation and the worst tragedy in Jewish history inflicted by the cannibalistic Nazi rulers of Europe during World War II.

25

Jew-Hatred in America

It is estimated that at the time of the Revolution in 1776 the Jewish population in America was no more than two to three thousand out of a total population of approximately four million.[1] Most of these Jews were engaged either in trade or handicrafts, and took part in all the actions against England.[2] Very few Jews were loyal to the Crown. George Washington valued this support highly. His replies to greetings sent to him by Jewish congregations in Savannah, Charleston, and Newport have remained as testaments of Jewish emancipation in the new, free land.[3]

In the first quarter of the nineteenth century the total number of Jews in the country was still small. By 1825 there were no more than ten thousand Jews in all of the colonies.[4] The Jews at that time had the same rights as the rest of the population in almost every respect. However, the anti-Jewish feelings that Christian immigrants brought over with them from Europe did not disappear overnight. Muted, they hid in the corners. In general it can be said that the non-Jewish population in the United States never displayed any rabid Jew-hatred. It can also be said that even during the stormy twentieth century, Jew-hatred in America was restrained. At times, anti-Jewish feelings did reach high levels, but the Jews were never subjected to the kinds of persecutions and restrictions they experienced in Europe.

In the 1830s and 1840s, when many people came to America from central and southern Europe, a movement arose against this stream of immigrants, particularly Catholics and Jews. Later, the destruction caused by the Civil War, the scarcity of products, and the high prices of necessities were used to arouse Jew-hatred. Propaganda against "Jewish speculators" increased. Jews were accused of being secretly friendly to the other side, of transmitting information to the enemy.[5]

On 17 December 1862 General Grant issued his Order No. 11 expelling all Jews from the war zones. The Order was directed specifically against Jews, not against spies, smugglers, or speculators. When the Jews appealed to President Lincoln, he immediately countermanded the Order, but after the war, Jews continued to be accused of all sorts of "unpatriotic" activities. These libels were particularly widespread in the South, where the population after the Civil War was still smarting from defeat and needed a scapegoat.

Among the embittered elements in the South were secret groups whose purpose was to keep the Blacks socially and economically oppressed and politically powerless. One of those groups was the Ku Klux Klan, whose white-hooded members staged cross burnings in an attempt to frighten their opponents. Lynchings of Blacks occurred periodically as the Klan terrorized the emancipated slaves, as well as Catholics and Jews. Protests throughout the country were raised against their criminal activities and laws were passed to curb them.

The sharpened anti-Semitism in Germany, France, Austria, and Russia in the last quarter of the nineteenth century inevitably affected the United States, especially as masses of Jews fled from the pogroms and the poverty. The effects of industrialization and the concentration of capital were also felt by agriculture. Farmers suddenly realized that the bankers and stock market speculators in the large cities had become their active partners, virtually the real masters of their labor and their land. In the farm areas a suspicion developed of the bankers and the "foreigners" in the big city.[6] When William Jennings Bryan ran for senator of Nebraska in 1894 he called for the free coinage of silver. His slogan was "don't crucify humanity on a cross of gold."[7] The words "crucify . . . cross . . . gold" became popular and suggested what they were supposed to suggest.

Dozens of pamphlets appeared describing how Jews had already swallowed up the countries of Europe and were now doing the same thing in America. One such pamphlet was written by a Greek immigrant named Timainis, who came to the United States in the 1870s. Having lived for several years in France, he became a teacher of French, as well as a journalist. Envious of the success of Drumont, the French anti-Semite, Timainis published *The Original Mr. Jacobs* and other books, in which he plagiarized entire passages from Drumont's *La France Juive*. The main theme of his books was that the Jews now controlled the "naive Americans." He repeated all the stale libels: the Jew is a swindler, the Jew is uncreative and unproductive, the wealth of every country always ends up in the Jew's pocket. Timainis's advice to Americans was to stop the immigration of Jews into the country. The books were illustrated with pictures taken mostly from Christian liturgical texts.

Many reviews of these books were printed in American magazines and newspapers branding the author as a bigot and a Jew-hater. A "Miss Johanna von Bohn" published a pamphlet and mailed it to the legislators in Washington, "This type of literature," she wrote, "is much worse than the obscene pornographic pictures and books which are prohibited by law." The *New York World* called the books extremely dangerous. The leading exception was the *Saturday Evening Post,* which described Timainis as "an anti-Semite who spreads hatred," but added that "historically, politically and socially it is an interesting and important book. . . ."[8]

Timainis was not the only anti-Semite in America in those days. A large segment of American intellectuals had been taken in by Gobineau's pseudo-scientific race theories. His four-volume *Development of the Human Race* was published in the United States in several editions, as were Drumont's *La France Juive*. Pamphlets appeared attacking the Zionist Congresses which took place in Switzerland at the end of the nineteenth century. "The Jews are uniting," these pamphlets warned, confirming the anti-Semitie charges that Jews are not patriotic citizens of the countries in which they live.

Early in the twentieth century the most popular racist book in Europe, *The Foundations of the Nineteenth Century* by Chamberlain, was printed in the United States in several editions. The principal theme of the book, that the Semitic race is a low and harmful one, gradually became part of the American scene. Pamphlets and books appeared emphasizing racial differences and urging restrictions on Jewish immigration, In 1908 a book appeared by Al Schultz called *Race or Mongrel: A Theory that Mixed Marriages Destroy a People*. The book saw several editions. Several years later, *The Passing of the Great Race* by Madison Grant appeared and went through more than ten editions. Americans were informed that the "best" Nordic race in the country was being contaminated with the blood of lower races—Latins and Jews. All these publications called for the cessation of immigration of "lower races" into America.

The Jewish population in the country up to 1881 had reached approximately 250,000; by 1900 it was 1.5 million.[9] Reactionaries and anti-Semites began comparing the "old" immigrants with the "new." In the old days, only "good" immigrants came to America— Nordics, Protestants, blonds. Now there were "too many from the southeast of Europe—Latins, Catholics, Slavs and Jews."[10]

Only isolated individuals were affected by these anti-human ideas. One such victim was Henry Cabot Lodge, Sr., senator from Massachusetts from 1893 to 1924, who proposed that no immigrant should be admitted who could not sign his or her name. The law was passed, but no Jews were thereby barred, because almost every Jew could sign his or her name in Yiddish. A few years later Senator Lodge offered a new bill which would have barred immigrants who could not read or write the language of their country of origin. This bill was so patently anti-Semitic that it was defeated in Congress by a large majority.[11]

The "moneyed aristocrats" in the United States not only refused to associate socially with Jews, but many of them even avoided business dealings with "those people." In the private clubs, no Jews were admitted. Exclusive resorts in those days posted signs announcing "No Jews or dogs allowed." (Some of these signs also included the word "Catholics.")

In 1877 the manager of the Grand Union Hotel, the largest in Saratoga Springs, New York, informed Joseph Seligman, a Jewish banker, that the hotel did not accept "Israelites." Seligman, who had been a personal friend of President Lincoln and General Grant and who had helped finance the Union Army during the Civil War, determined not to keep quiet about the insult. The result was a "sensation" in the public press, as leading newspapers condemned the action of the hotel.[12]

In 1891 the then influential *North American Review* carried an article charging that no Jews had served in the Union Army, that Jews had grown rich out of the tragedy of the Civil War. In 1908 Chief of Police Bingham of New York City wrote an article for the *North American Review* claiming that although the Jews were only 25 percent of the population in New York, they committed 50 percent of all the crimes in the city. The American Jewish

Committee, led by Louis Marshall and Cyrus Sulzberger, called him a liar and demanded to see his facts. It turned out that Jews were committing only 7 percent of the crimes. Bingham had counted as "criminals" Jewish peddlers without licenses and Jewish pickets around shops that had secured injunctions against strikes. The American Jewish Committee compelled him to print a retraction in the newspapers, but the lie was repeated by anti-Semites. In several speeches in Congress, the "criminal elements" were cited as reasons for stopping immigration.

When the terrible pogrom took place in Kishinev in 1903, American Jews reacted vigorously with mass demonstrations. The government in Washington queried Ambassador McCormick in Russia as to what it could do to help the victims. Petitions were sent to St. Petersburg demanding an end to the pogroms. One petition, with 12,000 signatures, contained the names of most of the congressmen, senators, governors, professors, and leading clergymen in America. The czarist government countered that it did not recognize the document and would not respond to it.

The pogroms two years later again aroused tremendous protest in the United States. The Jewish flight from Russia assumed a mass character. From 1903 to 1907 more than 400,000 Russian Jews migrated to America.[13] The Russian rulers, who were more than happy to see the Jews go, treated visiting American Jews as if they had no rights either, barring them from Moscow, St. Petersburg, Kiev, and other cities. During the Mendel Beilis trial in 1913, all commercial relations between Russia and the United States were broken off.[14]

1912 and 1913 were crisis years in America. Unemployment was at a record high. Masses of new immigrants were arriving from Italy, Austria, and Germany. From Russia and Rumania came many Jews. The American Federation of Labor demanded a halt to immigration. The newcomers, they argued, were a reserve of cheap labor. Anti-Jewish groups demanded that Jewish immigration be the first to be restricted. In those years discrimination against Jews was intensified in hotels, resorts, and "better neighborhoods" in the cities. Help wanted advertisements in newspapers cautioned: "Only Christians Need Apply." Ivy League universities rejected the applications of Jewish students.

In 1915–16 the Ku Klux Klan grew to an estimated four or five million members. In Georgia, in 1915, they lynched an innocent young Jew named Leo Frank, accused of murdering a young woman who worked with him in a pencil factory. A court having sentenced him to death on the testimony of an ex-convict, the governor commuted the sentence to life imprisonment. On 15 August 1915 a band of Klansmen broke into the prison and lynched him.[15] Ten years later an inmate of a federal prison confessed that he and the witness against Frank had killed the woman.

In 1916, when President Wilson nominated the popular liberal Jewish attorney, Louis D. Brandeis, to the Supreme Court, a powerful anti-Semitic campaign was mounted against the president. During World War I most of the newly arrived Jewish immigrants from Russia were eager to see a defeat of the czarist regime. In government circles and in the country generally, sympathy from the outset of the war was on the side of the Allies. The anti-Russian sentiment among Jews was no secret. In various quarters Jews were accused of being enemies of "our allies." However, by the time the United States entered the war in 1917 the czarist regime had already been overthrown. Jewish sympathies changed in favor of the Allies.

The course of the revolution in Russia aroused great alarm in America. The fear of bolshevism strengthened the mistrust of "ex-Russians" throughout the country. The world-famous Jewish names prominent in Bolshevik leadership caused many Americans to regard Jews as "allies of communism." Throughout the country and the world anti-Semites raised the cry of "Jewish communism." A reaction against any kind of radicalism set in. Combined with the isolationist mood against "foreign entanglements," public opinion in the United States turned against unlimited immigration. Agitation by the Ku Klux Klan and other anti-Semites led to the passage of the Johnson-Lodge Act by Congress in 1921. This law was adopted in accordance with the racist theory that the gates of America were open only for "Nordics" and people of the "Aryan" race. The quota system specifically limited immigration from Eastern Europe, home of the so-called lower races.

This discrimination against the Jews of Eastern Europe struck them precisely at a time when they were in dire need of a place of refuge. The Jews of the Ukraine had just experienced the devastating pogroms of the civil war.[16] More than a million Jews in Russia had been declassed by the Bolshevik government and reduced to beggary. In the Baltic countries, in Poland, Galicia, Rumania, where there were populous Jewish centers, the anti-Semitic temperature had risen steeply. In Germany, which had lost the war, galloping inflation and rising unemployment produced the Nazi movement.

The chauvinist agitation in Germany obviously boded the Jews no good. Masses of Jews in Europe were trying desperately to escape from the inferno developing all around them.

In the early 1920s Henry Ford popularized the *Protocols of the Elders of Zion* in America. His regrets and apologies came too late. Anti-Semitic pressure undoubtedly had something to do with the tightening of the immigration laws in 1924. However, Jew-hatred never became deeprooted among the masses of Americans. As a result, Jews felt free and secure here. Restrictions were rare, although they did exist upon Jews with "new capital." The large financial and industrial combines usually refused to accept them as partners. Discrimination also existed against American-born Jews seeking admission to Ivy League universities. With few exceptions, Jewish scholars were not given teaching positions in most institutions of higher learning. Hospitals avoided hiring Jewish physicians. The prestigious law firms stayed *Judenrein*.[17]

Rise of Anti-Semitism in the 1930s

The protracted economic crisis of 1929-36 threw millions of American workers out of their jobs. Banks closed. Thousands of small businesses went bankrupt. The blame for the Depression was placed upon abstract causes—Wall Street, the banks. Anti-Semitic groups, which began to sprout like mushrooms after a rain, added Jews to the abstract causes. Thus, the bankers and Wall Street also became part of the "Jewish conspiracy," which was in accord with the lies of the *Protocols* that were being more widely disseminated throughout the country.

The German-American Bund, led by agents of the Nazi government such as Hans Spanknoble and Fritz Kuhn, received funds, uniforms, and flags from Germany, plus a mass of anti-Semitic literature printed in English. With this support, many Fascist groups were organized among various elements in the United States, not all of them German. Many unemployed workers began to pay attention to Fascist slogans, as did middle class people who had lost their livelihood or their savings. Led by anti-Semitic demagogues like Gerald L. K. Smith and Charles Winrod, large and influential anti-Jewish organizations such as the National Economic Council, Christian National League, White Citizens Councils, and the Constitutional Party were formed. The Ku Klux Klan enjoyed a revival. Its former slogan, "Down with Niggers, Catholics, and Jews" was changed to "Down with Jews, Niggers, and Catholics." The Constitutional Party began distributing the *Protocols* (and was still doing so in 1950). From 1933 to 1941, when the United States entered the war against Germany and Japan, a total of one hundred and twenty Fascist organizations operated in the country.[18] The "big gun" in their propaganda arsenal was the warning that the Jews were pushing the United States into a new war.

In the 1930s an important addition was made to the growing army of anti-Semites in the "golden-tongued orator" Father Charles Coughlin, a Catholic priest in Detroit. In 1936, after Roosevelt's election to a second term, Coughlin began attacking the president, the Jews, the radicals, the Communists, as well as the international bankers and the warmongers. Much of his "material" was lifted from speeches made by Hitler, Goebbels, and other Nazis. The *Protocols* were printed in his magazine, *Social Justice*, which had a mass circulation. His radio programs reached an even larger audience.

At the same time, the Protestant minister Charles Winrod, the novelist Theodore Dreiser, and the national hero Charles Lindbergh, had joined the chorus that was blaming the Jews for all the ills of the world. American financiers and monopolists, unhappy with Roosevelt's liberal reform program, began a campaign of slander against the Democratic president and his New Deal, which they sneered at as "Jew Deal." Anti-Semitic propaganda in America flowed from many sides. Hate leaflets were distributed to American homes, newspapers printed anti-Jewish stories, anti-Semitic speeches could be heard on the radio and at streetcorner meetings. It must be added, however, that widespread as this propaganda was, it never penetrated very deeply into the consciousness of the American people. President Roosevelt was reelected for a third term and then a fourth.

Yet the anti-Jewish slanders did not completely disappear even during the war years. Not until the final years of the conflict, and immediately afterward in 1944–46, when it became clear that the bestial anti-Semitism of the Nazis was an excuse to conquer the world, when the Nazi crimes against humanity were exposed, when the murder of six million Jews was revealed, including more than a million children, not until then did the anti-Semitic agitation come to an end, as its perpetrators retreated deeper into their holes. By the end of the 1940s, national polls showed a sharp decline of Jew-hatred in the United States and many other countries in the world, although this was not true everywhere. In the Soviet Union, for example, anti-Semitism was given a new lease on life at precisely that time.[19] In 1962, in a poll taken in the United States, 60 percent of those questioned said they would not vote for an anti-Semitic candidate for Congress. To the question, "Do you think Jews are a danger to America?" 14 percent had answered yes in 1946; in 1962, only 3 percent answered yes.[20]

And so, in the early 1960s it seemed that anti-Semitism in the United States was on its deathbed. John Higham, a history professor at the University of Michigan, wrote: "It is hoped that anti-Semitism will disappear completely in America. . . ."[21] Morton Keller, sociologist at Brandeis University, said that there were signs that Jew-hatred in America would grow even weaker, that this was because Jews were being assimilated very rapidly, that cultural pluralism would be victorious in the United States, and that this process would be hastened as minorities were assured equal rights.[22]

The flame of Jew-hatred was not completely extinguished, however. Tolerance of the Jewish minority is not a static phenomenon. Social crises have always caused a rise in anti-Semitism, sometimes even to the point of violence.

Anti-Semitism and the Political Extremists

For the last two hundred years Jews have sided with the liberals who have supported them through their struggle for emancipation. Conversely, reactionary forces in all countries have been opposed to Jews emancipation. It has become a truism that reaction is the source of all the trouble that befalls the Jews. Anti-Jewish decrees, libels, pogroms have always come from the Right. The Radical Right in the United States, as evidenced by the words and deeds of such groups as the John Birch Society and the America First Party, has always supported anti-liberal and anti-Semitic laws and attitudes. Recently, however, the anti-Semitism of the Radical Right is echoed by the Radical Left. The various Communist parties and their offshoots, such as the Trotskyists, the Maoists, the New Left, spread Jew-hatred at a pace as intense as the parties of the Right. Radical leftists often spread their hate beneath the guise of anti-Zionist propaganda. The Communist Party of the United States, for example, unreservedly supports the discriminatory policy of the Soviet Union against Jews.[23] Publishing anti-Semitic books in hundreds of thousands of copies, printing Nazi-type articles in leading journals in the Soviet Union and other countries is not considered anti-Semitism by the Communists of the United States. Nor do they consider as anti-Semitic the Soviet state's denial of the right of Soviet Jews to their ethnic identity, to the study of Jewish history, to the raising of their children as Jews.

One of the important components of the Radical Left in the United States has been the Trotskyist Socialist Workers Party (SWP). The main theme of their propagandists who traveled around the campuses of America during the Vietnam War was to draw a parallel between the Palestinian revolutionaries and the North Vietnamese, who were fighting to "liberate" their country.[24] The Jews of America who supported Israel were (and still are) smeared by all of the leftist groups as "imperialists and fascists." In general, the Left in the United States has planted the idea that American Jews are part of "The Establishment." The young leftists, many of them well-intentioned, repeat these lies word for word and imagine they are fighting for justice and socialism.

In 1971, when Hyman Lumer, editor of the Communist journal, *Political Affairs*, attacked the American Jewish community, he named the bankers—the "Morgenthaus, Rosenwalds and War-burgs . . . Kuhn-Loeb and Lehman Brothers."[25] These names have appeared repeatedly in the pages of anti-Semitic propaganda of both the Left and the Right in the United States.

For their part in exploiting extreme leftist sentiment in the United States, the Soviets have been quick to use anti-Jewish, anti-Israel rhetoric in public. In a blatant address to the Security Council of the United Nations in 1971, the Soviet ambassador Yakov Malik said:

> . . . Try to prove that you are the chosen people and the others are nobodies . . . . I must only regret that some political leaders— including those in the city in which we find ourselves [i.e., New York City]—under the influence and pressure of the Zionists, because of mercantile and electoral considerations, follow on the leash of the Zionists and support them by every means.[26]

Much of the post-World War II sympathy for Jews has evaporated. Throughout the world, the younger generation of progressive leftists, including many Jews, are ignorant of the facts concerning the death camps such as Auschwitz and Maidanek. They know even less about the persecutions, expulsions, pogroms, massacres, and poverty and destitution to which Jews have been subjected for the last two thousand years.

Some of the leftist rhetoric has filtered down into the radical element within minority communities. For instance, in the Black communities, where cooperation between Black and White and Black and Jew has been carefully nurtured by such progressive institutions as the National Association for the Advancement of Colored People (NAACP) and the National Urban League, the radical element took on a militant stance.

When in the late 1950s and early 1960s a number of Black Christians in the United States adopted Islam in protest to discrimination by a Christian society, they assumed all the Arab charges against Israel. Some of the extremists among them then transferred this Arab hatred of Israel to American Jewry. "Jewish Establishment" and "Jew-pig" became clichés in their writing and speeches.

During the New York teachers' strike of November 1968, Black extremists distributed more than a million anti-Semitic leaflets among the Black population. In one particularly vicious attack against Jews, Leslie Campbell, Brooklyn coordinator of the African-American Teachers Association (ATA) went on WBAI-FM in December of that year and read a poem supposedly written by a fifteen-year-old girl. Entitled "Anti-Semitism" it says in part:

Hey, Jew boy, with that yarmulke on your head
You pale-faced Jew boy—I wish you were dead; . . .
I'm sick of hearing about your suffering in Germany,
I'm sick about your escape from tyranny,
I'm sick of seeing in everything I do
About the murder of six million Jews;
Hitler's reign lasted for only fifteen years—
For that period of time you shed crocodile tears.
My suffering lasted for over 400 years, Jew boy,
And the white man only let me play with his toys . . . . [27]

Before the smoke had cleared from the furor caused by this event, another ATA representative, Tyrone Woods, spoke out against Jews on WBAI-FM and said, "As far as I'm concerned, more power to Hitler. He didn't make enough lampshades out of them. He didn't make enough belts out of them."[28]

Such virulent Jew-hatred did not disappear with the end of the New York teachers' strike. Many anti-Jewish diatribes were printed in militant Black publications, among them *Black News*, closely associated with the ATA. One typical attack which appeared 10

April 1970 and entitled "The Unholy Sons of Shylock," reads in part:

> The American Jew today spends a great deal of time financing the imperialist war effort by Israel against the Arabs, when he is not ransacking the pockets of black people . . . .
>
> Our communities are sucked dry and exploited by a Jewish Mafia, which has its tentacles in our groceries, our dwellings, in our schools, indeed in every area of our lives . . . . It stands to reason, therefore, that black people in our community will not throw off the shackles of poverty until they drive these Jewish parasites and vile money-changers from our community by any means necessary. Let the Jew-boys take their thievery into the white community where it belongs![29]

Extremists have tried to convince American Blacks that their worst enemy is liberalism, that liberal ideas have created nothing but illusions and vain hopes. Many Blacks began to look upon liberals as obstacles in the way of social progress. Since many Jews are liberals, this propaganda brought about a crisis in the individual Jew's understanding of his or her social position and his or her philosophic outlook. Some Jews have begun to feel uncomfortable with their liberalism—it has become a dirty word.

At full circle of these extreme leftists are the American rightwing anti-Semitic groups who had spread Hitler's propaganda and had lain low until the mid-1960s. Since then they have gradually come out of their holes.

The John Birch Society, whose founder and president, Robert Welch, argued several years ago that the Jews should not be accused of communism because they are not to blame for it, circulated an anti-Semitic book by Gary Allen entitled *None Dare Call It Conspiracy*.[30] It is filled with lies and distortions about Jews, most of them lifted from the *Protocols of the Elders of Zion*. The publication appeared during the 1972 national elections and has subsequently been reprinted in the hundreds of thousands of copies. During that campaign, Welch boasted that the John Birch Society had 60,000 members.[31]

The attacks of the rightist groups on the State of Israel closely resemble the tirades of the Soviet Union and the American Communist Party: all the turmoil in the world is caused by Israel and Zionism. At its Louisville convention in 1972 the rightwing American Party adopted a resolution which reads " . . . that: America declare its neutrality in the Middle East and that it repudiate any commitment expressed or implied to send U.S. troops to participate in the Middle East conflict."[32]

The Liberty Lobby, an extreme rightwing and openly anti-Jewish group based in Washington, D.C., has published a newsletter, *Liberty Lobby*, since the mid-1960s. They claim to have a mailing list of at least 200,000.[33] Willis A. Carto, founder and leader of the group and deeply involved in the outrightly anti-Semitic newsletter *RIGHT* published in the 1950s, is an enthusiastic disciple of Adolf Hitler.[34] They also issued a booklet, *America First*, which is strongly anti-Semitic. Israel, they submit, is a "bastard-state," organized and supported by "atheistic Jews." The "Zionists," they continue, control the United States Congress and the media. They contend that "Almost all of the early Bolsheviks were Jewish."[35]

Even popular culture is not immune to the infiltration and perpetuation of anti-Jewish attitudes and stereotypes. In 1972, Norman Jewison (who is not Jewish), the talented producer-director of *Fiddler on the Roof,* filmed the spectacle *Jesus Christ Superstar,* a grotesque imitation of the anti-Semitic Passion Play.[36] Philip Roth's novel of self-hatred, *Portnoy's Complaint*, did not pass unnoticed by the anti-Semites in America. The sex-crazed Alexander Portnoy proved a very useful stereotype for them. The classic method of generalizing the negative features of one Jew into prototype was applied here in full measure and "Portnoy" thus became a popular epithet.

It is not difficult to see how easily these anti-Jewish stereotypes permeate the public mind. Statements by highly placed United States officials can reflect how deeply rooted these canards are. For instance, the late General George Brown, after a speech at Duke University on 10 October 1974, in reply to a question about the anti-Israel lobby in Washington, said, "The Jews, you know, own the banks and the newspapers in this country." Answering a question about the oil embargo, he predicted, "If the Arab countries impose a second oil embargo, Americans will get mad and put the Jewish lobby out of business, along with Jewish influence in the country." His comments, printed on 13 November in the Washington *Post*, caused great outrage. The following day, President Ford summoned the general to the White House. Their conversation was not reported, but a day later General Brown expressed regrets, calling his remarks "accidental, unfounded and ill-considered." He also apologized to the Jewish War Veterans. But he was not dismissed from his high office in either the army or the government.

Such attitudes in high places on an international scale lead to policies harmful to the Jews in Israel and in the Diaspora. For the nineteen years that the Transjordan held the captured Old City of Jerusalem, desecrated and vandalized the Jewish holy places, and would not allow Jews to go near the Western Wall, the whole world kept silent. But when Israel vanquished its enemies in 1967, liberated the borders, and made the Old City accessible to all faiths, the Vatican insisted, and still insists, that Jerusalem must not remain under Israeli rule. To this day nations hostile to Israel use and abuse the power of the United Nations against Israel. A threat against Israel is a threat to Jews worldwide.

26

Jews in the Smaller Centers in the Twentieth Century

France. In the period between the two World Wars, until the Nazis came to power, there was no acute Jew-hatred in France. In 1936 Leon Blum, a Jew, became premier. Many Jews fled to France from the pogroms in the Ukraine and the persecutions in Poland and Rumania. After 1933 many Jews from Germany and Austria arrived. Most of them went on to America, Palestine, and other countries. Inside France, anti-Semitic organizations began to surface.

On 10 May 1940 Germany invaded France. On 14 June the Nazis entered Paris and divided France in two: one part under the authority of the Germans and another part under the authority of the Vichy government. Germany annexed Alsace-Lorraine, and the Jews there came under the Nazi laws. Before 1939 the number of Jews in France was estimated at 300,000, around half of them recent arrivals from Germany, Austria, Czechoslovakia, Holland, Belgium, Denmark, among other places. Approximately 90,000 Jews were deported to the gas chambers. Only three thousand of the deportees survived.[1] It is true that the French anti-Semites did not themselves send Jews to their death, but without their help the Nazis would not have been able to find so many "foreign" Jews (the recent immigrants).

The German regulations in France were practically the same as all the anti-Jewish laws in Nazi-occupied countries. All Jews were registered, including converts; Jewish property was registered; Jews were fined large sums of money; they were required to wear the yellow patch. Jews played an important role in the Resistance in France. The majority of the non-Jewish population sympathized with the Jews; many helped to hide Jews, especially children.

After World War II the Jewish population in France increased from 180,000 at the end of the war to 550,000 in 1970, among them many survivors of the concentration camps and refugees from North Africa.[2] When Algeria won its independence in 1962, about 110,000 Jews left and went to France. (The Algerian Jews were French citizens.) Following the peace with Algeria, Charles de Gaulle began to curry favor with the Arabs and cool off relations with Israel. As early as 1966 de Gaulle imposed a partial embargo of munitions to the State of Israel. In 1967, on the pretext that Israel had broken an agreement, he declared a total embargo and stopped a shipment of planes for which Israel had already paid.[3]

The main charge the anti-Semites made against the Jews was that they are also loyal to Israel and are therefore guilty of dual national loyalty. On 27 November 1967 de Gaulle made a speech in which he characterized the Jews as "an elite people, an arrogant and domineering group." The speech served to inflame anti-Jewish and anti-Israel sentiment in France. De Gaulle's approval of Soviet policy in the Middle East was part of this new approach.

The Arabs have invested a greater effort in their anti-Israel and anti-Jewish campaign in France than anywhere else in Europe. Along with the numerous left wing groups in France sympathetic to the Third World, a large number of anti-Semitic organizations have appeared. Many young Jews have also been swept up by this propaganda. De Gaulle's death brought no change in the anti-Israel policy of the French government. On the other hand, pro-Israel sentiments among the population have not diminished either.

England. Early in the twentieth century more Jewish refugees from eastern Europe went to England than to France. Eastland and Whitechapel, at the eastern end of London, were crowded with Jewish immigrants. Most of them looked upon England as a way station to America; others stayed there. In 1910 there were a quarter-million Jews in England, most of them new immigrants from eastern Europe. The largest Jewish community, which numbered about 150,000, was in London. Eventually, most of the Jews in the East End of London emigrated to America. Since most Jewish immigrants were working people, the British workers began to object to their presence in the work force. Anti-Jewish feelings began to be expressed more openly and occasionally turned into violence. In Ireland a priest called for a boycott on Jews. In August 1911, during a strike in a coal town, a mob attacked Jewish homes and stores.[4] Newspapers accused Jewish government ministers Herbert Samuel and Rufus Isaacs of using their office for personal gain.

It was around 1930 that Oswald Mosley's Black Shirts made their appearance in British cities. In 1936 the government banned the wearing of "political" uniforms and the Black Shirts lost some of their strength. During World War II, when German planes were bombing London, the native Nazis apparently became disenchanted.

In the period immediately following the war, anti-Semitism was rarely encountered in England. This was true even in 1948, when England was helping the Arabs in their fight against the independence of Israel. When Foreign Minister Ernest Bevin in 1940 proposed to Palestine that it return the Negev to Egypt, Parliament voted him down.

Italy. At the turn of the century, Italy was comparatively free of anti-Semitism. In 1910, Luigi Luzzatti, a Jew, became prime minister. Ernesto Nathan, a Jew and mayor of Rome from 1907 to 1913, even felt free to criticize the manner in which the Vatican had ruled the city up to the mid-1800s. From 1922, when Mussolini and his Fascists seized power, up to 1936, when he became Hitler's partner, anti-Semitism had a low profile in Italy. In 1935, when Italy attacked Abyssinia, and England protested, Italian Fascists began agitating against the Balfour Declaration and the Zionists who had become "partners of the imperialists" in oppressing the Arabs.

1936 was the beginning of militant anti-Semitism in Italy. Fascist "scientists" demonstrated that the Italians are a branch of the Aryan race, and from this, anti-Jewish laws were adopted on the model of Nazi Germany.[5] Many of the old Jewish families, who considered themselves "pure" Italians, could not understand why they were being treated as enemies, unless it was their "sin" of still being Jews. Some four thousand Italian Jews became Christians at that time.[6] Five thousand Jewish families migrated to France. Of the 35,000 Jews who remained, about eight thousand perished in Nazi death camps, among them a number of converts. Some two thousand Jews fought in the Resistance alongside other anti-Fascists. After the war, the Jewish community in Italy numbered fewer than 30,000. These survivors experienced relatively little anti-Semitism.

In the mid-1960s there was a growth of neo-Fascist anti-Semitic groups in the country, influenced by the Arabs living in Italy. The Italian Communist Party, however, had not subscribed to the anti-Semitic line of the Soviet Union. In general, anti-Jewish feelings in Italy have been minimal. Jews remain active in all the political parties.

Scandinavian Countries. The anti-Semitic wave in the larger European countries at the turn of the century did not have very much influence in the Scandinavian lands. When the Nazis conquered Norway at the beginning of World War II, a local Fascist named Vidkun Quisling became nominal head of the country. There were only around eighteen hundred Jews in Norway at that time, many of whom fled to Sweden. With the assistance of the local Nazis, the Germans succeeded in murdering seven hundred Norwegian Jews.

The Balkans. In the summer of 1908, the government of Turkey was overthrown by the Nationalists, who were vehemently opposed to the separatist tendencies among the Greeks, Armenians, and Arabs living in the Turkish cities and provinces. In 1912, when a movement began in Turkey for decentralization and national autonomy, the Jews identified with the Turkish Nationalists. In several provinces, especially among the Greeks and Arabs, anti-Semitism increased. In the fall of 1912, Greece, Serbia, and Bulgaria declared war on Turkey with the aim of severing her European provinces. The 200,000 Jews who lived in those European Turkish cities fought in this war as staunch Turkish patriots.

The victory, however, went to the Balkan states. When the Greeks captured the city of Salonika, they terrorized the Jews until they were stopped by orders from the Greek government, which was seeking consent from the larger European powers to its annexation of that city. Eventually the anti-Jewish activities ceased. A Greek regulation ordering the annual fair in Salonika to be held on Saturday instead of Sunday was rescinded by the government in Athens.[7]

The cities taken from Turkey contained about 100,000 Jews, some 80,000 of whom remained under the rule of Greece, which had previously contained only about 7,000 Jews.[8] Serbia acquired a Jewish population of 10,000. The other 10,000 were divided between Bulgaria and Rumania. The situation of the Jews in Serbia, where there had been very little anti-Semitism, remained the same. At the end of the nineteenth century the Jews in the Bulgarian cities had suffered murderous pogroms as a result of blood libels. But the Bulgarian Jewish situation gradually changed for the better.

For those Jews who remained under Greek rule, the situation took a turn for the worse. While the government in Athens tended to protect the Jews, the local Greek population was historically anti-Semitic, partly due to the indoctrination of the Greek Orthodox Church.

Rumania. Anti-Semitism in Rumania during the first quarter of the twentieth century was among the most virulent in Europe. Land-owners, merchants, and peasants vied with each other in spreading lies and slander against the Jews of Rumania, blaming them for all the ills of that country.[9] Many Jews migrated to the United States or other countries, including Palestine. The total Jewish population in Rumania, however, did not diminish. During the civil war in Russia in November 1918, Rumania seized Bessarabia, which had a large Jewish population. In 1919 Rumania helped to suppress the Communist Revolution in Hungary and annexed Bukovina and Transylvania, which were also densely populated by Jews. The same year, many Jews, escaping from the pogroms in the Ukraine, fled to Rumania, and from there to America and other places.

The teachings of Nazi Germany were rapidly absorbed by the Rumanians. The leaders of the Social Christian Party boasted that as soon as they came to power they would handle the Jewish problem the same way the Nazis had in Germany. In December 1937 King Carol appointed Goga, one of the party leaders, to the premiership. Proclaiming a policy of "Rumania for the Rumanians," he promised that he would do everything in his power to rid the country of those foreigners, the Jews. Early in January the Jewish newspapers in Rumania were shut down; the liberal newspapers were also shut down, on the pretext that they had too many Jews on their staffs. Medieval anti-Jewish laws were adopted on the model of Nazi Germany. Jewish physicians, lawyers, engineers, and other professionals were dismissed from their posts. Jewish handicraftsmen were boycotted.

Protests came from all over the world. The value of the Rumanian currency dropped on the world exchange. The government treasury was empty and no foreign loans were available anywhere. After forty days, the king removed the Fascist leader and appointed a more liberal cabinet. The Nazi-type program was stopped, but only temporarily. Jew-hatred in Rumania moved into the wings, waiting for a more opportune moment. The Jewish organization in Rumania—religious, Zionist, labor—united to form the Federation of

Jewish Communities, which began a successful battle against discrimination.

The "opportune moment" for the Rumanian Fascists arrived in 1939, when the Nazi juggernaut began World War II and the Rumanian government announced its "neutrality." Two years later, when Hitler invaded the Soviet Union, Rumania became one of his allies. Deportations of Jews began to Transnistria, a province in the Ukraine which the Germans had already occupied. The Jews were sent away with no preparation whatsoever having been made for them—no work, no housing, no food or clothing. The Federation managed to stop the deportations and began a struggle, legal as well as underground, for the return of the deported Jews. They stayed on good terms with Premier Antonescu, a Rumanian patriot, who complained to Hitler that his other allies, Hungary and Italy, were not carrying out all his orders, why must Rumania do so?[10] The Federation even defeated the decree of the yellow patch in most provinces.

In 1942, when Adolph Eichmann demanded permission of the Rumanian government to deport the Jews of that country to Auschwitz, it was immediately forthcoming. Large transports of Jews from several provinces were deported. However, the Federation put many obstacles in his way, even to the point of bringing back some of the deportees from Transnistria. Approximately 50,000 survived there and returned to Rumania at the end of the war. Most of them later emigrated to Israel.

When Rumania had annexed Bessarabia, Bukovina, and Transylvania in 1919, its Jewish population was around 800,000. Up until the outbreak of World War II, 100,000 Jews had left the country. When Russia in 1940 annexed Bessarabia and Bukovina, some 600,000 Jews remained in Rumania, with 100,000 under Soviet rule. When Rumania went over to the side of the Allies, there were 428,000 Jews there. Thus, approximately 200,000 Rumanian Jews perished at the hands of the Nazis.[11]

From 1944 to 1948, when the monarchy was replaced by a Communist government under the wing of Moscow, about two-thirds of the Rumanian Jews left the country, most of them going to Palestine. In June 1948, during the war which the Arabs forced upon the fledgling State of Israel, Zionist organizations in Rumania were declared illegal. Up until 1965 the situation of the Jews in Rumania was similar to that in all the Soviet dominated countries; but in that year, the government began steering a more or less independent course and improved its relations with Israel and the 100,000 Jews within its own borders. After the Six Day War in 1967, Rumania was the only country under Soviet influence which did not break diplomatic ties with Israel. This situation has continued until the present.[12]

Austria. Of the 200,000 Jews in Austria before the Anschluss with Germany in 1938, probably fewer than a thousand survived the Holocaust. Immediately after the war, tens of thousands of Jews streamed through Austria on their way to Israel and other countries. Only 10,000 to 12,000 stayed on in Austria itself, most of them former citizens of the country. Anti-Semitism, however, has not disappeared. Prominent government figures do not even bother to conceal their former Nazi connections.

Belgium. In the 1930s the Belgian Fascists (Rexists) were active in the dissemination of Nazi propaganda. When the Nazis invaded Belgium on 10 May 1940, there were some 90,000 Jews in the country, including 15,000 refugees from Germany. Most of the Belgian Jews fled to France, England and America. The rapid march of the German Army trapped many Jews, however, and they were forced to return. Fifty thousand Jews remained under Nazi rule in Belgium.[13] Many fought in the Resistance movement. The Belgians were largely in sympathy with the Jews in their country. The Nazi order in October 1941 requiring all Jews to register was obeyed by 42,000 people, leaving some 12,000 who did not register and who were hidden by their Christian neighbors. When the order of 15 May 1942 was issued requiring the wearing of the yellow patch, the Belgian administration refused to enforce it.

In 1942 the Nazis began deporting Jews from Belgium, ostensibly to labor camps. The Jews were sent first to concentration camps and from there to Auschwitz and Sobibor. Up until July 1944, when the Allied armies liberated Belgium, the Nazis deported around 25,000 Jews. Only twelve hundred fifty survived and returned to their homes, which had been preserved for them.[14] The post-war Jewish community in Belgium numbered about 25,000 people.

Holland. Anti-Semitism in Holland has always been minimal. Before World War I and during the years between the two wars, Holland served the Jews as a way station to America. In 1939 there were approximately 140,000 Jews in Holland, includng 25,000 refugees from Germany and more than seven thousand from other countries.[15] When the Nazis invaded the country, only two thousand Jews managed to escape. From May 1940 to midsummer 1944 the Nazis deported 106,000 Jews to death camps. Of that number, only five thousand survived. Of the 22,000 who hid, less than half survived. Of the 10,000 who converted, almost all survived, protected as they were by the Church. Thus, a total of 113,000 Dutch Jews perished at the hands of the Nazis.[16]

Denmark. When Germany annexed Denmark there were around 15,000 Jews in that country. The Danish government, its rights circumscribed by the Nazis, cooperated with them in many respects, but not in the persecution of Jews. Up until 1943 none of the German anti-Jewish laws were enforced there. In September 1943 the Nazis themselves began deporting Jews from Denmark to Theresienstadt. Some seventy-five hundred Jews escaped to Sweden. Most of the Jews deported to Theresienstadt survived the war and returned to Denmark. Altogether, some three hundred Danish Jews were murdered by the Nazis.

Canada. As early as the 1870s, small groups of Jews who had come to England from eastern Europe migrated to Canada. By 1880 there were several thousand Jews in Canada's larger cities. After the pogrom wave in Russia in 1905-1906, Jewish immigration to Canada reached massive proportions. From 1905 to 1914 approximately 75,000 Jews arrived; up to 1930, another 50,000. By 1950 the Jewish population of Canada was close to 200,000.[17]

Montreal, the closest city to the port of entry for Jews arriving from Europe, has a large French population, most of whom originated in Alsace, where Jew-hatred was more deeply imbedded than anywhere else in France.[18] The Jews who settled in Montreal were at first victims of certain restrictions and even violence. Many Jews then moved farther into the interior and settled in Toronto, Winnipeg, and other cities which were populated mostly by people of British descent.

The problem of educating children in Canada was related to the specific conditions there, where the population still consists of two main cultural groups: French Catholics and English Protestants. From the very beginning they could not unite either on a common language or a common school system. They were consequently left with two school systems, each supported by its own cultural group. The Jewish immigrants, as a very small minority group, sent their children to the English-speaking schools for their general education;

religious Jews built their own yeshivas, secular Jews their own day schools. Most of the Jewish children, however, attended the English schools, which were not as strongly dominated by Christian religious doctrine as were the French Catholic schools. At various times the Jews in Canada considered the feasibility of setting up their own parochial school system, but there were serious differences among the groups about the program of these proposed Jewish schools.

In the 1930s, with the advent of Hitlerism in Europe and the rise of hate-mongering in the States—Detroit, home base of Father Coughlin, is very close to Canada—the anti-Semitic temperature rose sharply among French-Canadians. In Quebec, Jewish students were expelled from universities. In 1935 Quebec Minister of Labor Arkand announced an anti-Jewish boycott, which received the support of the premier, Duplessis.[19] However, the leading industrialists in Quebec were English and did not support the boycott. With Hitler's rape of France in 1940, pro-Nazi sentiments among the French-Canadians chilled. During the war years, Arkand and Duplessis were ousted. After the war the situation of the Jews in Quebec showed no improvement. An organization calling itself The Social Credit Union (which still exists) appeared with the stated objective of developing an ultraconservative movement in Canada similar to the John Birch Society in the United States. An important component of its program is anti-Semitism.[20]

Since the increase of Arab and Soviet propaganda in recent years, anti-Israel expressions have been evident among French-Canadians. In 1976, when the French nationalist groups won the right of secession, anti-Semitism grew stronger in Quebec. In the summer of that year, the head of the Canadian teachers' union attended the conference in Libya which declared that "Zionism is racism." When he returned, he proposed that the children in the Quebec schools be taught that "fact." The Quebec government has taken no position on this.[21]

Argentina. Toward the end of the nineteenth century, Baron Maurice de Hirsch of Germany purchased several hundred thousand acres of land in Argentina for Jewish colonization. The Czarist government permitted the opening of a Jewish Colonization Office in Russia, which undertook to settle three hundred Jews a week in Argentina. This would have meant the resettlement of 3.5 million people in twenty-five years. As the news circulated throughout the Pale, groups of Jews set sail for South America.

The plan did not succeed. Jewish emigrants who had learned a trade were more attracted to the United States where it was possible to earn a living. From Jews who had settled in Argentina came discouraging letters about housing that was nonexistent and life that was extremely difficult. Most of the Jews who had come to Argentina to cultivate the land had given up and gone to live in the cities, particularly Buenos Aires.

By 1895 there were twenty-five hundred Jews on farms. Prior to World War I approximately 20,000 Jews had settled in the farm colonies. Tens of thousands of other Jews had made their homes in the cities. Both city and country groups made strenuous efforts to get their relatives out of Russia. Soon large Jewish communities began to take shape in Argentina.

The Bolshevik Revolution in 1917 alarmed the Argentine government. Therefore, almost all the Jewish immigrants there were looked upon as Russians and were not welcome. These feelings soon led to a restriction of immigration. Despite this, the intolerable situation of the Jews in eastern Europe and the need for ports of refuge (especially after the United States closed its gates) resulted in continuing immigration to Argentina. Each year some seven thousand Jews entered that country legally; a greater number entered illegally. During the 1920s, 80,000 Jews settled in Argentina. In 1948 all those who had entered illegally were also recognized as citizens.

The Jews in Argentina were relatively free of anti-Semitic harassment until the economic crisis of 1930. One-third of the country's labor force was idle. Among the new immigrants were recent arrivals from Italy and Germany. Nazi propaganda increased. In 1936, demonstrations for a boycott of Jewish merchants and workers took place in Buenos Aires and other cities. Restrictions on Jewish immigration were further stiffened. During the first years of World War II, with the military leaders of Argentina in sympathy with the Fascist regimes in Europe, Nazi propaganda was openly distributed. The minister of labor in the new cabinet was Juan Domingo Peron, a demagogue who played up to the Nazis and other Fascist groups in the country.

In 1943, when the Jewish Organizations in Argentina tried to persuade the government to allow the entry of thousands of orphans from Europe, the negotiations dragged on so long that nothing came of it.[22] Up until 1944 many anti-Jewish demonstrations took place in Argentina. In March 1945, at the war's end, when the Fascist armies were already smashed, Argentina entered the war on the side of the

Allies, but even then the anti-Semitic agitation continued. Restrictions on Jewish immigration remained in effect after the war was over. Nazi war criminals, however, were permitted to enter freely, and anti-Semitism reached a new high.[23]

In 1946 Peron was elected president of Argentina. Three years later he issued a law prohibiting anti-Semitic activities, but it was never enforced. In 1955, during a political upheaval, Peron fled the country. The Church, intensifying its anti-Jewish propaganda, accused the Jews of having persuaded Peron to institute a public school system.

During the 1950s, the Arab League in Argentina joined the Jew-hating chorus. In the early 1960s a radical movement appeared, led by the Communist Party, which repeated the anti-Israel incitement of Russia and the Arabs. Buenos Aires became the center for anti-Semitism in South America. In May 1960 this activity reached a fever pitch when the Israelis captured Adolf Eichmann and executed him for the mass murder of Jews. Of 313 anti-Semitic acts in the world in 1967, 147 took place in Argentina.[24]

Many of the current anti-Jewish activists are young leftists, Third World patriots, including some Jewish students who sympathize with the Palestine Liberation Organization (P.L.O.). Since the Six Day War, thousands of Jews, many of them young people, left Argentina and settled in other South American countries; some went to the United States or Israel. The half million Jews in Argentina today live in a precarious situation.

Uruguay. The partial limitation on Jewish immigration to Argentina in 1923 diverted a considerable number of eastern European Jewish refugees to Uruguay, Chile, Peru, and other smaller South American countries. By 1970 there were some 50,000 Jews in Uruguay. Anti-Semitism was not serious there until after World War II. There is a well-organized Communist Party in the country (of the Stalinist type) which influences a sizable number of young Jews, some of whom are sympathetic to the Arab terrorists.

Brazil. Jewish immigrants from eastern Europe began arriving in Brazil in 1923. By the middle of the decade their number had reached 50,000, most of whom settled in Rio de Janeiro and São Paulo. In 1937 the Brazilian consulates in Europe were secretly instructed to deny visas to Jews wishing to emigrate to Brazil.[25] Nevertheless, the Nazi plague in Europe forced many Jews to break down all the roadblocks that had been erected to keep them out of Brazil. By 1960 there were 120,000 Jews there; by 1970, 155,000 amid a total population of 100 million.[26]

In the early 1930s the coffee industry and its workers were hard hit by the worldwide depression, as were the coffee merchants, many of them Jews. Fascist groups began to blame the Jews publicly for the crisis, but President Vargas headed off any anti-Jewish violence. After the second World War, Nazi war criminals appeared in Brazil with their propaganda, including the *Protocols*. A branch of the Arab League has recently begun spreading anti-Jewish and anti-Israel propaganda. In 1972 Palestine Liberation Organization (P.L.O.) pamphlets and other slanderous materials were distributed throughout the country. More recently, Karl Marx's brochure, *Zur Judenfrage*, was also distributed in Brazil. (In this essay, written in 1844, Marx asserts that money is the god of the Jews.)

Chile. Despite a law against the entry of new immigrants, several thousand Jews from central Europe entered Chile during the 1930s. In 1939 and 1940 some nine hundred Jewish refugees from Germany were admitted to the country on condition that they settle in southern Chile, the colder part of the country.

Anti-Semitism appeared in Chile in the 1930s as Nazi propaganda spread throughout the world. When several of the above-mentioned German-Jewish families moved to the more populous centers of the country, a demand was raised by anti-Semites that all the German Jews be removed to the south or expelled from Chile altogether. In the 1940s many Arab emigrants arrived. The 1940 census reported 100,000 Arabs in Chile. The number of Jews is 30,000, with about 90 percent of them in Santiago.

Under the socialist government elected in January 1970, the Jewish situation remained unchanged. President Allende's attitude was friendly. When the Communist countries broke relations with Israel, Chile did not follow suit. In 1972 Allende protested against the Arab terrorist murder of the Israeli athletes in Munich. In September 1973 the militarists in Chile overthrew the Allende government and murdered the president. Chile today is a land that Jews are leaving.

Mexico. Groups of Sephardic Jews from the Balkans and the Middle East had settled in Mexico in the mid-nineteenth century. A larger Jewish immigration took place when the gates of the United States and Argentina were slammed shut. The Jewish population in Mexico has remained at around 45,000, with the largest community

with 40,000 in Mexico City.[27] In recent years many native-born
Mexican Jews have entered the professions. Mexico is a democratic
country where Jews enjoy equal rights.

In 1970 the police uncovered a terrorist anti-Semitic organization
known as Movement for Revolutionary Action and arrested twenty
young men and women. Almost all of them had spent time as
students at Patrice Lumumba University in Moscow, where students from non-Communist countries are trained in revolutionary
activism. Soon after this was revealed, the Mexican government
requested five high-ranking members of the Soviet Embassy to leave
the country.

The Jewish community in Mexico has not experienced a great
deal of anti-Semitism, although in the last two decades an Arab
group has been actively disseminating anti-Israel and anti-Jewish
material. On 10 November 1975 the Mexican delegation to the
United Nations voted in favor of the resolution equating Zionism
with racism.[28] When American Jews declared a tourist boycott
against Mexico, the government issued an apologetic statement to
the effect that they had not really meant it. On 25 December 1975 the
Mexican delegation again voted for a resolution condemning Zionism, and again apologized.

Colombia. The Jewish community in Colombia is a small one. In
1975 the Jewish population there was 15,000, out of a general
population of 25 million. Most of the Jews who arrived between the
two world wars are in business and the professions. During those
years, Germans also settled there, many of whom were actively anti-
Semitic. During World War II, anti-Jewish agitation in Colombia
was widespread and continued after the war's end.

In 1948, during a Pan-American conference, a leader of the liberal
party was assassinated. A pogrom broke out in Bogata, where most
of the Jews live. Some one hundred thirty stores were looted. Since
1948, and particularly after the Six Day War, Arab groups have
joined the anti-Jewish campaign. They are supported by the Communist Party of Colombia, which has agitated against American
control of the Panama Canal.

South Africa. South Africa was a distant, unknown land for Jewish
immigration until around 1870. In the 1880s, Jews began to arrive
there from eastern Europe. By 1890 there were about 10,000 Jews
there; in 1900, around 25,000; in 1950, 120,000.[29] Anti-Semitism
became visible as early as the 1920s and grew stronger in the 1930s,

when the Gray Shirts began stirring up prejudices. The local Nationalist Party also adopted an anti-Jewish program. An immigration quota was decreed in the mid-1930s which excluded Jews altogether.[30]

During World War II, South Africa joined the Allies and declared war on Germany. The anti-Jewish agitation subsided. Some six thousand Jews emigrated from South Africa to Israel, leaving 115,000 Jews in the country in 1967.

Jewish liberals, together with other white liberals, are strongly opposed to the racist apartheid policy of the government. More recently, anti-Semitic newspaper articles have been appearing in which Jews are labeled "white niggers."

27

Return to Zion: Arab Anti-Semitism

Through all the centuries after they were driven out of Judea by the Romans in 70 C.E., the Jews always held fast to their hope of "returning to Zion," but very few of them actually returned. The land was arid, desolate, and provided no opportunity for earning a living by farming, handicrafts, or commerce. During the last four hundred years mostly older Jews went to Eretz Israel to live out their years and be buried there. They lived primarily on charity collected in Jewish communities throughout the world.

In 1881, following the wave of pogroms in Russia, young Jews of the *Hibat Tzion* movement organized BILU groups (initials of *Bet Yaakov lekhu v'nelkhah*, "House of Jacob, come, let's go!")[1] In the summer of 1882 the first BILU group reached Palestine. When stories reached Constantinople that the new immigrants were planning to set up a Jewish state in Palestine, the Turkish government ordered all Jewish immigration into Palestine stopped.[2] Jews who came to the port of Jaffa were forced to proceed to Port Said, and from there make their way on foot or by camel through the Sinai Desert to Palestine.

During the early 1880s the colonies of *Rishon L'Tsion*, near Jaffa, and *Zikhron Yaakov* and *Rosh Pinah*, near Haifa and Safed, were founded. In 1883 another group from Russia revived the colony of *Petah Tikva*, which had been established and then abandoned mainly because of malaria. The new Jewish immigrants also settled in Jaffa, Haifa, Jerusalem, and other cities.

While the Turkish government maintained its ban on immigration, many Jews entered by bribing immigration officials and bought tracts of land from the effendis, the wealthier Arab land-owners. Most of the land sold by the effendis was either malaria-infested swamp or rock-strewn hills; when they did sell a tract of arable land (at an exorbitant price), they drove off the fellaheen.

By 1900 there were around thirty Jewish colonies in Palestine, with a population of five thousand. In the cities there were about 60,000 Jews, half of whom were older people living mostly on charity from abroad. Up until that time there were no conflicts between Jews and Arabs, but at the turn of the century, signs of Arab opposition to Jewish immigration began appearing. This opposition stemmed from two sources.

1. The effendis, owners of the largest areas of cultivated land, oppressed the fellaheen who worked the fields and orchards for starvation wages or as sharecroppers. The effendis were firm believers in the status quo. The new immigrants, the foreign Jews, industrious and innovative Europeans, devised ways of coaxing more and better products out of the wilderness with less laborious but more efficient human effort. They dried out the swamps and reduced the incidence of malaria; they cleared away the rocks, introduced irrigation, and planted their fields scientifically. Their general living standards, even in the first difficult years, were immeasurably higher than those of the fellaheen. In addition, the Arabs on the Jewish farms earned a higher wage than those who worked for the effendis. Such an example could have created trouble for the established order.

The effendis made use of anti-Jewish passages in the Koran to spread stories among the Arabs that the Jews had come to steal their wives and daughters, that the Jews had come to defile the Islamic holy shrines.[3] As an example of flagrant immorality they pointed to the Jewish women who walked around in public with their faces uncovered.

2. Along with protests against exploitation by foreigners, another source of Arab hostility to the Jewish immigration was the nationalist sentiment that was slowly awakening among oppressed peoples outside of Europe. For decades in the Middle East, French, English, and Italian propagandists (for their own imperialist purposes) had been agitating the Arabs against Turkish rule. Early in the twentieth century, Arab nationalism had already made inroads into the upper level of the Arab intelligentsia in almost all the countries in the Middle East.[4] In 1881–82 there was a serious revolt

against British domination. The mood in Syria against French rule was no less intense.

From the early twentieth century onward, Arab opposition to Jewish immigration was never absent. The effendis, the mullahs, and the nationalist intellectuals never ceased disseminating anti-Jewish slander. Arab mistrust gave the Jews no rest. First there were "petty annoyances" like knocking down orchard fences or setting fields on fire. Later Jewish homes were set on fire, and Arab snipers began shooting at Jews.

Soon after the harrowing pogroms in Russia in 1903–1906, a new stream of Russian Jewish youth arrived in Palestine. In this "second *Aliyah*" there were already young people steeped in socialist ideas. Many of these new immigrants became wage workers in the existing colonies, although the owners of the citrus orchards preferred Arab hands who were willing to work for less. Among the Jewish workers a movement known as *Kibbush Avodah* ("conquest of labor") was formed, which stood for the principle of "Jewish workers in Jewish colonies." They picketed Jewish employers, demanding that they dismiss Arab workers and hire only Jews.[5] Needless to say, this only exacerbated the hostility of the Arabs, among whom the anti-Jewish agitation began to find more receptive ears. Arab attacks on Jewish settlements became more frequent.

To repel these attacks, the Jews organized larger and better trained self-defense units, and in 1909 all these groups combined to form the Hashomer. During World War I, the Hashomer evolved into the Jewish Legion and subsequently the Haganah. Between the Arab terrorists and the Hashomer there was uninterrupted fighting, with victims on both sides.

In eastern Europe the pogroms and anti-Jewish decrees had not stopped. Jews continued to emigrate to Palestine. By 1914, when the first World War began, there were close to 90,000 Jews in the country.[6] With the growth in the population and the elimination of the swamps, more Arabs migrated to Palestine from Gaza, Trans-jordan, Syria, and Egypt. Infant mortality decreased sharply. The Arab population increased in greater proportion to the Jews. As a result, by 1914 there were 600,000 Arabs in Palestine as against 100,000 Jews.[7]

The war of 1914 put a stop to Jewish immigration into the country. Many young Jews were arrested or drafted into the Turkish army, among which most fled to Egypt.

At the end of 1915 an agreement between Sir Henry McMahon,

British commissioner in Egypt, and the ruling Hashemite family of Hussein, recognized the right of all the Arab countries to complete independence, but the language in the agreement (as in the Balfour Declaration) was vague. When the Arabs later argued that England was giving Palestine away to the Jews, England claimed that one of the conditions in the agreement was that Syria would rebel against the Turks. Since this had not happened, England was released from its pledge. The Arabs denied ever having agreed to any such condition.[8]

In 1916, England, France, and Russia began negotiations over the division of lands under control of the Central Powers after the war. England was to get Transjordan, France was given Syria and Iraq, and Russia was given Constantinople and the Armenian provinces bordering on the Caucasus. Unhappy with its share of the spoils, England began negotiations with the Zionist leader, Chaim Weizmann, concerning a homeland for the Jews in Palestine. On 2 November 1917 Lord Balfour, the British foreign minister, signed the declaration which raised the hopes of Jews throughout the Diaspora.

During 1915–16, under the leadership of Vladimir Jabotinsky and Joseph Trumpeldor, a Jewish Legion was organized. It comprised six hundred young Jews, most of whom had escaped from Palestine to Egypt when the war broke out. In the late months of 1917, the British army, with the help of the Jewish Legion, drove the Turks out of Palestine. Jewish volunteers from the United States and Canada later joined the Legion.

Soon after the war, Britain, which had promised the Arab leaders freedom from Turkish domination, found a way to appease the Husseini family: Abdullah, son of the Emir Faisal, was crowned kind of Transjordan, a territory which England carved out of the land promised to the Jews in the Balfour Declaration. This gift apparently served its purpose, because Faisal recognized the Jewish right to the western portion of Palestine. In the spring of 1919, in a letter to Felix Frankfurter, Faisal declared that he wished the Jews well, that they were welcome in the region, and that they would prove to be a blessing. The newspapers in Cairo and Lebanon greeted the Balfour Declaration and Chaim Weizmann. "The Jews," wrote King Hussein's newspaper in Mecca, "are entitled to their ancient homeland."[9]

In 1918 Weizmann made a special trip to Aqaba to meet with Faisal. "Jews and Arabs," said Faisal, "will work together for a free state. . . . Arabs need not fear the Jews. We are the best friends of the Jews." One year later he wrote in his paper that he was opposed to those Zionists who wanted a Jewish state. "We Arabs will not give up Palestine. We will fight to the last man to keep Palestine from being excluded from the Arab nation."[10]

At the end of 1919, hundreds of pioneer groups from Russia, Poland, Galicia, Rumania, and other European countries streamed into Palestine. In February 1920 a number of kibbutzim were attacked by Arabs. Among the dead was Joseph Trumpeldor, hero of the Jewish Legion. On 4 April, a two-day pogrom in Jerusalem left fifteen Jews dead and many others wounded. In May 1921 there were attacks on Jews in Jaffa, Tel Aviv, Petah Tikva, Kfar Saba, Hadera, and Rehovoth. The Jews defended themselves bravely everywhere.

At the peace talks in San Remo in April 1920, Britain was given the mandate over Palestine on the basis of the Balfour Declaration. As soon as they became masters of the country the British began placating the Arabs. In 1921 they issued a special report blaming the Jews for the May riots in Jaffa. Jewish immigration and land purchases were severely restricted.[11]

The situation of the Jews in the Soviet Union, Poland, Rumania, Germany, and Austria after World War I was intolerable. Many Jews found their way to Palestine in one way or another. By 1922 there were 100,000 Jews in the country; by 1939, 450,000. Neither Arab protests nor British restrictions had very much effect. The Mandate power concerned itself very little with improving Arab-Jewish relations in the country; the continuing concessions to the Arabs only encouraged them to increase their attacks on Jews.

In 1922 Herbert Samuel, British high commissioner for Palestine, permitted the Arabs to organize a Muslim Council for religious affairs, under the leadership of Haj Amin al-Husseini, who had been involved in the pogroms of 1920–21. In April 1921, after he was chosen Mufti of Jerusalem, he organized a staff of leaders of the most important terrorist groups in the country and became the guiding spirit behind the Arab anti-Jewish movement.

As a result of the struggle against Arab terrorists in the early 1920s, and because the Mandate authority did nothing to protect Jews, the Hashomer evolved into the Haganah. During the summer of 1929 there were several clashes between Arabs and Jews near the Western Wall. In this overheated atmosphere the Mufti circulated rumors among the fellaheen that the Jews were preparing to destroy the Muslim temple in Jerusalem. On 15 August 1929 the Arabs carried out sudden attacks on Jewish settlements in many cities and villages, killing 133 Jews and wounding hundreds of others.[12]

Soon afterward the colonial minister, Lord Passfield (Sydney Webb) sent two commissions to Palestine to investigate the "disturbances." Both commissions reported that the Arabs had been the aggressors, but that the Jews were guilty of bringing in too many illegal immigrants and purchasing too much land from the effendis. It was the Mandate's reponsibility, chided the commissions, to protect the interests of the Arabs in Palestine.[13]

At that time, Lady Passfield (Beatrice Webb) put the following question to Chaim Weizmann: Why were the Jews in England and throughout the world making such a fuss about a few score Jews murdered in Palestine? In Great Britain, she said, more people than that are killed each week by automobile accidents.[14] In 1930 Lord Passfield released a White Paper prohibiting Jews from buying any more land in Palestine and halting Jewish immigration completely.

During the 1930s, nazism drove new masses of Jews to the shores of Eretz Israel, but England refused to lift the ban on immigration. Almost all the immigrants now entered Palestine illegally. A particularly virulent anti-Jewish campaign was whipped up among the Arabs by Germany and Italy. Powerful broadcasts urged Arab rebellion against "imperialist England, France, and Zionism." German news agencies supplied the Arabs with plenty of anti-Zionist propaganda. Arab newspapers reprinted Streicher's blood-thirsty articles, as well as the speeches of Hitler and Goebbels. It should be kept in mind that the British were still in control of the country, including censorship of the press—especially the Jewish press.

In April 1936 an all-out attack began on the Jewish settlements. From Syria, Lebanon, Iraq, and Egypt came volunteers to help the aggressors. In Germany, Arab Nazis trained for *Der Tag*. The Jewish leaders made a decision to defend themselves only when attacked, and not to take reprisals on Arab settlements. This policy was known as *Havlagah* ("patient self-restraint"), but it did not last long.[15] The British continued to blame "the Jews and the Arabs," always with the Jews listed first. The Arab attacks grew bolder and more frequent. Indeed, the Arabs now began to attack the British, also. But instead of sending larger army units to Palestine, London permitted a strengthening of the Haganah, even sending them a British officer, Captain Charles Orde Wingate, who was an outspoken friend of the Jews, and an excellent military instructor.

In November 1936 England sent a commission (headed by Lord Peel) to Palestine to investigate the complaints of both sides. A detailed report in June 1937 categorically denied the Arab charge of exploitation by Jews; rather, said the commission, since Jews had begun settling in Palestine, the living standard of the Arabs had improved significantly. The Peel Commission, however, recommended the partition of Palestine into two states, one Jewish and one Arab. After long discussion, a majority of Zionists accepted this plan. The Arabs refused even to consider it.[16]

In May 1937, at the traditional Arab celebration of Muhammad's birthday, Arabs everywhere hung out Nazi and Fascist flags and pictures of Hitler and Mussolini. The *Protocols of the Elders of Zion* were being translated and distributed in millions of copies throughout the Middle East. From the Fascist countries came arms and military instructors. During the summer, the Arabs launched another series of attacks on Jewish settlements. The British government invited both sides to send representatives to London to make an effort to understand and discuss the issues. Since the Arabs refused to sit in the same room with the Jews, the discussions were conducted through intermediaries. The conference ended with no results after the Arabs made it clear that they would not agree to any plan that would allow Jewish immigration into Palestine.[17]

In May 1939 the British government issued another White Paper prohibiting future Jewish immigration into Palestine. The plan provided that 75,000 Jews would be admitted over the next five years, and that would be the end of it.

When World War II began, the Arabs were squarely in the camp of the Nazis. The Mufti sat in Europe, working loyally with the Germans. In 1942 and 1943, Arab leaders tried to persuade Arab landowners to sell their property to the Jews because very soon the Germans would come and kill all the Jews anyway, and the Arabs would get their land back for nothing. From the mid-1930s until after the war, there were pogroms against Jews in almost all the Arab lands. In 1941, one hundred ten Jews were murdered in Baghdad. In May 1941, seven hundred Jews were massacred in Tripoli. Pogroms took place in Damascus, Beirut, Cairo, Libya, and Yemen.[18]

Adolf Eichmann's close associate, Captain Wisliceny, revealed that beginning in 1941 the Mufti repeatedly appealed to Hitler, to von Ribbentrop, to Himmler, that they exterminate European Jewry. He also appealed to the Nazis to bomb Tel Aviv, Haifa,

Jerusalem, and all the Jewish settlements. In May 1943, with the Nazi death camps already in operation, the Mufti sent a sharp protest to King Boris of Bulgaria because he proposed to let four thousand Jewish children leave Bratislava. When Antonescu wanted to release 80,000 Jews from Rumania, again the Mufti objected. He demanded also that Italy and Hungary stop permitting Jews from those countries to go to Palestine and recommended they be sent to Poland instead, where they would be "properly taken care of."[19]

In June 1944 the Mufti wrote to Himmler complaining that the elimination of the Jews was proceeding too slowly. He urged them to do the Arabs a service and kill more Jews, the quicker the better. In his diary the Mufti wrote: "The best friend the Arabs have is Adolf Eichmann; he is really brilliant."[20] Captain Wisliceny also stated that the Mufti pleaded with Himmler to "lend" him Eichmann after the German victory, because with his methods, Eichmann would be very useful to the Arabs.

After the war the Mufti was to have been tried with the other Nazi war criminals at Nuremberg, but he slipped out of the hands of the British and French police. Eichmann, at his trial in 1961, testified that he had met several times with the Mufti; the latter, however, "could not recall" ever having met with Eichmann.

As a young officer in the Egyptian army, Anwar el-Sadat (now president of Egypt), worked with General Rommel against the British until the summer of 1943. In 1953, eight years after the war, Sadat was still an admirer of Hitler and his "achievement" of wiping out European Jewry.[21]

In 1945–46, when tens of thousands of miraculously surviving Jews were clamoring to enter Palestine, the British government again refused to allow Jews entry. When President Truman proposed to England that 100,000 Jews be permitted to settle in Palestine, the British counterproposal was one thousand.[22] Thus the illegal immigration intensified. British authorities stopped ships carrying homeless Jews and put the passengers behind barbed wire on Cyprus. In 1947 forty-five hundred illegal Jewish immigrants on the *Exodus* were forced to return to a French port, and when the Jews refused to disembark there, the British forced the ship back to Hamburg, where the Jews were placed in camps.[23]

When the United Nations General Assembly on 29 November 1947 adopted the recommendation of a special commission to create two states on the land remaining out of the original mandate in Palestine, the Jewish representatives overcame their dissatisfaction and accepted the plan. The Arab countries voted against it, insisting that if the plan were adopted, all the Arab countries would join together to destroy the Jewish state.[24]

Attacks on Jews began even before the vote in the United Nations was taken. On 30 November, the day after the vote, Arabs shot up a bus in Israel, killing five Jews and injuring several more. The next day Jewish homes were set on fire in Jerusalem as British soldiers stood by and did nothing. In the week following the United Nations vote, one hundred five Jews were killed by Arabs.[25] Arab volunteers from Jordan, Syria, and Egypt were permitted by the British to enter the country freely. By the end of 1947 the war against the Jews in Palestine was in full swing. The Haganah had only limited arms, and even these had to be concealed from the British. When the Arabs attacked, the Haganah truly faced a life-or-death struggle. In early April of 1948 Israel received a large (illegal) transport of arms from Czechoslovakia.[26] The Haganah then took the offensive and cleared several roads leading to Jerusalem and Haifa.

In 1947, as Arab radio broadcasts kept threatening the Jews with an Armageddon, many wealthy Arab families left their homes and went to Cairo, Beirut, and other far-off places to "sit out" the war. When the fighting erupted, more Arabs left for neighboring countries. For a while the Arab leaders were worried that no one would remain to fight. One Arab newspaper in Jaffa wrote on 20 January, "Our own fifth column is deserting the struggle."[27] By April, Arab military units were already pleading with the Arabs to leave their homes, so that the army could freely bomb the Jewish settlements without endangering Arab lives.

After 2 October 1947, when wealthy Arabs started leaving, the Jews issued this call to their Arab neighbors:

> The Jews hold out to you a hand of friendship and brotherhood; cooperate with us, let us work together for peace and progress, for the good of both our countries.[28]

Salim Zubron, an Arab citizen of Israel, related in 1962 how the Arabs fled from Haifa.

> We received an appeal from the Arab leaders to leave our homes for two weeks, so they could more easily fire at the Jews. The Haganah appealed to us to stay. . . . The Histadrut distributed leaflets pleading with us to stay. I still have one of those leaflets.[29]

In a report to the Mandate General Staff, the British police in Haifa stated: "The Jews are doing everything they can to convince the Arabs to stay. . . . The Jews are promising them safety." The British, however, continued to state publicly that they were giving up the Mandate, that they were no longer responsible for the peace of the country, that they were leaving. This only made the panic among the Arabs worse. Whole villages were abandoned.

In the fall of 1947 the United Nations delegates from Cairo, Iraq, and the North African countries, repeatedly warned that if the partition plan were adopted, they would "settle accounts" with the Jews in those countries.[30] Most of the Jews in Beirut, Tripoli, Baghdad, Cairo, and other Arab centers fled to Israel. Approximately 800,000 Jewish refugees came from the Arab countries, most of them penniless, not having been permitted to take any property. Israeli society absorbed them all. In addition, there were tens of thousands of survivors of the Nazi Holocaust who had also come to Israel seeking refuge. The Arab countries, however, refused to accept their homeless relatives from Palestine. Furthermore, they crowded the Arab refugees into camps near the borders of Israel in order to keep open the wound of Arab homelessness, and to use the refugee camps as recruiting grounds for terrorists. Out of the original 600,000 Arabs who left their homes, about one-fifth, the more well-to-do, established themselves in other Arab lands. To the remaining 480,000 were added poor Arabs who lived in areas which Jordan had captured in the war. When they discovered that homeless people were being given ration cards entitling them to free food and clothing—even though they were still living in their own homes—they became "refugees." Tens of thousands of unemployed Arabs from Egypt, Syria, and Jordan were also added to the already swollen list. The United Nations was unable to keep an accurate account of these "homeless" Arabs, whose numbers increased from year to year.

In the 1960s the United Nations was supporting 1.3 million Arab "refugees" and the total was still rising. The fact that the United Nations Organization was supporting them gave the Arabs in the camps the legitimacy of being "wronged by Israel." Many young, naive, well-meaning fighters for justice throughout the world blame the State of Israel for the plight of the refugees.

Two weeks after a cease-fire was signed by Israel and the Arab countries in June 1948, Egypt, Syria, and Jordan renewed their attacks.[31] From the borders of Egypt, Syria, and Jordan, terrorists repeatedly attacked Jewish settlements. From their positions of safety in the Golan Heights, Arabs fired down upon kibbutzim in the valley around the Sea of Kinneret. From Gaza, where Arab refugees had settled, fedayeen terrorists daily assaulted peaceful Jewish villages. The Soviet Union and its allies supported the crimes of the Arabs against Israel and their violations of United Nations resolutions, and encouraged the Arabs to continue their attacks.

Israel began responding to Arab attacks in kind, but after every such action, the United Nations almost always condemned Israel, not the terrorists. The agreement among Egypt, Syria, and Israel had stressed that the cease-fire must lead to a real peace treaty. The first sentence of Paragraph 4 reads: "The cease-fire is adopted in an attempt to liquidate the war situation and establish a lasting peace."[32] While Israel accepted the cease-fire as a step to peace, the Arabs saw it as a temporary truce, and never ceased proclaiming that they were in the midst of a war with the State of Israel.

In 1954 Egypt fortified its borders on the eastern shore of the Sinai Peninsula and prevented Israeli ships from passing through the Straits of Tiran at Sharm al-Sheikh. Even Israeli air traffic over the straits was obstructed. With greater frequency, armed Egyptian fedayeen attacked Israeli settlements and mined Israeli roads. In a speech to the United Nations on 10 October 1956, Abba Eban, Israel's foreign minister, reported that in the six years up to the end of 1955 there had been 1,339 armed attacks on Jewish settlements by Egypt, resulting in the death of 101 Jews and the wounding of 364; and that in the first nine months of 1956, 28 Jews had already been killed in Arab attacks.[33] The attacks from Gaza were unremitting.

In 1955 Egypt received large transports of arms from the Soviet Union. In 1956 President Gamal Abdel Nasser nationalized the Suez Canal and blockaded Eilat, Israel's outlet to the Red Sea. In October, Egypt signed a military pact with Syria. The leader of the Arab Legion, Abu Navar, stated: "Not Israel, but we, shall decide the time and place of a new war. . . ." On 29 October 1956 Israeli forces attacked the Egyptians in Sinai and within several days reached the Suez Canal. The Eisenhower-Dulles administration in the United States, cooperating with the Soviet Union, forced the Israeli army to retreat to the previous borders. Walter Lippmann wrote at that time:

> To ignore the Egyptian attacks on Israel, as if Israel, not Egypt, were the aggressor, is a bad error, aside from being unjust. Such a position is indefensible. Such a position is false, impractical and unrealistic.[34]

Accusations have been made that Israel, together with England and France, planned the attack on Egypt to help them retake the Suez Canal. The truth is that Israel's reasons for attacking Egypt had nothing to do with the motives of England and France. For Israel it was a matter of breaking the blockade in the Red Sea, of ending the incursions across its borders. It is not difficult to imagine that since it would obtain the rights of transportation through the Suez Canal, the Jewish State was not unhappy that Nasser had provoked France and England into a war.

Having been bailed out by Eisenhower-Dulles and the Soviet Union, Nasser pledged never again to block Israel's passage to the sea and to allow Israel's shipping through the Suez Canal. He promised to prevent fedayeen attacks on Israel's borders, and he permitted United Nations peacekeeping units on his land. When the Israeli army withdrew from Sinai, the prime minister of Israel declared that any future attempt by Egypt to block to Red Sea and obstruct Israeli shipping at Eilat would be viewed by Israel as an act of war.

The Six Day War

The promise that Nasser made in 1957 to permit Israeli shipping through the Suez Canal was broken the very same year. In 1965 there were thirty-five terrorist raids across Israel's borders; in 1966, forty-one; in the first four months of 1967, thirty-seven.[35] From the Golan Heights came an incessant barrage. Israel's complaints to the United Nations went unheeded as the Soviet Union used its veto power. On 7 April 1967 after Syrian artillery in the Golan Heights had heavily bombarded the Jewish kibbutzim below, Israeli planes replied with a concentrated attack. Six Syrian aircraft were shot down. The Soviet government accused Israel of serving American imperialism by attacking the progressive Syrian government. The same month the Soviet Union informed Egypt that Israel was massing a large army on the Syrian border. Israel denied it.

In May the Soviet ambassador to Israel awakened Prime Minister Levi Eshkol in the middle of the night and delivered a Soviet protest against the massing of an army at the Syrian border. The premier again denied it and offered to take the ambassador along the whole length of the border, so he could see for himself. The ambassador refused, replying he was certain Moscow had a reason for its protest. Moscow radio kept repeating the story that Israel was amassing for an attack on Syria. On 19 May U Thant, secretary general of the

United Nations, assured that body that reliable sources had informed him that Israel was not gathering troops on the Syrian border.

On 14 May Nasser began massing a large army at the border of Israel on the pretext that Egypt was pledged to come to the aid of Syria. On 16 May Cairo radio announced that Israel had already existed too long. Triumphantly the announcer proclaimed: "The hour has struck! In the battle which we are preparing we will destroy Israel totally."[36] In Cairo, radio broadcasts and newspaper articles called upon the people to be ready for the final battle against Israel.

On the same day Nasser demanded that the United Nations remove its forces from Gaza, Sinai, and Sharm al-Sheikh, which had been there since 1956. On 19 May the commander of the United Nations peacekeeping force acceded to the demand of the Egyptian government and removed his troops from the borders. On 23 May U Thant flew to Cairo. The same day Nasser ordered the reimposition of the blockade of the Tiran Straits and of all shipping bound for Eilat. Prime Minister Eshkol announced that Israel regarded this as an act of war.[37] In turn, Nasser replied that Egypt was ready for a full-scale war with Israel.

On 30 May, King Hussein of Jordan turned the command of the Jordanian Army over to the Egyptian general staff. Egyptian, Saudi Arabian, and Iraqi army units came to Jordan to help in the war against Israel. Troops came from Algeria and Kuwait. On 3 June the Egyptian radio announced that the hour of the Holy War against Israel had struck, that Palestine would be liberated and the Jews driven into the sea. On 5 June the Israeli air force attacked Egyptian air bases and smashed more than four hundred planes. The same morning, the Israeli army attacked Egyptian forces in the Sinai and Gaza, drove the Syrians out of their positions in the Golan Heights and occupied the fortifications. The Israeli government appealed to King Hussein to keep Jordan out of the war, but his troops took the offensive. In a war that lasted six days Israel was victorious on all fronts west of the Jordan. Jerusalem was liberated.

While the war was in progress, the United Nations Security Council met every day, with the Middle East on its agenda. On 5, 6, and 7 June the United States proposed that the United Nations call for a cease-fire. The Soviet Union (apparently believing the Arab reports that they were winning on all fronts) vetoed the cease-fire proposal. Not until 10 June did the Soviet delegate agree to the proposal. Israel, Egypt, Syria, and Jordan accepted on 12 June.

Soon after the war, the Soviet Union began sending enormous transports of modern weaponry to Egypt and Syria. At the Khartoum Conference of Arab States in August 1967, resolutions were adopted against negotiating with Israel, against a peace treaty, against recognizing Israel, and against renouncing the right of the Palestinian Arabs to return to their land. These four conditions have remained the essential position of most of the Arab countries toward Israel and peace in the Middle East until this day.[38]

Anti-Israel incitement on the Arab radio after the Six Day War grew even worse than it had been before. In Egypt, Syria, Lebanon, and throughout the Middle East the *Protocols of the Elders of Zion* were reprinted and distributed in millions of copies. Arab terrorists increased their activities along the borders, in Jerusalem, Tel Aviv, and other cities. Attacks on Israeli citizens took place also in European cities.[39]

In 1969 Egypt began its sixteen-month war of attrition against Israel. The shooting across the canal reached war-like proportions. In the spring of 1970, four Soviet planes were shot down by Israeli fighters. As a result of the political tension which arose between the United States and the USSR, President Nixon called for a cease-fire between Egypt and Israel, and the shooting stopped.

In 1972 Egypt had a falling out with the Soviet Union and ordered most of the Russian military personnel out of the country. Despite this, the Soviet Union continued to sell arms to Egypt and Syria. It was these arms which enabled those two countries to launch their surprise attack on Israel in October 1973.

The attack came on Yom Kippur and caught Israel unprepared. The Arab side was joined by nine other countries—Jordan, Iraq, Sudan, Tunisia, Morocco, Kuwait, Saudi Arabia, Libya, and Algeria. In addition, the P.L.O. terrorists attacked villages in the north of Israel. The Egyptian army succeeded in crossing the Suez Canal with a large armada of tanks and numerous well-equipped military units. The Syrians captured the Golan Heights during the first hours of the war. Many thousands of young lives were lost on all sides. After two weeks of bitter fighting, Israel managed to halt the Arab offensive and cross the Suez Canal, trapping the Egyptian Third Army. Israeli troops also retook the Golan Heights.

In March of 1973 the Soviet Union had promised President Nixon to cooperate in every way possible to bring about peace in the Middle East.[40] However, in the October War the Soviet Union refused to demand a cease-fire in the early days of the conflict.

Soviet leaders even threatened to send several of their own divisions to help the Arabs. To this threat the United States replied by putting its European forces on the alert. The United States government then compelled Israel to stop its counterattack and lift its siege of the Third Army.

The hatred of the Arabs for Israel continued at fever pitch. Between 1967 and 1973 the leaders of the Arab countries, together with the Soviet Union, conducted an unceasing agitation throughout the world against the Jewish state.

In October 1975 a majority of countries in the United Nations voted for the shameful resolution equating Zionism with racism. That resolution was proposed by the Arab countries and supported by the Soviet Union, China, and the smaller Communist countries.

28

Jew-Hatred in Poland and Germany Between the Two World Wars

When Poland became an independent state after World War I, one-third of its population were national minorities. Of the approximately thirty million people in the country, six million were Ukrainians, three million were Jews, and one million were Germans.[1] In the former Russian areas of the new Poland—Volhynia, Byelorussia, and Lithuania—the peasants had been impoverished since the czarist days. The villages, forests, and pasturelands all belonged to the Polish landowners. Under the impact of the revolution in Russia, a mood of rebellion stirred the Ukrainian peasantry. Trying to head off a revolt, the landowners began spreading anti-Jewish slanders, blaming the poverty of the peasants on the Jewish storekeepers.[2]

The Polish Catholic Church, like the Greek Orthodox in the eastern regions, had no qualms about doing its own hate-mongering. The Polish intellectuals, exulting chauvinistically in their newly won national independence, saw, as enemies of Poland, all foreigners, particularly the Jews, who were "foreigners" of long-standing, Russifiers, and most recently also Bolsheviks. Most vicious in their anti-Jewish campaign were the Endeks (National Democrats), whose leader, Roman Dmowski, while still in the Czarist Duma, had joined forces with the anti-Semitic *Soyuz*.[3]

Almost immediately after Poland was declared an independent nation, and the forces of General Haller defeated the Ukrainians in Lwow, a pogrom was organized in that city on the pretext that the Jews had cooperated with the Ukrainians. This pogrom on 22

November 1918, in which 52 Jews were killed and 463 wounded, quickly spread to other cities in Galicia.[4]

During the war with the Bolsheviks in 1919-20, Polish soldiers terrorized Jews wherever they found them. In April 1919, eighty Jews were killed in Vilna and more than two thousand homes were ransacked. In Pinsk on 5 April 1919 they attacked a Jewish meeting where plans were being made to allocate the assistance provided by the Joint Distribution Committee. Hundreds of Jews were arrested and forty summarily shot.[5] Sixty innocent Jews were released after months of imprisonment.

In their march on Kiev and return, the Polish troops passed through many Jewish towns and took vengeance on the population. When the facts were brought to the *Sejm*, the anti-Semites there accused the Jews of spreading slanders in order to sully the good name of Poland.

As the day neared for the Versailles Peace Conference, where the Western powers were to approve Poland's independence, Premier Ignace Paderewski (an anti-Semite himself) convened a Jewish conference on 18 February 1919 to consider ways of improving the lot of the Jews. Yitzhok Greenbaum and Noah Prilutsky, two of the delegates, demanded that the government put a stop to anti-Semitic propaganda, including the boycott movement, and guarantee the Jews national cultural autonomy, including schools using Yiddish. Paderewski replied that Poland would never permit cultural autonomy for any national minorities within its borders.

Attacks by Polish soldiers on Jews continued during the entire period of the war against the Bolsheviks; one hundred fifty such pogroms took place from 1918 to 1920.

After the Peace of Riga in 1921, Poland regained large parts of Volhynia, Byelorussia, and Lithuania. Added to the Galician and Lithuanian Jews, there were now three million Jews in Poland. The government continued to institute anti-Jewish laws. In the period between the two world wars Polish anti-Semitism was expressed in all sorts of ways, but most effectively by economic regulations which grew more oppressive, driving Jews out of one economic position after another.[6]

As early as 1874 a Polish anti-Semite, Jan Jelenski, had published a pamphlet advocating "a drive to abolish the Jewish commercial monopoly erected through the centuries."[7] This theme was now taken up by the Endeks and developed to its logical conclusion that the Jews were utterly superfluous in Poland.

Independent Poland began its existence with a heritage of economic devastation resulting from the World War I occupation by Germany and Austria. Then came the Polish-Bolshevik war, which completed the destruction. Before the war, Poland was politically and economically part of the Russian empire; now, as a separate state, it found itself economically isolated. Starvation drove the Polish peasants into the cities and smaller towns, where they tried their hand at some of the traditionally "Jewish" occupations.

The Polish government itself organized cooperatives which employed large numbers of Christian workers. It also set up state monopolies in important consumer articles such as tobacco, alcohol, salt, and matches, and prohibited Jews from participating in these monopolies.[8] In 1929, with the outbreak of the world economic crisis, the situation of the Polish Jews reached catastrophic levels. With the combination of economic crisis and restrictive government policies, the Jewish population in Poland continued to grow more impoverished with each succeeding year. Jews were forced out of the export-import business; grain export was forbidden to them. Jewish government employees in Galicia were dismissed, and even Jewish state employees who went to serve in the military were not restored to their jobs when they returned.[9] This process continued systematically through the 1920s and 1930s. Even conversion to Christianity was not a way out. In Warsaw, for example, three converted Jews were dismissed from the courts.[10]

With the official approval of the government, anti-Semitic groups openly agitated for boycotts against Jewish businesses and articles made in Jewish shops. A boycott movement was also instituted against Jewish handicraftsmen. In the late 1920s a law was passed requiring artisans to have a "Master's diploma" in the particular trade. The judges at the "examination" were always Christian craftsmen whose primary interest was in eliminating Jewish competition.

The boycott also extended to Jewish professionals. In the early 1920s Polish authorities introduced a Jewish quota of 10 percent in the universities which was based on the number of Jews in the country as a whole, and despite the fact that 98 percent of the Jews in Poland lived in the cities and that the proportion of Jewish students in universities had always been more than 30 percent. Polish students, mostly sons of government officials, and often the vanguard of the anti-Semitic movement, objected even to the 10 percent quota and created their own way of eliminating Jews from the universities. In addition to insults, threats, and beatings, they refused to sit on the same benches with Jewish students. Jews were consequently assigned separate seating, a kind of ghetto within the school. Jewish students refused to submit to this indignity and stood during classes.

In 1931, anti-Semitic students at Warsaw University formed an organization to strengthen the general boycott against Jews and called it The League of the Green Ribbon. The League's statutes contained these four paragraphs: (1) not to buy in Jewish stores, not to employ Jewish tailors and other handicraftsmen, not to use the services of Jewish attorneys or physicians; (2) not to have any business or social dealings with Jews; (3) it is the duty of every League member to agitate for the anti-Jewish boycott everywhere; (4) to fight for the introduction of quotas in all Polish universities.[11] The wearing of the green ribbon spread like wildfire. The number of anti-Semitic newspapers increased. Even skywriting was used for this purpose.

On 11 October 1936 Bishop Lukomski of the Lomz diocese wrote in the Catholic press:

> The Jews are a boil on the body of Poland. They are busy everywhere. In the press they are fighting against the Catholic faith. . . . Abroad they sully Poland's name. . . . They spread smut and immorality in our cultural life.[12]

In 1919 the government acceded to a demand of the Church for the introduction of compulsory Sunday rest laws. In addition to the boycott and other forms of discrimination, the government instituted a tax system which drove masses of Jewish businessmen and artisans to beggary and desperation. All over Poland trucks were dispatched to confiscate, for nonpayment of taxes, furniture from Jewish homes, merchandise from Jewish stores, sewing machines from Jewish tailors, horses and wagons from Jewish teamsters.

The Nazi brutalities in Germany in the 1930s encouraged the Polish anti-Semites even further. Beginning in 1935 and particularly after the death of President Pilsudski, the poison of anti-Semitism was just as thick in the air of Poland as it was in Nazi Germany. In 1934 Joseph Goebbels was received in Poland with great pomp. Hitler's aide, Hermann Göring, was also a frequent guest in

Warsaw.[13] In the mid-1930s most of Poland's professional and economic societies adopted the infamous "Aryan paragraph" which excluded from membership Christians who stemmed from Jewish converts four generations back.[14] The last remaining Jews in the villages were expelled. In some villages warnings were posted: "Jews are forbidden to enter."[15]

Soon this hatred turned to violence. In June 1935 there was a pogrom in Grodno; in March 1936, in Przytyk; in June 1936, in Minsk-Mazowiecki; in May 1937, in Brisk; in June 1937, in Czenstochow. "The wave of pogroms," wrote the historian Isaiah Trunk, "engulfed all parts of Poland from Slonim to Lodz, from Poznan to Vilna."[16] A Jewish self-defense group was organized which put up effective resistance. In the large cities there was almost a state of war, with the police usually taking the side of the pogromchiks.

At the same time, virtually the entire press was conducting a campaign urging the Jews to leave Poland. *Zhidze du Palestinu* ("Jews to Palestine") became a popular slogan of the anti-Semites. The Peasant Party advised the Jews:

> The Jewish problem can be solved only by the emigration of the Jews. . . . Don't the Jews understand that their obstinate refusal to leave Poland will only aggravate the anti-Semites? The villages are crowded with a surplus of hands and mouths. If we must push somebody out of here, it is really much fairer that it be the Jews who, after all, are foreigners in Poland. . . . Those Jews who insist that they will not leave only contribute to the growth of anti-Semitism in Poland.[17]

The Polish Fascists soon saw the fulfillment of their dream. When the German troops marched into Poland in 1939 and began "solving the Jewish problem," the Polish patriots enthusiastically placed themselves at the service of the Nazis. Together with the Schutzstaffeln, known as the SS, armed Polish executioners searched out Jews in their hiding places and drove them pitilessly to the boxcars destined for the death camps. And when Poland, with the help of the Soviet army, was liberated from the Nazis, and several thousand Jews returned to Poland, the Polish Fascists, some of whom had become "Communists," began driving out the last remnants of Jews. That story is a chapter unto itself, one of the most shameful in the history of Poland. In that last chapter, however, the Polish Fascists already had the blessing of the Kremlin in Moscow.[18]

Anti-Semitism in Germany

A quip current in early twentieth century Germany divulged that "every decent German is an anti-Semite." There was an element of truth in it. Jews had no access to positions in government or institutions of higher learning. A Jew who earned the title of "professor" was given the title but not a chair on the faculty. In Socialist circles, which by the end of the nineteenth century were quite prominent in Germany, anti-Semitism was officially combatted as being a concomitant of political reaction. But like other sections of the population, the Socialists also were impatient with the "stubbornness" of the Jews in maintaining their own identity. Karl Kautsky, a leading Socialist theoretician, argued that the Jews are not a nation and must therefore assimilate with the rest of the population, and the sooner the better, for them and for society.[19]

Assimilation was widespread. The Yiddish language had been forgotten. Jewish religious worship was almost completely Reform. Education in the public schools was free of any "Jewish values." Most German Jews considered it beneath them to associate with Jews from Eastern Europe. The finest complement you could pay a Jew in Germany was to tell him that he looked like a "real" German. Many Jews converted in order to secure government positions. In 1904 some five hundred Jews were converted in Berlin alone. In 1905-1909 about 25 percent of all Jewish marriages in Germany were mixed. In the larger cities the number was closer to 50 percent. The German Jews themselves did not attempt to combat anti-Semitism, except for publishing several apologetic pamphlets showing that anti-Semitism is a "mistake." Jewish national life was suppressed and denigrated. Only isolated Jews were active in the Zionist movement, which had already captured the imagination of large sections of East European Jewry. Most assimilated German Jews were fearful that Zionism would hurt their image as loyal citizens. Ludwig Geiger, editor of the *Allgemeine Zeitung*, a Jewish newspaper, wrote anti-Zionist editorials averring that the government had a right to deprive Zionists of their citizenship rights because "Zionists are not good German citizens."[20]

Werner Sombart (1863-1941), a German historian and author of *Modern Capitalism*, wrote that the Capitalist system originated in the early Middle Ages, and that most of the important initiators and developers of the system were Jews; this, he asserted, was because they were better equipped to do it, owing to a special characteristic which they possess, a characteristic which is odious to the "Nordic race." Sombart welcomed the new Jewish nationalism in Eastern Europe, while he castigated the German Jews who were stubbornly trying to gain access to government positions.

> The new anti-Semitism is a product of the conflict between the Jews and those around them. This conflict always grows more acute after efforts at closer relationships. It will grow weaker when the Jews stop pushing themselves into Christian society.[21]

Sombart's theory that Jews "originated" capitalism is essentially anti-Semitic. This theory has been assiduously advanced by Jew-haters of every stripe, including Adolf Hitler. It is true that as an urban element in society, deprived of all the conventional ways of earning a living, Jews participated in the new mercantilism in order to survive. But the Jews did not "invent" capitalism. In 1934, when Hitler was already ruling Germany, Sombart was professor of history and economics in Germany and published his "German Socialism" in which he argued for the Nazi program of excluding Jews from the nation's economic and cultural life.

In 1914 there were approximately 600,000 Jews in Germany, of whom 100,000 served in the armed forces. Twelve thousand German Jews were killed in World War I.[22] This did not modify the attitude of the Junker government toward Jews one iota.

With the continuing inflation, a drastic political reaction set in. The lost war, coming after the illusory faith in the German *Reichswehr*, the tremendous number of casualties, the war-maimed on the streets, the hunger and privation which the German people suffered during the protracted war, the destitution resulting from the inflation, and above all, the wounded pride after the defeat—all this raised in every section of German society a mood of desperation and revanchism. Dozens of nationalist groups and sects sprouted at this time with diverse political programs; but they all had one common feature: anti-Semitism.

The program of one such group, which called itself by the grandiose name of National Socialist Party, was a vague mixture of chauvinism, socialism, and anti-Semitism. One member of this group was a demobilized, disturbed soldier named Adolf Hitler. Hitler's ravings in the beer saloons, to the effect that Germany had not been defeated but betrayed from within, by the Jews, began to attract attention and followers. This in turn encouraged him further.

In the spring of 1923 he organized a *Putsch* against the Weimar Republic, an abortive attempt which was easily put down. During the year he spent in prison, Hitler wrote *Mein Kampf*, in which he outlined his plan for putting Germany back on its feet. Several times in this book he cited the *Protocols of the Elders of Zion*, which had been translated into German in 1920 and printed in 100,000 copies.

In *Mein Kampf* Hitler concluded that as the first step, Germany must rid itself of the Jews. He assures Germans that they have the full moral and historical rights to rule the lower Slavic races of the East. His ideas were not new: the Jews sold out Germany to its enemies. Jews are internationalists, bankers, Communists, and such. Jews are a misfortune for the pure and noble German race. They corrupt the German blood. Democracy is a Jewish idea. There is no true equality. The German people must abolish the Versailles Treaty and the Jewish Weimar Republic.[23]

This program of the "hero" Adolf Hitler, who went to jail for his beliefs, a program which offered both consolation for the defeat of the German army and a hope for revitalizing the German nation, attracted many followers, and their number multiplied manyfold during the crisis that struck Germany and the entire Capitalist world in 1929.

During the late 1920s, when the grip of inflation eased, Jews in the free political atmosphere of the Weimar Republic achieved economic and social position that had not been accessible to them before the war. At the same time, anti-Jewish feelings grew stronger, and during the economic crisis of 1929–33 the Jews found themselves the targets of a deadly anti-Semitic barrage.

Hitler's raving "solutions" hypnotized millions of Germans. The Socialist and Communist parties in Germany were at loggerheads as they separately tried to counter the success of the Nazis. Street fights broke out in the cities between Nazis and leftists. In 1930, when unemployment in Germany rose to 40 percent, Nazi representation in the Reichstag jumped from twelve to one hundred and seven. The number of Nazi followers increased daily, accompanied by attacks on Jews in the streets, on trolleycars, in synagogues, in homes. Nazis demonstrated against Jewish businesses, smashed windows, pillaged, agitated for boycotts. In September 1931, as Jews in Berlin were leaving a synagogue, the Nazis began a pogrom in the center of the city. The cry of "Germany Awake—Death to the Jews!" resounded through the capital.

In 1931 the Nazis organized the Storm Troopers, who put on

brown shirts, sewed swastikas on their sleeves, and lived in their own camps, as if they were part of an army. While the Nazis lost votes in the election of 1933, German political leaders, alarmed by the prospect of a left wing victory, hastened to put the reins of government into the hands of that archenemy of humanity, Adolf Hitler.[24] On 30 January 1933 President Hindenburg appointed Hitler Reichschancellor. A few weeks later, after the Nazis had burned down the Reichstag building and blamed it on the Communists, Hitler proclaimed himself dictator and outlawed all the other political parties.

In May 1933 a book burning was organized in the center of Berlin, where all German works written by Jews or former Jews were thrown into the flames. When the League of Nations characterized the Nazi acts as "barbarism," Hitler withdrew from the organization and began building up the Reichswehr. The leaders of England and France did nothing to stop him. On 15 September 1935 the Nazis convened a conference at Nuremberg to compile a special code of anti-Jewish statutes. The Nuremberg Laws decreed that Jews could no longer be citizens of Germany, that the Aryan blood of the Germans was to be kept pure, that marriages between Germans and Jews were forbidden, that Jews were forbidden to employ female German servants in their homes, that Jews could no longer hold public office or occupy any position wherein they would supervise Germans. The Nazi code was to remain forever as a bulwark against the "lower Jewish race."[25]

In municipal buildings, in public squares all over Germany, one could read, in giant letters, the worst anti-Semitic utterances of the leading Jew-haters in German history, particularly Treitschke's slogan: "The Jews are our misfortune." Doors of hotels and restaurants proclaimed: "Jews Not Welcome Here!" The Jews of Germany found themselves more deeply entrapped as the Nazi mass murderers readied the cruelest disaster in Jewish history.

Jews in Austria (1914–38)

After the St. Germain peace treaty in 1919, there were approximately 200,000 Jews in the truncated Austrian state, 175,000 of them in Vienna alone.[26] The racist Pan-Germanism captured the imagination of the six million Germans in Austria. The unemployment and starvation of the early 1920s gave rise to Jew-baiting in the Vienna beer halls, streets, churches, and universities. Boycotts and physical assaults inevitably followed. During the 1920s, when Nazi groups were springing up in Germany, the anti-Semites in Austria became more blatant. Attacks on Jewish students increased. The anti-Jewish boycott intensified.

Premier Dollfuss, who would not permit an *Anschluss* with Germany, was assassinated in 1934 by Nazi thugs. The anti-Jewish campaign grew worse. Catholic priests again became active in disseminating anti-Semitism. By the beginning of 1937 many Austrian Jews were desperately seeking a place of refuge, but America, Palestine, Argentina, were all closed to Jewish immigration.

In February 1938, Hitler summoned Premier Schuschnigg to Germany and ordered him to appoint Nazis to his government, otherwise the German army would occupy Austria.[27] Schuschnigg hesitated. On 13 March 1938 the Nazi armies invaded Austria, completed the *Anschluss* and made Austria a province of Germany. Very soon thereafter, Hitler's deputy, Göring, came to Vienna and announced that Austria must become *Judenrein*. The brutalities of the Austrian Nazis toward the Jews of Vienna outstripped even those of their German mentors. Many Austrian Jews fled to Palestine and entered illegally by one means or another.

29

Anti-Semitism and Hitler's Final Solution

The flareup of Jew-hatred in Germany and all of Europe in the last quarter of the nineteenth century was not a sudden phenomenon. Though not the only cause, the seeds of bigotry which the Church had sown in Europe throughout the centuries were still bearing fruit. Martin Luther's sixteenth century teaching—"The Jews have been our misfortune for 1400 years"[1]—had never been retracted. The unspeakable bestiality known as Hitlerism was actually an offspring of the union between medieval religious Jew-hatred and nineteenth century racist German nationalism.[2]

Hundt-Radowski, one of many anti-Semitic pamphleteers in the nineteenth century, wrote: "Killing a Jew is not a crime; but it only causes a commotion and becomes inconvenient."[3] He proposed, instead, castrating all male Jews, placing Jewish women in brothels, and deporting the rest to England to be used on plantations.[4] The composer Richard Wagner said: "Emancipation from the yoke of Judaism appears to us the foremost necessity."[5] And Adolf Hitler, noting in his diary that Wagner belonged in the same category with Frederick the Great and Martin Luther, added: "Whoever wants to understand National Socialist Germany must know Wagner."[6]

Theodor Fritsch (1844–1933), in his *Anti-Semite's Catechism*, listed ten racist commandments, among which are:

Thou shalt keep thy blood pure. Avoid all contact with the Jew and keep him away from thyself and thy family, especially thy daughters, lest they suffer injury of body and soul.[7]

During the Hitler years this catechism, under the title of *Handbook on the Jewish Question*, was reissued in millions of copies and, together with *Mein Kampf*, became the new German "gospel."

The Jews did not expect this resurgence of anti-Semitism nor did they take it seriously. The Germans, after all, were a civilized people. Given time and education, this unjustified hatred would disappear. But it did not disappear. Apart from all the other causes of anti-Semitism, the need for a scapegoat never vanished. Anti-Semitism in Germany and Austria became a political issue, a vote-getter; it became legitimate and respectable, and its poison spread rapidly through the German body politic. In 1890, 47,500 Germans voted for anti-Semitic candidates; in 1901, 461,000 voters elected sixteen anti-Semites to the Reichstag.[8]

With the exception of the Social Democratic Party, which condemned the dissemination of anti-Semitic propaganda, not one group in Germany remained free of Jew-hatred. In the 1912 elections to the Reichstag the Social Democratic Party drew a large number of votes, and it appeared that anti-Semitism in Germany might be on the decline. By 1916, as the war dragged on, voices were heard blaming the Jews for all of Germany's troubles.

Adolf Hitler was born in 1889 in a small Austrian town not far from the German border. His father, a local politician of the anti-Semitic stripe, had been an illegitimate child, reportedly the son of a Jewish father. When Hitler was fourteen, his father died. A friend of Hitler's recalled that at this age he was already an avid reader of the anti-Semitic press and acquainted with Wagner's writings. Two years later Hitler quit school. As a young man, Hitler considered himself an artist. When he showed his work to the people at the Vienna Academy, they rejected it. His mother, who had been supporting him, died in 1908. Through 1913, Hitler stayed in Vienna, living from hand to mouth. It was a time when anti-Jewish propaganda could be heard on all sides, and Hitler absorbed it all.

At the time there was a political struggle between two German nationalist groups—Schonerer's Pan-Germanism and Lueger's Christian Socialists. In *Mein Kampf*, Hitler discusses the difference between these two systems of Jew-hatred. Lueger's anti-Semitism, he said, stems from religious concepts, not "pure racial science." This was a foolish approach, Hitler believed. Conversion had always been an escape route for Jews. A Jew could permit himself to be sprinkled with a little holy water, stay alive, and keep his stolen wealth.[9]

When World War I broke out, Hitler was in Munich. He volunteered for army service. On the French front he was wounded, and in 1918, while he was in the hospital, the war ended in defeat for Germany. When he left the hospital, Hitler returned to Munich and launched his campaign against the Marxists and the Jews, who had "sold out" Germany. Soon after the suppression of the Communist uprising in Munich he was given a job by the army as a propagandist against Marxism and radicalism.[10]

In his new position, Hitler made the acquaintance of some "important" people. One of them was Alfred Rosenberg. Born of German parents in Latvia in 1897, Rosenberg attended the Russian Technological Institute in Riga. In 1918, when the Germans retreated from the Ukraine, he went back to Germany with them. Alfred Rosenberg, the "intellectual" among the anti-Semitic leaders, wrote "scholarly" articles about nationalism, about the *Protocols*, about the race question and about *Lebensraum* for Germany. Fluent in the Russian language, he became an authority on Soviet affairs and wrote *The Myth of the Twentienth Century*, in which he "proved" that the Jews are the backbone of Bolshevism and democracy.

In 1920 Adolf Hitler already knew how he wished to solve the "Jewish problem." In a reply to a letter, he wrote: "Anti-Semitism must not become an emotional issue. . . . Rational anti-Semitism must lead to disposing of the Jews altogether."[11] In *Mein Kampf* he stated:

> The Aryan race is the source of human cultural development. The very existence of world civilization depends on the purity of the Aryan race. The obstacle to a pure Aryan race is the Jew. The Jew spreads disease, plagues. Jews are bacilli which poison the blood of other peoples. It is the Jews who have spread syphilis in Germany. The Jews are parasites, bloodthirsty leeches that degrade the Aryan race. The Jews strive to rule the world and enslave the nations.[12]

As examples of his "truths" Hitler pointed to what "the Jews had done in Russia." Through Russian bolshevism, he argued, the Jews are obviously planning to become the rulers of the world in the present century.[13]

From 1923 to 1930 unprecedented inflation in Germany, unemployment, together with unbridled nationalism, drove masses of working people and middle class citizens into the embrace of Nazi ideology. The larger anti-Semitic groups numbered four hundred and thirty throughout the country, with seven hundred periodicals. The young people in particular were swept up by the hate-mongering. In 1921 two-thirds of all the students in institutions of higher learning elected active anti-Semites to lead them.

In June 1922 Walter Rathenau, a Jew and a minister in the Weimar Republic, was murdered by a Nazi. Attacks on Jews in the streets multiplied. Hitler's speeches, his "evidence" from the *Protocols* that the Jews were preparing to destroy Germany and the world, his threats about Jewish bolshevism, and his charge of Jewish responsibility for all the misfortunes of Germany all caused a volcanic eruption of Jew-hatred. The German Socialists, Communists, and liberals, fought against Hitler's political program, but not against the spreading anti-Semitism.

In the Reichstag elections of 1923 the Nazi party drew 800,000 votes. Seven years later they received 16.5 million, or 37 percent of all the votes cast. In 1932, the votes were divided as follows: Nazis, 14 million, 33 percent; Socialists, 9 million, 20 percent; Communists, 7,600,000, 17 percent; Catholic Party, 7 million, 15 percent; Monarchists (who supported Hitler), 4 million, 9 percent; the other 6 percent were divided among the smaller parties.[14]

Realizing that the Nazis had lost almost 2.5 million votes to the leftist parties, the ruling Capitalist circles of Germany turned the government over to the National Socialists on the pretext that they were the largest single party. On 30 January 1933 Hitler became Reichschancellor. In March, ten days after the Reichstag fire, 15,000 opponents of the Nazis, leading Socialists, Communists, liberals, and Jews, had already been arrested. On 14 July 1933 Hitler declared the Nazi Party the only legal party in the country.[15]

Earlier, in April, a boycott was announced against all Jewish businesses in Germany. Hoodlums in brown shirts took up positions outside of Jewish stores and allowed no one to enter. All Jews were dismissed from posts in courts, universities, public schools, newspapers, theaters, trade unions, the postal service, banks, railroads, and hospitals. Albert Einstein was declared a "cultural Bolshevik." Jewish children were expelled from schools. Books written by Jews were removed from libraries and thrown into bonfires in many cities in Germany.

In answer to protests throughout the world, Hitler accused the Jews of spreading lies to hurt the German economy. Hermann Göring, governor of Prussia, summoned Jewish leaders and warned them that he would hold them personally responsible if they did not deny the "lies" that Jews were spreading abroad. On 30 March 1933 the following telegram was sent by the Jewish community in Berlin to the American Jewish Congress:

> According to newspaper reports, atrocity and boycott propaganda against Germany is continuing overseas, apparently in part also by Jewish organizations. As Germans and Jews we must enter a decisive protest against this. The dissemination of untrue reports can only bring harm, affecting the reputation of our German fatherland, endangering the relations of the German Jews with their fellow citizens. Please try urgently to see to it that every atrocity and boycott propaganda is halted.[16]

From the Storm Troops, Hitler's aides selected the "best" Nazis and created the Schutzstaffeln (SS).[17] Placed over the SS was one of Hitler's most trusted watchdogs, Heinrich Himmler, who considered Hitler the greatest man of all time. In 1930, one year after he was appointed, the SS numbered 3,000. In 1933, when Hitler came to power, it numbered 50,000; in 1939, 250,000. The most trustworthy executioners were selected for the *Sicherheitsdienst* (SD), the special Security Services.

The SD had a handpicked detachment of "experts" on the Jewish problem. In 1934 they were joined by an "expert" on Zionism named Adolf Eichmann.[18] Another group of loyal Nazis, those with even more sadistic leanings, were selected for the *Totenkopfverbänd* (Death's-Head Organization), the security police for the concentration camps. In February and March 1933, when the prisons began to bulge with political prisoners and Jews, Himmler constructed concentration camps, the first of them near Dachau. At the end of that year there were several such camps in Germany, with 25,000 prisoners.

In Prussia, Göring established his own secret police, the *Geheime Staats Polizei* (Gestapo). In 1934 the Gestapo became part of the SS under Himmler. As head of the Gestapo, Himmler appointed one of his own aides, Reinhardt Heydrich, whose bloodthirsty treatment of the Jews exceeded that of the SS.

Toward those Jews who wanted to leave Germany, the SS at first had a more lenient approach; they wanted the Jews to emigrate. "Assimilationists" were arrested and warned. However, when the Arab Mufti came to Berlin in 1936, the situation changed. In 1937 Hitler's foreign minister announced that his government was opposed to making a Jewish country out of Palestine.[19] One year before that, Hitler had made a speech in which there were clear signs of what he had in mind for the Jews:

We shall see to it that these base creatures will never be able to introduce Jewish Bolshevism into Germany, the heart of Europe. We shall relentlessly destroy the subversive forces today, or a little later, or even if it takes a hundred years.[20]

In March 1935 Hitler abrogated the 1919 treaty prohibiting German rearmament, and immediately instituted compulsory military service. Neither England nor France protested, although according to that treaty they had a right to stop him. That year a new phase began in the reign of terror against German Jewry. Jews were not admitted to theaters, swimming pools, and other public places. Attacks on Jews in the streets again became a frequent occurrence. The boycott against the few remaining businesses was intensifed. Jewish newspapers were shut down.

In October and November 1936 the "Berlin-Rome-Tokyo" axis was forged. Speeches against "Jewish Bolshevism" and the "Jewish Comintern" flowed out of Germany as the Nazis terrorized the nations of the world with the "menace of Moscow." "From their base in Russia, the Jews are preparing to conquer the world. . . ."[21]

The Nazis in Austria

When the economic crisis struck Austria in 1929, the resultant unemployment, together with the propaganda spread by the Nazis who were sent by Hitler to agitate for the *Anschluss,* placed the 200,000 Jews in that country—175,000 of them in Vienna alone[22]— in the same peril as the Jews of Germany. The enforcers of Hitler's terror against the Jews of occupied Austria were not Germans but native Nazis. Adolf Eichmann was sent to Austria to carry out his plan of expulsion. Jews were arrested as "criminals" and in order to be released they had to promise to leave Austria. The plan worked. In a few months, 45,000 Jews had emigrated. A year later, only 50,000 Jews remained in Austria.

In late September 1938, Neville Chamberlain and Edouard Daladier, prime ministers of England and France, came to Germany to sign the infamous Munich Pact with Hitler. 300,000 Jews in Czechoslovakia fell under the Nazi jackboot. More than 30,000 Jews were expelled from that country by Eichmann before World War II began.

In May 1938 masses of Jews in Germany and the occupied lands were sent to concentration camps. The Nazis were feverishly mobilizing for their long-planned attack. The war industry needed more hands. On 1 June 1938 Heydrich ordered his Storm Troopers to arrest all ablebodied Jewish males in Germany "with criminal records" and put them to work in camps. In October 1938 the Nazis rounded up 12,000 "foreign" Jews from Poland, many of whom had lived in Germany since before World War I. Most of them were middle-aged and older. They were taken to the Polish border near Poznan, to be deported to Poland. The Polish government promptly cancelled their citizenship and refused them entry. Homeless, many of them became ill or died. Finally, the protests from abroad forced the Polish government to admit them.[23]

In Paris, on 7 November 1938, a seventeen-year-old boy named Hershl Grynszpan, whose parents were among the "foreigners" driven out of Germany, shot and seriously wounded Ernst von Rath, a minor official in the German embassy. Two days later, when von Rath died of his wounds, a savage reprisal began against the Jews in Germany. Joseph Goebbels, screaming that Grynszpan's act was proof of an international Jewish plot to destroy Germany, gave his SS the signal to do whatever they pleased with the German Jews. On the night of 9 November an orgy of violence left Jewish homes and shops looted and destroyed. This pogrom has become known as *Kristallnacht*, the night of the broken glass. Scores of Jews were murdered, hundreds more injured. At least two hundred synagogues were burned to the ground.[24]

When the pogrom was finally stopped, the Jews themselves— under Nazi truncheons—were forced to clean up the debris and pay a fine of a billion marks. For not paying this fine, 50,000 Jews were thrown into concentration camps. "The news from Germany in the last several days," said President Roosevelt, "has shocked public opinion in Ameica. I myself cannot believe that such things could happen in our century, in a civilized country."[25]

Masses of Jews in Germany, Austria and Czechoslovakia, anxious to escape from the Nazi hell, found that it was now almost impossible. Up until 1938 Jews could emigrate from Germany legally and even take some of their possessions with them. Early in 1938 Jews were still permitted to leave, taking nothing out with them, but only if they had a specific destination. Of the 600,000 Jews in Germany in 1933, some 350,000 were left by 1938. Not all had emigrated. Many died. Many "foreign" Jews were expelled. Many committed suicide. (An average of one hundred suicides a month were recorded in Germany during 1938.)

On 24 January, Marshal Göring had given Heydrich full authority to expel as many Jews as possible. Thousands of Jews were imprisoned in the camps at Dachau, Buchenwald, Mauthausen, and other places. Thousands more were forced to clean the streets and public latrines in German cities. In mid-1939 all Jewish emigration was halted. Months before the start of World War II, Hjalmar Schacht, president of the Reichsbank, went to England to negotiate a ransom deal for the Jews of Germany. The essence of his plan was that 150,000 Jews a year would be let out of the country over a three-year period in exchange for $600-million and trade privileges.[26] Nothing came of the plan.

On 21 January 1939 Hitler informed the Czech foreign minister that he was preparing to liquidate the Jews. On 30 January he told the Reichstag:

> If international finance Jewry within Europe and abroad should succeed once more in plunging the peoples into a world war, then the consequence will be not the Bolshevization of the world and therewith a victory of Jewry, but on the contrary, the destruction of the Jewish race in Europe.[27]

The Stalin-Hitler Pact and World War II

On 28 April 1939, five weeks after he annexed Czechoslovakia, Hitler annulled his non-aggression pact with Poland and threatened her with war unless she returned the city of Danzig and the Polish Corridor to Germany. In return for a promise of assistance from England and France, Poland had pledged not to allow the Red Army to help her in event of a German attack. This was followed by secret negotiations between the Soviet Union and Hitler's Germany.

On 23 June Marshal Göring summoned the top Nazi leaders to an important meeting. Workers would be needed in the event of war. Himmler promised to supply enough workers from the concentration camps, where there were many Jews and prisoners from the conquered peoples. On 23 August the Stalin-Hitler pact was signed, containing three secret points: (1) Poland would be divided between Russia and Germany; (2) Lithuania would be given to Germany; and (3) Latvia, Estonia and Finland would be given to Russia. Both parties agreed not to attack the other, neither alone nor in alliance with anyone else.[28]

In the war which he started on 1 September 1939 Hitler set for himself the two goals of *Lebensraum* for Germany and a "final solution" to the Jewish problem, by which he meant the total destruction of the Jews. The second goal was no less important to him than the first.

By 27 September 1939, Poland was crushed and divided between Germany and Russia. On 27 October Hitler instructed General Keitel that all the Jews, Gypsies, Poles, and other non-Aryans must be cleaned out of the old and new Germany (the recently occupied territories). Polish intellectuals, political leaders, teachers, and professionals, must be eliminated. All other Poles must be used as slave labor for the Germans. The Jews must be segregated from the Poles in concentration camps, preparatory to liquidating them.[29] The implementation of this plan was entrusted to Himmler, who in turn appointed Heydrich as his aide. To govern Poland they both chose a tested Nazi, Hans Frank.

From his SS divisions, Heydrich selected the most experienced killers and created six units known as *Einsatzgruppen* (backup groups). Each army column was assigned such a group, which had the task of rounding up the Jews in the smaller towns into a number of larger concentration points. This process was accompanied by beatings, murder, rape, robbery, synagogue burnings. Before he locked the Jews into ghettos in the larger Polish cities in 1940-41, Hans Frank ordered them to put on identifying arm bands. The younger and stronger Jews were sent to do forced labor, either in their own or more distant cities. Jews were used in the war industry and in constructing the concentration camps.[30] Many died of starvation, disease, injuries; suicides increased. Half a million Jews perished in Poland even before the death camps began operating in 1942.

Late in 1941 these camps were ready, all six located on railroad lines: Chelmno, in Posen, in a forest between Lodz and Poznan; Treblinka, in a forest between Bialystok and Warsaw; Sobibor, between Wlodowa and Chelm; Maidanek, in a forest near Lublin; Belzec, in a forest in Eastern Poland near Przemysl; Auschwitz, in a forest south of Krakow.

Eichmann, the "expert on Zionism," continued his plan of deporting Jews—this time to death camps. Late in December 1941, groups of Jews were deported from the ghettos in Poznan and Prussia to the camp in Chelmno. In March 1942, Jews were deported from Poland to Belzec and Maidanek. From July to September 1942, 300,000 Jews were moved by train from the

Warsaw ghetto to Treblinka. From Byelorussia and the Ukraine, hundreds of thousands of Jews were deported in 1942–43 to Maidanek and Sobibor. Belzec and Sobibor also contained masses of Red Army prisoners. From Germany, the Balkans, and West Europe, hundreds of thousands of Jews were deported to Auschwitz in 1942–44. The Jews were told that they were being transported to work sites or to Switzerland. Though they did not believe the Germans, the Jews could not be sure. It was inconceivable to them that the Nazis intended such an unprecedented crime. The conditions of life in the ghetto, the murder and starvation, the terror and uncertainty, had created in the Jews a state of mind where anything was preferable to staying where they were.

At the end of 1942, Jewish slave laborers were replaced by Poles and other non-Aryans; the liquidation of the ghettos began. In March 1943 the ghettos in Krakow and Czenstochow were liquidated. In April 1943 it was the turn of the ghetto in Warsaw. Somewhere the few thousand surviving Jews in Warsaw, starved and debilitated, found the strength to begin an armed uprising against their tormentors. They fought with everything they could put their hands on—a few scattered guns, knives, clubs, iron pipes, hot water. It was not until mid-May that the Nazis were able to complete the liquidation of the Warsaw Ghetto. The Lodz ghetto held out until August 1944.[31] In many towns and cities Jews resisted, enabling hundreds to escape into the forests and join friendly partisan groups fighting the Germans. Uprisings also took place in the death camps at Sobibor, Treblinka, and Auschwitz.[32]

Of the 3.3 million Jews in Poland before the Nazis invaded, only 300,000 miraculously survived, including a few thousand who worked in the slave labor camps. Several thousand survived in the larger cities on the "Aryan side," disguised as Poles. Most of these survivors fought in the general Warsaw uprising in August 1944. Many Polish Jews who had escaped from the ghettos tried to make contact with the partisans in the forests. If they did not meet up with Polish partisans they had a good chance of surviving to take vengeance on the Nazis. Tragically, many Jewish escapees were murdered by anti-Semitic Polish partisans whom they mistook for friends.

A total of 50,000 to 70,000 Jews survived within Poland itself. Many others who had been in the Polish army were taken as prisoners of war by the Soviet Union and survived that way. Approximately 180,000 Jews who had crossed the Soviet border when the Nazis invaded Poland returned to Poland after the war. With the assistance of anti-Semitic Poles, Ukrainians, and Lithuanians, the German Nazis murdered three million Polish Jews, more than a fifth of them children.

Jews in the Holocaust

Russia. When the Nazis invaded the Soviet Union in 1941, most of the Jews living in the Baltic states, Byelorussia, the Ukraine, Bessarabia, Galicia, and Crimea were trapped by the swiftness of the advance. The civil administration established by the Germans in these areas locked most of the surviving Jews into ghettos in Vilna, Kovno, Shavl, Riga, Dvinsk, Minsk, Mogilev, Zhitomir, Berditchev, and many other towns and cities. In Kiev the *Einsatzgruppen*, in the course of two days in September 1941, massacred tens of thousands of Jews in a ravine at Babi Yar. Many Ukrainians there helped the Nazis in this particular atrocity.[33]

In hundreds of towns in the Ukraine, Byelorussia, and Lithuania, the Nazi killers attacked Jewish quarters at dawn and drove the Jews at gunpoint to the outskirts of town, where mass graves had already been dug. Here special Nazi murder squads finished the task, shooting men, women, and children in cold blood. As the mass graves were covered over, many of the victims were buried alive. Hundreds of mass graves in Eastern Europe today are reminiscent of the "Jew-hills" or "Jew-ditches" that were created in a similar way in medieval Germany.[34]

In the summer of 1943, after their defeat at Stalingrad, the Nazis began stepping up their extermination schedule. In September 1943 they liquidated the ghettos of Minsk, Lida, Vilna; in October, Bialystok; in November, Riga; in July 1944, Kovno and Shavl. In most of last-mentioned ghettos there were uprisings. In the Ukraine, Byelorussia, and the Baltic countries, 1,250,000 Jews were massacred. In Byelorussia more than 66 percent of the Jewish population was destroyed; in the Ukraine, 60 percent; in the Baltic states, no less than 90 percent.

France. On 10 May 1940 the Germans launched a blitzkrieg against Belgium; some days later on Holland; and on 17 May on France. In mid-June 1940 Hitler entered Paris and divided France into two parts: one part occupied by the Germans and another ruled by a pro-Nazi government in Vichy. When the Germans attacked, most Jews in Paris and other cities fled to southern France. Approximately

120,000 Jews were trapped under Nazi rule. On 4 October the police arrested and sent to forced labor camps 25,000 "foreign" Jews who were refugees from Nazi-occupied countries. Many Jews died in those camps of starvation, cold, sickness, and injuries. In July 1941 the Jews and their property in Vichy were registered.

In Nazi-occupied France the Jews were forced to wear armbands with the Star of David. Many were seized for slave labor in the camp at Drancy, near Paris. On 28 March 1942 the first transport of Jews from Drancy was sent to Auschwitz. In mid-July around 13,000 foreign Jews were rounded up. The younger and healthier Jews were sent to Drancy; the rest were deported to Poland to die in the gas chambers. Jews who were caught in hiding places or who were known to be in the Resistance were shot on the spot. After the liberation of France in August 1944, 260,000 Jews were left. Ninety thousand French Jews had been annihilated.[35]

Belgium and Holland. The Germans invaded Belgium and Holland on 10 May 1940. In the former, there were some 90,000 Jews; in the latter around 140,000, including many refugees from Germany, Austria, and Czechoslovakia. One-fourth of the Jews in both countries fled to France. The Fascist Rexists in Belgium were more than willing to cooperate with the Nazis. In Holland the Nazis had fewer collaborators. Late in 1941 the Jews and their property were registered. At the beginning of 1942 the property was confiscated. In March many Jews were deported to camps in Poland. According to German records, more than 140,000 Jews were deported from Holland and Belgium to the death camps. Three-quarters of the Jews in those two countries perished.

One-third of the three thousand Jews in Luxembourg escaped to France. Most of the remainder were deported to Auschwitz. Some four hundred survived in hiding places.

Italy. In Italy there were about 57,000 Jews in 1938, including 10,000 refugees. Up until 10 June 1943, when the Allies landed in Sicily, the Fascist government had not deported any Jews to the death camps. After the landing in Sicily, however, the Nazis occupied large sections of the country and began deporting Jews. In October, a thousand Jews were rounded up and deported, but most Jews in Italy were hidden by their neighbors and survived. The Italian police succeeded in arresting some seven thousand Jews, many of whom died in prison even before they could be deported. Altogether, around eight thousand Italian Jews perished at the hands of the Nazis.[36]

Norway, Denmark, and Finland. Norway has a community of eighteen hundred Jews when the war began, including some three hundred refugees from Germany. Eight hundred Norwegian Jews were deported to Auschwitz, a few more than that escaped to Sweden, and Norway was *Judenrein*.

On 8 April 1940 the Germans occupied Denmark, where there were about eight thousand Jews, among them fifteen hundred refugees from Germany. Denmark remained under German rule, but with its own government and with some autonomy. Up until 1943 the Danish government refused to cooperate with the Nazis in carrying out any anti-Jewish decrees. In October 1943 the Nazis ousted the government and began sending Jews to concentration camps. Some four hundred Jews were placed in Theresienstadt; fifty-one of them died a "natural" death, the rest survived.[37]

In Finland, with about two thousand Jews, the government refused to carry out the German order to deport them or even restrict their rights. The small Jewish community of Finland escaped with nothing more than a bad scare.

Germany and Austria. When the Nazis came to power, Germany had a Jewish population of half a million. From 1933 to 1938, 150,000 Jews left the country. After the Kristallnacht pogrom in 1938 another 150,000 Jews fled. In Austria, at the time of the *Anschluss*, there were about 185,000 Jews, most of them in Vienna. Approximately 120,000 fled the country before the war began and another 6,000 Jews escaped before the end of 1939.

In 1940 the Nazis began deporting Jews from Germany and Austria to cities in Poland, to Riga in Latvia, and as far away as Minsk in Byelorussia. 40,000 Jews were deported to Theresienstadt. By May 1943, Berlin was *Judenrein*. At the end of the war, only 28,000 "racial" Jews remained in Germany, that is, those who stemmed from mixed marriages going back several generations.[38]

Czechoslovakia. In Bohemia and Moravia, the two provinces occupied by the Germans, there were about 118,000 Jews before the war. From March 1939, when the Germans occupied Czechoslovakia, to September, when the war began, some 26,000 Jews managed to escape from these two provinces, leaving around 90,000 under Nazi rule. Only 10,000 Czech Jews survived.[39]

When the Nazis took the two provinces, Hungary seized one part of Slovakia with 40,000 Jews, but 5,000 of them fled. Around 90,000 Jews were left in all of Slovakia, whose autonomous government collaborated with the Nazis; their police were organized on the model of the SS. In March 1942, 75 percent of the Jews in Slovakia were deported to death camps, mostly to Auschwitz. Only 10,000 survived.

Hungary. Hungary, with 650,000 Jews, was an ally of Germany from the beginning of the war. In 1941 the Hungarian army took part in the invasion of the Soviet Union. The government, however, was a little slow in implementing Hitler's order to deport Jews to death camps. In March 1944, when there was no longer any doubt about Germany's eventual defeat, the Nazis occupied Hungary. Along with the regular army came Eichmann and his SS. By 7 July 1944, 437,000 Jews had been deported to death camps, including 50,000 from Budapest alone. On 14 February 1945 the Red Army marched into Budapest and rescued 200,000 Jews who had been either hiding or fighting in the Resistance movement. A total of 450,000 Hungarian Jews perished.[40]

Rumania. At the beginning of the war, in which Rumania claimed to be neutral, there were 750,000 Jews in the country, including the 150,000 in Bessarabia. With the seizure of power by the Iron Guard, a series of pogroms took place and many Jews were deported to labor camps. At the end of 1940 the Jews of Rumania were registered. In 1941 a civil war erupted between the Rumanian army and the Iron Guard, with the Fascists taking advantage of the chaos to carry out pogroms. In Bucharest alone, 170 Jews were killed.[41]

In June 1941 the army, now allied with Germany, participated in the invasion of the Soviet Union. Rumanian anti-Semites joined the *Einsatzgruppen* in murdering tens of thousands of Jews in Bessarabia and the towns of the Ukraine. In the summer of 1942, Gustav Richter, one of Eichmann's aides, came to Rumania to supervise the deportation of the Jews. However, the Rumanian leaders were no longer in a hurry to carry out their obligations. General Antonescu advised Himmler that instead of deporting the Jews to the camps, he would rather permit them to buy their way out and let them emigrate. In 1943 negotiations took place between Rumania and Jewish leaders, but with no result. Of the 600,000 Rumanian Jews outside of Bessarabia, 300,000 were murdered by the Nazis and their Rumanian collaborators. An equal number survived.[42]

Bulgaria. Early in the war, although Bulgaria was supposedly neutral, its government—in exchange for certain territories—permitted German army units to pass through the country on the way to

Greece and later also to Italy. By the end of 1941, Bulgaria was an ally of Germany. At that time Bulgaria had a Jewish population of 50,000, plus 14,000 in annexed areas. Until the Nazis took over Germany there was no marked anti-Semitism in Bulgaria. After that, the social climate in Bulgaria also became poisoned, but there was a large and influential group of people in the country who actively fought against nazism. The agreements with Eichmann's aides to deport the Jews were not carried out. From the annexed territories, 14,000 Jews were deported to death camps. Almost all the original 50,000 Bulgarian Jews survived.[43]

Yugoslavia. On 6 April 1941 a combined attack by Germany, Italy, Bulgaria, and Hungary was launched against Yugoslavia. Many Serbs and Croatians fled to the forests and organized partisan units, which then received arms from England and the Soviet Union. Before the war there were 72,000 Jews in Yugoslavia. As in most Balkan countries, anti-Semitism was minimal until the 1930s. In October 1940, while Yugoslavia was still neutral, several anti-Jewish laws were adopted.

Soon after the Nazi invasion, most Jewish males in Belgrade and other cities were arrested and put into camps. Since the death camps were not yet operating, five thousand Jews were shot in a few days. In December 1941 the Jewish women and children were also locked up in the camps. Many were later killed. Serbian Fascists searched out several hundred hidden Jews and turned them over to the Nazis. In August 1942, nine thousand Jews were deported to Auschwitz. Of the 45,000 Jews in Serbia and Croatia, 26,000 were murdered by the Nazis. In March 1945 the Red Army entered Yugoslavia. Many Jews who had been fighting in the partisan brigades survived.

Greece. In May 1941 Germany occupied Greece, which then had a Jewish population of 76,000. The younger Jews were rounded up for labor camps. In mid-August 1942 they were sent to several of the islands to dry out the malaria swamps. Many died there.[44] In February 1943 Eichmann's aides arrived in Greece. The following month the Jews in Salonika and Thrace were deported to death camps. In October, SS General Strupp ordered all the remaining Jews in the country to register on pain of death. For hiding a Jew, the punishment was immediate execution. Many hidden Jews were thus discovered and deported to Auschwitz. A total of 60,000 Greek Jews were killed by the Nazis.[45]

**ESTIMATED NUMBER OF JEWS KILLED
IN THE FINAL SOLUTION**

Country	Estimated pre-Final Solution Population	Estimated Jewish Population Annihilated	
		Number	*Percent*
Poland	3,300,000	3,000,000	90
Baltic countries	253,000	228,000	90
Germany/Austria	240,000	210,000	90
Protectorate	90,000	80,000	89
Slovakia	90,000	75,000	83
Greece	70,000	54,000	77
The Netherlands	140,000	105,000	75
Hungary	650,000	450,000	70
SSR White Russia	375,000	245,000	65
SSR Ukraine*	1,500,000	900,000	60
Belgium	65,000	40,000	60
Yugoslavia	43,000	26,000	60
Rumania	600,000	300,000	50
Norway	1,800	900	50
France	350,000	90,000	26
Bulgaria	64,000	14,000	22
Italy	40,000	8,000	20
Luxembourg	5,000	1,000	20
Russia (RSFSR)*	975,000	107,000	11
Denmark	8,000	—	—
Finland	2,000	—	—
Total	8,861,800	5,933,900	67

* The Germans did not occupy all the territory of this republic.

From *The War Against the Jews* by Lucy S. Dawidowicz. © 1975 by Lucy S. Dawidowicz. Reprinted by permission of Holt, Rinehart and Winston, Publishers.

30

Jew-Hatred in the Soviet Union

Immediately after the February revolution in 1917, the Provisional Government in Russia abolished the Pale of Settlement and all other restrictions against Jews. Many Jews settled in previously forbidden cities. They entered factories, schools, universities. Jewish political parties were legalized. There was a rapid development of Jewish publishing of all kinds. The October Revolution continued this equality of Jewish rights. With Poland seceding from the Russian Empire and appropriating parts of the Ukraine, the six million Jews of Russia were split in half, three million remaining in Poland and a half million in each of the Baltic countries and Bessarabia, which Rumania had seized during the war.[1]

The protracted conflict of 1914–18, the civil war, and the "Military Communism" introduced by the Bolshevik regime had left Russia's economy severely impaired. In addition, the military dictatorship and the terror of the Cheka led to peasant revolts against the Soviet government, especially in the Ukraine. The March 1921 mutiny of the Kronstadt sailors alarmed the Soviet leaders. In that rebellion one could again hear the familiar anti-Semitic slogans of the White Guardists—the new system was the work of the damn Jews!

Even worse than the situation of the general population was that of the Jews. The problem of anti-Semitism sharply confronted the fledgling Soviet government, which issued strict laws against the dissemination of anti-Semitism, condemning it as counterrevolutionary. Lenin never deviated from the principle that nationalism is an obstacle in the path of socialism. Nor did he ever question the thesis concerning the Jewish Labor Bund, which he himself had propounded at the Russian Social Democratic Party convention in 1903: ". . . the absolutely inconsistent idea (in a scientific sense) that there is a separate Jewish people is a reactionary one. . . ." Moreover, "the Jewish question is indeed one of assimilation or isolation. The idea of a Jewish nationality bears a clearly reactionary character not only among Zionists but also among those who wish to couple it with the Social Democratic camp."[2]

However, in order to satisfy the minorities with whom he wished to stay at peace during the civil war, Lenin temporarily permitted a certain degree of expression and development among the non-Russian peoples in the country. Accordingly, the Jews were also permitted to designate themselves as a national group with special cultural rights.

But the economic condition of the Jews was far worse than that of the rest of the population. The "productive" elements among the Jews—the factory workers and handicraftsmen—began adapting themselves to the new system. Most of the Jews in the Soviet Union, the merchants, the petty traders, and the unemployed, together with the various Jewish religious functionaries, were officially labeled unproductive and became *lishentses* or people without rights, which automatically meant without any means of livelihood. In the early 1920s there were more than a million such declassed Jews in the Soviet Union.[3] The New Economic Policy (NEP) temporarily eased the plight of these people, but it was not long before hundreds of thousands of Jews were soon without means of support again.

In 1921–22 several thousand Jewish families began to occupy themselves with farming in the villages near their home towns in the Ukraine and Byelorussia. Several thousand others moved to the Kherson area and the Crimea, where Jewish colonies had been in existence since the days of the czar. In 1924 the *Komzet* was established with a plan to settle at least 100,000 Jewish families on the soil. However, because of the insufficiency of land and the scarcity of farm equipment, only a small percentage stayed. More than half of the 2.5 million Jews in the Soviet Union remained declassed and uprooted. Many of them emigrated. Some died. Most of them eventually adjusted themselves to the new economic system. A considerable number of younger Jews went into the army, the police, or the Party leadership. In the 1920s, Jews felt no interference with their participation in any facet of activity, at least from official sources.

In 1929 the Soviet government designated Birobidjan, an area along the Far Eastern Chinese border, as a Jewish Autonomous Region. In time, when it acquired a Jewish majority, it was to become a Jewish Socialist Republic. The goal was a hundred thousand Jews in ten years. The conditions for Jewish settlement in this region were extremely difficult. The harsh climate, the intractable terrain, the absence of living quarters, the lack of farm machinery, all created a situation which led most of the immigrants to give up and leave.[4]

The guardians of Jewish cultural life in the Soviet Union were the *Yevsekes*, loyal Communist Party people who watched over the "line" promulgated from above. The ideological leadership of the *Yevsektsie* isolated Soviet Jewry from Jewish communities in the rest of the world. Yiddish schools were indeed established where Jewish children were taught reading, writing, arithmetic and science in the Yiddish language. But "Jewish history" began with the Russian Revolution, and the curriculum was generally devoid of Jewish content. Jewish parents preferred to send their children to Russian or Ukrainian schools, where they were better prepared for future careers.

The entire traditional Jewish way of life, including holidays and customs of a folk or secular nature, were declared counterrevolutionary and anti-Soviet. Religious education of the young was strictly forbidden. As a result, a generation of assimilated Jews arose in the Soviet Union without a spiritual physiognomy, divorced from its Jewish historical roots and values. In the census of 1897, 97 percent of the Jews in Russia had listed Yiddish as their mother tongue. In 1926 only 70 percent gave Yiddish as their language; by 1959 only 18 percent; in 1970 the percentage as almost the same.[5]

In general, however, the situation of the Jews who adapted themselves to the new system was no worse than that of the rest of the population. Together with everyone else they suffered and helped to "build socialism." Anti-Semitic propaganda was illegal, and during the first dozen years or so, this law was more or less enforced. Jew-hatred, which had previously been such a widespread phenomenon, was not too visible. Up until the end of the 1920s the Soviet government conducted educational campaigns against anti-Semitism, so whatever Jew-hatred existed among the populace was mostly concealed. This was the situation until Joseph Stalin seized control of the Party and government.

Then, very gradually, official agencies began to overlook and hush up anti-Semitic incidents. As early as 1926, the Moscow Party leader, Uglanov, instructed the agitation and propaganda cadres to wage a struggle against the influence of "alien elements" in the party—meaning Trotsky, Zinoviev, Kaminiev—all Jews.[6] Stalin himself was extremely skillful in concealing his criminal plans from the eyes of strangers. The British writer, H. G. Wells, a man of wide experience and hardly naive, had a long conversation with Stalin in 1934. Later that year he wrote: "I am convinced that it was not through fear that he attained his high position, but because people trust him and no one fears him."[7] In 1931 Stalin granted an interview to a representative of the Jewish Telegraphic Agency. Replying to a question about anti-Semitism, Stalin said: "Anti-Semitism is a serious crime against our system. It is a remnant of cannibalism."[8] This interview, widely printed in the world press, did not appear in any Soviet newspaper. No one in the USSR even heard that Stalin had equated anti-Semitism with cannibalism.

In 1932, when the internal passport system was introduced into the Soviet Union, Point 5 of the passport regulations concerned itself with nationality. From that time on, the word *Yevrei* ("Jew") had been recorded on the identity cards of Jews. This results, on the one hand, in discrimination against Jews, and on the other, in favoritism to members of other nationalities in their own regions.

During the 1930s, Stalin sent hundreds of thousands of innocent citizens into Siberian exile, "criminals" whose guilt consisted only in expressing independent opinions, or even in having held a heretical view two decades earlier. Among these victims were tens of thousands of prominent Jews accused of "Trotskyism" or nationalism.[9] They were arrested and they vanished. Dr. Israel Zinberg, author of the classic *Di geshikhte fun literature by Yidn* ("History of Jewish Literature"), disappeared this way, as did the gifted poets Moishe Kulbak and Izzy Charik, the writer Isaac Babel, and the lexicographer Zalman Reisin. Some of the most loyal *Yevsekes*, devoted Bolsheviks like Moishe Litvakov, Esther Frumkin, Shimon Dimanstein, and many other dedicated followers of the "line," disappeared one after the other and became non-people.

By the end of the 1930s the Jewish national rights which had been permitted up until this point were denied openly and cynically. Jewish institutions were shut down one after the other. Stalin began to regard the Jews as enemies of the Soviet Union. His daughter related that when she told her father she was going to marry a Jew, he considered it a subversive act.[10] A Soviet official who defected to

Canada, Igor Guzenko, said that in 1939, secret instructions were issued by Moscow to establish quotas for Jewish students in the universities.[11]

After the Stalin-Hitler Pact, when the Red Army took over sections of Poland and the Baltic countries, the Soviet government shut down the Jewish children's schools, teachers' seminaries, scholarly institutions, and all other organizations which Jews had built in those areas. Prominent Jewish leaders were arrested.

When Hitler's armies invaded the Soviet Union, almost a million Jews fled toward the hinterland. Masses of Jews joined the Red Army. In battle and behind enemy lines, they displayed exemplary courage. Nevertheless, throughout the Soviet Union and in the ranks of the Red Army itself, anti-Semites spread lies about Jews evading military service. The Soviet press never attempted to expose these rumors, allowing them to sink deeper and deeper into the popular mind. Ilya Ehrenburg, the most widely read Soviet war correspondent, related that during the war, Cherbakov, Stalin's aide, instructed him to play down Jewish participation in the Red Army and among the Partisans.[12]

After the war, the Jews in the Soviet Union were condemned to total assimilation and eventual disappearance as a cultural and ethnic entity. The Yiddish publishing house *Emess* was shut down. The last Yiddish newspaper, *Eynikayt*, ceased publication. The Yiddish tongue grew mute. In 1948 a roundup of Jewish writers, teachers, cultural workers, actors, and scholars, took place. The most prominent Yiddish authors vanished without explanation. The world-renowned actor Solomon Mikhoels was maneuvered into a back street in Minsk and "accidentally" run over by a truck.[13] Throughout the world Jews began to ask worried questions, but no one in the Soviet Union had an answer. Rumors continued to spread, and Jews outside the USSR began to protest.

This did not stop Stalin's anti-Jewish campaign. The Soviet press began carrying stories which put Jews in an increasingly bad light. On 12 August 1952, in a Moscow prison, twenty-six of the most distinguished Yiddish writers in the Soviet Union were shot to death, among them David Bergelson, Peretz Markish, Itzik Feffer, and Leyb Kvitko.[14] By the end of that year Stalin had arrived at the decision to transport all the Jews in the European areas of the USSR to specially prepared concentration camps in Siberia. Like all other such decrees which the Soviet despot dreamed up, this one, too, was to have been implemented under some sort of deceitful pretext.

On 13 January 1953 Harrison Salisbury telegraphed the *New York Times* from Moscow:

> *Pravda* had published an urgent news item which electrified the populace. The Government had arrested nine of the most prominent physicians in the Kremlin, on charges of plotting to assassinate the political and military leaders of the country. The names of the criminals are: Vinogradov, Wafsi, Kagan, Klein, Feldman, Greenstein, Ettinger, Yagarov and Meyerov, six of them Jews. The doctors are agents of foreign governments; most of them were connected with the Jewish Joint Distribution Committee.[15]

Everyday, newspapers in all parts of the USSR featured reports of arrested "saboteurs." Wherever names were listed, most of them were Jewish. Where the last name did not sound Jewish enough, the patronymic was included. The insanity reached an advanced stage. On 21 January a feature article in *New Times* stated that "the entire Zionist movement has sold itself to American imperialism. . . . They are creating a Fifth Column in the Soviet Union and other socialist countries."[16]

In February the accused doctors "confessed." It was clear that some drastic step was about to be taken by the Soviet government. But in early March, Stalin died. The doctors were released, the charges against them dismissed as complete fabrications. On 8 June 1953 the *New York Times* printed a story attributed to the Soviet ambassador in Poland. It has a plausible ring to it, bizarre as it is:

> In late February Stalin summoned the Presidium of the Soviet Communist Party and informed them that as a result of the Zionist-imperialist plot, he was preparing to deport all the Jews of European Russia to Siberia. The Presidium members sat there dumbfounded. The first to speak up was Kagonovich, who asked hesitantly whether this included all Jews or would there be exceptions.
>
> In a trembling voice Molotov said that such an act would produce a bad reaction in the world. It would not be to the credit of the Soviet Union. Marshal Voroshilov jumped up, threw his Party card on the table and expostulated: "If this monstrous thing is carried out I will be ashamed to remain a Party member!"
>
> In a rage, Stalin shouted at Voroshilov: "Comrade Clementi, I will be the judge of whether you are fit to be a member of the Party or not!" As he uttered these words, Stalin fell to the floor unconscious.
>
> The irony is that Stalin's personal physicians, who had always been

within call, were now all in prison. It took some time before a doctor was located. Stalin never regained consciousness. On March 5th he died.

At the Twentieth Congress of the Soviet Communist Party, on 24 February 1956, Nikita Khrushchev recited a long list of crimes which Joseph Stalin had committed against citizens of the Soviet Union going back to the 1930s and continuing beyond World War II. There was not a single word in this report about crimes committed by Stalin against Jews and Jewish culture.

The change in leadership from Stalin to Khrushchev and later to Brezhnev brought very little difference in matters relating to Jews. The laws which Stalin had introduced to suppress Jewish identity— the Jewish schools that had been closed, the publications that had been stopped, the Yiddish theaters that had been shut down—none of this was corrected. On the contrary, new hardships were added.

From 1961 to 1964 approximately two hundred fifty individuals were sentenced to death in the Soviet Union for "economic crimes." Fifty-four percent of them were Jews. In the Ukraine it was 80 percent. The names of the Jewish "criminals" were widely publicized on the radio and in the press.

New ways of harassing Jews were devised. Kosher slaughtering of animals was prohibited; religious articles were unobtainable, nor was their importation permitted. Synagogues were closed on the pretext that Jews conducted business there. In 1957 government-owned bakeries stopped baking matzos. In 1958 this regulation was extended to all of the Ukraine. From 1959 to 1963 the baking of matzos was prohibited anywhere in the Soviet Union.

In the 1950s and 1960s anti-religious books directed at Judaism in particular appeared. In 1962 an eighteenth century work by Paul Holbach was reprinted. The thesis of the book was that in the course of eighteen hundred years, Christianity had corrupted all the European peoples, and since Judaism had been such a strong influence on Christianity, obviously the faults of the latter stemmed from the former. The book was published in 75,000 copies that were distributed throughout the USSR.[17]

In 1963 a book called *Catechism without Embellishment* by A. Osipov was published in an edition of 105,000. The message of this book is that the Jewish God is the biggest murderer in history and the Jews have been his instrument. The same year saw the publication of Trofim Kichko's infamous *Judaism without Embellishment*, the essence of which is not the text but the accompanying drawings. Taken from Christian liturgical books of the Middle Ages, they feature the odious figure of the hooknosed Jew, the same caricatures which the Nazi Julius Streicher used in his *Sturmer*. Sharp criticism of the Kichko book came from distinguished world figures such as Bertrand Russell and a number of Communist leaders. Eventually it was withdrawn from circulation and an unfavorable critique even appeared in the Soviet press. Kichko, however, was not removed from his position as professor of scientific studies. Four years later he was rewarded for his "scholarly" work by public recognition and a handsome prize.[18] In 1964 came the Mayatsky pamphlet, "Contemporary Judaism and Zionism," which led the British writer Emanuel Litvinoff to observe: "The Soviet Union has become the leading supplier of anti-Semitic material in the world."[19]

Since 1929 no one in the USSR has been punished for disseminating anti-Semitic propaganda, although it is officially against the law. Jews have been excluded from leadership of the country; there is not one Jew in the Politburo, in the Army high command, in the diplomatic corps, except for Benjamin Dimshitz, the token Jew. Stalin's plan of expunging Jews from the "apparat" has been fulfilled.

Jewish culture in the Soviet Union has been condemned to disappearance. There is no legal way for Jews there to learn their language or traditions or their history. The old books and periodicals from Czarist times and even from the early years of the Soviet system have been hidden from the public. Even the *Soviet Encyclopedia* of 1932, with its one hundred sixty columns on "Jews," and an extensive bibliography, is accessible only to authorized researchers.[20] In the 1952 *Encyclopedia* the entry on "Jews" was down to four columns, or one-fortieth of its original length. In the 1975 edition, it was down to two columns. Jewish newspapers and magazines from abroad are not permitted in the country. The magazine *Sovetish Heymland*, though printed in the Yiddish language, has very little Jewish content. Most of its 25,000 monthly copies probably go for foreign distribution.[21] Even if *Sovetish Heymland* were to print a reply to anti-Semitic lies (as has happened once or twice) such a criticsm would never be reprinted or even mentioned in other Soviet periodicals. The publication itself has nothing but exaggerated praise for the treatment of Jews in the Soviet Union.

That *Sovetish Heymland* is published mainly as a means of mollifying opinion abroad can be seen from a comment by minister of culture Furtseva in 1961 to Andrei Blumel, head of the French Society of Friends of the Soviet Union. "If the Soviet government does anything for Jewish culture," she said, "it is not for domestic purposes but to satisfy our friends abroad."[22] Soviet leaders and their apologists continue to mouth the lie that Soviet Jews no longer need or want Jewish culture, that they are already fully assimilated. But two years after Khrushchev told J. B. Salzberg that the Jews in the Soviet Union did not want Yiddish culture, the deputy minister for culture, Danilov, boasted to a French-Jewish delegation that in 1957 three million Soviet Jews attended Jewish concerts. When Dr. Haim Sloves, a member of the delegation, immediately responded that this was contradictory to the official view that Soviet Jews were not interested in Jewish culture, Danilov stammered: "We shall solve the problem . . . have patience . . . things will normalize themselves. . . ."

The oppressive attitude of the Soviet government toward Jewish culture is evident when one looks at other minority cultures in the USSR. The Yakuts, for example, totaling 250,000 people, have their own grade schools and scores of newspapers in their own language, as do the Tatars and the Chukchi, a people of perhaps 20,000. Everyone except the Jews seems to have certain cultural rights.

The mass grave at Babi Yar, near Kiev, had no memorial stone for thirty years; now the inscription says only that "people" are buried there, victims of facism. It is forbidden to mention the word "Jews" on a public symbol. On the wall of a house in Kiev, Number 5 Red Army Street, there was a plaque in the 1930s: "Here lived a great Jewish writer, Sholem Aleichem." Today the house still has a plaque, but it says: "Here lived a great writer, Sholem Aleichem."[23]

In the "Socialist" Soviet Union one must avoid such terms as "anti-Jewish," which is too reminiscent of nazism. So Soviet leaders are not against Jews as such; they are merely combatting an international counterrevolutionary movement called "Zionism," an "important weapon in the hands of the imperialists." Even before 1967 there was an anti-Israel campaign in the Soviet Union, with newspaper stories about Arabs being herded into ghettos, and such. But after the Israeli military victory in 1967 the anti-Semitic wave in the Soviet Union mounted higher than ever. "Zionism," wrote *Pravda*, "is today the most dangerous weapon of the imperialist West. Zionism is the bloody enemy of the working class, of all the people in the world."[24]

Zionism is so often linked with fascism and nazism in Soviet writing that the terms have become synonymous. Soviet newspapers refer to Israelis as "Zionist murderers. . . . Tel Aviv fascists. . . . Israeli Nazis. . . . Hitlerite military leaders of Israel. . . ." On 16 June 1967, *Izvestia* published an interview with an Italian reporter who had just returned from Cairo. The reporter wrote: "Israeli troops doused Egyptian prisoners with gasoline and set them afire."[25] The name of the reporter is not given.

Horror stories like these were printed in all the Soviet newspapers. From these sources the hate propaganda was reprinted by Soviet papers from Arab sources. The stories were then reprinted and rebroadcast in Poland, Hungary, East Germany, and other Socialist countries. The result was a raucous chorus of hate. Soviet professors dragged out the old, discredited anti-Semitic *Protocols of the Elders of Zion*. In the 4 October 1967 issue of *Komsomolskaya Pravda*, Yevgeny Yevseyev "revealed" the source of all the evils in the world, as excerpted below.

The war clouds of the Israeli aggressors are being spread with the help of a mighty empire. This empire is invisible but it exists and is a powerful force. It is the power of capitalist barons and Zionist industrialists, but you will not find it on any map. . . . Even a superficial knowledge of the activities of Zionist organizations in various countries reveals the imperialist nature of Zionism. . . . There are between 20 and 25 million Zionist sympathizers in the United States alone, Jews and non-Jews. . . . Around 70% of all American lawyers are Zionists; 69% of the physicists engaged in secret preparation of weapons of mass destruction are Zionists. 43% of the industrialists in America and 80% of American news agencies are Zionists. 56% of the large publishers serve Zionist ends. . . .

The Zionists can very easily turn public opinion in many countries in whatever direction they wish, since they publish 1036 newspapers and magazines throughout the world. . . . Among the leading Zionists you could not find one worker, one peasant, one handicraftsman. They are all merchants, bankers, senators, or even members of the highest courts in America. . . .

There is really no difference between the Zionist preachers of "racial purity" and the American racists. . . . The president of one of the most reactionary Zionist organizations, B'nai B'rith, publicly expressed support for the activity of American racists. . . . [26]

Komsomolskaya Pravda comes into the homes of millions of Komsomol members, the largest youth organization in the Soviet Union.

In the leading theoretical journal *International Affairs*, two Marxist scholars named Beleyev and Frumakov explain the "Lessons of the 1967 War in the Middle East":

> On the surface it might appear that the Israeli aggressors attacked their Arab neighbors because they wished to secure their own existence. But this was not the case. National features were indeed present in the war, but they were not the essential thing. The main object of the aggressors was to destroy the progressive-national regimes that had come to power in the Arab lands. . . . The Soviet Union was alert and did not permit this to happen.[27]

Early in 1969 a book was published by Yuri Ivanov, another "specialist" on Zionism, with the "scholarly" title, *Beware: Zionism!* Repeating essentially what Yevseyev had said, Ivanov's book was issued in 75,000 copies and reviewed enthusiastically by leading Soviet periodicals. One year later a second edition of 200,000 copies was printed and the book was translated into Polish, German, Hungarian, and Czech.[28]

In 1970 two anti-Semitic novels appeared, written by Ivan Shevtsov. The first one, *In the Name of the Father and the Son*, was issued in 65,000 copies. *Komsomolskaya Pravda* attacked the book as vulgar, a banal collection of filth, poison for the young. The Central Committee of the Communist Party rejected this criticism. The facts in the book, they argued, are true. The author has a great deal to say about the international Zionist conspiracy, including the "fact" that Trotsky (the Jew Bronstein) was actually a Zionist agent, an international provocateur exposed by Stalin.

Shevtsov's second book, *Love and Hate*, was issued in 200,000 copies—by the Ministry of Defense! The negative characters in this novel have typical Jewish names. One of them, Nahum Holtzer, rapes women, deals in drugs, and murders his mother by slashing open her belly and strangling her with her own intestines. In the course of the story he reminds the reader that Trotsky-Bronstein was associated with Fanya Kaplan, who shot Lenin in 1919.[29]

In an interview in France at the end of 1966, when Soviet premier Kosygin announced that the Soviet government would permit members of separated families to join their relatives abroad, the Department of Emigration was inundated with applications of thousands of Soviet Jews for visas to Israel. Soviet Jewish citizens found, however, that when they applied for exit visas to Israel, they were automatically deprived of all their civil rights, dismissed from their jobs, expelled from universities. If the family had recently been granted better living quarters, they were evicted. This did not mean that the application was thereby approved. The visa application was usually rejected and the family was left stranded.

In 1970 the secret police in Leningrad arrested twelve Jews who, according to the official charge, were planning to hijack an airplane and fly it to Israel. That the whole idea of hijacking the plane was the brainchild of an informer became clear when the police, less than an hour after the arrest of the twelve people in Leningrad, conducted searches and arrested scores of people in many cities across the Soviet Union, as if on a pre-arranged schedule. All the searches were made in the homes of Jews who had applied fo visas to Israel.[30]

With the possibility of détente between the two great powers, the Soviet government in the early 1970s permitted several thousand Jews to leave. But in 1971 the authorities invoked a new law: Jews who wished to emigrate must repay the thousands of rubles it had cost the government for their education. Protests from abroad resulted in a relaxation of the law.

In 1972, in Yuri Kalesnikov's book, *The Promised Land*, Soviet readers are told about a rabbi who runs a brothel where Zionist bankers, manufacturers and wealthy merchants hold their conspiratorial meetings. The *London Jewish Chronicle* labeled this book "unbridled anti-Semitism." But on 2 October 1974 the Soviet weekly *Ogonyuk* carried an article by Dmitri Zhukov which went beyond anything the Russian anti-Semites—and even the Nazis—had ever invented about Jews. Among other things, Zhukov "disclosed":

> Zionism is a reactionary ideology. The Zionist organizations are similar to the gangster organizations in America: they liquidate their shaky elements, they are strictly conspiratorial, and they obey their leaders blindly. Their activity, however, is not confined to Chicago, nor to any one country, but to the entire capitalist world. At the end of the last century, a significant majority of the capital and industry in the developed countries fell into the hands of the Jewish bourgeoisie.
>
> The foundation of Zionism always was and remains the Jewish religion. The Zionists start with the theory that God selected the Jews to be His chosen people. The Talmud taught religious Jews to hate "the goyim"—to swindle them wherever they could and, if possible, to destroy them. It is this, indeed, which now inspires the Zionist hoodlums to "heroic deeds," to wipe entire settlements off the map, to have no mercy on women and children, to rape little girls, to force

defenseless Arabs to crawl on their hands and knees for hours at a time.

With the Jews being raised from early childhood to have this arrogant attitude toward "goyim," and to believe that they would eventually conquer the whole world, it has often led to persecutions and attacks upon the Jews themselves.

The Zionists distributed a brochure in London. The brochure was accompanied by a map bearing the caption, "Israel As It Will Look in the Near Future." On this map the borders of Israel include Lebanon, Syria, the entire Arab peninsula, and also areas of Iraq west of the Euphrates River. In Israeli schools the children are taught that God promised them in the Bible: "And you shall consume all the peoples that the Lord your God delivers unto you; your eye shall not pity them."

The effrontery and the predatory strivings of the Zionists depend on the fact that the largest part of industry, commerce and the means of communication in the capitalist countries is subservient to the Zionist bourgeoisie. In the United States alone, the Zionists receive more than a billion dollars a year in the form of technical military equipment, and in unlimited quantities. In the post-war years, 70 billion dollars were extracted from the countries in Latin America. Three-quarters of this sum went to the monopolies that are run by the Zionist elite such as Lehman, Lazare, Bluestein, Stillman, Warburg, Guggenheim, Kahan, Lowe, Kuhn, Rosenwald and Schiff.[31]

The anti-Semitic slanders and brazen lies that are spread by the Soviet Union are accepted in many countries of the Third World as absolute truth. Together with similar material from the Arab countries, this is resulting in a new and extremely dangerous wave of anti-Semitism around the world. The anti-Israel expressions in the United Nations, the shameful resolution which was adopted in 1975, the pairing of Zionism with racism—none of this happened accidentally. The original source is in the Soviet Union. As early as 1971 the Soviet delegate at the United Nations, Yakov Malik, furious because the delegate from Israel had dared take the side of the Soviet Jews, screamed: "Why did the Israeli representatives have to mention Soviet Jews again? That is not your business, Mr. Tekoah. Don't stick your long nose into our Soviet garden."[32]

Anti-Zionism, the boycott against Israel and world Jewry, stem from the combination of Arab chauvinism and Soviet anti-Semitism. In addition to everything else, the bureaucracy in the

Soviet Union needs the Jews as a scapegoat, because of the difficult problems into which their system and their policies have led them. For the foreseeable future, therefore, they will continue to foster Jew-hatred and use it as a justification for their failures.

31

Anti-Semitism in the Soviet-Dominated Countries and the Third World

Jew-hatred in Poland, Czechoslovakia, and the other Soviet-dominated countries in the Balkans did not begin with the march of the Soviet Union into those areas after the defeat of Nazi Germany; it had been deeply rooted there for a long time. Up until World War I the Balkans were the powder-keg of Europe and the world. The borders established in that area after the war created difficult problems for national minorities. In 1939 the population of that part of Europe consisted of approximately 110 million. Of that number, some 22 million were minorities ruled by other peoples.[1] One of those minorities were the Jews.

In the mid-nineteenth century the peoples in that region had fought to liberate themselves from the Turks. The nationalism which was then already a characteristic of those ethnic groups led to bitter clashes among the Balkan peoples. These disputes frequently dragged in the Jews, many of whom were linguistically assimilated with the larger and stronger peoples. Jews who lived among the smaller and weaker peoples—Serbs, Bulgarians, Czechs, Slovaks— were accused of advocating linguistic assimilation. The result was that after the Nazi "final solution," only 750,000 Jews survived out of the five million who had lived in those countries. In Poland itself, only 50,000 Jews remained out of 3.3 million.[2]

After 1945, Poland, Rumania, Hungary, Yugoslavia, and Bulgaria were ruled by Communist governments. In February 1948 Czechoslovakia also fell under Communist rule. Despite the fact that there were very few Jews left in those countries, anti-Jewish attitudes continued to gain strength. Evidently anti-Semitism is not incompatible with socialism or communism. In addition, the peoples that are now ruled by Communist parties have their own special history of Jew-hatred.

In Czarist Russia, Jews were "foreigners" and interlopers. Lenin was not an anti-Semite. His view was, however, that the Jews are not a people.[3] This position was also adopted by his disciple Stalin, who was an anti-Semite, and given a "Marxist" foundation.[4] According to Stalin, the fact that "Jews stick together" proved they are not trustworthy citizens either of the Soviet Union or of the countries under its influence. The prominent Jewish Communist leaders of those countries—Berman in Poland, Rakosi in Hungary, Anna Pauker in Rumania, Rudolph Slansky in Czechoslovakia—all became a thorn in Stalin's side.

Before World War II the Communist parties in the smaller East European countries were weak, and in comparison with the indigenous ethnic groups, Jews (as liberals with universalist leanings) were disproportionately represented in those parties. Many Jews placed great hope in socialism as the salvation of all the peoples. Anti-Semitism, they believed, was a by-product of an unjust social order, of exploitation, of capitalism; socialism would bring the end of anti-Semitism along with all other injustices.

When the countries in Eastern Europe fell under Soviet influence, the Communist parties there recruited many new members. In Rumania, for example, the Communist Party grew from 1,000 in 1939 to 250,000 in 1948; in Hungary, from a few thousand to 250,000; in Czechoslovakia from 50,000 to 2.5 million.[5] Many of these new members were former Nazis or Fascists. In 1950, during the Cold War, a purge of these parties took place, but in line with Stalin's directive, it was mostly the democratic elements who were eliminated—former Social Democrats, liberals, many of whom were Jews. Generally, those who agreed with the hard line were not expelled.

Conditions in the Eastern European countries following the war were incredibly difficult. The result was a rising anti-Communist, anti-Moscow mood among the people, who began to look upon their own leaders, many of whom had spent the war years safely inside the Soviet Union, as Soviet agents. The underlying anti-Semitic prejudices had never disappeared. In 1945 and 1946, pogroms took place in Kielce (Poland), Slovakia, and Hungary. In Kielce, forty-three Jews were killed.

Jewish Communist leaders in these countries were doubly hated, as Jews and as Soviet agents. The Communist parties did nothing to combat this. The few surviving Jews in those countries began to leave. In 1952 alone, 300,000 Jews (out of 740,000) emigrated. In the fifteen years after 1952, a few hundred thousand more left. With the Arab-Israel war in 1967, Bulgaria, Czechoslovakia, and Yugoslavia became almost *Judenrein*. Some 25,000 Jews remained in Poland.

In his last years, when Stalin adopted a policy of outright anti-Semitism, he also turned his attention to the Jewish Communist leaders in the socialist countries. Investigators came from Moscow to ferret out the slightest disagreement with Stalin or the official line. "Heretics" were arrested, tried, and punished. Where such leanings could not be found, they were invented. The charges were usually Trotskyism, Titoism, espionage. Jewish "deviationists" were accused also of being Zionists.

In Bulgaria in 1951, the victim was Traicho Kostov, a leading Jewish Communist. In Hungary, in order to demonstrate his own loyalty, Matyas Rakosi (a Jew) fabricated a lie against his colleague, Laslo Raik (also a Jew) and sentenced him to death. In 1952 in Rumania, Anna Pauker, the Jewish secretary of the Party, was expelled from the Party. In Poland it was Jakub Berman, a leading Communist and a Jew. In Czechoslovakia, the Jewish secretary general of the Communist Party, Rudolph Slansky, was tortured and sentenced to death. In 1956, after the death of Boleslaw Bierut, leader of the Polish Communist Party, Khrushchev flew to Poland to advise them on a choice for secretary general. Roman Zambrowski, a long-time, dedicated Communist whom the Polish Politburo had chosen for the post, but who was of Jewish descent, was turned down by Khrushchev because "you already have too many Abramovitches."[6]

Poland. In 1961–62 Wladyslaw Gomulka, leader of the Polish party, agreed to keep a watchful eye on Jewish Communists there. A secret file was set up containing the records of all those with Jewish-sounding names. Offices were bugged. In 1965 he adopted a secret plan by which eventually not one Jew would remain in an important government post in Poland. As Premier Cyrankiewicz later ad-

mitted, this was all being done with the advice and approval of
Soviet leaders.[7] In 1966, more than a year before the hate campaign
that followed the Six Day War, a new edition of the *Protocols of the
Elders of Zion* was printed in Poland and distributed among
students in military academies and universities, army officers and
Party functionaries.[8]

One week after the Six Day War, on 19 June 1967, speaking to the
Trade Union Congress, Gomulka publicly labeled the Jews of
Poland a "fifth column." In order not to offend the Soviet Union,
Adam Mickiewicz's national drama, *Dziady* ("The Forefathers")
was ordered closed, even though it had been attracting large
audiences.[9] Students and liberals demonstrated in the streets against
this act of censorship. Several people were arrested, among them
eight Jews. There were only two hundred Jewish students among a
total student population of 270,000 in all of Poland's colleges and
universities, but the press featured most prominently the names of
the Jewish protesters as the "real instigators" of the unrest among
the students. *Trybuna Ludu*, organ of the Communist Party, wrote:

> It was enough to glance at the names of the ringleaders of the student
> riots—Szlaifer, Michnik, Blumsztain, Werfel, Lasota (alias Hirsz-
> owicz), Topolski (alias Toerman), etc.—to realize that most of the
> troublemakers were Zionists to whom the interests of the Polish
> nation are alien.[10]

ZBOWID (Union of Fighters for Freedom and Democracy)
organized "spontaneous" demonstrations of workers, peasants, city
neighborhoods, army personnel, and party members to protest
against the "Zionists." Kazimierz Kakol, editor of the Lawyers'
Association journal, accused the "Zionists" of having for years
"sucked the blood of the nation and the state."[11] The anti-Zionist
campaign grew more hysterical, even using anti-Semitic cartoons on
television. On 9 March 1968 Gomulka said in a speech:

> We are combating Zionism as a political program, as Jewish
> nationalism, and this is correct. This is quite different from anti-
> Semitism.[12]

The mood of the populace was such that a Yugoslav
correspondent wrote to his paper that after Gomulka's speech,
Zionism has become the number one problem for the Communist
Party of Poland. A joke current at the time was: What is the

difference between today's anti-Semitism and the anti-Semitism of the 1930s? Answer: Today it is obligatory.[13]

Several days after Gomulka's speech, six leading professors were dismissed from universities; four of them were Jews, the other two were known as liberals. All of them had supported the right of the students to protest the ban on Mickiewicz's play. In the space of a few months, hundreds of Jews were fired from important positions in the government, party, army, press, universities, hospitals, courts.[14] During the first seven or eight months of 1968 most of the Jewish government officials in Lodz were dismissed, as were Jewish weavers from the factories.

Hieronim Reniak, head of agitation and propaganda in Lodz, published two pamphlets on Zionism. In one of them he blamed former leaders of Jewish origin for the Stalinist terror in Poland prior to 1956.[15] In the other he confirmed the main thesis of the *Protocols* that Zionism is a world conspiracy to oppress the *goyim*. In the 12 May 1968 issue of *Glos Robotniczy* ("Workers' Voice"), a certain Piotr Goszcynski wrote an open letter to Golda Meir:

> Please answer my last worry: Is it true that your supreme commander, Moshe Dayan, is not Dayan at all but Otto Skorzeny, the well-known specialist in murder and kidnapping from Uncle Adolf's SS, hiding under the name of Dayan and concealing one of his eyes under an eye patch? Furthermore, Mrs. Meir, I have heard that—for a lot of money—you are hiding in your closet Hitler's deputy, Martin Bormann. Is this true?[16]

The author of this letter received a prize for "outstanding journalism."

An oppressive pall of Jew-hatred hung over Poland, which could easily be compared to the race hatred rampant in Germany thirty-five years earlier. In all the media the Zionists were accused of being a fifth column, agents of imperialism and of West Germany. Thrown our of their jobs, their children expelled from schools, frightened, and morally shattered, thousands of Jews submitted applications for visas to France, the United States, South America, and Israel. The Polish government refused to issue visas for any country but Israel. For this privilege, a Jewish emigrant had to sign a statement relinquishing Polish citizenship. Each visa cost 5,000 zloty (about two months' wages). In addition, there was air fare to Vienna, plus baggage charges. Arriving in Vienna, all the emigrant had left was about five American dollars (given to him by the Polish government) and a document showing that he was a man without a country.

By the end of 1969 more than 12,000 Jews had left Poland. From 1969 to 1975 another few thousand left. In Poland now are perhaps six thousand old, sick, and invalided Jews, most of them living on meager pensions. Many cities in Poland are completely *Judenrein*.[17]

Czechoslovakia. On 31 July 1951 the Czech Communist newspaper *Rude Pravo* printed, on page one, a letter of the Communist Party congratulating Rudolph Slansky, its secretary general, on his fiftieth birthday and praised him as an indefatigable fighter for communism ever since his youth. The newspaper called him "the most faithful collaborator of President Gottwald." On 17 August a factory was named for him. Less than four months later the same paper carried a brief announcement:

Hitherto unknown circumstances have recently been established which prove that Rudolph Slansky has been guilty of anti-State activities. He has been detailed for purposes of investigation.[18]

One year later he and thirteen other important leaders of the Party and government were convicted as "Titoist, Trotskyist, Zionist, bourgeois-nationalist traitors, enemies of the Czech people." Slansky and ten of the thirteen were hung on 3 December 1952.[19]

Ten years later, on 14 May 1963, the Czech Supreme Court announced that there never had been an anti-state, Zionist conspiracy in Czechoslovakia, that the "criminal acts" of which the fourteen leaders had been convicted were a frameup, that they and sixty other accused people were forced to confess by the use of physical and psychological pressure.[20]

The trial of Slansky and his comrades was undoubtedly anti-Semitic. The Jewish names were always prominently featured. Where the name was not Jewish-sounding enough, the Jewish name was added, for example: Ludvik Freika, alias Ludwig Freund; Rudolph Slansky, alias Saltzmann. The "Zionist traitors" had all "confessed" that they received assistance from Israel, America, France, and Yugoslavia. The initiative for the Prague trial came from the Soviet Union six weeks before the "Doctor's plot" was announced there. Soviet investigators, invited to purge the Czech Party of dangerous elements, came from Moscow and arrested a few people on "suspicion." President Gottwald, incredulous, was considering stopping the investigation. In November 1951, Anastas Mikoyan, a member of the Soviet Politburo, came to Prague with a message from Stalin: Arrest Slansky.[21]

Arthur London, the Jewish deputy minister who was later freed,[22] related that when he was arrested, the prison guard, a Communist, greeted him with these words:

> You and your dirty race, we shall eliminate you! You are all the same! Not everything that Hitler did was bad, because he killed the Jews and that was a good thing. Too many of you escaped the gas chambers. What he did not finish, we shall complete. We'll bury you ten meters under the earth—you and your filthy kind.[23]

The "Zionist conspiracy" trial was planned in Moscow, but the anti-Zionism remained in Czechoslovakia as an important component of a political program for the future, to be used when needed. Immediately after the outbreak of the Six Day War, the Czech government became one of the loudest agitators against the "Israeli aggressors." However, with the memory of the Slansky trial still lingering in the minds of many people, the exaggerated and false accusations against Israel and Zionism weighed heavily on the conscience of a large section of the Czech intelligentsia and led to the Czech political uprising of 1968.

At the writers' congress in June 1967 the Czech playwright Pavel Kohout compared the situation of Israel in May with the situation in Czechoslovakia in 1938 and he asked: "If in 1938 the Czechs, instead of capitulating, had fired the first shot, could they be regarded as the aggressors by fair-minded judges of this conflict?"[24] Ladisav Mnacko, prominent Czech writer, and not a Jew, flew to Israel and left a statement that his act was in protest against the disgraceful position of his government, against its pro-Arab, anti-Israel, and anti-Semitic declarations, which reminded him of the false accusations against Slansky in 1952, and that "the people responsible for the events of those days are still around."[25]

Mnacko's protest flight to Israel and his statement made a deep impression on the Czech people and throughout the world. Inside the country a mood of protest soon surfaced in violation of censorship regulations. The Novotny government tried desperately to stem this tide, but failed. In August the vice president of the American JOINT, Charles Jordan, on a visit to Prague, was found murdered. The press openly accused the government of anti-Semitism and murder. In January 1968, when the Communist Party removed Novotny from leadership and moved toward a more liberal position, the official Polish press accused the Czech Party of being dominated by Zionists and cosmopolitans.

Actually there were few Jews in Czechoslovakia and fewer in the Party or government. Early in 1968, during the period of liberalization, two Jews gained prominence—Dr. Frantisek Kriegal, who had fought in the Spanish Civil War, was elected to the Party presidium and Professor Eduard Goldstuecker, a literary critic, was elected chairman of the Writers' Union.

Goldstuecker, born in Slovakia in 1913, became a Communist in 1933 and spent the war years in England. After 1945 he was a professor of literature and a Party activist. From 1949 to 1951 he was ambassador to Israel. As one of the accused in the Slansky trial, he was sentenced to life imprisonment. After eight years, including two at hard labor in the uranium mines at Jachimov, he was released in 1960 and "rehabilitated," but he then became the target of Fascists inside the Communist Party. Of the many letters he received, he made one public to illustrate how low the counterrevolutionaries had sunk:

> Mr. Goldstuecker, rascal, Zionist hyena, on your birthday we send millions of curses on behalf not only of the working class of our country but also in the name of other socialist countries. . . . You should have been given the rope along with Slansky. Honest Communists know that you are a Western agent. We have photocopies of documents which we shall very soon put at the disposal of the competent authorities. . . . You can write your last will. You are the instigator of recent events, which you and your kind had prepared a long time ago. . . . You want to rule, you Jews, not only in Israel, but as a Zionist you wish to dominate the whole world. Don't worry, your time will come; your days are numbered, you filthy Jew.

In his reply to the letter, Goldstuecker commented:

> It may be the product of the pathological periphery of political life found in every country. But men of my generation cannot forget that it was in such a pathological atmosphere that, for example, the Nazi Party emerged. . . . I know its vocabulary, phraseology, and stylistic principles. It is the language of my investigators from Ruzyn in 1951–53, of my guards in 1953–55, of my indictment and the speech of the prosecutor.[26]

With the invasion of Czechoslovakia by a Soviet army on 20 August 1968 came a renewed campaign against Zionism. The hatred which had begun to appear among the Czechs against the Soviet Union was now diverted to the Jews. Anti-Semitism became a vital tool of the Communists in allaying popular anger against themselves. The most rabid anti-Zionist attacks came from East Germany. *Neues Deutschland*, a leading Communist newspaper, wrote:

> Zionist forces had captured the 1,700,000 member Czech Communist Party. . . . West Germany was actively assisting counterrevolutionary and Zionist forces in Czechoslovakia.[27]

A resolution of congratulations to the Soviet forces which had "saved Communism" was sent by the Ukrainian Writers Union, condemning "world imperialism and militant Zionism."[28] The Soviet newspaper *Izvestia* attacked the Czech foreign minister, Jiri Hajek, but the attack boomeranged. Soon after the Soviet troops invaded Czechoslovakia, Hajek addressed the United Nations and declared that the Soviet action was sudden and without the knowledge of the government or the Communist Party leadership. In response, the Soviet press accused Hajek of collaborating with the worst imperialist forces in the world, and furthermore, his name was not even Hajek, he was a Jew who had changed his name from Karpeles. The Austrian Communist *Folkstimme*, however, reported the next day that *Izvestia* had made a gross error of fact. Jiri Hajek was not a Jew and had never changed his name. They had confused him with another Hajek who had changed his name from Bedrich Karpeles and fought in the Czech liberation movement.

The campaign against the liberals and Zionists continued in the Soviet press with attacks on Goldstuecker, Kriegel, Hajek, and Sik. Ota Sik, an economist for the Czech government, replied with an open letter to the Prague newspapers and noted, among other things:

> It is shocking if one considers that the German fascists, who held me in the Mauthausen concentration camp for four years for illegal activity in the Communist movement, did not regard me as a Jew even according to their racial laws. Apparently the epithet "head of the counterrevolutionaries" is no longer effective and therefore new variants of a somewhat heavier caliber, appealing to the basest instincts, are resorted to, namely, that I am supposed to be a Zionist.[29]

On 1 October 1968, Alexander Dubcek, who was still premier, stated publicly that Soviet representatives had been trying to force the Czech government to stage trials of Kriegel and Goldstuecker.

At a press conference in Vienna, Simon Wiesenthal compared two anti-Semitic speeches, one written by Nazis in 1938 and the other by Communists in 1968, and he pointed out that if the words "Zionist" and "progressive forces" were replaced by "Jews" and "National Socialists," the speech heard on the East Berlin radio could easily be mistaken for one delivered by Goebbels, Hitler's propaganda minister.[30]

The technique of spreading the "Big Lie" became an art with the Soviet press, for which purpose they worked closely with the Arabs. For example, an Arab newspaper prints a piece of "authentic" news: eight West German doctors have come to Tel Aviv to sterilize Arabs. An East German paper reprints this "news" as a proven fact; several months later the Soviet radio broadcasts the same story in Arabic and "authenticates" it by citing the East German newspaper. Then the East German press reprints it with the introductory phrase, "as is well known."[31]

After Dubcek was removed in April 1969, Dr. Gustav Husak, a Slovakian patriot, became first secretary of the Czech Communist Party. Under his leadership the Party put a stop to criticism of anti-Semitism by the press, and the Prague Communist press itself now began publishing anti-Zionist propaganda, accusing the liberals of having connections with the Israeli aggressors.

Between August 1968 and February 1969 some thirty-five hundred Jews left Czechoslovakia. A small number of Jews remained in Prague. One Jewish writer described their situation: "Prague Jewry has become a tourist attraction, like the Indians on the U.S. reservations, like bears in some Central European countries whose species must be preserved for the sake of coming generations."[32]

The Third World. With the exception of the Arab countries in the Middle East, the North African countries, and several countries in South America, most of the underdeveloped nations of the world had no Jewish population, no Jewish problem, and no anti-Semitism. Yet a large majority of the delegates in the United Nations voted on 10 November 1975 for the anti-Semitic resolution which describes Zionism as a "form of racism." The resolution was approved by seventy-two nations with twenty-nine opposed, thirty-two abstentions, and three absent. Congressman Rosenthal of New York commented aptly that Hitler would have been very happy with the resolution and the vote.[33] Only three or four years earlier many of those countries had been on friendly terms with the Jewish state, having invited Israeli specialists to come and help develop their economies. Hundreds of Africans had gone to Israel to study various agricultural and organizational techniques. It was easy to turn to Israel, a small, independent nation, and the Jewish state met them halfway. In 1972, thirty-two underdeveloped nations received assistance from Israel.

As early as the 1950s it became evident that the USSR would try to influence the undeveloped countries. Lenin himself had written in 1920:

> Our policy must be to join with the national liberation movements throughout the world. If the European nations are late with their revolution, we shall awaken the national feelings among the colonial peoples for their liberation. This will weaken the imperalist nations. [And in 1923 he added:] The victory of Bolshevism throughout the world will depend largely on our cooperation with the Asian peoples. With their cooperation we shall win a hundred times more than we have lost in Europe.[34]

At the Bandung Conference of Third World nations in the mid-1950s, Israel—which had already been recognized by several of those governments *de jure*, and by others *de face*—was not present. U Nu of Burma was strongly in favor of inviting Israel. Representatives of Pakistan and Indonesia, both Islamic nations, warned that if Israel were invited, the Arab countries would boycott the conference. This argument won the day.

To counter this isolation, Israel began seeking ties with underdeveloped nations that had already achieved independence. The first success in this direction was with Ghana. Kwame Nkrumah, head of the Ghanian government, expressed gratification that the Israeli specialists who were working in his country did not act as if they owned it, nor were they above getting their hands dirty in the practical work.[35] In 1958 Nkrumah invited Golda Meir, then foreign minister of Israel, to a conference of African countries in Accra, capital of Ghana. Golda Meir's words made a good impression on the African leaders, and many of them established links with the State of Israel. In 1960 only six African countries were receiving help from Israel; by 1972 the number had risen to thirty-two.

Soon after the Bandung Conference, Khrushchev and Bulganin visited several countries of the Third World. In India, they said they had not come there to propagandize for communism, but only to seek friendship. In the underdeveloped nations the Soviet leaders emphasized that they were in absolute agreement with the principles of the Bandung Conference concerning peaceful coexistence among nations with differing economic systems. After 1955, when relations between the Arab countries and England and France were strained, and the United States was not willing or quick enough to fill that vacuum, the Soviet Union succeeded in establishing a foothold in the area.[36]

Knowing that the Arab peoples were still smarting from their defeat by Israel in 1948, the Soviet leaders launched a program of arming the Arabs for a new war. In Soviet propaganda the Arab governments suddenly became "progressive," virtually socialist. That these same Arab nations had supported the Nazis before and during World War II, that they had provided refuge for Nazi war criminals, and that thousands of Arab Communists and Socialists were rotting in their prisons did not seem to matter to the Soviet leaders. From 1955 until after the Arab-Israeli war in October 1973, the Soviet Union supplied the Arabs with massive quantities of modern weapons. Some estimates of this matériel range as high as $4.5 billion.[37]

After the Six Day War the Soviet-Arab campaign against Israel was stepped up and began to take effect in many of the underdeveloped nations, particularly where the population was Muslim. In the non-Islamic countries the process was slower. The help which Israeli technicians were giving acted as a buffer against this propaganda.

For over fifteen years the Arab countries waged a campaign to isolate the State of Israel. In this effort they have been aided by the Soviet Union and its Eastern European allies. In turn, with the help of the Arab countries, the prestige of the Soviet Union has risen among the underdeveloped nations and in the United Nations. Most of the Third World nations have no concept of Jewish history or Jewish claims to Israel and Jerusalem. In addition, the prism through which these nations see the Arab-Israeli conflict was that of anti-imperialism and anti-racism. They have been highly suspicious of white Europeans, their recent oppressors. And millions of radios in these countries have poured out an endless stream of pro-Soviet, anti-imperialist, and anti-Israel propaganda. The friendship which the Jewish state had earned for itself among those peoples during the 1960s slowly deteriorated. By the early 1970s, Israel found itself isolated from these former friends.[38]

At conferences of Third World nations during the 1960s and 1970s, more abusive resolutions were adopted against Israel, the most vitriolic one being at Algiers in September 1973. At that conference, last-minute, secret meetings of Arab leaders were held to plan their attack on Israel the following month. After the Yom Kippur War, the speeches of Third World delegates at the United Nations condemned Israel as the aggressor, but none of the Arab governments denied that they had planned and carried out the initial attack.[39] In 1974 many delegates of those countries at the United Nations applauded the Arab terrorist Yassir Arafat when he appeared before that body. In 1975 the shameful resolution labeling Zionism a form of racism was adopted.

Hostility toward Israel and Jews remains at high levels in Egypt, Syria, and other Arab countries. During the Six Day War, Israeli soldiers found hate propaganda in school textbooks in Jordan, Syria, and Egypt. When the question was asked at the United Nations as to why the minds of school children were being poisoned this way, the Syrian minister of education replied: "The hatred which we implant in the minds of our children is a holy one."[40]

Anti-Semitic propaganda in many places is being disseminated by Communist and other left wing groups who support the Arabs. Most vicious has been the anti-Semitic agitation in South America. Prior to World War II, Jew-hatred there was the "monopoly" of right wing, Fascist groups. Lately the Fascists have been competing with the Communist and Arab groups in this field. By this time it is difficult to tell the difference between the two "approaches."

In the United States, which is still experiencing the disillusionment that followed the Vietnam War, Communist and Arab propaganda accuses Israel and the Jews of seeking to drag America into a new war in the Middle East. The Soviet news agency *Tass* informs the world that all Jews in the United States are millionaires and that they exert tremendous pressure on Congress to support Israel. As one *Tass* release said:

> The Zionist lobby is pushing the United States and the whole world into an atomic disaster. What is good for the Jews is bad for America. The Jews in the U.S. are the vanguard of the Israeli racists.[41]

It is no longer only Israel; it is also "the Jews." And now this anti-Semitic agitation is being spread by Soviet writings in a number of European countries too.[42]

Postscript

Hostility toward Jews, or toward Zionism, by those in the Third World, in the Soviet Union, and in numerous other places, including Germany, where the mindless variety of anti-Semitism led to the unspeakable "Final Solution," are without exception, an integral part of the fused mass of hate which was originally formed in the early centuries of the Jewish diaspora. As Yehezkel Kaufmann observed, all of these man-made disasters—the persecutions, libels, pogroms, and massacres to which Jews have been subjected—occurred within their own historical perspective. The seeds of anti-Semitism sown so many centuries ago are deep-rooted and still flourishing today. It will suffice to iterate a few examples, which have been covered in this book:

(1) The Crusades, the blood libels, and the violent persecutions through which Jews suffered after the turn of the twelfth century all began at a time when the Church in Europe was experiencing a severe crisis. The civil authorities in central Europe opposed the hegemony of Rome and drove the pope out of the city. This was the period of the antipopes.

A bit earlier, the Islamic tribes defeated the Eastern Roman Empire and occupied stretches of territory in the Near East, including Jerusalem. Rumors spread throughout Christian Europe that the "infidels" had vandalized the holy church on the grave of Jesus. At this point in history, Jew-hatred had already been deeply rooted for generations in almost all the countries of Christendom.

(2) The expulsion from Spain at the end of the fifteenth century, the Inquisition which began at that time, the blood libels and host desecration charges, as well as the expulsions and pogroms everywhere reflected the chaos in the Catholic world. The widespread heresy in Catholic Europe—the Waldensians and Albigenses in France, Wycliffe in England, the Hussites in Bohemia—all led to Luther and the Reformation in central Europe.

In that period the fused mass of Jew-hatred throughout the Christian world was already dense and glowing. As the humanist Erasmus formulated it at the beginning of the fifteenth century: "If hatred toward the Jews is an important part of Christianity, then we are all good Christians today."

(3) Modern anti-Semitism, the terrible Jew-hatred which surged forth in most countries in Europe in the last quarter of the nineteenth century, was also a result of a specific historical development in Europe at that particular time.

During the nineteenth century, capitalism had already become the dominant economic system in all the major countries of the world. Exploitation of workers in the industrial countries was unrestricted. The four wars in the middle of that century, which involved England, France, Turkey, Russia, Italy, Austria, and Prussia, only intensified the poverty in those countries and exacerbated the prevalent chauvinism. Gobineau's racial theory became the order of the day. The deep economic crisis of 1873 in most countries of Europe threw masses of defenseless working-people out into the street.

Jew-hatred was spread throughout society, from the reactionary political Right to the radical Left. Marx, Bakunin, Dühring, and Proudhon, on the Left, were no less active in disseminating Jew-hatred than Stöcker, Wagner, Treitschke, and so many others on the Right. Drumont's agitation in France was no less poisonous than that of Schönerer and Lueger in Austria. The Tisza-Eszlar blood libel in Hungary was of a piece with the pogroms in hundreds of cities in Russia, and with the Dreyfus trial in France.

With comparatively little resistance, this fused mass of hatred erased the memory of the "Enlightenment" which had blossomed more than a century earlier, with its so-called truth that "all human beings are brothers. . . ."

(4) The unprecedented, malevolent anti-Jewish incitement in eastern and central Europe after 1914–18; the thousands of victims of the bloody pogroms during the civil war in Russia; the widespread dissemination of the *Protocols of the Elders of Zion* in every country in the world; the "cold" pogrom against the Jews of Poland and Rumania during the period between the two world wars; the bloodthirsty anti-Jewish incitement in Germany during those two decades— none of these things happened by accident.

World War I left almost all the warring countries in ruins—the "conquerors" as well as the "conquered." The revolutionary storm in those countries, itself a result of the breakdown of the old system, in turn caused the collapse of the foundations which had supported the old, "normal" world. The massive hatred of Jews during that tempestuous period of history flared up with a hellish fire which led to the resulting conflagration of the Holocaust.

This fused mass of hatred, if only because of its weight, could be neither dissolved nor halted. No geographical, political, or cultural borders could block its way. The leaders of the democratic countries, had they really wished to, could have at least partially helped to extingush the flames, but apparently they too were infected by the virus of anti-Semitism.

Nothing the Jews could do, or whatever others in retrospect think they should have done, could have eliminated in any way that dense mass of Jew-hatred, or prevented the hostile decrees and the bloody attacks. Conversion could not dim the Jewish stereotype. The forced conversions in Spain in 1391 and 1412 and the massacres of the Marranos in 1470–72, several years before the Inquisition was installed, are the best evidence that conversion was unable to ameliorate the lot of the Jews.

The United States is an exception to the excesses of the past. It is one of the few countries where democratic principles still abide and all its citizens are guaranteed their personal freedoms. American Jews are the best witnesses to this fact. Yet we dare not depend on the positive mood of yesterday. Anti-Semitism is again on the rise throughout the world, and we begin to see traces of this disease infecting the society in this country. The ever-present hate groups are again spreading their malicious rumors blaming the Jews for the social and economic problems we are now experiencing.

Jews today have a choice that has not been available to them for almost 2,000 years. When Jew-hatred appears we must immediately react with direct and bold measures to confront the source and keep these vicious lies from spreading.

The official leadership of the Christian world must also be constantly pressed to actively oppose the dissemination of all malevolent lies no matter what the source. An appropriate beginning would be to revise the liturgy which would at least partially weaken the roots of anti-Semitism.

The new thrust of today's anti-Semitism is political in nature. Countries throughout the world, particularly the Soviet Union, Poland, and the Arab nations, are equating Zionism with racism and are seeking to transfer the mass of Jew-hatred to the State of Israel. But it is essential to Jewish well-being throughout the world that Israel survive and flourish. Strong measures must be taken by all Jews to ensure this goal.

Therefore, despite their long history of persecution, suffering, blood libels, expulsion and massacres, the Jews devoted a large portion of their national energies toward strengthening and spiritually enriching the cause of Jewish survival. This is the main reason Jews have so devotedly safeguarded and advanced Jewish culture in all periods, peaceful or otherwise, and in all languages which they spoke, and still speak, in the Diaspora. Jewish survival also has been the driving force which supported and strengthened the interconnection of the Jewish people through all periods in all corners of the world.

Notes

Notes to Chapter 1

1. See Chapter 2.
2. 1 Kings, 11 to 2 Kings, 17.
3. Josephus, *Antiquities* 14, 7, 2.
4. Book of Esther, 3:8.
5. Josephus, *Antiquities* 19, 5, 3.
6. Exod. 20:5; Deut. 4:16, 23, 25; 5:8, and many other books of the Bible.
7. Zach. 8:21–23.
8. Josephus, *Antiquities* 12, 1, 1.
9. Simon Dubnow, *Di velt-geshikte fun yidishn folk*, v. 2, p. 296; see also Salo W. Baron, *A Social and Religious History of the Jews*, v. l, p. 171.

Notes to Chapter 2

1. Dubnow, v. l, p. 342.
2. Josephus, *Antiquities* 14, 10, 20; *Wars of the Jews* 5:2; *Anti-Apion* 2, 4.
3. Josephus, *Anti-Apion* 2:8.
4. Josephus, *Antiquities* 14, 10, 8.
5. Josephus, *Anti-Apion* 2:34–37.
6. Josephus, *Antiquities* 12:8. All six paragraphs.
7. Dubnow, v. 2, pp. 299–304.
8. Josephus, *Antiquities* 18:9.

Notes to Chapter 3

1. Harry J. Leon, *The Jews in Ancient Rome*, p. 257.
2. Dubnow, v. 2, pp. 440–44.
3. Baron, v. l, p. 191.
4. Ibid. v. l, p. 190.
5. Dubnow, v. 3, p. 96.
6. Josephus, *Anti-Apion* 2, 40.
7. Josephus, *Wars* 2:1, 3.
8. Josephus, *Antiquities* 17, 10, 10.
9. Leon Poliakov, *A History of Anti-Semitism*, vol. 1, p. 7.
10. Josephus, *Antiquities* 20, 11, 1.

Notes to Chapter 4

1. Ben-Zion Katz, *Perushim, Zadokim, Kanaim, Notzrim*, 2:50–51.
2. Cecil Roth, "Notes," *Revue De Qumran*, no. 6 (February 1960), p. 262.
3. Hasmoneans, 1, is the most important source for Hasmonean history, Josephus, in his time, referred to this book. The book ends with the life of Shimon, last of the five Maccabeans who ruled independent Judea for seven years (141–135 B.C.E.). His son John Hyrcanus was head of the Sanhedrin and high priest in Judea for thirty years (135–105).
4. In *Perushim*, Katz gathered many passages in the Talmud which confirm the disagreements among the ultrapious hasidim and the Hasmonean fighters.
5. Hasmoneans A 14:45–50.
6. Dan. 11:36. From the scrolls found in the Judean Desert we also learn that the ultrapious hasidim had a fatalistic outlook.
7. *Brith Hadashah* is also the Hebrew name of the New Testament.
8. Dead Sea Scrolls, "Manual of Discipline," Col. 10, line 20.
9. S. Glassman, *Megiles fun Yam HaMelekh*, p. 253.
10. W. F. Albright, *From the Stone Age to Christianity*, p. 398.
11. Malcolm Hay, *The Foot of Pride*, pp. 3–32.

Notes to Chapter 5

1. Baron, v. 2, p. 73.
2. Josephus, *Antiquities* 20, 8, 6; *Wars* 2, 4, 5.
3. Dubnow, v. 2, p. 334.
4. Later Christian leaders seem to have censored the writings of the Qumran Sect. The Dead Sea Scrolls testify to another origin of Christianity and perhaps to another Christian Messiah than the one revealed in the New Testament.
5. H. Graetz, *History of the Jews*, v. 2, pp. 397–98.
6. Ibid., p. 409; Dubnow, v. 3, p. 51.
7. Graetz, *History*, pp. 418–19; Dubnow, v. 3, p. 54.
8. Dubnow, v. 3, p. 143; see also James Parkes, *Conflict of the Church and the Synagogue*, p. 84.
9. Poliakov, p. 23.
10. A. Kahana, *HaSeforim HaHizonim l'Torah*, Chaps. 5, 7.
11. Dubnow, v. 3, p. 208; Graetz, v. 2, p. 625.
12. Graetz, v. 2, p. 562; see also Jacob R. Marcus, *The Jew in the Medieval World*, p. 103

Notes to Chapter 6

1. Dubnow, v. 3, p. 16.

2. The word *min* (singular from *minim*).
3. Graetz, v. 2, p. 561.
4. Dubnow, v. 3, p. 181.
5. Parkes, p. 119.
6. Marcus, pp. 4–5.
7. Baron, v. 2, p. 169.
8. Marcus, pp. 3–7.
9. Hay, pp. 3–32.
10. Parkes, pp. 163–65; see also Hay, p. 28.
11. Due to the poor communications of that time, and particularly because of the restrictions on the Jewish people, Jews in the Diaspora were confused about calendar matters; they did not know when a new month began or what day to begin a holiday. In 359 C.E. Hillel the Second, patriarch of Palestine Jewry, published an intercalation to equalize the solar and lunar years, thus making it possible for the Jewish calendar to be determined without actual observation of the lunar phases. This system computed seven leap years in nineteen years.
12. Hay, p. 28.
13. Ibid., p. 24.
14. Baron, v. 2, p. 168.
15. Dubnow, v. 3, p. 208.
16. Edward H. Flannery, *Anguish of the Jews*, p. 73.
17. Graetz, v. 3, p. 47.
18. Ibid., v. 3, pp. 22–23; see also Flannery, p. 68.
19. Baron, v. 3, p. 41.
20. Graetz, v. 3, p. 103. The solemn oath, abbreviated, is cited in the source book, *The Jew in the Medieval World*, by Marcus, pp. 20–22. The severe punishment for breaking a promise to the king was not new. It was the acknowledged right of the king to punish by death or sell into slavery anyone who acted insubordinately to him.
21. Dubnow, v. 4, p. 40.
22. Ibid., v. 4, p. 45.

Notes to Chapter 7

1. Dubnow, v. 3, p. 177; see also Baron, v. 2, p. 210.
2. Dubnow, v. 3, p. 98.
3. Ibid., v. 3, p. 252.
4. Ibid., p. 254.
5. This was the same King Khosrau II who conquered Jerusalem with the help of the Jews and later expelled them from the Holy City.
6. Dubnow, v. 3, p. 336.
7. Ibid., pp. 336–37; see also Graetz, v. 3, p. 73.
8. See Chapter 6; also Graetz, v. 3, p. 19.
9. Ibid.
10. Dubnow, v. 3, p. 343.
11. Graetz, v. 3, pp. 80–81.
12. Ibid., pp. 84–85.
13. Ibid., pp. 87–88.

14. Dubnow, v. 3, p. 346.
15. Baron, v. 3, p. 97.
16. Graetz, v. 3, p. 109.
17. Baron, v. 3, p. 100; see also Dubnow, v. 3, p. 369.
18. Dubnow, v. 3, p. 370; see Graetz, v. 3, pp. 176–77.
19. Ibid., p. 371.
20. The *Shiites* are pious Muslims who venerate the Koran but not the *suna* (the added statutes).
21. Graetz, v. 3, pp. 247–48.
22. Dubnow, v. 3, p. 422.
23. Graetz, v. 3, p. 109.
24. Dubnow, v. 4, p. 160.
25. Ibid., p. 161.
26. Ibid., p. 162. The "Rabad" (Rabbi Abraham ben David) relates that Shmuel HaNagid maintained an entire staff of scribes to copy Hebrew and Arabic books. Before the invention of printing, books were rare and very expensive.
27. Dubnow, v. 4, p. 166.
28. Graetz, v. 3, p. 278–79.
29. Dubnow, v. 4, p. 266.
30. Graetz, v. 3, pp. 358–59.
31. The "Rambam" (Rabbi Moshe ben Maimon, also known as Maimonides) was among the Jewish scholars who fled Islamic Spain at that time.

Notes to Chapter 8

1. Flannery, p. 86. The Jews were not expelled then from Mainz. No historical sources mention an expulsion from Mainz in those years.
2. Baron, v. 4, p. 259.
3. The worst anti-Semites of the Middle Ages, Bishop Agobard and his disciple, Bishop Amolon, were active during the reign of Louis the Pious and his son Charles the Bald. It does not appear that they were able to influence the kings to disdain the Jews.
4. Graetz, v. 3, p. 161.
5. This was a pretext to deny slaves to Jews. Bishop Agobard insisted that the Jews be prohibited from owning Christian slaves, in accordance with the Justinian code.
6. Poliakov, p. 310; Hay, pp. 26–32.
7. The Bishop translated his curses from the *Tokhekha* (curses of the Bible) verbatim.
8. Dubnow, v. 4, pp. 92–93.
9. Flannery, p. 84.
10. Dubnow, v. 4, p. 104.
11. See Chapter 7.
12. Baron, v. 4, p. 57.
13. Dubnow, v. 4, p. 128.
14. Ibid., pp. 129–30.
15. Graetz, v. 3, pp. 139–40.
16. Ibid., p. 254.
17. Pictures of Jews that were circulated by the Nazis were copied from

church paintings of the Middle Ages. So too were the cartoons of the Soviet "scholar" Kichko, in his book, *Judaism without Embellishment*, faithful copies of the hate art of the Medieval age.

18. The custom of *Pro Judaeis non flectant* has remained in the Catholic Church up to the second Vatican council.
19. Adolf Hitler, *Hitler's Secret Conversations, 1941–1944*, p. 457.

Notes to Chapter 9

1. Dubnow, v. 4, p. 209.
2. Baron, v. 4, p. 99.
3. Graetz, v. 3, p. 301. In the chronicles of that period no mention is made of money that the Jews paid to the Bishop of Worms for protection. However, the fact that only the rich were admitted into the castle, and many Jews were left unprotected in their homes, is sufficient testimony that the Jews did indeed pay a great deal of money for their protection.
4. Dubnow, v. 4, p. 211; see also Graetz, v. 3, p. 302.
5. Graetz, v. 3, p. 303.
6. Dubnow, v. 4, pp. 331–32.
7. Ibid., p. 216.
8. Graetz, v. 3, p. 308.
9. Hay, pp. 37–38.
10. See the beginning of Chapter 10.
11. Baron, v. 4, p. 120; also Graetz, v. 3, p. 351.
12. Graetz, v. 3, p. 354.
13. Dubnow, v. 4, p. 220.
14. Ibid., p. 230.
15. Ibid., p. 234; Graetz, v. 3, p. 411.
16. Marcus, pp. 131–36; see a shortened account of the riots in York; p. 417-421.
17. Baron, v. 4, p. 129.
18. Ibid., p. 134.
19. Poliakov, p. 104.
20. The *Jacquerie* (peasant uprising) in France in 1358; the Reformation under Wycliff in England in 1360; John Huss at the beginning of the fifteenth century in Central Europe; Martin Luther at the beginning of the sixteenth century and the peasant uprising in Germany in 1525.

Notes to Chapter 10

1. Dubnow, v. 4, pp. 217–18.
2. Only Christian slaves were prohibited to Jews. Pagans were permitted. However, as soon as an idolator accepted Christianity, he was automatically freed. See Marcus, p. 5.

3. Poliakov, v. 1, p. 75.
4. Dubnow, v. 5, p. 51.
5. Exod. 22:24; Levit. 25:35, 37; Deut. 23:20, 21.
6. Dubnow, v. 4, p. 252.
7. *Sefer HaKashidim*, a work on ethical behavior, was completed in the early thirteenth century and remained a code of law for generations. See I. Zinberg, *Di geshikhte fun literatur by Yidn*, v. 2, pp. 43–63.
8. Flannery, p. 25.
9. Hay, p. 122.
10. Dubnow, v. 4, p. 222.
11. Ibid., pp. 224–25; see also Graetz, v. 3, p. 404.
12. *Emek Habokha* (*Vale of Tears*), describes the massacres of Jews during the first crusade. It was compiled in the sixteenth century. See Zinberg, v. 4, p. 92.
13. I. Kornhendler, *Yidn in Pariz*, p. 143.
14. Baron, v. 1, p. 170.
15. Graetz, v. 3, pp. 247–48; also Chapter 7.
16. Poliakov, p. 66.
17. Kornhendler, pp. 38–104.
18. Ibid., p. 58.
19. Flannery, p. 119.

Notes to Chapter 11

1. Graetz, v. 3, p. 403.
2. Kornhendler, p. 101.
3. Dubnow, v. 4, p. 225.
4. Ibid., v. 5, p. 27.
5. Graetz, v. 3, pp. 578–79.
6. Before the invention of printing, copies of the Talmud were handwritten and scarce. Paper was expensive and hard to get. It took months, sometimes years, before a tractate of the Talmud was copied.
7. Dubnow, v. 5, pp. 45–46. At that time the Inquisitors were not empowered to punish their victims, only to try them.
8. Ibid., p. 44.
9. Hay, pp. 142–43; also Werner Keller, *Diaspora*, p. 233.
10. Dubnow, v. 5, p. 238. Poliakov cites the work *Sheyvet Yehuda*; 140 Jewish communities were destroyed.
11. Graetz, v. 4, p. 57; also Dubnow, v. 5, p. 239.
12. Graetz, v. 3, p. 591.
13. Dubnow, v. 5, p. 58.
14. Ibid., p. 59.
15. Hay, pp. 98–100.
16. Dubnow, v. 5, p. 63.
17. Graetz, v. 3, pp. 642–43.
18. Ibid., pp. 645.

Notes to Chapter 12

1. Dubnow, v. 5, p. 145–46.
2. Ibid., pp. 145–46.
3. Graetz, v. 3, pp. 639–40.
4. Dubnow, v. 5, p. 151.
5. Ibid., p. 153; Graetz, v. 4, pp. 35–37; Flannery, pp. 106–107.
6. Dubnow, p. 156.
7. Ibid., pp. 162–63.
8. Ibid., p. 255.
9. Ibid., p. 257.
10. Graetz, v. 4, p. 108; Poliakov, p. 111.
11. Graetz, v. 4, p. 109.
12. Ibid., v. 4, pp. 164–65.
13. Dubnow, v. 5, p. 270.
14. Graetz, pp. 222–23.
15. Dubnow, v. 5, p. 281.
16. Ibid., pp. 283–85.
17. Ibid., p. 178.
18. Graetz, v. 5, p. 359.
19. Dubnow, v. 5, p. 369.
20. Ibid., p. 372.
21. Ibid., pp. 375–76.
22. *Encyclopaedia Judaica,* v. 9, p. 1124.
23. The word "ghetto" is derived from a metal factory by that name on the outskirts of Venice. Many poor Jews lived close to that factory in a few narrow, dirty streets. In 1517 the city magistrate of Venice forced those Jews who were living among Christians in better neighborhoods to move into the ghetto. Somewhat later, many city governments in Europe prohibited Jews from living among Christians. Ghetto entered the language as meaning "Jews' Street."
24. Isaac Unterman, *The Talmud*, pp. 266–67.
25. Dubnow, v. 6, p. 97.
26. *Encyclopaedia Judaica,* v. 5, p. 54; they were kept in the Catechumenate until they converted and could be trusted as Christians.
27. Dubnow, v. 6, p. 101.

Notes to Chapter 13

1. Graetz, v. 3, p. 387.
2. Marcus, pp. 34–39.
3. Dubnow believes that the number of Jews in Castile was around 234,000, not 850,000 as estimated by Graetz. Castile was not the only province in Spain where Jews lived. There were sizable Jewish communities also in Catalonia and Aragon. See Dubnow, v. 5, n. on p. 73.
4. Dubnow, v. 5, p. 208.
5. Graetz, v. 4, p. 126.

6. Zinberg, v. 3, p. 182.
7. Graetz, v. 4, pp. 77–78.
8. Flannery, p. 133; also Graetz, v. 5, pp. 166–69.
9. Flannery, p. 132.
10. Graetz, v. 4, pp. 170–71.
11. Ibid., pp. 171–72.
12. Dubnow, v. 5, p. 300.
13. Ibid., p. 315.
14. Graetz, v. 4, p. 279.
15. Ibid., pp. 281–82.
16. Ibid., pp. 313–14.
17. Dubnow, v. 5, p. 334; also Abraham L. Sachar, *A History of the Jews*, p. 211.
18. Graetz, v. 4, p. 318.
19. Dubnow, v. 5, p. 335.
20. Ibid., p. 341.
21. Ibid., pp. 341–42.
22. Ibid., pp. 342–44; also Marcus, pp. 51–55.
23. Dubnow, v. 5, p. 344.
24. Ibid., p. 347.
25. Ibid., p. 345. Dubnow states that 200,000 Jews were driven out of Spain. Graetz estimates closer to 300,000.
26. Ibid., p. 345.
27. Graetz, v. 4, pp. 353–54.
28. Ibid., pp. 401–05.

Notes to Chapter 14

1. See Chapter 11.
2. Dubnow, v. 6, pp. 214–22; Graetz, v. 4, pp. 414–17.
3. Graetz, v. 4, pp. 415–16.
4. Dubnow, v. 6, pp. 216–17.
5. Graetz, v. 4, pp. 439–40; Dubnow, v. 6, pp. 218–19.
6. Dubnow, v. 6, pp. 219–220.
7. Graetz, v. 4, pp. 468.
8. Stefan Zweig, *Romain Rolland*, p. 15.
9. Dubnow, v. 6, p. 229.
10. Ibid., pp. 229–31.
11. Ibid., p. 233.
12. Ibid., p. 257.
13. Ibid., p. 258.
14. Ibid., pp. 258–59.
15. Ibid., p. 264.
16. Ibid., p. 275; also Werner Keller, *Diaspora*, p. 300.
17. Dubnow, v. 6, pp. 267–68; Graetz, v. 4, pp. 686–87.
18. Dubnow, v. 6, p. 245.
19. Graetz, v. 4, p. 586.
20. Dubnow, v. 6, p. 278–79.

Notes to Chapter 15

1. I. Shipper, *Yiddishe geshikhte (Wirtschaftsgeschichte)*, p. 50. See also I. Brutzkus, "Di erste yedios vegn Yidn in Polen" in *Historishe Shriftn*, pp. 55–72. Brutzkus maintains that Jewish settlements existed in the cities of southern Poland as early as the first half of the eleventh century, and that these settlements were established as way stations for Jewish merchants who traversed Europe from west to east.
2. Dubnow, v. 5, pp. 390–91.
3. Shipper, p. 150.
4. Ibid., pp. 284–85.
5. Dubnow, v. 6, pp. 303–304.
6. Ibid., p. 305.
7. Ibid., p. 306.
8. Ibid., p. 311.
9. Ibid., p. 319; see Chapter 12.
10. Ibid., pp. 327–29.
11. Ibid., v. 7, p. 22; also Graetz, v. 5, p. 6.
12. Graetz, v. 5, pp. 7–8.
13. Ibid., pp. 8–9.
14. Ibid., pp. 9–10; also Keller, pp. 304–305.
15. Graetz, v. 5, p. 11; also Dubnow, v. 7, p. 28.
16. Dubnow, v. 7, p. 28. *Yovon metzulah* is a phrase from the Psalms (*metzulah* means "an abyss"). With these words the Jews described the Greek Orthodox Ukrainians (*Yovon* means "Greek") after the pogroms in 1648–49. The pamphlet *Yovon Metzulah* by N. N. Hanover may therefore be called *The Abyss of the Cossacks*. For a full description of this work see the essay in *Historishe Shriftn* by Israel Israelson, "Natan Hanover: Zeyn leben un literarishe taytekeyt," pp. 1–26.
17. Graetz, v. 5, p. 12.
18. Ibid., p. 15.
19. According to Graetz, about 250,000 Jews were murdered in 1648–49. Dubnow, in his essay "Der zweiter hurbn fun Ukrainia" in *Historishe Shriftn*, pp. 27–54, sets his estimate between 100,000 and 250,000.

Notes to Chapter 16

1. Dubnow, v. 7, p. 79.
2. Ibid., p. 87.
3. Ibid., p. 101.
4. Marcus, pp. 179–80.
5. Graetz, v. 5, p. 285; also Dubnow, v. 7, p. 393.
6. Graetz, pp. 124–25.
7. Ibid., pp. 129–30.
8. Dubnow, "Der zweiter hurbn fun Ukrainia" in *Historishe Shriftn*, pp. 27–54.
9. Dubnow, v. 7, p. 364; also Graetz, v. 5, p. 387.
10. Dubnow, p. 373.
11. Ibid., v. 8, p. 288.
12. Ibid., v. 8, p. 293.

Notes to Chapter 17

1. Graetz, v. 5, p. 173.
2. Dubnow, v. 7, p. 182.
3. Ibid., pp. 185–86.
4. Ibid., p. 192; also Graetz, v. 5, p. 252.
5. Dubnow, v. 7, p. 197.
6. Zinberg, v. 7, p. 114.
7. Dubnow, v. 7, pp. 342–43.
8. Ibid., v. 8, p. 254.
9. Joseph II, Emperor of Austria, a follower of the physiocratic doctrine, believed agriculture to be the only source of wealth. He considered the Jews, who had been prevented from farming for centuries, to be a useless element in society, calling them *Betlerjuden*. He expelled the Jewish merchants and tavern-keepers from the villages.
10. Zinberg, v. 7, pp. 114–15.
11. Dubnow, v. 8, p. 246.
12. Ibid., p. 250.
13. Graetz, v. 5, p. 191; also Dubnow, v. 7, pp. 199–200.
14. Dubnow, v. 7, p. 202.
15. Graetz, v. 5, p. 188.
16. Ibid., pp. 192–93.
17. Eisenmenger's book was reprinted in several editions in Hitler's Germany. In the hundreds of thousands of anti-Jewish books and pamphlets which circulate today in the Soviet Union—the works of Kichko, Evseyev, Ivanov, Begun, among many others—one can find "incontestable" facts and quotations from Eisenmenger, Streicher, and other world-renowned Jew-haters before them.
18. Dubnow, v. 8, p. 24.
19. Ibid., v. 8, p. 27.
20. Graetz, v. 5, p. 344.
21. Christian Wilhelm von Dohm, *Uber die bürgerliche Verbesserung der Juden*, quoted in Dubnow, v. 8, pp. 22–23.

Notes to Chapter 18

1. Poliakov, p. 180.
2. Dubnow, v. 7, p. 247.
3. Graetz, v. 5, pp. 342–43.
4. Dubnow, v. 8, pp. 56–57.
5. Graetz, v. 5, p. 352.
6. Max Margolis and Alexander Marx, *A History of the Jewish People*, p. 609.
7. Dubnow, v. 8, p. 90.
8. Graetz, v. 5, p. 448.
9. Dubnow, v. 8, pp. 123–24.
10. Ibid., p. 125.
11. Ibid., p. 129–30; also Graetz, v. 5, p. 480.

12. Dubnow, p. 135.
13. Ibid., p. 147; also Graetz, v. 5, pp. 498–99.
14. Dubnow, v. 9, pp. 211–12.
15. Howard M. Sachar, *Course of Modern Jewish History*, p. 228.
16. J. L. Talmon, "European History—Seedbed of the Holocaust" in *Midstream* (May 1973), pp. 3–25.
17. Robert F. Burns, *Antisemitism in France*, pp. 118–20.
18. Ibid., p. 119.
19. Ibid., pp. 137–40.
20. Ibid., pp. 331–33.
21. Dubnow, v. 10, p. 194.
22. Ibid., p. 196; also I. Elbogen, *A Century of Jewish Life*, p. 187.
23. Dubnow, p. 197.
24. Ibid., pp. 199–200; also Elbogen, pp. 188–89.

Notes to Chapter 19

1. Dubnow, v. 7, pp. 300–301.
2. Ibid., p. 303.
3. Raphael Mahler, *A History of Modern Jewry*, p. 351.
4. Dubnow, v. 10, p. 211.
5. Ibid., v. 7, p. 266.
6. Graetz, v. 5, pp. 337–38; Dubnow, v. 7, pp. 272–73.
7. Elbogen, p. 142.
8. Dubnow, v. 10, p. 208.
9. *Encyclopaedia Judaica*, v. 4, p. 417.
10. Kornhendler, pp. 118–145; also see Chapter 10.
11. Kornhendler, pp. 118–145.
12. In addition to the promise not to multiply unduly, they also agreed not to permit marriages among the poor; that a bride brought from afar must contribute a sizable dowry; that they would not engage in real estate dealings or become landlords; and that they would not share a dwelling with a non-Jew.
13. Dubnow, v. 8, p. 169.
14. Mahler, pp. 471–74.
15. Dubnow, v. 9, p. 372.
16. Ibid., v. 7, pp. 280–81.
17. Ibid., pp. 282–85.
18. Ibid., v. 8, p. 65.
19. Ibid., v. 7, p. 288.
20. Ibid., v. 8, p. 162.
21. Ibid., v. 8, p. 168.
22. Ibid., v. 9, pp. 219–20.
23. Ibid., v. 9, p. 363.
24. Elbogen, p. 67.
25. Dubnow, v. 9, p. 379; Elbogen, p. 71.
26. Dubnow, v. 9, p. 380.
27. Ibid., v. 7, pp. 322–23.
28. Ibid., p. 313.

29. Graetz, v. 5, p. 643.
30. Dubnow, v. 9, pp. 384–85.
31. Ibid., v. 9, p. 388.
32. Ibid., v. 7, p. 324.
33. Ibid., v. 6, p. 203.
34. Marcus, pp. 69–70.
35. Dubnow, v. 7, p. 276.
36. In the 1790 census there was no data about the various religious groups in the thirteen states. See Mahler, p. 85; Dubnow, v. 8, p. 75.
37. Dubnow, v. 8, pp. 72–73.
38. Ibid., p. 73.

Notes to Chapter 20

1. Dubnow, v. 8, p. 177.
2. Ibid., p. 178; also Margolis and Marx, pp. 620–21.
3. Dubnow, v. 8, pp. 223–29. Moses Mendelssohn's daughter, Dorothea, converted under the influence of one of these salons.
4. Graetz, v. 5, pp. 468–70; Dubnow, v. 8, p. 184.
5. Ibid., p. 500.
6. Dubnow, v. 8, pp. 199–200.
7. Ibid., pp. 202–203, see note.
8. Graetz, v. 5, pp. 504–505.
9. Dubnow, v. 8, pp. 209–10.
10. Graetz, v. 5, pp. 519–20.
11. Ibid., pp. 516–17; Dubnow, v. 9, pp. 16–17.
12. Dubnow, v. 9, p. 21.
13. Graetz, v. 5, pp. 528–29.
14. Dubnow, v. 9, p. 21.
15. Ibid., p. 31.
16. Graetz, v. 5, p. 600.
17. Dubnow, v. 9, pp. 44–45.
18. Ibid., p. 51.
19. Ibid., p. 61.
20. Ibid., p. 248.
21. Ibid., p. 252.
22. Elbogen, p. 12.
23. Dubnow, v. 9, p. 261.
24. Ibid., p. 263; see also *Jewish Emancipation* by R. Mahler, pp. 57–58.
25. Dubnow, v. 9, pp. 106–108; also Elbogen, p. 18.
26. Dubnow, v. 9, p. 110.
27. See Chapter 17.
28. Dubnow, v. 9, p. 116.
29. Ibid., v. 9, p. 118.
30. Ibid., pp. 283–84.
31. Ibid., pp. 284-85; see the wording of the emancipation in Mahler's *Jewish Emancipation.*
32. Dubnow, v. 9, p. 287.
33. Ibid., p. 288.
34. Ibid., pp. 290–91; also Elbogen, p. 26.

35. Dubnow, v. 9, p. 294; also Elbogen, pp. 27–28.
36. Max Weinreich, *Tzwantzik Yor noch Czernowitz*.

Notes to Chapter 21

1. See Chapter 17.
2. Dubnow, v. 10, p. 53.
3. Walter Laqueur, *A History of Zionism*, p. 22.
4. Ibid., p. 27.
5. Hay, p. 174.
6. Talmon, pp. 3–25.
7. Ibid.
8. Burns, pp. 121–25; also Talmon.
9. Burns, p. 65.
10. Eugen Dühring in H. M. Sachar, pp. 225–27; see also Lucy S. Dawidowicz, *The War Against the Jews*, pp. 38–39 and Dubnow, v. 10, p. 120.
11. Eugen Dühring, Adolf Stöcker, and Karl Marx in Germany; Karl Lueger and Georg von Schönerer in Austria; Eduard Drumont in France; Tichamirov and Romanenko, leaders of the *Narodniki*, in Russia.
12. Laqueur, p. 28; Elbogen, p. 162.
13. Laqueur, pp. 28–29.
14. Ibid., p. 29.
15. Dubnow, v. 10, pp. 26–28. In these discussions the voice of Graetz was not heard. On one side, he was attacked by Treitschke and other anti-Semites; on the other, the assimilated Jews accused him of exposing them to the charge of Jewish nationalism by his interpretation of Jewish history.
16. Dubnow, v. 10, p. 42.
17. Dawidowicz, p. 38.
18. Burns, p. 16; Dawidowicz, pp. 32–33.
19. Dubnow, v. 10, p. 44.
20. The quota system in Russian universities excluded the majority of Jewish students, who were compelled to attend schools in foreign countries. Many went to Germany and America.
21. Dawidowicz, p. 44; see also Elbogen, p. 164.
22. Dubnow, v. 10, p. 64.
23. Ibid.; also Burns, pp. 91–92.
24. Burns, pp. 82–84.
25. Dubnow, v. 10, pp. 67–69.
26. Ibid., v. 10, pp. 73–74.
27. William Korey, *The Soviet Cage*, p. 12, n. 18.
28. Dubnow, v. 10, p. 78.
29. Ibid., pp. 82–83.
30. Ibid., pp. 85–88; Elbogen, pp. 155–59.
31. Dubnow, v. 10, p. 342.
32. Ibid., p. 343.
33. Ibid., p. 345.
34. Ibid., p. 347.

Notes to Chapter 22

1. Dubnow, v. 6, pp. 333–34.
2. Ibid., p. 334.
3. Ibid., v. 7, p. 142.
4. Ibid., p. 143.
5. Ibid., p. 152.
6. Ibid., pp. 145–46.
7. Ibid., pp. 148–49.
8. Ibid., p. 385.
9. Ibid., v. 8, pp. 300–301, see note.
10. Ibid., pp. 304–306. At that time the governor received many reports and denunciations of the Hasidim from the Misnagdim and vice versa. This was a period of great dissension among these sects.
11. Ibid., p. 320.
12. Ibid., p. 321.
13. Ibid., p. 331.
14. Ibid., v. 9, pp. 133–34, see note. No exact data is available. The figure of two million is an estimate ca. 1840.
15. Ibid., pp. 139–40.
16. Ibid., p. 145.
17. Many Jewish children were tortured and martyred for refusing baptism. The historian A. Tcherikower documented the struggle of the "cantonists" against baptism in his essay, "Fun di russishe archiven" in *Historishe Shriftn*, pp. 789–92.
18. Elbogen, p. 57.
19. Dubnow, v. 9, pp. 157–58.
20. Ibid., p. 168.
21. Ibid., pp. 172–76.
22. Ibid., pp. 312–13.
23. Ibid., pp. 182–83.
24. Ibid., pp. 186–87.
25. Ibid., p. 325.
26. Ibid., p. 327, see note.
27. Ibid., p. 381.
28. The story is told about Chwolson that when he was asked whether he converted for the sake of his career or out of conviction, he answered: "Conviction. I'm convinced that it is much better to be a professor in St. Petersburg than a *melamed* in Shnipeshok."

Notes to Chapter 23

1. Baron, *The Russian Jew Under Tsars and Soviets*, p. 52.
2. Dubnow, v. 10, p. 99. The same outcry against the Jews at the end of the nineteenth century could be heard in Germany, Austria, and France.
3. Elbogen, p. 201.
4. Dubnow, v. 10, pp. 106–107.
5. Baron, *Russian Jew*, p. 56.

6. Dubnow, v. 10, pp. 116–17; Korey, pp. 12–13.
7. Dubnow, v. 10, p. 123.
8. Ibid., p. 121. Lord Beaconsfield (Disraeli), Prime Minister of England, 1868–80, prevented Russia from spreading its influence into the Balkan Peninsula.
9. Ibid., p. 123.
10. Elbogen, pp. 210–16; also Dubnow, v. 10, pp. 128–29.
11. Dubnow, v. 10, pp. 132–33.
12. Ibid., pp. 136–40; Baron, *Russian Jew*, p. 57.
13. Elbogen, p. 214.
14. Dubnow, v. 10, p. 145.
15. Baron, *Russian Jew*, p. 61.
16. Dubnow, v. 10, p. 150.
17. Ibid., pp. 151–54; also Elbogen, pp. 218–19.
18. Ibid., pp. 160–61.
19. Ibid., pp. 163–65.
20. Ibid., p. 169.
21. Ibid., p. 170.
22. See Moshe Katz, *A dor, vus hot forlorn di moyre*.
23. Dubnow, v. 10, p. 303.
24. Laqueur, pp. 103–106. The first Zionist world congress was held in Basel, Switzerland in 1897.
25. Ibid., p. 124; Dubnow, v. 10, p. 308.
26. Dubnow, v. 10, p. 319.
27. Ibid., pp. 320–21.
28. Ibid., pp. 321–22.
29. Ibid., p. 324.
30. Ibid., p. 325.
31. Elbogen pp. 398–99; Dubnow, v. 10, pp. 328–29.
32. Dubnow, v. 10, p. 331.

Notes to Chapter 24

1. William Ebenstein, *Great Political Thinkers*, p. 290.
2. Herman Bernstein, *The Truth About the Protocols of Zion*.
3. This was written at the time when the Jews were emancipated in most European countries. Disraeli became prime minister in England. Many Christians opposed equal rights for Jews. Goedsche repeats the arguments of the European anti-Semites. The demand that Jews must not hold government positions was popular among anti-Semites everywhere.
4. We have no information whatsoever about this document. Those who knew about it did not discuss it. Nilus mentions only the person from whom he received the *Protocols*, nothing more.
5. Dubnow, v. 10, p. 485.
6. Bernstein, p. 286.
7. Ibid., p. 36.
8. Ibid., p. 46.
9. Dubnow, v. 10, p. 51.

10. Ibid., p. 486.
11. Bernstein, pp. 259–64 and p. xxix.
12. Ibid., p. x.
13. Ibid.
14. Ibid., p. 297.
15. Ibid., p. 302.
16. Bernstein, p. 304.
17. Ibid., p. 312.
18. Ibid., pp. 371–79.
19. A. Tcherikower, *Ukrainer pogromen in yor 1919*, p. 11. See also N. Gergel, "Di pogromen in Ukrainia in di yorn 1918–21" in *Ekonomishe Shriftn*, pp. 106–13.
20. Dubnow, v. 10, p. 352.
21. Elbogen, p. 459.
22. Dubnow, v. 10, p. 421.
23. Ibid., p. 430.
24. Tcherikower, p. 28.
25. Ibid., pp. 81–87.
26. Ibid., p. 126.
27. Ibid., pp. 158–59.
28. Gergel, p. 112.
29. Ibid.

Notes to Chapter 25

1. Oscar Janowsky, *American Jew*, p. 6; also Mahler, p. 85. Dubnow estimates that there were five thousand Jews in the United States at the time of the Revolution. Considering the size of the Jewish communities, the smaller number makes more sense. Jack S. Levin, former president of the Jewish Historical Society, estimates the number as between two and three thousand, in his article, "Judaic Roots of the American Revolution" in *Congress Monthly* (October 1976), pp. 10–11.
2. Mahler, pp. 100–101.
3. See title page of Charles H. Stember, *Jews in the Mind of America*; also Levin.
4. Dubnow, v. 9, p. 231.
5. John Higham, "American Anti-Semitism Historically Reconsidered" in Stember, p. 248.
6. Ibid., p. 242. Xenophobia was, and still is, a widespread sentiment.
7. Oscar Handlin, *Adventure in Freedom*, p. 186.
8. L. A. Greenberg and H. Jonas, "An American Anti-Semite in the 19th Century" in Joseph L. Blau, *Essays on Jewish Life and Thought Presented in Honor of Salo Wittmayer Baron*, pp. 265–83.
9. Dubnow, v. 10, p. 228; also C. Bezalel Sherman, *Jew Within American Society*, p. 270.
10. Handlin, p. 192.
11. Higham, pp. 251–52. There was a great deal of sympathy in the United States for the Jewish refugees from Russia.
12. Grayzel, pp. 701–702.

13. Dubnow, v. 10, p. 400. From 1903 to 1907 about 400,000 Jews came to the United States. Although immigration into the United States ceased during World War I, the Jewish population reached four million in 1920.
14. Ibid., pp. 401–403.
15. Higham, p. 249.
16. See Chapter 30, n. 2; also Elbogen, pp. 399–400.
17. Handlin, p. 205.
18. Ibid., p. 207.
19. See Chapter 30.
20. Stember, p. 228.
21. Higham, p. 243.
22. Stember, p. 269.
23. Arnold Forster and Benjamin R. Epstein, *The New Anti-Semitism*, pp. 146–47.
24. Ibid., pp. 128–37.
25. Ibid., p. 142.
26. Ibid., p. 243.
27. **Ibid., p. 61; from the broadcast discussion of "Great Proletarian Revolution," moderated by Julius Lester, 26 December 1968.**
28. Ibid., p. 62.
29. Ibid., p. 61.
30. Ibid., p. 287.
31. Ibid., p. 286.
32. Ibid., p. 291.
33. Ibid., p. 296.
34. Ibid., p. 293.
35. Ibid., p. 294.
36. Ibid., pp. 91–101.

Notes to Chapter 26

1. Dawidowicz, p. 403.
2. *Encyclopaedia Judaica*, v. 7, p. 36.
3. Ibid., pp. 41–42.
4. Dubnow, v. 10, p. 381.
5. Ibid., p. 462.
6. *Encyclopaedia Judaica*, v. 9, p. 1135.
7. Dubnow, v. 10, pp. 390–93.
8. Ibid., p. 393.
9. Ibid., p. 394.
10. *Encyclopaedia Judaica*, v. 14, p. 408.
11. H. M. Sachar, p. 451.
12. Paul Lendvai, *Anti-Semitism Without Jews*, p. 326.
13. Dawidowicz, p. 364.
14. *Encyclopaedia Judaica*, v. 4, p. 421.
15. Dawidowicz, p. 367.
16. Ibid., p. 403.
17. H. M. Sachar, pp. 401–402.
18. See Chapter 18.

19. H. M. Sachar, pp. 503–504.
20. *Encyclopaedia Judaica*, v. 5, p. 111.
21. Ruth R. Wisse and Irwin Cotler, "Quebec's Jews: Caught in the Middle," *Commentary*, September 1977, p. 58.
22. *Encyclopaedia Judaica*, v. 3, p. 416.
23. H. M. Sachar, p. 514.
24. *Encyclopaedia Judaica*, v. 3, p. 416.
25. Ibid., v. 4, p. 1328.
26. H. M. Sachar, p. 518.
27. *Encyclopaedia Judaica*, v. 11, p. 1458.
28. *Facts on File*, D-1 (1975), p. 838.
29. H. M. Sachar, p. 507.
30. Ibid., p. 508.

Notes to Chapter 27

1. Laqueur, p. 75.
2. Ibid., p. 76.
3. H. M. Sachar, p. 413; see also Chapter 7.
4. Ibid.
5. Laqueur, p. 28.
6. Dubnow, v. 10, p. 395; also Laqueur, pp. 220–21.
7. Laqueur, p. 213.
8. Ibid., p. 235.
9. Ibid., p. 236.
10. Ibid., p. 237.
11. Dubnow, v. 10, pp. 443–44.
12. Laqueur, pp. 255–56.
13. Ibid., pp. 492–93.
14. H. M. Sachar, pp. 386–87.
15. Laqueur, pp. 261–62.
16. Ibid., pp. 514–20; also H. M. Sachar, p. 390.
17. H. M. Sachar, pp. 319–92.
18. Saul S. Friedman, "Arab Complicity in the Holocaust," *Jewish Frontier*, April 1975, p. 17.
19. Ibid., p. 13.
20. Ibid., p. 13. In June 1944, when the Red Army was at the gates of Warsaw, Hitler's defeat was evident. The Mufti's only fear was that too many Jews would survive.
21. Ibid., p. 10.
22. Laqueur, p. 571.
23. Ibid., p. 586.
24. "The Twenty-Five Year War—The War of 1948," *Near East Report*, 6 February 1974, p. 25.
25. Ibid.
26. The arms from Czechoslovakia came with the approval of the Soviet Union. Stalin was looking for a way to weaken the position of Britain in the Middle East.
27. "Two Refugee Problems," *Near East Report*, 6 February 1974, p. 50.

28. Ibid., p. 51.
29. Ibid., pp. 51–52.
30. Ibid., p. 50.
31. J. Zineman, *Di geshikte fun Zionism*, p. 618.
32. *Near East Report*, p. 28.
33. Ibid., p. 28.
34. Ibid.
35. Ibid., p. 29.
36. Ibid., p. 30.
37. *Encyclopaedia Judaica*, v. 9, p. 414.
38. Ibid., p. 414. In November 1977 the President of Egypt, Anwar el-Sadat, for the first time in the history of Arab-Israel relations, told the Israeli Knesset: "We recognize you and we wish to live in peace with you." However, he proposed impossible conditions and refused to compromise on them. In July 1978, he issued several warnings that if his demands were not met, he would withdraw his offer of peace.
39. Some of these terrorist attacks include that on the Israeli Olympic athletes in Munich in October 1972, or the hijacking of planes carrying Israeli citizens.
40. Eugene Rostow, "The American Stake in Israel," *Commentary*, April 1977, p. 45.

Notes to Chapter 28

1. Leon Brandes, "The Juridical Position of the Jews in Poland Between the Two Wars" in *YIVO Bleter*, v. 42, p. 147.
2. Pawel Korzec, *Antisemitism in Poland*, pp. 13–14.
3. Dubnow, v. 10, p. 466.
4. Brandes, p. 171.
5. Dubnow, v. 10, p. 438; also Isaiah Trunk, "Economic Antisemitism in Poland Between the Two World Wars" in *Studies on Polish Jewry, 1919–1939* (Yiddish section), pp. 6, 13–25.
6. Dubnow, v. 10, pp. 436–37; also Brandes, pp. 174–75.
7. Trunk, p. 50.
8. Ibid., p. 13; also Brandes, p. 176.
9. Trunk, p. 17.
10. Ibid., p. 18.
11. Ibid., p. 49.
12. Ibid., p. 41.
13. Dubnow, v. 10, p. 465.
14. Trunk, pp. 57–59.
15. Ibid., p. 53.
16. Ibid., pp. 54–55; also Brandes, pp. 172–73 and Dubnow, p. 468.
17. Trunk, p. 38.
18. See Chapter 31.
19. Karl Kautsky, *Are the Jews a Race?*, p. 246.
20. Dubnow, v. 10, p. 368.
21. Ibid., pp. 337–38. Dubnow presents Sombart's views in almost positive tones, virtually as an advocate of Jewish nationalism. That Sombart was a dyed-in-the-wool anti-Semite is evident also from the fact that in 1974 the

Soviet anti-Semite, Dmitri Zhukov, in an article in *Ogonyok* (12 October 1974), offered Sombart's ideas as "testimony" that the Jews had seized economic power in Europe.

22. *Encyclopaedia Judaica*, v. 7, p. 483; Dubnow, v. 10, p. 420.
23. Dubnow, v. 10, p. 455.
24. Dawidowicz, pp. 48–49.
25. Dubnow, v. 10, p. 460.
26. H. M. Sachar, p. 433.
27. Ibid., p. 435.

Notes to Chapter 29

1. Hay, p. 167.
2. Dawidowicz, p. 23.
3. Dubnow, v. 9, p. 21.
4. Laqueur, p. 20.
5. Dawidowicz, pp. 32–33.
6. Ibid., p. 7.
7. Ibid., pp. 39, 64.
8. Burns, p. 82.
9. Dawidowicz, p. 11.
10. Ibid., p. 14.
11. Ibid., p. 17.
12. Ibid., p. 18.
13. Ibid., p. 20.
14. Ibid., pp. 47–48.
15. The one-party dictatorship was not Hitler's original idea. This "lesson" he learned from the October Revolution in Russia and from Mussolini in Italy.
16. Dawidowicz, p. 53.
17. Ibid., p. 50.
18. Ibid., p. 80.
19. Ibid., p. 35.
20. Ibid., pp. 87–88.
21. Ibid., p. 94.
22. Dubnow, v. 10, p. 442.
23. H. M. Sachar, p. 429.
24. Ibid., p. 430.
25. Elbogen, p. 664.
26. H. M. Sachar, p. 432.
27. Dawidowicz, p. 106.
28. Ibid., p. 110.
29. Ibid., p. 112.
30. Ibid., p. 145.
31. Ibid., p. 397.
32. About the uprisings in the ghettos, see Yuri Suhl, *They Fought Back*.
33. Dawidowicz, p. 400.
34. See Chapter 12.
35. Dawidowicz, pp. 359–63.
36. Ibid., pp. 370–71.

37. Ibid., p. 373.
38. Ibid., pp. 374–75.
39. Ibid., p. 377.
40. Ibid., pp. 380–82.
41. Ibid., p. 383.
42. Ibid., pp. 383–86.
43. Ibid., pp. 388–89.
44. Ibid., p. 393.
45. Ibid., pp. 393–94.

Notes to Chapter 30

1. Dubnow, v. 10, p. 435.
2. V. I. Lenin, *Ausgevelte verk*, v. 8, pp. 54, 55.
3. Dubnow, v. 10, p. 447.
4. Baron, pp. 242–45.
5. Korey, pp. 25–26.
6. Ibid., p. 65.
7. H. G. Wells, *Experiment in Autobiography*, p. 689.
8. Roy A. Medvedev, *Let History Judge*, p. 493.
9. Ibid., pp. 192–239.
10. Svetlana Alliluyeva, *Only One Year*, p. 152; also, Medvedev, pp. 495–97.
11. Korey, p. 68; also, Medvedev, p. 493.
12. Korey, p. 67.
13. Alliluyeva, p. 154.
14. **Esther Markish, "Mit Peretz Markish un on im" in *Di Goldene Keyt*, no. 88 (1975), pp. 22-40.**
15. Medvedev, pp. 494–95.
16. Harrison Salisbury, *Moscow Journal*, pp. 312–18.
17. *Encyclopaedia Judaica*, v. 8, p. 817.
18. B. Smolar, *Soviet Jewry Today and Tomorrow*, p. 30.
19. Gunther Lawrence, *Three Million More?*, p. 160.
20. Smolar, pp. 7–9.
21. Lawrence, pp. 100–101.
22. Korey, p. 35.
23. Lawrence, p. 103.
24. Ibid., pp. 135–36.
25. Ibid., pp. 137–38.
26. The shortened article by Yaakov Sharet was translated from the Hebrew periodical, *Yomim VeLaylot* (27 October 1967).
27. I. Belyev and Y. Primakov, "Lessons of the 1967 Middle East Crisis" in *International Affairs* (Russian), no. 3 (1968), pp. 40–46.
28. Lendvai, pp. 5–12.
29. Ibid., p. 12.
30. Lawrence, p. 196.
31. Note the accusations made by a Soviet United Nations Representative to the people of South America in order to inflame anti-Semitism in their countries.

32. This speech is quoted in *The New Anti-Semitism* by Arnold Forster and Benjamin R. Epstein of Security Council records for 25 September 1971. The ambassador attempted to incite New Yorkers against the Jews. This speech is also quoted in William Korey's article in the *American Zionist*, "Bigotry in the Hall of Brotherhood" (January 1972), pp. 12–15.

Notes to Chapter 31

1. Lendvai, p. 40.
2. Ibid., pp. 24–25; also, Dawidowicz, p. 397.
3. See Chapter 30, n. 6.
4. Ibid., n. 27.
5. Lendvai, pp. 72–73.
6. Institute for Jewish Affairs, p. 39.
7. Ibid., pp. 22–23.
8. Lendvai, pp. 144–45.
9. Adam Mickiewicz (1798–1855), a Polish patriot, was exiled by the Czarist government. His play, *Dziady*, which was always very popular with the Poles, contains many anti-Russian statements.
10. Lendvai, p. 90.
11. Ibid., p. 117.
12. Ibid., p. 131.
13. Ibid., p. 125.
14. Ibid., p. 149.
15. Ibid., p. 155.
16. Ibid., p. 159.
17. Ibid., p. 160.
18. Ibid., p. 243.
19. Ibid., p. 244.
20. Ibid.
21. Ibid., pp. 249–51.
22. Arthur London was sentenced to death together with Slansky and the others. His brother-in-law, a member of the Politburo of the French Communist Party, saved his life.
23. Lendvai, pp. 253–54.
24. Ibid., p. 263.
25. Ibid., p. 264.
26. Ibid., pp. 276–77.
27. Ibid., p. 281.
28. Ibid.
29. Lendvai, pp. 291–92.
30. Ibid., p. 283.
31. Ibid., p. 289.
32. Ibid., p. 296.
33. *Facts on File* (1975), p. 775.
34. Mario Rossi, *The Third World*, p. 139.
35. Michael Curtis and Susan A. Gitelson, eds., *Israel in the Third World*, p. 183.
36. Eugene V. Rostow, "The American Stake in Israel" in *Commentary* (April 1977), pp. 32–46.

37. K. London, *Soviet Impact on Africa*, p. 261.
38. Curtis and Gitelson, pp. 254–58.
39. Ibid., p. 258.
40. Forster and Epstein, p. 163.
41. Curtis and Gitelson, p. 368.
42. A French court convicted a French citizen who reprinted an anti-Semitic article from a French-Soviet magazine. The court found him guilty of disseminating race-hatred in France. See Forster and Epstein, p. 164.

Appendix

A Chronicle of the First Crusade, by Shlomo ben Shimeon (abridged from the text in *Doyres dertseyln*, by Ezekiel Lifschutz, 1944, pp. 30-41). The chronicler relates that he wrote this in Mainz in 1140, where he heard the details from older people.

And now I will tell how the attacks spread to the other communities which were martyred in the sanctification of God's name.

In the year 1096 the attacks spread to the other kehillas. All the plagues in the world descended upon us. An angry, motley army of Frenchmen and Germans appeared on their way to Jerusalem to find the grave of the Christ, drive out the Ishmaelites, and rule the country. The Cross was their emblem. There were men, women, and children, more numerous than the locusts on the face of the earth. One could say about them: There is no king over the locusts. When they passed cities where Jews lived, they spoke among themselves: "Look, we are going on a long journey to find Jesus' grave and take vengeance on the Ishmaelites. Here among us live Jews whose ancestors crucified our Lord. Let us first take vengeance on them and destroy them, so that the name Jew shall no longer be remembered. Or let them become like us and accept our faith."

When the kehillas heard this, they—like their ancestors—began to repent their sins, pray to God, and give charity. The hands of our people have grown weak and helpless. . . . They hid in hiding-places and tormented themselves with fasts for three days in succession, day and night, besides fasting on other days, until their skin withered and barely stuck to their bones. They cried aloud to God, and God moved away from them.

In that year, on the eighth day of Iyar [3 May] the enemies attacked Speyer and put to death eleven holy souls. They were the first to be martyred rather than be converted. Among them was a respected woman who, in order to sanctify God's name, took her own life. The remaining Jews of Speyer were saved by Bishop Johann, even though they were not converted.

On the twenty-third day of Iyar [18 May] the murderers attacked the Jews of Worms. The community split into two camps: those who remained in their homes and those who went to the castle of the bishop, who was ruler over the city. The wolves of the desert savagely attacked the Jews who had remained in their homes. They slaughtered everyone—men, women and children, young and old. They destroyed the homes, plundered and pillaged. They trampled the sacred Torah scrolls in the dirt, ripped them to shreds and burned them.

Seven days later, on the first day of the month of Sivan [25 May], tragedy struck those who had taken refuge in the castle. Strengthened by the example of their brothers, they also sanctified God's name and stretched out their necks to the executioners. Some took their own lives. One man killed his brother, another his wife and children. Bridegrooms slew their brides and merciful mothers killed their own children. All accepted their fate willingly and gave up their souls to their Creator with a *Shema Yisroel* upon their lips. The enemy did not spare anyone, except a few who were forced to convert. Around eight hundred souls were killed in two days and were brought to their graves naked.

When the Jews of Mainz heard that their brethren in Worms had fallen by the sword, their hands grew weak and their hearts dissolved. They cried to God: "Eternal God of Israel! Do you wish to put an end to us, the remnant of Israel?" The leaders of the Jewish community gathered together and took counsel. One said to the other, "Let us choose from among our elders those who will tell us what we must do, because this great misfortune will swallow us up." And the elders decided to ransom the Jews with money, to give up all their possessions as a bribe to the nobleman, the governors, the bishops and the barons.

The esteemed leaders of the kehilla, who were in the good graces of the bishop, went to his lords and servants to speak with them and told them, "What shall we do, after we have heard about our massacred brothers in Speyer and Worms?" And they replied, "Take our advice, put all your money in our treasury, and you, with your wives and sons and daughters stay in the bishop's castle until those armies have passed through. In this way, you will save yourselves from the crusaders." But they only gave us that advice in order to hand us over to the murderers, in order to steal our property, which they indeed finally did.

The bishop gathered his lords, servants and princes and knights to defend us. At first he really did want to save us, with all the power that he had. We had given him and his lords money for that purpose. The bribe, however, did not help us in the days of fury and tragedy.

At noon on the first day of Sivan [25 May 1096], when Baron Emicho, the villain and scourge of the Jews, arrived at the gates with his army, the Christians opened the gates for him. Those enemies of God said, "See, they have opened the gates for us, now let us avenge the blood of Christ!"

When the Jews saw the large army that was as numerous as the sands of the shore, they all put on armor, armed themselves, and Rabbi Klunymos ben Meshullam, the leader of the community, stood at their head. But because of the many fasts they had subjected themselves to, they lacked the strength to withstand the onslaughts of the enemy. The Jews in the bishop's castle moved to the gate in order to resist the crusaders and the city folk, and they fought each other until halfway to the gate. The hand of the Creator fell heavily upon his people.

All the Christians gathered in the bishop's court to exterminate the name of Jew. The bishop's people, too, who had promised to help, were the first to run away and hand the Jews over to their enemies. . . . The bishop himself, Bishop Rothard, also ran away and hid in his church, because they wanted to baptize him too, since he had tried to defend Jews.

(The chronicler relates further how the Jews were martyred. The scenes he describes, of mothers killing their own children, of a child pleading with his mother not to kill him, are simply shattering. It is worth citing the comment of E. Lifschutz: "King Henry IV had permitted the Jews who were forced to convert to return to their faith. Pope Clement III and the Catholic Church opposed the king vigorously on this. The Jews themselves received the 'penitents' coldly. They refused to intermarry with the former renegades, to associate with them socially; in general, they avoided contact with them whenever possible.")

The Pogrom in York (1190). Account of the Monk, William of Newburgh.

The wrath of the Christians against the Jews was released in a savage manner. But the wrath was not because of religious reasons. It was greed and avid envy which caused the cruelties. Many Christians envied the Jews for being luckier than they. Thieves and murderers persuaded themselves that by robbing and killing Jews they were doing God's will. Nothing could stop the people of York, neither the fear of the king, nor the breaking of the law of the land, nor any human and Christian feelings. They robbed and murdered their misguided enemies, God's enemies, as freely as they wished. That which took place in York during those few days must be written down in all its details, so that it should not be forgotten.

When the king went off to France to organize the crusade, several citizens of York conspired to get even with the Jews. The Christian citizens who were in debt to the Jews began murdering people and stealing their property, like wild animals, without any Christian conscience. The leaders of the robbers were several noble lords, like the family Furstey, who were in great debt to the moneylenders. The Furstey family had pledged their estates with the Jews for the money they had borrowed. Now they were in need of new loans to pay their debts to the king's moneylenders. The government used to help the Jews collect the debts, and they would take a portion for themselves. The property of the moneylenders was of course the property of the royal treasury.

Some of the York people who had joined the crusaders believed that the expenses of the holy mission should be met by stealing from God's enemies, here on the spot, especially when they could do it without fear of punishment. One night, during a stormy wind, a fire broke out in the city. Many houses went up in flames. As we now know, it was not an accidental fire, but was set with a purpose. While the city officials were busy putting out the fire and trying to save the buildings, no one interfered with the robbers.

An armed band, which had equipped itself for the purpose, broke into the home of the wealthy Jew, Benedict, who had died in London. They murdered Benedict's wife and children and whoever they found in the house. They set the roof on fire and when the flames had spread, they grabbed everything they could carry and got away.

The Jews of York, with their leader, Rabbi [Joseph] Gotshe had previously brought a large sum of money to the warden of the city to protect them.

A few days later the nocturnal robbers returned. Many of the York people had joined them. They beseiged Rabbi Gotshe's home, which looked like a walled castle, so strongly had it been built. The murderers broke into the house and killed whoever they found there. They stole everything they could carry out and then set fire to the house. Rabbi Joseph had not been at home. He apparently expected this and had taken his wife and children into the nobleman's castle. With him went a good number of other Jews. Only a few remained defenseless inside their homes. They were the first victims.

When the robbers left with their booty, a savage mob entered the city and began plundering, smashing and destroying whatever was left after the fire. The enemies of the Jews were now raging openly, without fear of anybody. Not satisfied with the robbing and destruction they had done, they now herded together all the Jews they could find in the city, dragged them into churches, and converted them by force. Some Jews submitted in order to stay alive. Those who hesitated were murdered without pity on the spot.

The Jews who were in the castle were safe for the time being. With them was the warden. When he left the castle for a while and wished to return, the frightened Jews inside refused to let him in. They did not trust him. They were afraid that, having taken their money, he had made an arrangement with their enemies. The warden immediately went to the Chief of Police to complain against the Jews for seizing the castle. The Sheriff was furious. The leaders of the attack incited the Sheriff still further, convincing him that the Jews had rebelled against the king and captured a nobleman's castle. The Sheriff ordered the band to surround the castle.

As soon as the order was given, the angry mob, who were well armed, (they were mostly people from the city and villages), surrounded the castle. The Sheriff almost immediately regretted his order and pleaded with the crowd to disperse. But he could not now cool their excited minds and restrain them from doing what they were so intent on doing—killing Jews.

It is true that a number of the most prominent citizens of York did retreat. The masters and their workmen, and many young people of the city, however, refused to leave the area of the castle. There were many villagers and a good number of crusaders, all of them with an urge to murder. Among the crowd were also some priests and even one monk, who was even more incensed at the Jews than the others.

The besieged Jews in the castle did not have much food. Had the siege lasted much longer they would have starved to death anyway. Nor did they have enough arms to defend themselves with. They resisted the mob with stones which they threw from behind the protected walls. The castle lay under siege for few days more. The mob gradually prepared and set up machinery to smash the walls of the fortress. When the machinery was ready and in place, it became clear to the Jews that they had no alternative. They bravely conferred on their course of action. The mob outside was gleeful; they were about to be victorious.

In accordance with the advice of the rabbi, the famous Rabbi Yom Tov, many of the Jews committed suicide after they set fire to the castle. Those who remained were ready to convert. But the mob murdered all of them.

The appearance of the city and the castle after the massacre was appalling. Corpses lay all around the castle. Soon after the mass murders the conspirators marched to the city hall where the official city documents were kept. Here they threatened to kill the frightened guards unless they turned over the notes which the debtors had given the Jews. When the documents were surrendered and burned, the conspirators who had joined the crusade then crossed the Channel to France, before they could be called to account for their crimes. The others remained in the country, having nothing to fear.

This tragedy happened in the city of York on Good Friday, in the evening and Saturday morning, March 16 and 17, in the year 1190.

Sources

Albright, William Foxwell. *From the Stone Age to Christianity*, New York: Doubleday, 1957.

Alliluyeva, Svetlana. *Only One Year*, trans. Paul Chavchavadze, New York: Harper & Row, 1969.

———. *Twenty Letters to a Friend*, trans. Priscilla J. McMillan, New York: Harper & Row, 1967.

Baron, Salo W. *The Russian Jew Under Tsars and Soviets*, rev. ed., New York: Macmillan, 1976.

———. *A Social and Religious History of the Jews*, 16 vols., 2nd rev. ed., New York: Columbia University Press, 1952-73.

Belyev, I., and Primakov, Y. "Lessons of the 1967 Middle East Crisis" in *International Affairs* (Russian) no. 3, Moscow: Tue Mezdunarodnaya Kniga, 1968, pp. 40-46.

Bernstein, Herman. *The Truth About the Protocols of Zion*, rev. ed., New York: Ktav, 1972.

Brandes, Leon. "The Juridical Position of the Jews in Poland Between the Two Wars" in *YIVO Bleter*, vol. 42, New York: YIVO Institute for Jewish Research, 1962, pp. 147-86.

Brutzkus, I. "Di erste yedios vegn Yidn in Polen" in *Historishe Shriftn* (Yiddish), ed. A. Tcherikower, vol. 1, Warsaw, 1929, pp. 55-72.

Burns, Robert F. *Antisemitism in France*, New Brunswick, NJ: Rutgers University Press, 1950.

Curtis, Michael, and Gitelson, Susan A., eds. *Israel in the Third World*, New Brunswick, NJ: Transaction Books, 1976.

Dawidowicz, Lucy S. *The War Against the Jews: 1933-1945*, New York: Bantam, 1976.

Dimenshteyn, S., ed. *Yidn in SSSR (Zamlbuch)*, Soviet ed. (Yiddish), Moscow: "Emes," 1935.

Dubnow, Simon [Semen Markovich Dubnov]. *Di velt-geshikte fun yidishn folk* (Yiddish), vol. 1, New York: A. Loeb Verlag, n.d., vols. 2-10, Buenos Aires, n.d.

———. "Der zweiter hurbn fun Ukrainia" in *Historishe Shriftn* (Yiddish), ed. A. Tcherikower, vol. 1, Warsaw, 1929, pp. 27-54.

Ebenstein, William. *Great Political Thinkers*, 4th ed., New York: Holt Rinehart & Winston, 1969.

Elbogen, Ismar. *A Century of Jewish Life*, trans. Moses Hadas, Philadelphia: Jewish Publication Society of America, 1944.

Sources / 423

Encyclopaedia Judaica, 16 vols., New York: Macmillan, 1971–72.

Flannery, Edward H. *Anguish of the Jews: Twenty-Three Centuries of Anti-Semitism*, New York: Macmillan, 1965.

Forster, Arnold, and Epstein, Benjamin R. *The New Anti-Semitism*, New York: McGraw-Hill, 1974.

Friedman, Saul S. "Arab Complicity in the Holocaust" in *Jewish Frontier*, vol. 42, no. 4 (April 1975), pp. 9–17.

Gaster, Theodor Herzl. *The Dead Sea Scrolls* (English), Garden City, New York: Doubleday, 1956.

Gergel, N. "Di Pogromen in Ukrainia in di yorn 1918–21" in *Ekonomishe Shriftn* (Yiddish), vol. 1 (1928), pp. 106–13.

Glassman, S. *Megiles fun Yam HaMelekh* (Yiddish), New York, 1965.

Goldberg, I. "Antisemitism in Russia" in *Yiddishe Cultur* (Yiddish), trans. Dmitri Zhukov from *Ogonyok* (Russian; 12 October 1974).

Graetz, Heinrich. *History of the Jews*, 6 vols. (1898), Philadelphia: Jewish Publication Society of America, n.d.

Grayzel, Solomon. *History of the Jews*, New York: New American Library, 1975.

Greenberg, L. A., and Jonas, Harold J. "An American Anti-Semite in the 19th Century" in Joseph L. Blau, et al, *Essays on Jewish Life and Thought Presented in Honor of Salo Wittmayer Baron*, New York: Columbia University Press, 1959, pp. 265–83.

Habermann, Abraham Meir. *Megiloth Midbar Yehudah* (Hebrew), Jerusalem: Mahberot l'Sifrot, 1959.

Halpern, Ben. "Anti-Semitism in the Perspective of Jewish History" in Charles Herbert Stember, et al, *Jews in the Mind of America*, New York: Basic Books, 1966, pp. 273–301.

Handlin, Oscar. *Adventure in Freedom: Three Hundred Years of Jewish Life in America*, New York: McGraw-Hill, 1954.

Hay, Malcolm Vivian. *The Foot of Pride: The Pressure of Christendom on the People of Israel for 1900 Years*, Boston: Beacon Press, 1950.

Higham, John. "American Anti-Semitism Historically Reconsidered" in Charles Herbert Stember, et al, *Jews in the Mind of America*, New York: Basic Books, 1966, pp. 237–58.

Hitler, Adolph. *Hitler's Secret Conversations, 1941–1944*, New York: Octagon, 1953.

Israelson, Israel. "Natan Hanover: Zeyn leben un literarishe taytekeyt" in *Historishe Shriftn* (Yiddish), ed. A. Tcherikower, vol. 1, Warsaw, 1929, pp. 1–26.

Janowsky, Oscar I., ed. *American Jew*, facs. ed., New York: Arno Press, 1942.

Josephus, Flavius. *The Life and Works of Flavius Josephus*, trans. William Whiston, New York: Holt, Rinehart and Winston, 1957.

Kahana, A. *HaSeforim HaHizonim l'Torah* (Hebrew), 3 vols., Tel Aviv: Hoziat Mikorot, 1936–37.

Katz, Ben-Zion. *Perushim, Zadokim, Kanoim, Notzrim* (Hebrew), Tel Aviv: N. Twersky, 1947.

Katz, Moshe. *A dor, vus hot forlorn di moyre* (Yiddish), 1956.

Kaufmann, Yehezkel. *Goleh V'nekhar* (Hebrew), 3 vols., Tel Aviv: Dvir, 1929–32.

Kautsky, Karl. *Are the Jews a Race?*, repr. of 1926 ed., Westport, CT: Greenwood Press, 1972.

Keller, Werner. *Diaspora: The Post-Biblical History of the Jews*, New York: Harcourt Brace Jovanovich, 1971.

Kipnis, Itzik. *Tsum lebn: Dertseylungen* (Yiddish), Moscow: Sovetski Pisatel', 1969.

———. "Untervegns" in *Dertseylungen* (Yiddish), YIKUF, 1960.

Korey, William. "Bigotry in the Hall of Brotherhood" in *The American Zionist*, vol. 62, no. 5 (January 1972), pp. 12–15.

———. *The Soviet Cage: Anti-Semitism in Russia*, New York: Viking Press, 1973.

Kornhendler, Yehezkel. *Yidn in Pariz* (Yiddish), Paris, 1970.

Korzec, Pawel. "Antisemitism in Poland as an Intellectual, Social and Political Movement" in *Studies on Polish Jewry, 1919–1939*, New York: YIVO Institute for Jewish Research, 1974, pp. 12–104 (English section).

Laqueur, Walter. *A History of Zionism*, New York: Holt, Rinehart and Winston, 1972.

Lawrence, Gunther. *Three Million More?*, Garden City, NY: Doubleday 1970.

Lendvai, Paul. *Anti-Semitism Without Jews: Communist Eastern Europe*, Garden City, NY: Doubleday, 1971.

Lenin, Vladimir Ilich. *Ausgevelte verk* (Yiddish), 8 vols., Moscow. 1925–30.

Leon, Harry J. *The Jews in Ancient Rome*, Philadelphia: Jewish Publication Society of America, 1960.

Levin, Jack S. "Judaic Roots of the American Revolution" in *Congress Monthly*, vol. 43, no. 8 (October 1976), pp. 10–11.

Lewis, Bernard. "The Anti-Zionist Resolution in the U.N." in *Foreign Affairs* (October 1976), pp. 54–64.

Lifschutz, Ezekiel. *Doires dertselyn* (Yiddish), New York, 1848.

Mahler, Raphael. *A History of Modern Jewry, 1780–1815*, New York: Schocken Books, 1971.

———. *Jewish Emancipation: A Selection of Documents,* New York: The American Jewish Committee, 1941.

Marcus, Jacob R. *The Jew in the Medieval World: A Source Book, 315–1791*, New York: Atheneum, 1969.

Margolis, Max, and Marx, Alexander. *A History of the Jewish People*, New York: Atheneum, 1969.

Markish, Esther. "Mit Peretz Markish un an aym" in *Di Goldene Keyt* (Yiddish), no. 88 (1975), pp. 22–40.

Mazrui, Ali A. "Black Africa and the Arabs" in *Foreign Affairs* (July 1975), pp. 725–42.

Medrash Eicha Rabbah (Hebrew), Jerusalem: Torah l'Am, 1958.

Medvedev, Roy A. *Let History Judge: The Origins and Consequences of Stalinism*, ed. David Joravsky and Georges Haupt, New York: Random House, 1973.

Milik, Jozef Tadeusz. *Ten Years of Discoveries in the Judean Desert*, Naperville, IL: Alec R. Allenson, 1959.

Parkes, James. *Conflict of the Church and the Synagogue: A Study in the Origins of Antisemitism*, New York: Atheneum, 1969.

Poliakov, Leon. *A History of Anti-Semitism*, vol. 1: *From the Time of Christ to the Court Jews*, New York: Vanguard, 1964.

Rossi, Mario. *The Third World: The Unaligned Countries and the World Revolution*, Westport, CT: Greenwood Press, 1974.

Rostow, Eugene V. "The American Stake in Israel" in *Commentary*, vol. 63, no. 4 (April 1977), pp. 32–46.

Roth, Cecil. *A History of the Jews: From Earliest Times Through the Six Day War*, rev. ed., New York: Schocken Books, 1970.

―――. "Notes: Talmudic Reference to a Qumran Sect" in *Revue de Qumran*, no. 6 (February 1960), pp. 261–65.

Rowe, Leonard. "Jewish Self-Defense: A Response to Violence" in *Studies on Polish Jewry, 1919–1939*, New York: YIVO Institute for Jewish Research, 1974, pp. 105–49 (English section).

Sachar, Abraham L. *A History of the Jews*, New York: Alfred Knopf, 1967.

Sachar, Howard M. *Course of Modern Jewish History*, London: Weidenfeld & Nicolson, 1958.

Salisbury, Harrison. *Moscow Journal: The End of Stalin*, Chicago: University of Chicago Press, 1975.

Schappes, Morris U., ed. *A Documentary History of the Jews in the United States, 1654–1875*, New York: Schocken Books, 1975.

Sharet, Yaakov. "Ziknei-Zion Hosru l'Moscow" in *Yomim v'Laylot*, supp. *Ma'ariv* (Hebrew), (27 October 1964); also trans. Evse'ev in *Comsomolskaya Pravda* (Russian), (4 October 1967).

Sherman, C. Bezalel. *Jew Within American Society: A Study in Ethnic Individuality*, Detroit: Wayne State University Press, 1961.

Shipper, Ignaz. *Yiddishe geshikhte* (*Wirtschaftsgeschichte*, Yiddish), 4 vols., Warsaw, 1930.

Smolar, B. *Soviet Jewry Today and Tomorrow*, New York: Macmillan, 1971.

Stalin, Joseph. *Marxism and the National-Colonial Question*, Chicago: Proletarian Publishers, 1975.

Stember, Charles Herbert, et al. *Jews in the Mind of America*, New York: Basic Books, 1966.

Suhl, Yuri, ed. and trans. *They Fought Back: The Story of the Jewish Resistance in Nazi Europe*, New York: Schocken Books, 1975.

Talmon, J. L. "European History—Seedbed of the Holocaust" in *Midstream* (May 1973), pp. 3-25.

Tannenbaum, Mark H. "Oberammergau" (pamphlet), New York: The American Jewish Committee, 1970.

Tcherikower, A. "Fun di russishe archiven" in *Historishe Shriftn* (Yiddish), vol. 1, Warsaw, 1929, pp. 778-804.

———. *Ukrainer pogromen in yor 1919*, Bibliotek fun YIVO (Yiddish), New York: YIVO Institute for Jewish Research, 1965.

Trunk, Isaiah. "Economic Antisemitism in Poland Between the Two World Wars" in *Studies on Polish Jewry, 1919-1939*, New York: YIVO Institute for Jewish Research, 1974, pp. 3-98 (Yiddish section).

Turok, Nancy. "The Arab Boycott of Israel" in *Foreign Affairs* (April 1977), pp. 472-93.

"The Twenty-Five Year War—The War of 1948" in *Near East Report*, vol. 18, no. 6 (6 February 1974), pp. 25-27.

"Two Refugee Problems" in *Near East Report*, vol. 18, no. 6 (6 February 1974), pp. 50-53.

Unterman, Isaac. *The Talmud, an Analytical Guide to Its History and Teachings*, New York: Bloch, 1952.

Vishniak, Mark. "Antisemitism in Tsarist Russia" in *Essays on Antisemitism*, ed. Koppel S. Pinson, Jewish Studies Publications, no. 2, New York: Conference on Jewish Relations, 1946, pp. 121-44.

Weinreich, Max. *Tzwantzik Yor noch Czernowitz* (Yiddish), Vilna: YIVO, 1928.

Wells, H. G. *Experiment in Autobiography: Discoveries and Conclusions of a Very Ordinary Brain*, New York: Macmillan, 1934.

Wisse, Ruth R., and Cotler, Irwin. "Quebec's Jews: Caught in the Middle" in *Commentary*, vol. 64, no. 3 (September 1977), pp. 55-59.

Zeitlin, Solomon, "The Hebron Pogrom and the Hebrew Scrolls" in *Jewish Quarterly Review*, vol. 43, no. 2 (1952), pp. 140-52.

Zinberg, Israel. *Di geshikhte fun literatur by Yidn*, 10 vols., Buenos Aires: 1927-70.

Zineman, Jacob [Jacob Taffet]. *Di geshikhte fun Zionism* (Yiddish), 2 vols., Paris: Imprimerie S.N.I.E., 1947-49.

Zweig, Stefan. *Romain Rolland* (Yiddish), Warsaw, 1929.

Index